The Suppression
of the
Society of Jesus

In memoriam
The Month
(July 1864–April 2001)
with all its past Editors and Staff

... on either side of the river stood a tree of life,
which yields twelve crops of fruit;
one for each month of the year;
the leaves of the trees serve for the healing of the nations ...
　　　　　　　　　　　　　　The Book of Revelation 22:2

The Suppression of the Society of Jesus

Sydney F. Smith, S.J.

edited
by Joseph A. Munitiz, S.J.

with an Afterword
by R. W. Truman

GRACEWING

Text first published in *The Month* February 1902–August 1903 as a series of nineteen instalments.

This edition first published in 2004

Gracewing
2 Southern Avenue
Leominster
Herefordshire HR6 0QF

All rights reserved. No part of this publication may be reproduced, stored in a retrieval system, or transmitted in any form, or by any means, electronic, mechanical, photocopying, recording or otherwise, without the written permission of the publisher.

Text of the late Sydney Smith, SJ

© Trustees for Roman Catholic Purposes 2004

The right of Sydney Smith, SJ to be identified as the author of this work has been asserted in accordance with the Copyright, Designs and Patents Act, 1988.

ISBN 0 85244 630 6

Printed and bound by Antony Rowe Ltd, Eastbourne

Typesetting by
Action Publishing Technology Ltd, Gloucester, GL1 5SR

Contents

Preface *J. Munitiz*		vii
Bibliography	1. Used by Sydney Smith	ix
	2. Published after Sydney Smith	xii
Chapter 1	In the Portuguese Dominions	1
Chapter 2	In France	18
Chapter 3	In Spain	74
Chapter 4	The Harassing of Clement XIII	133
Chapter 5	The Conclave of 1769	158
Chapter 6	The Bullying of Clement XIV	200
Chapter 7	The Execution of the Brief of Suppression	253
Chapter 8	The Brief of Suppression	289
	Conclusion	307
Afterword *The Suppression of the Society of Jesus viewed from the twenty-first century* by R. W. Truman		319
The Bourbon States		319
The Process of Expulsion		322
The Case of Spain		323
The Brief of Suppression		325
Sydney Smith and the Nineteenth-Century Debate		327
Modern Studies Consulted		338
Index		341

Preface

The fascination of this work, first presented to readers one century ago, derives from a variety of causes. It deals with an episode in the history of the Church from which a great deal can be learned, as much about the Church as about the Society of Jesus; it is still the longest monograph on the subject despite the passage of time; it represents a mentality long out of date but which only a century ago was dominant in ecclesiastical circles; and it is written in a clear, if stilted, style that retains a certain panache. Its author was probably aware of its limitations, but in any case by the time of his retirement, when he would have had the leisure needed for its publication in book form (instead of the articles in which it was first published), he had lost the drive and capacity needed. And yet if accepted without illusions, as a piece of high-class propaganda journalism, his work deserves to be better known.

Fr Sydney Fenn Smith (1843–1922) was the son of a well-to-do Anglican vicar. Privately educated (and taught Hebrew by his mother), he began to study architecture in London, but at the age of twenty-one was received into the Roman Catholic Church by the Jesuits at Farm Street in 1864, and two years later was accepted into the Society of Jesus as a novice. His subsequent career is soon told: appointed a theology professor (specializing in biblical studies) for six years as a young man, he then had some pastoral experience in Wimbledon for a couple of years, but at the age of forty-eight (1891) took over as editor of *The Month* and held that post for almost thirty years (until 1921), when he moved from Farm Street to the Jesuit novitate in Roehampton, dying in the following year. A very prolific writer of articles[1] from early in his Jesuit life, he also threw himself

---

[1] E. F. Sutcliffe, *Bibliography of the English Province of the Society of Jesus 1773–1953*, The Manresa Press, Roehampton, 1957, pp. 169–175, lists 339 pamphlets and articles, but he also contributed to the Scripture Manuals for Catholic Schools, apart from many unsigned reviews and notes.

into pastoral work – missions, retreats, spiritual direction, instruction of those interested in joining the Roman Catholic Church[2] – while sedulously attending 'gatherings to promote Catholic interests'.[3] Despite his open criticism of Anglican orders, he seems to have had many friends amongst the Anglican clergy and in general was noted for his 'kindliness of thought and courtesy of manner'.

His aim in writing a score of articles on the suppression of the Society[4] was plainly apologetic, and he admits that he does not pretend to have made the sort of in-depth research on archival material that would be needed to produce a scholarly work. He draws mainly on second-hand sources, or on already published state documents (e.g. for the chapters on France and Spain). However, within his limits he is scrupulously fair and balanced. If nothing else, his work shows clearly what are the limits that need to be overcome. In this re-publication the original spellings (e.g. 'tenour'), punctuation, capitalization, and abbreviations (e.g. 'apud' and 'ap.' = 'cited from') have been retained.

Special thanks are due to Mr R. W. Truman, formerly lecturer in Spanish studies at Oxford University and a student of Christ Church. My intention in inviting him to write the *Afterword* was to provide readers with a disinterested appraisal of the 'defence speech' presented to them by a Jesuit. In my opinion he fulfilled his role admirably. The final verdict remains, of course, with the jury: the readers of this book.

Joseph A. Munitiz, S.J.

---

[2] Between 1894 and 1920 he instructed 254 persons at Farm Street alone: cf. 'The late Fr Sydney Smith, S.J.', *The Month*, 140, August 1922, pp. 97–102; cf. p. 101, note 1.

[3] *Ibid.* p. 101.

[4] They were published in *The Month*, of which he was then editor, in nineteen instalments between February 1902 and August 1903; these are mentioned in the footnotes to the chapters. The text published here remains basically unchanged, except that references to the article form have been removed.

Bibliography

1. Used by Sydney Smith
*** main sources used

Alembert, Jean Le Rond d', *Sur la Destruction des Jésuites*, Edinburgh ed., 1765 [originally the article: *Jésuites* in the *Encyclopédie*, Eng. trans., *The Destruction of the Jesuits*].
Anonymous
  Apologie Générale de l'Institut, 1762 [anonymous Jesuit publ.].
  Colección general de las providencias ... sobre el estrañamiento ... de la Compañía, Madrid 1767.
  Destruction des Jésuites en France, Anecdote politique et intéressant trouvé dans les papiers d'un homme bien instruit des intrigues du temps. Publ. London 1766 [published in Saint-Victor: see below].
  Documents concernant la Compagnie du Jésus [cf. Auguste Carayon; and cf. Saint-Priest].
  Il est temps de parler, 1764, 2 vols [anonymous Jesuit publ.].
  Mémoires historiques et anecdotes de la Cour de France pendant la faveur de Madame de Pompadour, 1802.
  Nouvelles Observations sur les Jugements rendus contre les Jésuites, Bordeaux, 1763 [anonymous Jesuit publ.].
  ****Recueil par ordre de dates, de tous les Arrêts de Parlement ... concernant les ci-devant soi-disant Jésuites*, vol. 1, 1762.
  Reflexions des Cours des Bourbons sur l'affaire des Jésuites, c. 1770.
  Réponse au livre intitulé 'Extraits des Assertions', 1763 [cf. Grou].
Beccatini, Francesco, *Storia di Pio VI*, 2 vols, Venice, 1841.
Benevenuti, Carlo (S.J.), *Irreflessioni*, Rome, n.d. [c. 1772].
Biographie Universelle Ancienne et Moderne (52 vols), Paris, 1811–1828, s.v. Clémencet, Charles (vol. 9 [1813], pp. 12–14); Terray, Joseph Marie (vol. 45 [1826], pp. 175–190).

***Boero, Giuseppe (S.J.),[1] *Osservazioni sopra l'istoria del Pontificato di Clemente XIV scritta dal P. A. Theiner*, Modena, 1854 (2nd ed.).

Boero, Giuseppe (S.J.), *Vita del V.P. Pignatelli*, Rome, 1856.

Caballero, Ramón Diosdado (S.J.), *Bibliothecae Scriptorum Societatis Supplementum*, Bologna, 1814.

Cahour, Arsène (S.J.), *Des Jésuites, par un Jésuite*, Paris, 1843-1844.

Cánovas del Castillo, Antonio (ed.), *Historia General de España*, (18 vols), Madrid, 1891-1898.

Capefigue, Jean-Baptiste, *Louis XV et la Société du XVIIIme Siècle*, (4 vols), Paris, 1842.

Caraccioli, Louis-Antoine, Marchese de, (ed.), *Lettres intéressantes du Pape Clément XIV*, 1775/1776.

Carayon, Auguste (S.J.), *Documents inédits concernant la Compagnie de Jésus*, 23 vols (1863-1886), Doc. xviii. p. 183.

Carné, Louis-Marcien de, 'La Monarchie de Louis XV', *Revue des Deux Mondes*, 15 January, 1859.

Charlevoix, Pierre-François-Xavier (S.J.), *History of Paraguay*, (2 vols), London, 1769.

Clément, Abbé, *Journal d'un voyage et correspondence en Italie et en Espagne*. [cf. Ravignan, *Clément XIII et Clément XIV*, vol. 1].

***Cordara, Giulio Cesare [cf. Döllinger for the version used by Sydney Smith; subsequently publ. *On the Suppression of the Society of Jesus. A Contemporary Account*, trans. and notes by John P. Murphy, Chicago, Loyola Press, 1999]

Coxe, William, *Memoirs of the Kings of Spain of the house of Bourbon* (3 vols, 1st ed.), London, 1813 [later edition, 4 vols, used].

***Crétineau-Joly, J.,[2] *Clément XIV et les Jésuites, ou histoire de la destruction des Jésuites*, Paris, 1844.

***Crétineau-Joly, J, *Histoire religieuse, politique et littéraire de la Compagnie de Jésus*, Paris, 1851-9, 6 vols (esp. vols 5-6).

Cunninghame Graham, R. B., *A Vanished Arcadia being some account of the Jesuits in Paraguay, 1607-1767*, London (Heinemann), 1924 [1921].

***Danvila y Collado, Manuel,[3] *Reinado de Carlos III* (6 vols), Madrid, 1893-1896 [published in Cánovas del Castillo, *Historia de España*, see above].

Döllinger, F., *Beiträge zur politischen, kirchlichen und Cultur-Geschichte*, vol. 3, part 1, Cordara, *Commentarii de suis et*

---

[1] Cf. *Afterword*, p. 330.
[2] Cf. *Afterword*, p. 329.
[3] Cf. *Afterword*, p. 331.

suorum rebus usque ad occasum Societatis Jesu.
Döllinger, F., *Fortsetzung der Handbuchs der Christlichen Kirchengeschichte von Hortig.* II, Bd. 2 Abth.
Duclos, Charles Pinot, *Voyage en Italie*, 1791.
***Duhr, Bernardus (S.J.), *Jesuiten-Fabeln. Ein Beitrag zur Culturgeschichte*, Freiburg i. Br., 2nd ed., 1892.
El Observador Católico (Mexico, 1849, tom. iii, Appendix) British Library press mark, PP. 909, c.2.
Epistolae Praesulum Generalium ad Patres et Fratres Societatis Jesu, vol. 2, Edit. of Ghent, 1847.
***Ferrer del Río, Antonio, *Historia del Reinado de Carlos III en España*, 2 vols, Madrid, 1856 [though Sydney Smith (p. 114) gives the date 1857].
Grou, Jean Nicolas (S.J.), *Réponse au livre intitulé 'Extraits des Assertions'*, 3 vols, Paris, 1763-1765, 9 vols, Paris, 1773 [work begun under the direction of H. M. Sauvage].
Gutiérrez de la Huerta, F., *Exposición y Dictamen del fiscal del consejo y cámara de Francisco Gutiérrez de la Huerta*, 1815 [publ. in *El Observador Católico*, 1849; (Sydney Smith does not seem to have had access to the Madrid, 1845, edition)].
Institutum Societatis Jesu, Prague edition, 1759, vol. 1.
Laffrey, Arnoux, *Siècle de Louis XV*, 2 vols, Paris, 1796 [referred to as *Vie privée de Louis XV* perhaps under the influence of the work of Mouffle d'Angerville, *Vie privée de Louis XV, ou Principaux évenements, particularités et anecdotes de son regne*, 4 vols, London, 1781].
Mahon, Lord, *History of England*, vol. 5. Append., 1857 ed.
Martin, Henri, *Histoire de France jusqu'en 1789* (19 vols, Paris, 1838-1853; 2nd ed. revised, 17 vols, Paris, 1878).
***Masson, Frédéric, *Le Cardinal de Bernis depuis son Ministère*, 1884.
***Miguélez, M. F. (O.S.A.), *Jansenismo y Regalismo en España*, Madrid, 1895.
Montézon, Fortuné de (S.J.), *Mémoire sur les jansénistes et les jésuites* [published as an Appendix in Sainte-Beuve (4th ed., vol. 1, 1858) see below].
Muratori, L. A., *Cristianesimo Felice.*
Murr, Christopher, *Journal zur Kunstgeschichte*, vol. 9.
Navarette, Juan Andrés (S.J.), *De viris illustribus in Castella Veteri Societatem ingressis*, Bologna, 1793.
Nonell, Jaime (S.J.), *Vida del V. P. José Pignatelli*, 3 vols, Manresa, 1893-94.
Norbert, *Mémoires Historiques* [cf. Parisot, Pierre-Curel].

Pacca, Card., *Memorie Storiche*.
idem, *Notizie sul Portagallo* [quoted by Alfred Weld].
Parisot, Pierre-Curel, *Mémoires Historiques du R.P. Norbert*, 4 vols, 1745.
Peramas, José Emmanuel (S.J.), *De vita et moribus sex sacerdotum Paraguaycorum*, Faenza, 1791.
***Ravignan, Xavier La Croix de[4] (S.J.), *Clément XIII and Clément XIV,* 2 vols, and Pièces Justificatives, Paris, 1854.
Sainte-Beuve, Charles-Augustin de, *Port-Royal*, 1840-1860.
Saint-Priest, Alexis Guignand, Comte de, *Histoire de la Chute des Jésuites*, 1844 [published in Ravignan].
Saint-Victor, Jacques B. M., Comte de, *Documents historiques concernant la Compagnie de Jésus*, tome 1, 1827.
Sauvage, Henri Michel (S.J.), *Le Oui et le Non, ou Lettres sur la Procédure faite contre les Jésuites au Château Saint-Ange*, Paris, 1777. [cf. p. 283].
idem, cf. Grou.
Schoell, Maximillen S. F. [1766-1833], *Cours d'Histoire des Etats Européens,* vol. xliv.
Sommervogel, Carlos (S.J.), *Bibliothèque des Ecrivains de la Compagnie de Jésus*, Bruxelles/Paris, 1890-1898 [Supplem., 1960, vol. XII].
Southey, Robert, *History of Brazil*, 1810-1819, 3 vols.
***Theiner, Augustin,[5] *Histoire du Pontificat de Clément XIV*, vol. 1., French ed., [Paris, 1852].
von Reumont, Alfred, *Ganganelli - Papst Clement XIV - seine Briefe und seine Zeit*, 1847.
Weld, Alfred (S.J.), *The Suppression of the Society of Jesus in the Portuguese Dominions*, London (Burns & Oates), 1877.
Zalenski, Fr. (S.J.), *Les Jésuites de la Russie-Blanche* (2 vols), Paris, n.d. [1886?], vol. ii, chs. i-viii.

2 published after Sydney Smith[6]

Astráin, Antonio (S.J.), *Historia de la Compañía de Jesús en la asistencia de España*, 8 vols, Madrid, 1902-1925.
Aveling, J. C. H., *The Jesuits*, London (Blond & Briggs), 1981, ISBN 0-85634-110-X [his bibliography includes useful comments].

---

[4] Cf. *Afterword*, p. 330.
[5] Cf. *Afterword*, p. 329.
[6] A random selection that may assist those interested in further research. In addition, cf. 'Modern Studies consulted' supplied by R. W. Truman in the *Afterword*.

Cejudo, Jorge and Egido, Teófanes, *Pedro Rodríguez Campomanes. Dictamen fiscal de la expulsión de los jesuitas de España, 1766-1767*, Madrid, 1977 [with an extensive bibliography on the controversy about the Jesuits].
Desautels, A. (S.J.), *Les Mémoires de Trévoux et le mouvement des idées au XVIIIe. siècle*, Rome, 1956.
Diccionario Histórico de la Compañía de Jesús, eds. Charles E. O'Neill (S.I.), Joaquín M. Domínguez (S.I.), Rome and Madrid, 2001 [many useful entries, e.g. that by Isidoro Pinedo mentioned below].
Edwards, Francis (S.J.), *The Jesuits in England from 1580 to the present day*, Tunbridge Wells, Burns & Oates, 1985, ISBN 0 86012 137 2 [Appendix 1, pp. 298-302, extracts from Cardinal Manning's papers giving his views on the Suppression of the Society[7]].
Ferrer Benimeli, José Antonio (S.J.), [extensive publications based on the French diplomatic sources] e.g. 'El Motín de Esquilache y sus consecuencias según la correspondencia diplomática francesa', *Archivium Historicum Societatis Iesu*, 53 (105), 1984, pp. 193-219.
Giménez López, Enrique (ed.), *Expulsión y Exilio de los Jesuitas Españoles*, Alicante, Universidad de Alicante, 1997, ISBN 84-7908-329-8.
Harney, Martin P., *The Jesuits in History*, Chicago, 1962.
Holt, Geoffrey (S.J.), [several articles dealing mainly with the suppression of the English Province and previously published in the *Archivum Historicum Societatis Iesu* are now available in *'Promising Hope'*, ed. T. M. McCoog (S.J.), 2003].
Kley, Dave van, *The Jansenists and the Expulsion of the Jesuits from France 1757-1765*, New Haven and London, Yale University Press, 1975, ISBN 0-300-01748-0.
March, J. M., *El restaurador de la Compañía de Jesús, beato José Pignatelli y su tiempo*, vol. 1, Barcelona, 1935.
McCoog, T. M. (S.J.), ed., *'Promising Hope': Essays on the Suppression and Restoration of the English Province of the Society of Jesus*, Rome, 2003.
Palmer, R. R., *Catholics and Unbelievers in 18th century France*, Princeton, 1939.
Pastor, Ludwig von, *The History of the Popes*, ed. Kerr, London, 1930, vol. XXXVI.
Pinedo, Isidoro (S.J.), 'Supresión [de la Compañía de Jesús]', eds

---

[7] Cf. *Afterword*, p. 336.

Charles E. O'Neill (S.I.), Joaquín M. Domínguez (S.I.), *Diccionario Histórico de la Compañía de Jesús*, I, Rome and Madrid, 2001, pp. 878-884 [with a good bibliography].

Williams, Michael B., *The Venerable English College Rome, A History 1579-1979*, London, 1979.

Chapter One

In the Portuguese Dominions[1]

When the Jesuits protest their innocence of the gross and wholesale iniquities with which they are charged, it is considered a peculiarly effective reply to point to the many Catholics, Bishops and others, clergy and laity, who have been their adversaries, to the many rulers of Catholic countries, who have expelled them from their midst, and most of all to their entire suppression by that very Apostolic See of which they have always proclaimed themselves to be the devoted servants and special champions. 'What,' say our adversaries, 'can be the explanation of this universal and persistent dislike for the Society on the part of so many highly representative Catholics unless it be that the charge of private ends, political intrigues, plots and conspiracies, poisonings and regicides, of obscurantist and immoral doctrines, is fully justified?'

There is doubtless a speciousness about this mode of putting the question, and it has the advantage of dispensing those who trust in it from the troublesome task of weighing arguments and verifying disputed facts. But it is forgotten that, if there are Catholics – Bishops, priests, and laymen – who have been hostile to the Society, there have been others still more numerous, belonging to these several classes, who have been its firm friends and advocates; that if there have been rulers in Catholic countries who have expelled it and tried to suppress it there have been others still more numerous who have invited it into their dominions, have built colleges and churches for its use, and have spoken of it in terms of the highest praise; and if there was a Pope, just one Pope, who suppressed it, there have been more than twenty Popes who have protected it, and have set high store on its services, among them being those most recent Popes who, step by step, have restored to it all that it had lost of spiritual faculties and privileges by the act of Clement XIV. What all this

[1] *The Month*, **99** (1902), 113–130.

points to is the impossibility of arriving at the truth by the summary and superficial method above described. In this, as in all other controversies of a complicated nature, a sure conclusion can be reached only by those who are prepared to take each allegation separately, and apply to it the ordinary and indispensable tests for determining historical and doctrinal truth.

In regard to the most recent instance of such an expulsion of the Society by the rulers of a Catholic country,[2] our readers can judge whether, when a country is in a certain sense Catholic, it necessarily follows that its rulers can be credited with a genuine zeal for the welfare of the Catholic religion, and whether the bare fact of a large body of Religious being expelled from such a country is always conclusive evidence that they had given justifiable provocation to their rulers – unless indeed it be justifiable provocation to have stood in the way of a determined movement for de-christianizing their country. Given the interest shown in the contemporary controversy, we shall perhaps be meeting the wishes of our readers by taking up the question of the Suppression of the whole Society by Clement XIV in 1773. It has been more than once thrown in our faces during the last few months by those who have defended the French Associations Law, one writer even going so far as to maintain that that single Papal Letter in itself is sufficient to settle beforehand the question of Jesuit guilt, not only as regards Jesuits who lived in the times before it was published, but even as regards those who live now or may live in centuries yet to come. Such a suggestion is of course foolish, but it is worth a passing notice, inasmuch as people are not wanting whom it unconsciously influences, though they would be ashamed to formulate it. However, the Brief of Suppression is an historical fact which needs to be taken into account by those who would form their minds on the Jesuit question, and we propose to consider it under the three following heads: (1) What is the precise verdict which the Brief *Dominus et Redemptor* passes on the Society, and in view of which it proceeds to suppress it? (2) Was the publication of the Brief a spontaneous act on the part of Clement XIV, representing his unfettered judgment on the needs of the Church, or was it extorted from him by the threats of the Bourbon Courts, and did it only represent his judgment of what the welfare of the Church required in the sense that he felt he must either grant this much to his tormentors or expect from their resentment still more serious injuries to the Catholic populations? (3) What were the motives animating those who pressed for the

---

[2] [Sydney Smith is referring to the expulsion of the Jesuits from France in the late 19th century. *Ed. N.*]

extinction of the Society – for whether the pressure of the Bourbon Courts went to undue lengths or not, no one will dispute that it existed or that it was most persistent? We have arranged these questions in an analytic order, but it will be more convenient to investigate them in their historical sequence; and in explaining the motives of the Bourbon Courts it will be necessary to recount at some length the history of the expulsion of the Jesuits by civil authority from the French, Spanish, and Portuguese dominions – since, as will appear, the object of these Courts in demanding the total suppression was that their own previous campaigns against the Society might be justified and completed.

The Courts which towards the close of the eighteenth century, after having expelled the Jesuits from their own dominions, laboured so energetically for its total Suppression by the Holy See, were those of France, Spain, and Portugal, together with the lesser Courts of Naples and Parma. It is customary to speak of them as the Bourbon Courts. The King of Portugal, indeed, was of the House of Braganza, though his wife was a Bourbon, but the Kings of France and Spain were both grandsons of the Grand-Dauphin, the son of Louis XIV, whilst the King of Naples was a son of Charles III of Spain, and the Duke of Parma the son of his younger brother. It is, however, not so much to these Sovereigns as to the Ministers and favourites who dominated them that the movement for the suppression was primarily due. Louis XV was personally more inclined to favour the Jesuits than to harass them, and he did make some feeble efforts to stay or temper the persecution inflicted on them in his name. But his character had been enfeebled by years of debauchery, and he was too weak to resist for long together the wishes of his strong-willed mistresses and *Parlements*. Joseph I of Portugal was also not personally opposed to the Jesuits, but on the contrary, kept them about his person, until his Minister, Carvalho, gained the entire control over him by playing on his fears and credulity. The rulers of Naples and Parma were mere boys, and besides, their sovereignties were but appanages of the Spanish crown. Carlos III of Spain contrasts favourably with Louis XV and Joseph I. He was a man of pure morals and high character, and was animated by a sincere desire to rule for the welfare of his people, an end which in many respects he pursued successfully. Nor did he treat the Jesuits otherwise than with favour, for until some six years after his accession to the Spanish throne he had been their friend and protector. Of the mysterious circumstances under which he then suddenly became their chief foe we shall have to speak in due course.

Hostility to an institution like the Society of Jesus may proceed from many causes. We are, for instance, sometimes told that Catholics as well as Protestants, and good Catholics as well as bad, are to be found among their opponents, and in a sense this may he true. Within the limits of essential belief and practice marked out by the authority of the Catholic Church there is still a wide margin left for the varieties of individual taste as to work and methods. It is in large part to meet these varieties that the distinction between seculars and regulars, and again between the different Orders and Congregations of regulars, has been sanctioned by the Church among her workers. The inevitable result of such a distinction among Catholic institutions must be that there will be dislikes as well as likes, and that, human nature being what it is, these will tend to become intensified at times by the opposition of interests, for there must be opposition of interests when the members of these various bodies work side by side, and gather round them friends and supporters. In short, in this way an Order tends to become unpopular in one quarter just in proportion as it becomes popular in another, and that is how it has often been with the Society of Jesus. Still, this kind of antagonism, which is possible in persons whom both sides would acknowledge to be good Catholics, is comparatively mild in its character, and belongs to an entirely different order, both as regards its motives, its bitterness, and the lengths to which it is prepared to go, from the hostility to the Society which characterized those – we are referring to their Ministers rather than to the Sovereigns themselves – who pressed for its extinction by Clement XIV.

The motives of these latter may be suitably described in words used by Clement XIII in January 1768, in his protest against the invasion of ecclesiastical rights by the Government of Parma. 'The end in view,' he then said, 'is to detach the faithful and keep them apart from the Head of the Church, the sheep from their shepherd, and the result is to oppress the ecclesiastical jurisdiction, to overthrow the sacred hierarchy, to diminish the rights and privileges of the Holy See, to subordinate his authority to the civil power, and reduce to slavery the Church of God which is free.' This has been the dominant note of the world's conflict with the Holy See and the Catholic Church all through, being one in which all the classes of the disaffected naturally unite – worldly-minded statesmen who desire to manage everything in their own way, the advocates of unsound doctrine who desire to avert the condemnation they have merited, and those downright enemies of the Christian name whose purpose, as they cannot destroy the Holy See altogether, is to reduce its power for good as far as possible. And if the same classes of men have generally sought to precede their assaults on the Church's spiritual liberty, by attempts to destroy the Society of Jesus, it is because they have recognized the Society to be a body of men who will always use whatever influence they may possess, not indeed as political agents, for that is beyond their scope, but as teachers and spiritual advisers, in defence of the Holy See and of that free exercise of its jurisdiction which is so necessary for the discharge of its high mission. That these are the motives animating the present persecutors of the Society across the Channel has been shown clearly, and it will be found that they were also the motives animating, not indeed the Sovereigns themselves, but their Ministers at the end of the eighteenth century. It will be found, too, that the methods employed by these earlier persecutors are the same as those which we have observed in their modern imitators. To put forward their real motives would clearly be inexpedient, and they have preferred, partly by perverting the meaning of real facts, partly by downright inventions, to overwhelm the Society with a load of calumnies; on the one hand, firmly refusing it every judicial test which could cast the light of truth on their allegations, and, on the other, organizing the reiteration of the calumnies on such a scale as to create the semblance of consentient witness. In this way they have been able to pose as upright rulers, anxious only to guard their subjects from the wolves. To trace adequately the history of the action, thus conceived, of the Bourbon Courts at the time of the Suppression would require a more detailed treatment, and we must be content with a mere outline. It was in France only that the hostility to the Society had taken root in an influential class of the people, but it was in Portugal that administrative measures were first taken against it, and it was the King of Spain who eventually took the lead in demanding its total suppression of the Holy See. We begin with Portugal.

Joseph I ascended the throne of Portugal in July 1750, and appointed to be his chief Minister Sebastian Joseph Carvalho, better known by his subsequent title as the Marquis of Pombal. Pombal during the previous reign had been disliked at Court, but he had had occasional diplomatic employment which took him first to London and later to Vienna. It was in these Courts probably that he imbibed the principles to which he afterwards strove to give effect, and which Cardinal Pacca, who became Nuncio at Lisbon shortly after the close of Pombal's administration, thus summarizes:

> To make war on the Holy See and oppress the clergy, he adopted those measures and used those arms which, employed dexterously by the irreligious men of our time, have hitherto done, and are still doing, so much mischief, and are inflicting such serious wounds on religion and the Church. He corrupted and perverted public education in the schools and

universities, especially in that of Coimbra, which soon became a seat of pestilence. He took from the hands of youth the works of sound doctrine hitherto used in instruction, and substituted others of schismatical and heretical tendency, and amongst these, Dupin and the celebrated book of von Hontheim under the name of *Justinus Febronius,* lately condemned by the Holy See and by the greater part of the Bishops in those places in which the secular power had not shut the mouths of the sacred pastors. He facilitated the introduction into Portugal of the so-called Regalist writers, and refused it to the works of those who supported the rights and authority of the Holy See ... He published various writings... in which, with Jansenistic perfidy, he undertook to exalt the episcopal authority in order to lower the Pontifical primacy, and enlarged and extended the authority of Sovereigns in Church matters to such a degree that his doctrine differed little from the system of the Anglican Protestant Church.[3]

In short, he strove to do what Henry VIII actually did in England, and what M. Waldeck-Rousseau[4] is aiming at in France, to found a schismatic Church, in which Royal or State authority should be substituted for that of the Holy See.

These are just the motives already indicated as those dear to the persecutors of the Jesuits, and explain why Pombal should have wished to direct the first blows against them. As, however, at that time, all classes of the nation were thoroughly Catholic, and much attached to the Jesuits, whose services as teachers and confessors at home and as missionaries in the colonies were highly appreciated, it was necessary for him to conceal for a while the purposes he was cherishing in his heart. His policy was to commence his tenure of office by professing himself to be their fervent admirer, which was the easier because he had received from them several services. Later, when he had sufficiently destroyed their reputation by calumnies, would be the time for him to play the part of one sorrowfully disillusioned, and compelled to protect the kingdom against them.

The first act of his campaign against them was in connection with troubles provoked by his maladministration of the Indian settlements in South America. Mr Cunninghame-Graham[5] has brought under the notice of English readers the history, so bright in itself so sad in its termination, of the Jesuit missions or Reductions in Paraguay, and

---

[3] Pacca, *Notizie sul Portogallo,* p. 10. Ap. Weld, *Suppression of the Jesuits in Portugal,* p. 15.

[4] [Pierre M. R. Waldeck-Rousseau, 1846–1904, who introduced legislation to expel the Jesuits, and separate Church and State in France. *Ed. N.*]

[5] R. B. Cunninghame-Graham, *A Vanished Arcadia being some account of the Jesuits in Paraguay, 1607–1767,* London (Heinemann), 1924 (new ed., 1st publ. 1901).

other parts of South America. It is notorious how hard is the task of Christianizing and civilizing a savage race, and many men of judgment have pronounced it impossible. The Society has then a just title to take pride in its management of these South American missions of the seventeenth and eighteenth centuries, missions which were conducted on the rational principle of governing races still in their childhood by methods adapted to that stage in their mental development.[6] For a century and a half, by self-sacrificing and persevering endeavours, they reclaimed thousands of natives from savage life, trained them to habits of labour, agricultural, mechanical, and even artistic, and above all trained them to live lives of innocence and purity, of peace and industry, and of solid Christian piety. The one great danger to the permanence of this happy state threatened not from within so much as from without, that is to say, from the character of the many European emigrants who were seeking to make their fortunes in the new country. Even in these days the class is not noted for its orderly habits and high principles, and then it was far more wild and unscrupulous. The only chance for the Reductions was to keep the natives apart from these Europeans, who otherwise would have defrauded them, corrupted them, and if possible enslaved them, turning their paradises into hells. Accordingly, the missionaries had, with the sanction many times repeated of the Portuguese and Spanish monarchs, established a system by which these Europeans were forbidden to enter the Reductions, and this imposed on them the necessity of themselves administering the exchange of the produce of the natives' labour with the European goods required for their use. As the natives numbered many thousands these transactions were necessarily on a large scale, but the accounts were carefully kept, nor was anything whatever deducted from the profits for the benefit of the Fathers, who gave their services gratuitously, and relied for their maintenance exclusively on alms sent over to them for that purpose by their Sovereign, and by friends in Europe. It must be added that the Fathers had also Papal and Royal sanction for undertaking these procuratorial duties.

It was inevitable that the European colonists should resent their exclusion from the Reductions, and should put their own interpretation on its purport and intent. There were gold mines, they said, on

[6] The primary authorities on the history of these Reductions are Muratori's *Cristianesimo Felice* and Charlevoix's *Histoire de Paraguay*. A good popular account may be found in Crétineau-Joly's *Histoire de la Compagnie de Jésus*, and also in Father Weld's *Suppression of the Society of Jesus in Portugal*. Southey's *History of Brazil*, though in some respects hostile, renders important testimony on the subject.

the mission territories, which the Jesuits wished to keep to themselves, and by exploiting which they were acquiring vast wealth. On this foundation of misconstruction imagination naturally built other calumnies. Whilst depriving the colonists of their natural rights – as they described their claim to enslave the natives – the Jesuits, so they said, themselves enslaved their neophytes, and even treated them with gross cruelty. Then, too, this vast system of exchange of goods, what else was it but trade,[7] in which, by the laws of the Church, the clergy, and especially the Religious, were forbidden to engage? Further, it had been found necessary to enable the Reductions to defend themselves against invasion by the uncivilized tribes around them, and sometimes even by these European immigrants and their half-breed progeny; the Jesuits had provided their neophytes with arms, which they were taught to make and to use. Doubtless, this was an undertaking which, under ordinary circumstances, would have been deemed unbecoming in members of a religious order. But the occasion fully justified it and it was done with the knowledge and approbation of the authorities, civil and ecclesiastical, at home. These native troops, too, had from time to time, at the bidding of their European Sovereign, flocked to his standard and proved themselves to be his loyal soldiers. None the less, the enemies of the Reductions sought to make out that the Jesuits were forming for themselves an independent nation in which they might hold sovereign power.

These were the pre-existent conditions on the South American continent when Pombal was appointed to be the chief Minister. Till then the Kings of Portugal, like their brother-Kings of Spain, had conscientiously investigated all complaints against the Fathers and their Reductions, by appointing governors and visitors, and securing Bishops, in whom they could trust. The reports of these had been invariably, if we except such as came from notoriously unscrupulous persons, like de Cardenas, in justification of the Fathers and in condemnation of their accusers, and the Kings had frequently written back in the same sense, and so the mission work could go on. Now,

---

[7] Trade, in the sense in which it is forbidden by the Canon Law, is buying in order to sell, advantage being taken of the difference of price of the same article in different times or places, to make a profit. It does not then touch, and has never heen held to touch, those who sell the produce of their own lands. In exactly the same sense an English country gentleman does not consider himself a trader when he sells his corn or his turnips, his peaches or his cattle. Indeed, the only difference between the Jesuit Procurators of the Reductions on the one hand, and an English country gentleman, or the Abbot of a monastery on the other, is that in the former case the operations were on a much larger scale, and were for the sake not of themselves, but of many thousand natives too inexperienced to act for themselves.

however, that Pombal was in power at Lisbon, he saw only in these contentions the opportunity for initiating his intended campaign against the Society.

His chance soon came. In 1750, one Gómez Pereira, a resident at Rio Janeiro, asserted once more that the Jesuits were working gold mines in the Reductions east of the Uruguay river, in the northern part of the province of Rio Grande do Sul. These Reductions, seven in number, at that time belonged to Spain, but misled by the representations of this man, Pombal proposed an exchange of territory, Portugal to take the district in which lay these Reductions, and Spain to receive in return the Colony of San Sacramento on the north bank of the Rio de la Plata. Foreseeing to some extent what the transaction might mean for his Indian subjects, King Ferdinand VI, then King of Spain, hesitated to accept the Portuguese proposal, but the temptation was great, as quite recent inquiries by the Spanish authorities had established that there was no gold in the territory coveted by Portugal, or any richness of soil to make it valuable, whereas the colony of San Sacramento was really valuable, and the more so as it commanded the entrance to the La Plata. The exchange was accordingly accepted, and with it the condition exacted by the Portuguese Government, that the Indians in the seven Reductions should evacuate their settlements and migrate to other lands, west of the Uruguay. This was because the Portuguese desired to have all to themselves this Uruguay district in which they expected to find gold, but for the Indians it meant abandoning the farms on which they and their ancestors of now several generations had expended their care and toil, the homes round which gathered so many cherished associations; and it meant migrating with their families, some thirty thousand in number, to a distant and unknown land, where they would have to start life absolutely afresh, where they might not find the needful soil or produce, and where they would certainly be in danger from the savage tribes which would surround them and dispute possession with them. It must be a marvel to the present generation how Christian rulers could conceive a scheme so cruel and wicked, and it is easy to realize how the Indians would be prone to resist. The Jesuit Fathers, however, were ordered to see to its accomplishment, and their General, Father Retz, himself wrote to them in the same sense. It was indeed the only course he could recommend to his subjects, for to counsel resistance to the tyrannous measures, even if lawful, was foredoomed to be disastrous. The missionaries addressed themselves to the painful task, and they first represented to the Spanish authorities – for the territory was as yet under Spanish rule – that at least an interval of three years was indispensable to make proper preparations for the migration, and to sow the seed in the new lands. They then used their influence over the natives, and with such success that these became resigned to the sad necessity, and began their preparations. Pombal and his agents, however, were only too anxious to precipitate a catastrophe; and under pressure from them Valdelirios, the Spanish Governor of Paraguay, and Gómez Freire de Andrada, the Portuguese Governor of Rio de Janeiro, told the missionaries that not three years, but three months at most, would be allowed for the evacuation of the Reductions. This was more than the Indians could stand, and they turned on the missionaries themselves, whom they accused of betraying them into the hands of their cruel enemies, the Portuguese. Into the details of the ensuing struggle we need not enter. It is sufficient to say that the Indians rose, attained an initial success, but were soon subdued by an army of Spaniards and Portuguese united together. The missions were ruined, many of the natives carried off by the Portuguese into slavery, and of course the Jesuits accused by Pombal and his agents of having been the true authors and fomenters of the rising. As, however, these Jesuits were Spanish subjects, he could not touch their persons. Meanwhile, gold was not found in the territory of the seven Reductions, and disputes arose between the two Governments, which ended by a dissolution of the Treaty of exchange, and the Uruguayan territory reverting to Spain. The Indians were then able to return to their now ruined homes. Spanish Jesuits were again sent to take charge of them. Thus these missions might in time have resumed their peaceful course, had it not been for the expulsion of the Society from Spain in 1767, the effects of which were felt in Paraguay in 1768, by the withdrawal of all the Jesuit missionaries from the Spanish colonies. Since then the fruits of so many years of patient solicitude and self-sacrifice have been lost, the natives gradually relapsing into their former uncivilized mode of existence.

The events we have been relating occurred between the years 1750 and 1756, and it was to be expected that the evil wrought in the Uruguay district would have a demoralizing effect on the Reductions lying westward of the Uruguay and Parana rivers. Nor was that the extent of the devastation wrought among the missions by Pombal's anti-Jesuit policy. All along the south bank of the Amazon, in the district then called Maranhão, were very many similar Indian settlements which had developed under the care of the Jesuit missionaries, since the beginning of the seventeenth century, when the first foundations were laid by Frs Pinto and Figueira. This vast territory belonged to Portugal, and thither in 1753 Pombal sent his brother, Francis Xavier Mendoza, as Governor, with instructions to harass the

Jesuits, and do his best to create a pretext for requiring their recall to Europe. This Mendoza at once proceeded to do, by lending credence to the accusations of the European colonists described above. He reported accordingly to his brother, and on 6 June 1755, received back orders to take away from the Jesuit Fathers altogether (as likewise from the Capuchins) the temporal administration of the missions, a measure which shortly after was followed by the deportment of many of them back to Lisbon.

Pombal's next step was to gain over the King to an unfavourable view of the Society, and, as the latter was credulous and incompetent, this was not so difficult. He first caused a pamphlet to be concocted out of the false charges against the missionaries, which was entitled *A Short Relation of the Republic established by the Jesuits in the dominions of Spain and Portugal in the New World, and of the War waged by them against the armies of the two Crowns, extracted from the Register of the Commissaries and Plenipotentiaries* [i.e., of Valdelirios, Freire de Andrada, and Mendoza, &c.] *and other authentic documents*. Having poisoned the King's mind by these accounts, and added to their effect by the suggestion that even the Jesuits in Portugal were disloyal to him, and were striving to divert the affections of his people from himself to his brother Don Pedro – a purely fictitious charge – Pombal next obtained leave to dismiss all the Jesuit confessors to the King and Royal Family, and to banish them altogether from the Court, that is, from all power to represent the true facts to his Majesty. Then, using the name of this miserable puppet of a Sovereign, he applied to Benedict XIV, recounting the offences he was imputing to the Jesuits, and demanding their suitable punishment. By way of instruction to Almada, the Portuguese representative in Rome, he sent a copy of the *Short Relation* – other copies of which he simultaneously distributed throughout Portugal, and sent to all the Courts of Europe. He also sent a second document of a similar kind, but more elaborated, and added an accompanying letter to Almada, under date 10 February 1758, in which he speaks in the following terms:

> Your Excellency will find in this Relation evident proof that for some years past these Religious have renounced the obedience they owe to the Bulls and commandments of the Popes, the observance of laws most necessary for the maintenance of public peace in these Kingdoms. They have sacrificed every Christian, religious, natural, and political duty to a blind, insolent and unbounded passion for possessing themselves of political and temporal governments, to the insatiable desire to acquire and amass the goods of others, and for usurping the authority of Sovereigns ... To such a deplorable state of corruption have these unworthy children

of a holy religion fallen in the Kingdom of Portugal, and still more in her dominions beyond the sea, that few Jesuits can be found who do not appear to be merchants, soldiers, and tyrants, rather than Religious.

Here we must interrupt the history for the moment to comment on the true character of this *Short Relation,* and its supplement – documents which lie at the root of very many of the base charges against the Society with which the books of its enemies are filled, documents which the Brief of Suppression has evidently in view in one or two of its clauses. As regards Uruguay, the bare fact of such an order of the Two Courts requiring the Indians to abandon their homes and migrate elsewhere, is enough to account for all the disastrous consequences that followed, nor is it needful to infer any improper conduct in the missioners to explain them. In regard to the missions of Maranhão, as likewise in regard to the missions in the vast district lying west of Paraguay in the diocese of Tucumán, these accusations of cupidity, of desire for sovereignty, of cruelty, are only such as were sure to be made by the greedy and unscrupulous European adventurers by whom the missions were surrounded. Often too before, as has been said, when persons of this class alleged their grievances against the missionaries, the result had been to elicit official inquiries, and reports from Governors, Bishops, and other trustworthy persons, all of whom testified from the fulness of their knowledge that accusations of this sort were entirely false, and that the conduct of the missionaries was worthy of all praise.

Thus in defence of the Paraguay Fathers may be cited the letter of Don Gabriel Peralta, Dean of the Cathedral of Paraguay, addressed to the President of the Royal Council of the Indies, on 18 May 1653, the letter of the Archbishop of La Plata to the King of Spain, on 3 March 1690, the Official Report of Don Balthasar García Ros, Governor of Paraguay, dated 15 June 1705, the letter of Philip V of Spain, to the Provincial S.J. of Paraguay, dated 26 November 1706, congratulating him on the good state of the missions, and attributing all to his care, and lastly the decree of the same King Philip V, dated 28 December 1743, which rehearses the various accusations against the missionaries, and declares that as the result of his inquiries he is thoroughly satisfied that the accusations are groundless, and in particular gives his entire sanction to the system of managing and selling the produce of the lands which had been called merchandize.

In defence of the Maranhão missions may be cited the decree of Alphonso VI of Portugal, of 1683, and the similar Royal Decree of 31 March 1680; the Report of John de Mala, Governor of Maranhão, to John V, dated 10 September 1725; and that of Eduardo dos Santos, who was specially sent out by John V in 1736, to make a full inquiry into the truth of charges laid before his Majesty by Paul de Silva-Nunez.

In defence of the missions under the pastoral care of the Bishops of Tucumán may be cited the letters written by successive bishops of that see, on 8 October 1658, to Pope Alexander VII, on 24 July 1720, to Philip V of Spain, on 20 April 1729, to Philip V, on 23 November 1730, to Pope Clement XII, and on 4 December 1750, to Benedict XIV.[8]

Though these numerous testimonies belong to dates previous to the time of Pombal, they are conclusive against his *Short Relation*, both directly, because it professes to indict the Jesuits of past generations, as well as his own, and indirectly, because it is not presumable, or even intelligible, that the accused and the accusers, the Jesuits and the European adventurers, should after all those years have suddenly interchanged their natures, the former from being upright and devoted to being self-seeking and unscrupulous, the latter from being self-seeking and unscrupulous to being upright and devoted. Still, as regards the Uruguay disturbances we have contemporary evidence, thanks to the inquiry made by General Cevallos in 1759. This General held a high reputation for integrity of character and military skill, and had been sent out to supersede Valdelirios. He was ordered to make a searching inquiry into the alleged guilt of the Jesuits by Wall, the chief Minister at Madrid, and, as Wall was a bitter opponent of the Society, it might have been more to Cevallos' interest to report against them. He was, however, an honest man, and he appointed his most capable officer, Don Diego de Salas, to conduct the process. Don Diego took innumerable testimonies, from the various royal officials, as well as the most respectable of the Indians, and wrote back thus on 30 November 1759:

> The process being now concluded, I have ascertained from it that not only did not a single Jesuit, and in particular not one of the eleven named in my instructions, in any way incite the Indians to disobedience, but on the contrary, as is established by all the depositions, the Fathers did all that was humanly possible to keep the Indians to the obedience incumbent on them. All this is confirmed by the declaration of the officers and generals of the army, the particulars of which your Excellency will see from the

---

[8] The text of this Letter of 1750 is to be found among Père de Ravignan's *Pièces Justificatives,* in his *Clement XIII and Clement XIV.* The text of the others may be found among the *Pièces Justificatives,* in Charlevoix's *History of Paraguay.* Extracts from them all may be read in Fr Weld's *Suppression of the Society of Jesus in Portugal.*

process, and the irresistible testimony of which is the clearest confirmation of what I wrote in my letters of 7 October 1758.[9]

It may seem superfluous to add anything further to this overwhelming testimony, but it was preceded by a decree of the Council of Castille, dated 5 April 1759,[10] pronouncing in favour of the Jesuits, and declaring their adversaries to be slanderers and forgers; also by a decree of the Spanish Inquisition of 13 May 1759, forbidding any one to read the libels against the Society circulated in Spain by Pombal and others. Also we have told how the *Short Relation* was disseminated in many countries of Europe, and it should not be overlooked that the effect of this wide circulation of the libel was to elicit from many Bishops in Spain and throughout Europe letters written to the Sovereign Pontiff, protesting against Pombal's libellous pamphlets, and recording their testimony of the exact observance and active labours of the Society in their respective dioceses. Père de Ravignan, in the work already cited, gives the text of fifty of these letters, which unquestionably form a wonderful testimony to the healthy state of the Order on the eve of its suppression.

We may now resume the thread of the history. When Pombal's letters reached Rome, Benedict XIV was near his end. If on some occasions he had found fault with certain Fathers, no Pope had awarded more glowing praise to the Society as a whole. He was now in his eighty-third year, and intensely pained at the representations made to him on behalf of the King of Portugal. He did not wish to protect evildoers from their merited punishment, but, on the other hand, he was sceptical about the truth of accusations so wholesale and so gross, and yet felt the difficulty of questioning allegations guaranteed by the testimony of a Sovereign. What he did was to appoint an Apostolic Visitor to inquire into the state of the Society in the Portuguese dominions, and he chose Cardinal Saldanha for the office. His letters to this prelate are extant; one being the Brief of Appointment, in which he gives the necessary powers and instructions, and the other a letter of a more private and personal kind, explaining how Saldanha is to understand and execute them. What is noticeable about the Brief of Appointment is that it states as the only reason for its issue the demand of Joseph I and the *Short Relation* which had been given to himself and his Cardinals, and spread throughout the world; that it orders Saldanha to make one visit, either by himself or by suitable subdelegates, to each House, College, Mission, or Residence of the Society, and to see all the members; to

[9] Origin. Estado, Simancas Leg 7404; ap. Duhr, *Jesuiten-Fabeln,* p. 216.
[10] *See* Ravignan, op. cit. i. p. 505.

correct himself, if there should prove to be need, any lesser evils, but if anything grave should be discovered to report it to the Pope, with all information, that he might ponder the matter over carefully and at leisure. In this official letter which would have to be shown to the King and his Ministers, he speaks guardedly about the possibility of the charges proving unfounded, but what is noticeable in the private letter, is that he treats them as hardly credible, and is very insistent that the inquiry should be made only through such persons as might be trusted to examine impartially and dispassionately: also that it should be carried on secretly, so as to save the high and well-deserved reputation of the Society. He is most urgent too in this private letter that the terms of the Brief shall be strictly adhered to, and nothing of grave moment in the way of regulation or punishment done without its being first referred back to himself.

Benedict XIV signed this Brief on 1 April 1758, and it reached Saldanha by the end of the month. On 2 May he promulgated it, and on 3 May Benedict died. It was on 6 July of the same year that Clement XIII was elected, and Saldanha – or rather Pombal, to whom he showed himself entirely subservient – made good use of the interval of vacancy. No attention was paid to the private letter or even to the limiting clauses of the Brief. Saldanha was to inquire carefully, and by visits to each Jesuit house in the Portuguese dominions. In fact he made no visits of inquiry, submitted no interrogations to the Jesuit Superiors or subjects, gave them no opportunity of explanation or defence, kept nothing secret, made no distinctions of guilty and not guilty, but on 15 May, just a fortnight after his reception of the Brief, declared the Jesuits as a body guilty of having exercised an illicit, public, and scandalous commerce both in Portugal and the colonies in America, Spain, and Asia. Surely this was not to reserve graver matters for the Pope's consideration – nor was it consistent with the supposition that he had made any proper inquiry of his own into the facts on which he passed his precipitate judgment. Three weeks later Pombal made the Patriarch of Lisbon withdraw all faculties to preach and hear confessions from the Jesuit Fathers within his patriarchate.

But a still heavier blow was impending. On 14 September, the King was returning in a carriage from the house of the Marquis of Tavora, and was fired at. The rumour spread at once, and after a few weeks it was said that the Duke de Aveiro and the members of the Tavora family were guilty of the crime which they had conspired to commit. They were all arrested on 12 December, and on 12 January they were tried. The trial, however, was of a remarkable kind. The natural tribunal for such an offence was set aside, and Pombal devised a court of *Inconfidenza*, in which he himself was both the accuser and judge, two of his own creatures being added as assessors. The trial was secret, and we depend therefore for the account of it on Pombal's untrustworthy testimony, but there appear to have been no depositions of witnesses taken, and all that was done was to put the accused to the torture. This elicited nothing damaging from the others, but the Duke de Aveiro was said, when able to bear the pain no longer, to have assented to all that they suggested to him, and then accused not only these nobles, but also the Jesuits, of having been in the plot. The nobles were executed the next day in the cruellest manner, but whether they were really guilty, or whether there had been any plot at all, is at least doubtful, and on the accession of the next Sovereign the innocence of all said to be implicated was judicially pronounced.

When the execution was over several of the Fathers were cast into prison, and among them Father Malagrida. Neither he nor the others were ever tried for this imputed offence, nor was anything publicly alleged as connecting him with the supposed assassination. Nor again was he of all others a man likely to descend to such iniquity. He was one of the best-known and most venerated priests in the Portuguese dominions, who had spent nearly forty years amidst immense labours and hardships, on the Brazilian mission. His services had also been much in request among the royal family, and he had even been summoned by the Queen Mother to return from Brazil to assist her at her death. Nor again, if Pombal really thought him guilty, is it intelligible that he should have kept him in prison for two years, and then had him executed, not on this charge, but on a charge of heresy, alleged to have been committed during these two years of his imprisonment. As to any opinion he may or may not have expressed whilst in prison we have no trustworthy evidence to tell us. Pombal, when he wished to try him on this charge, took care, first of all, to displace the Grand Inquisitor and to appoint his own brother, Paul Carvalho, to the post, and similarly to change the subordinate officials. It does not seem that these persons even held a proper trial, for no depositions were ever found, only a Report, published in 1761, which accuses Malagrida of having written the *Life of St Anne* and the *History of Antichrist*, books which if they existed and contained the gross absurdities the Report ascribes to them, convict the Father not of heresy, but of madness brought on by his sufferings. And it is possible that he really was mad, though it is highly suspicious that the books in question were never produced, whereas it would have been in Pombal's interest to produce them if he could. On 20 September 1761, before an immense concourse of people, Father

Malagrida was burnt as a heretic, if, indeed, it is not truer to say that he suffered as a martyr.

The object of this chapter has been not so much to relate the history of the Suppression in Portugal, as to show the motives that inspired it, and how impossible it is to gather from the facts a conclusion discreditable to the Society, after the manner of those whose argument is set down in the opening paragraphs at the beginning. We must pass over therefore, in spite of its pathos, the story of the banishment of the Jesuits from every portion of the Portuguese dominions, and their deportation to Città Vecchia, and must pass over the still more cruel story of the harsh imprisonment of some two hundred in the dungeons of Almeida, of Belem, and of St Julien's, where they languished for eighteen years, that is, until the next reign commenced, when with their release came the declaration of their perfect innocence.

Chapter Two

In France

I.[1] [The opposing forces marshalled]

It has been already remarked that in France, unlike Spain and Portugal, the hostility to the Society of Jesus, to which it succumbed at the end of the eighteenth century, was strongly cherished by an influential class of the people, and had struck deep roots in the past. These words, however, need to be understood strictly, for in no country more than in France was the popularity and consequent influence of the Society more widespread, and that at the very time when it was about to be suppressed by the civil power. On this point Father de Ravignan appropriately quotes from two authors of the period, neither of whom is suspect through any undue partiality for the Jesuits.

> Established at the Court of France [says Duclos] the Jesuits had no rivals among the regular clergy, and found friends and protegés in the highest classes ... The Bishops as a body were on their side ... If the doings of the *Parlement* of Paris had not been confirmed by an Edict which was little less than wrested from the King, it is doubtful if in the provinces the other *Parlements*, except Rouen, would have followed the example set them by the *Parlement* of Paris. I do not hesitate to declare, and I have been a closely-placed spectator of the transactions, that the Jesuits had, and still have, more partisans than adversaries. La Chalotais and Monclar by themselves alone gave the impulse to their own companies [i.e., the legal bodies attached to their respective *Parlements*], and in the case of the other (companies) it was necessary to resort to many expedients. Speaking generally the provinces regret the loss of the Jesuits, and they would, if they were to reappear among them, be received with acclamation.[2]

---

[1] *The Month*, **99** (1902), 263–279.
[2] *Voyage en Italie*, p. 52

And, says Laffrey,

> the larger and sounder part of the nation regret the loss of the Jesuits, ... and even among their judges, along with certain firebrands, they counted many partisans forced to esteem them, and in their heart of hearts to do them justice.[3]

Such testimonies are of importance, for they contribute to expose the silly fallacy, to which allusion was made in Chapter 1, that the bare fact of the Jesuits being proscribed in so many countries proves them to be anti-social agents, and relieves their critics from the necessity of examining the details of their history.

The character of the influential party who, in contrast with the mass of the French nation, were hostile to the Society and carried their hostility to the length of working for its suppression, is thus estimated by Theiner, a writer in whose judgment the enemies of the Society place much confidence:

> The savage war against the Society of Jesus which broke out at that time is certainly the saddest event that ever happened. Too many impure passions were then at work. Infidelity, which under the name of toleration and philosophy, had invaded all classes of society, and had even captured those in the very highest positions, and Jansenism, carried to its most violent excesses – although immortal enemies to each other – entered into a firm and impious alliance to work for the destruction of the Society of Jesus.[4]

To form, however, a complete idea of the forces arrayed against the Society we must include in our enumeration the *Parlement* of Paris, the nature and history of which require to be understood. It would be a mistake to regard a French *Parlement* as resembling an English Parliament. The latter is a representative body and derives its influence from this fact. The former was very differently constituted, and could find a more suitable English analogue in the Benchers of one of our Inns of Court. The *Parlement* of Paris traced back its origin to a remote past. It seems to have developed out of the early mediaeval *Conseil du Roi*, and had originally sufficed for the whole kingdom, moving with the King from place to place, like our *Curia Regis*. Later, when it became sedentary at Paris, *Parlements* of a similar character were established in the provinces, which eventually became twelve in number, and these, whilst presiding over the affairs of their

---

[3] *Vie privée de Louis XV*, iv, 72.
[4] A. Theiner, *Clement XIV*, I, Tabl.

respective jurisdictions, were expected, as regards matters affecting the whole kingdom, to adopt and carry out the measures initiated by the *Parlement* of Paris. The latter by the eighteenth century had come to consist of one hundred and ten members, of whom part were clergy and part were laity, but all lawyers by profession, whether ecclesiastical or civil. Membership was for life, and was obtainable by purchase, and this provision had the practical effect of restricting it to certain families, which formed a class apart in the country, and were called *familles de robe,* so that the *Parlement* became in course of time practically an hereditary chamber. The functions of the *Parlement* were not merely judicial, but also to a large extent administrative, a fact apparently due to its derivation from the *Conseil du Roi* at a time when the three-fold distinction of a ruler's functions was not as yet clearly appreciated. Thus equipped with powers the *Parlement* of Paris constituted an authority which was indeed under the Sovereign, by whom it was liable to have its measures set aside, but which within the margin thus left to it could, in conjunction with its fellow *Parlements* in the provinces, interpose in affairs of all kinds, ecclesiastical as well as civil, throughout the country, and cause its *arrêts* to be enforced. It had even acquired by usage the power to put a check on the exercise of the Royal prerogative, for one of its functions was to register the King's Edicts, which only thus became promulgated and acquired the force of laws. Having the right to register, it naturally claimed the right to remonstrate against any Edicts which it might deem injurious to the welfare of the country, and the remonstrance would on occasion be so prolonged as to amount to refusal. In this case the King, if he chose to use it, had his remedy in a *lit de justice,* a ceremony by which he came to a meeting of *Parlement* in person and in full state, and caused the obnoxious Edict to be registered in his presence. It will be easily understood that what resulted from this imperfectly ordered arrangement was that under strong Kings like Henri IV or Louis XIV, or a strong Minister like Richelieu, the *Parlement* was kept in subjection to the Crown, whilst under weak Kings like the last three Valois, or Louis XV, or again in troubled times like the earlier portion of the reign of Henri IV, the *Parlement* often carried the day over the Crown.

It is due to these French *Parlements* to acknowledge that at times they conferred signal benefits on their country by their firm resistance to the abuses of arbitrary power, and that speaking generally they were characterized by a fine incorruptibility and a strong sense of duty carried into the public service. Still it is possible for a corporation which has these traditional merits to have also some traditional demerits, to become dominated by strong passions, prejudices and party views, to cherish antipathies and resentments, and such was unquestionably the case with the *Parlement* of Paris; and it was thus that it became from first to last the uncompromising foe of the Society of Jesus. Three causes of this hostility may be distinguished. In the first place, the *Parlement* had inherited the ideas of the Pragmatic Sanction of 1438, ideas of which the Gallican Declaration of 1682 was but the reassertion, and which meant in practice the enslavement of the Church by the State, with the consequent subordination of spiritual to temporal interests. The Society of Jesus, on the other hand, had imbibed from its saintly Founder a spirit of wholehearted loyalty to the Apostolic See, whose attitude to these Erastian principles was always one of uncompromising protest. In the second place, in the middle of the sixteenth century, when the Society first sought entrance into France and asked to be allowed to open a College in Paris, it found itself in necessary competition with the University of Paris. The University was at that time in sad need of reform, both intellectual and moral, and it was not wonderful that the parents should show a disposition to transfer their children to a school where they would be better taught, and trained to habits of piety and purity. Yet all the more on this account did the University resent the intruder, and as its personnel was largely identified with that of the *Parlement*, they, of course, turned to the latter to use its powers on their behalf. Thirdly, when in the next century Jansenism appeared, it took its rise in the midst of the *familles de robe,* for such was the Arnauld family, as well as that of the Pascals, and of some other Jansenist leaders; and to this family connection was doubtless due the fact, which is in any case unquestionable, that Jansenism throughout its career of influence had its stronghold among the Parlementaires, and could always count on the *Parlement* to fight its battles of defence and offence; and so, as the Jesuits were recognized as the special combatants against Jansenism, they and the *Parlements* again found themselves brought by the force of circumstances into direct opposition.

It was in 1552 that the Jesuits first sought admission into Paris, and asked for authorization to open a College there. Letters Patent were then granted them by Henri II, which were followed by a succession of others during that and the next three reigns, but these all failed of their effect owing to the persistent opposition of the *Parlement*, so that the existence of the Society in the country was for more than half a century precarious – indeed, for a time the Fathers were actually expelled and their property confiscated. But with the commencement of the seventeenth century Henri IV found himself at last firmly seated on the throne, and, as he had come to know something of the

Jesuits and esteemed them highly, he issued a Royal Edict in 1603 in their favour, the registration of which he compelled. It was on this occasion that Achille de Harlay delivered his famous Remonstrance, to which Henri IV made his famous reply. The two together set forth excellently and in a nutshell a collection of the usual charges against the Society and the conclusive answers to them. From that time onward Henri IV was their firm friend – indeed the best friend on a throne that they ever had – and under his protection, and the favour of the French nation by whom their schools were always appreciated, they were able to open churches and colleges throughout the country; and lay the foundations of a future development and progress, not surpassed, if equalled, in any other kingdom.

Richelieu also was on the whole their protector, and so was Louis XIV. Accordingly, during these reigns the *Parlements* had little power to injure them, but with the death of Louis XIV their position became less secure. During the first three decades of the reign of Louis XV the Jansenist agitation was in an acute stage owing to the struggles consequent on the issue of the Bull *Unigenitus,* the final and most crushing condemnation of Jansenist errors. As long as Cardinal de Noailles was Archbishop of Paris he resisted the publication of this Bull in his diocese. He even joined the Appellants, or those who appealed against it to a future General Council, but published it in 1717, and in 1720 it was also registered by the *Parlement*. This was a severe blow to the Jansenists who, nevertheless, continued to disregard the Bull in practice until Christopher de Beaumont, a prelate respected universally for his virtues and the purity of his zeal, acceded to the archbishopric. De Beaumont at once ordered his clergy to refuse the sacraments to any Appellant who would not first make a formal retractation of his appeal. As the result was that some notable persons died without the sacraments, the *Parlement* took the matter up, and went to the length of arresting those of the clergy who obeyed their Archbishop's order. Such an outrage was more than the Court could stand, and in 1753 the *Parlement* of Paris was banished by royal authority to Pontoise, and a Royal Chamber was established at Paris to administer justice in its stead. As the advocates refused to plead at this new bar, and the King was too weak in character to insist on his will being carried out, the drastic measure failed of its effect, and the *Parlement* returned after an exile of only a few months. Still Archbishop de Beaumont was not the man to yield on a matter of principle, nor the *Parlement* on a matter affecting its prejudices and *amour propre*. Hence, as Voltaire put it, 'nothing was more common in the kingdom than for persons to communicate *par arrêt de Parlement*', and the next few years saw continual sentences of banishment, condemnations to the galleys, and confiscations of property executed on a crowd of *curés, vicaires,* vergers, and others by the *Parlement*s of Paris, Aix, Rennes, and Toulouse.

The Jesuits were of course held responsible both for the *Unigenitus* itself, and for whatever efforts to enforce it were made by the Church and State authorities. It appeared as inconceivable to their enemies then as it does still, that Pope or Bishop or King should be capable of any initiative or strength of purpose to exact obedience to the Church's authority, even in regard to matters of vital consequence for faith and conduct, except in so far as they received the impulse from the General of the Jesuits or his lieutenants. Against the Jesuits therefore was chiefly directed the fierce outburst of passions which by the time of these measures taken by the Archbishop against the Appellants, and by the Crown against the *Parlement*, had risen to fever heat. The Jansenists and the magistrates were burning to retaliate on the Society in every way in their power, and, if they did not first think of working for its entire destruction, it was only because they deemed that to be a hopeless enterprise. The status of the Society in France was secured to it by a Royal Edict, and only by a counter-Edict emanating from the same source could it be successfully assailed. Yet, even if such an Edict were possible of enforcement, in view of the firm roots the Society had struck in all parts of the Catholic world, what chance had they of obtaining it from the King – at a time too when their recent resistance to his wishes had rendered them most unpopular in the eyes of all connected with the Court? Whilst, however, their minds were in this state two events were occurring which opened out a wider range of possibility for their schemes. One was the success of Pombal's campaign against the Jesuits of Portugal, the news of which was welcomed and studied with eager interest by these enemies of the Society in France – for, if the Society, hitherto deemed to be invincible, had fallen so easily beneath the blows of a weak power like Portugal, could it offer effectual resistance to a strong power like France? The other event was the fortunate occurrence of a Court intrigue which unexpectedly supplied them with the very force they needed, the co-operation of the Royal authority.

It has been said that the real governor of France is always a woman. Whatever truth or error there may be in such a general estimate, it is certainly true that during the last thirty years of the life of Louis XV the reins of power were in the hands of his mistresses. Particularly was this the case with Madame de Pompadour, whose period of office lasted from 1746 to 1764. Louis XV was by no means wanting in the capacity to govern. He was a keen and accurate observer of facts, and realized well the nature of the political and religious complications, at home and abroad, in the midst of which he lived. His secret Cabinet under the direction of the Comte de Broglie, with its network of secret agents at foreign Courts, if not a method to be admired, is at least a witness to the pains he took to be correctly informed. Historians have noted too the clear-sightedness with which he would appreciate the points of a discussion, and the propriety of the practical conclusions he would draw from it. What he lacked was the strength to resist the will of others and act on his own judgments.[5] A King thus constituted was sure to exercise his power under the control of his mistress, if only she proved ready and able to profit by the opportunity, and Madame de Pompadour was distinctly of that kind. She was a woman of soaring ambitions, bent on making the most of her position at the Court. She was young, only twenty-four, when she first came to Versailles, but she had talent and education, was quick in her perceptions and brilliant in her judgments, and she possessed in a high degree the art of persuasion. Finally, she was as bold and determined as Louis XV was timid and irresolute. When in 1744 she began her twenty years' reign – for it was nothing less – she quickly realized the conditions of her power.

> Madame de Pompadour [says M. Capefigue] understood clearly that if she wished to exercise authority, the first condition must be to surround herself with persons of talent whose devotedness would be secured by the fact of her having made their fortunes. The disgrace of M. de Maurepas had shown that Louis XV was prepared to sacrifice even his friends to the will of the Marquise, now become the source of all power and credit. The Secretaries of State were soon to be convinced that nothing could be done save through her influence. As she had accustomed the King to work, and prepared for him his ideals and his judgments, she became actually the mistress of the whole Council. She was looked up to as to the oracle of destinies. Soon she filled the Ministry with politicians wholly devoted to her.[6]

Among those who were thus her creatures, two men need to be specially mentioned because of the part they afterwards played in the

---

[5] 'With an intelligence most just and prompt,' says M. Capefigue (*Louis XV et la Société du XVIIIme Siècle,* iv. 101), 'Louis XV was indolent: he hated all which disturbed his leisure and quiet. His judgments were always thoroughly reasonable, but he abandoned them at once on the first opposition from his *Conseil*; he followed perfectly the course of a debate, but natural timidity hindered him from taking a prompt resolution; he conceived but could not execute.'

[6] *Ibid.,* iv, 54

Suppression of the Society. These were the Abbé, afterwards the Cardinal, de Bernis, and the Duc de Choiseul. The former, when he first came to Versailles as an *Abbé du Cour,* made himself conspicuous as a writer of amatory verses, and was an habitual guest at the *petits soupers* of Madame de Pompadour at Choisy, where he did not hesitate to compromise himself by improvising such verses in her honour.[7]

This poetical Abbé showed some real political talents, but he owed his advancement to the Ministry in 1756 to his advocacy of the Austrian Alliance. It was a disastrous alliance, which involved France in the Seven Years War, but it pleased Madame de Pompadour – whom the Empress Maria Theresa had flattered by sending her a personal communication – and finding her previous advisers against it, she advanced her *protégé* to the portfolio of Foreign Affairs. It is due to Bernis to acknowledge that, two years later, realizing the evils of the alliance, he spoke out boldly against it. It was then that the favourite dismissed Bernis and gave his portfolio to Choiseul.

If Bernis was an ecclesiastic not too careful about his morals, Choiseul was a man with no religious convictions at all. He belonged to the party of the Philosophers, and his wife, 'so ridiculously worshipped, kept quite a court of Encyclopaedists, where essays full of learning and mocking impiety were read,' says M. de Capefigue, who adds that 'the Duc de Choiseul's project was to destroy the convents, one after another, and take over their property for the State, in order to restore the finances.'[8] He was a devoted admirer of Madame de Pompadour – as he might well be, since it was to her he owed his promotion – and he was prepared to lend himself a willing instrument to the prosecution of all her designs.

With the advent to this influential post in the Ministry of a Philosopher who was destined to play a primary part in procuring the

---

[7] For instance:
>Sais-tu pourquoi ce vin brillant
>Dés que ta main l'agite
>Comme un éclair étincelant
>Vole et se précipite?
>En vain Bacchus dans le flacon
>Retient l'Amour rebelle,
>l'Amour sort toujours de prison
>Sous la main d'une belle.
>   (Capefigue, *ibid.*, p. 5.)

[8] *Ibid.*, v.40. The 'Philosophers' were also called Encyclopaedists on account of the Encyclopaedia which they brought out under the editorship of d'Alembert, and which was intended to give expression to their theories of life.

Suppression, not in France only, but in Spain and throughout the world, it will be convenient to interrupt the course of the narrative for a moment in order to explain what class of men these Philosophers were, and what was their attitude towards the Society of Jesus. The term 'Philosophers' in this connection does not denote students of philosophy, but the adherents of that particular school of anti-Christian philosophy of which Voltaire, d'Alembert, Didérot, and d'Holbach, were the leaders and best known representatives. Having first sprung into existence in the licentious days of the Regency, they had, through their literary and social eminence, acquired an immense influence in the country by the time of which we are speaking. Their social ideal was an anti-Christian republic, which they identified with an age of enlightenment, and, though they were cautious about what they said openly, in their private correspondence they spoke freely of their intentions to work for this ideal. *Écrasez l'infame* – 'Down with the infamous one', was the chief entry in their programme; that is to say, 'Down with the Catholic Church', or, as at other times they interpreted it – for the two things were equivalent in their eyes – 'Down with Jesus Christ.' And when the Church was once destroyed it would be an easy thing to destroy the Kings ; 'to hang the last King with the guts of the last priest,' as Didérot elegantly expressed it. Such men were bound to wish for the destruction of the Jesuits, and they tell us they regarded it as the first fortress of the enemy requiring to be attacked. When that was taken the country beyond could be occupied with comparative ease; and they looked on with delight to see the Parlementaires and the Jansenists doing their work for them, and in doing it preparing their own ultimate ruin. We are anticipating a little in giving the following quotation from d'Alembert, for it is from a letter written to Voltaire in 1762, when the final onslaught on the Jesuits of France was being made, but the words obviously express what was throughout the mind of the writer and his friends. He says, then:

> The Parlementaires are not doing their work drowsily. They imagine they are serving religion, but without thinking it they are serving Reason; they are the executioners of high justice in the employ of Philosophy, from whom without knowing it they receive their orders ... You are always saying, *Écrasez l'inf*... but let the *Infame* go down of itself, for it is doing so more quickly than you think. Do you know what Astruc says, ... As for me I see everything *couleur de rose* just now, for I see the Jansenists dying a quiet death next year, after having put the Jesuits to a violent death this year; and after that toleration established, the Protestants returning home, the priests married, the confessional abolished, and fanaticism destroyed before anyone has become aware of the fact.

This quotation, which could be matched by others of the same sort, defines for us exactly the attitude of the Philosophers. They hated the Society and wished to see it destroyed, not because of any real faults they could find in it, but because they regarded it as a valiant legion in the army of the Catholic Church. At the time they were rather looking on, than actually joining in the campaign, which they rejoiced to see carried on so effectually by others. Later they were to join in themselves, namely, when the fighting area was enlarged and a Papal Suppression was being demanded. Even as it was, they had their representative at the sources of power in the Duc de Choiseul, and were further doing their best to aid the cause by pamphlets and private influence. But we are anticipating, and must resume the thread of the narrative.

It was hardly to be expected that at any time during her twenty years' residence at the Court, Madame de Pompadour should be friendly disposed towards the Jesuits. The King had a Jesuit confessor, and, though he was not in the habit of going to the sacraments, yet should he fall ill, as he might at any time, he might wish to confess, and then the confessor's first demand would be that the mistress should be sent away. Even apart from the actual time of confession, a royal confessor had an authorized position, and was on the lookout for opportunities of appealing to the King's conscience. Moreover, in another part of the palace were the Queen and her daughters, and the Dauphin, all good, earnest practising Catholics, all firm friends of the Society, and choosing their confessors from among its members. The chief preoccupation of this outraged family and their Jesuit advisers was about the King's evil life and the baneful influence exercised over him by his mistress. They, too, were always hoping and praying for an opportunity of reclaiming him, and always expecting that such an opportunity would come; the more so as, if he was weak and dominated by his passions, they knew that he had the faith strong in him, and a disposition to piety for grace to work upon.

Thus the Marquise could not but regard the Jesuit confessors to the King and his family, and their Society which stood behind them, as her natural enemies and her constant danger. And as time ran on the danger became more serious. She was no longer young, and there were young rivals anxious to succeed her; and though her power of resource was wonderful in devising new occupations and amusements, new artistic pleasures and entertainments, and new attractions to recommend the delicate little suppers he was so fond of, the fits of *ennui* to which he had always been subject became more and more frequent and depressing. Might not this experience of the weariness of sin sooner or later be the means of sending the Royal Prodigal back to his Father's house? Thus her position became increasingly precarious, and her aversion to the everpresent witnesses for God and conscience grew in proportion. On the other hand, there were reasons why she should not wish to enter the lists as an active opponent of the Jesuits. To act thus would be to lend support to their adversaries outside, the Jansenists and the *Parlement*, and that was what her position at Court made her still less inclined to do. As the practical ruler of the country her interests were on the side of those who supported the principle of authority and against those in revolt against it, whereas, throughout the perennial conflict between the Jesuits and their opponents, it was they who were contending for obedience to the injunctions of authority – Papal, Episcopal, and Royal – and the Jansenists and *Parlements* who were resisting and evading them. Of late, too, these latter had been making themselves particularly obnoxious to the Court, which had felt itself constrained to banish the Parlementaires from Paris, and institute a *Chambre Royale* to take over their functions; and though it had very soon recalled them, it had done so not willingly, but only under a compulsion which rendered them the more obnoxious in its eyes. In fact, the *Parlements* were all along the great thorn in the side of the Kings of France, and were felt to be not less but more so by weak Kings, like Louis XV, who were so ill able to hold them in check.

Such being the balance of antipathies in the favourite's mind, the Court influence might never have been lent to aid the resentments of the *Parlement*, had not a complication arisen in the course of her career which resulted in enkindling a woman's unreasoning fury in her breast and directing it against the Society.

In 1752 she made a change in her life. She felt that she had ceased to be personally attractive, and yet desired to maintain her position of influence. And so to prevent another from supplanting her, she resolved to remain at Court as the King's companion and confident adviser, and at the same time to take upon herself, in co-operation with his *valet-du-chambre*, the task of providing him with a succession of victims unable to harm her. It was with this intention that she induced him to purchase for her the *petite maison* in the Parc-au-Cerfs, close to Versailles, which became the scene of unspeakable turpitudes. There was not much indication of penitence here, none the less she took into her head to try and rehabilitate her reputation to some extent, and began to pose as a *dévote*. It was thus that she came to fall foul of the Jesuit Fathers.

D'Alembert, in his essay on *The Destruction of the Jesuits*, dimly alludes to the incident in the following terms:

They refused, through motives of human respect, to receive under their direction powerful personages who had not had cause to expect from them a severity in every way so singular. It is said that this indirect refusal helped to hasten their destruction by the very hands from which they should have been able to gain their support. Thus those men who had been so often accused of a lax teaching on morals, and who had been retained at Court only because such was their teaching, were ruined as soon as they wished to uphold rigorism.

Here we may disregard the assumptions that the Jesuits were kept at Court because of the laxity of their code of morals, and that pursuance of a different course in that one case was due to human respect. These are not facts, but only allegations for which the enemies of the Society were desirous to obtain currency. What is important in this passage from d'Alembert is his testimony to the fact that the Jesuits were ruined because they refused to administer sacraments to Madame de Pompadour save on conditions she was not prepared to accept.

A paper which M. Sainte-Priest transcribes in full in his *Chute des Jésuites*, and authenticates as having been found among the papers of M. de Choiseul, gives in the favourite's own words the story of what happened.[9] It is in the form of a memorandum sent to a secret agent at Rome, who was to bring it under the notice of the Pope and induce him to order the Jesuit confessors at the Court of Versailles to be more lenient. It is a long story, but the leading features are these. She states that as far back as 1752 she had, 'for reasons which it was useless to state,' determined 'to retain as regards the King only the sentiments of gratitude and the most pure attachment;' but that, as the King 'found her company necessary for the happiness of his life and for the sake of his affairs,' he had written to his confessor, the Jesuit Père Pérusseau, for him to suggest 'a way in which she might remain near the King without incurring suspicion of a weakness from which she no longer suffered.' Père Pérusseau's answer was, however, uncompromising, 'She must leave the Court altogether.' As the King would not consent to this, she continues, they remained as they were for three more years. Then 'long meditations on the misery that had pursued her even whilst her fortunes were at their zenith, the certainty that she could never be made happy with the goods of this

---

[9] The same account, though without reference to the application to Rome, is found in *Mémoires historiques et anecdotes de la Cour de France pendant la faveur de Madame de Pompadour*, published in 1802, see p. 105. These three authorities are independent, and as such guarantee the truth of at least the substance of the story.

world, ... but was forced to believe the sole source of happiness was in God,' caused her at last to apply for herself to Père de Sacy, another Jesuit, whom she begged to accept her conditions, and allow her to have absolution and Communion. But she found this Father as resistive as his *confrère*, so that eventually she had to leave him and never see him again. Her narrative does not, however, say whether she told him of her little doings just at that time at the Parc-au-Cerfs. She goes on to say that the following year the King applied again to his own confessor, who was now Père Desmaretz, Père Pérusseau having died by then, but found him as stubborn as the other two, the sad result being that the King 'relapsed into his former errors.' She herself however, had now found an Abbé who proved more reasonable, and allowed her to go to Communion, from which she experienced much consolation, though it was a trial to have to keep the matter secret lest the confessor's reputation should be blackened. But the difficulty about the King still remained, and it was this she wished to have referred to the Pope, who she felt confident would remove the difficulties the Jesuits had so unnecessarily put in the way, and allow Louis to edify his subjects by returning to the sacraments. Such is the tenor of this extraordinary document, which we may feel confident found Benedict XIV as uncompromising as the Jesuits of Paris. And, even if d'Alembert and others had not expressly informed us of the fact, we might have inferred that the enraged harlot would not allow the matter to rest there, but would join hands with the other adversaries of the Jesuits, and seek for the means of taking vengeance upon them. And it was not long before a convenient occasion presented itself.

So far the narrative has been brought down to the eve of the extinction of the Society in France, and has aimed at showing the nature of the forces arrayed against it, and the motives by which they were actuated. The way has thus been prepared for appreciating the inner spirit of the successive measures taken for its extinction, but the history of this last stage of the existence of the old Society in France is sufficiently full and complicated to require special attention.

In this further stage we shall have specially to consider the grievances against the Society alleged by the *Parlement* as justifying and demanding its suppression. In the meanwhile however, it will not be unprofitable to provide a slight survey of the real reasons by which its destroyers seem to have been actuated, and an invitation to the reader to judge whether they are reasons which do most credit to these destroyers or to their victims.

Of the motives which actuated Madame de Pompadour and induced her to join in the campaign there can be no two judgments. No one for whose opinion we need care, would acquit her and condemn the Jesuit confessors for their respective parts in the transactions which aroused her active hostility.

The Philosophers, as we have seen, desired the downfall of the Jesuits as a means tending to the ultimate destruction of the Catholic Church, which they professed to regard as the one great obstacle to human enlightenment. There are, no doubt, many of the generation now living who would express their judgment on the Catholic Church in similar terms; but not all these, and not the portion of them whose approval is worth having, would sympathize with the mocking, blatant, coarseminded, indecency-loving infidelity of the eighteenth-century Voltairians. Nor need the Jesuits count it to their dishonour that they should have suffered extinction at the hands of such a party as that, because it regarded them as an important outwork in the defences of the Catholic Church.

Were they then to blame for having incurred the wrath of the Jansenists – for, as we have seen, the Jansenists and the Parlementaires practically formed one party, and may be treated as such for present purposes? To this question the mass of English readers would say, 'Yes, certainly,' the view current among them being that the Jansenists represented the conscience of the country, and were harassed by the lax-minded Jesuits precisely on that account. But Catholics cannot take up this position, and do not acknowledge that the doctrine which the Jansenists rejected and the Jesuits defended was a specially Jesuit doctrine. It was the time-honoured doctrine of the Catholic Church, and as such was vindicated by the four Solemn Papal condemnations of the opposite error. As such, too, it was defended, both before and after the Holy See had spoken, not by Jesuits only, though it is the fashion to attribute all to them – but also by such men as St Vincent de Paul, M. Olier, Bossuet, Fénelon, de Beaumont, and others innumerable.

Nor did the controversy turn on mere speculative subtleties, as the following illustration may serve to show. A point on which St Cyran, the founder of French Jansenism, was particularly insistent was that to prove the sincerity of a penitent's dispositions, absolution should be deferred for a considerable time, and hence that Communions should be not frequent, but very rare; whilst Antoine Arnauld wrote a book strangely entitled, *Frequent Communion* – to encourage this abstention. This was to mistake the very purpose of the sacraments, which are not given to us as rewards of virtue but as strength and food to attain to it. And a letter of St Vincent de Paul to the Abbé d'Orgny, one of the priests of the Mission (dated 25 June 1648), tells us what were the practical results that followed: 'Several *curés* complain that they have much fewer communicants now than in former years; St. Sulpice has three thousand less ... We find hardly any one approaching the sacraments on the first Sundays of the month, and the feast-days, or very few, and hardly more even in the (churches of the) religious orders, unless perhaps some few at the Jesuit (churches);' and in another letter, dated 20 September of the same year,[10] he expresses his opinion that 'for a hundred who had been brought by the book on *Frequent Communion*, to make their Communions more carefully and fervently, ten thousand had been taught to discontinue them altogether.' Was there any impropriety in the Jesuits, along with others like St Vincent, combating the introduction of a system of spiritual devotion so baneful as this?

But, it is said, at least they might have conducted their opposition in a more Christian spirit, and have been less persecuting. To deal with this point adequately would require much space, but we may just note that the attempts to fix the charge of persecution on Père de la Chaise, Père Le Tellier, and others, break down for want of evidence, and as regards the question of Christian spirit we may call attention to the following contrast. M. Sainte-Beuve tells us that St Cyran, the day before his death in 1643, said to his doctor, M. Guérin, who was also the medical attendant to the Jesuit College near: 'Monsieur, please tell the Fathers not to triumph when I am dead, as I shall leave twelve stronger than I am to come after me.'[11] That, surely, was not quite a Christian sentiment for a man just about to go before his Judge. On the other hand, in 1653, on the publication of the Bull of Innocent X condemning the works of Jansenius, Father Goswin Nickel, then General of the Jesuits, wrote a circular letter to the Jesuit Provincials of France, exhorting them to see that their subjects were very careful indeed 'not to seem to triumph over (*insulter à*) those who had been their late adversaries.' 'Not only,' he added, 'would such conduct (as he forbade) be entirely opposed to religious moderation, but it would also be far from calculated to draw back their minds to sound doctrines, and, instead of making them milder and more tractable, would only serve to make them more bitter.'[12]

This shows the spirit animating the central government of the Society, and, though we are far from claiming that the salutary counsel was faithfully observed on every occasion by every Jesuit in

---

[10] The text of both letters is given by M. Sainte-Beuve in his *Port-Royal*, ii, 192.
[11] Op. cit., ii, 212.
[12] The text of this and the two following letters may be found in Père de Montézon, S.J.'s, *Les Jansénistes et les Jésuites* (pp. 534–537), which is printed as an Appendix to the first volume of M. Sainte-Beuve's *Port-Royal*.

France, there is at least evidence that it was received in a like spirit by the French Superiors and the mass of their subjects. For ten years later, Père Annat, then confessor to Louis XIV, and a leader among his brethren, writes to Father General Oliva, the successor of Father Nickel, to consult him as to the propriety of the Fathers answering the numerous writings of the Jansenists, the difficulty being that, if they do write, it keeps up the controversy, whilst, if they do not, the Jansenists are encouraged to press their attacks the more, and the general public are prone to take the silence of the Jesuits as tacit acknowledgment that the others are in the right. Incidentally Père Annat mentions that the Fathers have written nothing whatever for the last three years. He shows that it is his own mind that his *confrères* should write, but with the precaution that only those should be allowed to write who can be trusted to write becomingly. Father Oliva's answer is that 'at Rome so much writing on the subject is not approved of, and silence is thought more becoming.' He leaves this decision, however, to the discretion of Père Annat, but recommends him to take the advice of the King, his Ministers, and particularly the Chancelier, and of course to see that nothing is written save in a becoming style.

Probably our readers will agree with us that the spirit of the Jesuit opposition to Jansenism, as revealed in this domestic correspondence is not so disedifying as our adversaries would have men believe. And we may perhaps be allowed to conclude that, so far at least, not Jesuit iniquities, but, to use Theiner's own expression, 'too many impure passions,' raging in the breasts of their opponents, explain the extinction of the Society of Jesus in France under Louis XV. We are to see, however, what kind of a case could be made against it by those who at that time made its *procès*.

II.[13] [Steps towards the expulsion]

We have seen what forces were leagued together soon after the middle of the eighteenth century for the destruction of the Society in France. We have now to see these forces at work. It is the Jansenist party, as represented by the *Parlement* of Paris, that eternal enemy of the French Jesuits, which we shall find throughout in the forefront of the assault. Indeed, had we not learnt from the facts already indicated what were the feelings regarding the Society of the Royal Concubine and her agents, and of the Philosophers, we might have failed to perceive their part in the campaign. It is recognized, however, by all

---

[13] *The Month*, 99 (1902), 346–368.

the historians of the period – d'Alembert, Lacretelle, Schoell, Sismondi, Capefigue, Henri Martin, and others – that they were active interveners behind the scenes, now encouraging the *Parlement* to courses on which otherwise it would not have dared to venture; now using their social and literary influence to work up a public opinion favourable to their designs; now practising on the weak will of the monarch and staying his hand, when his better feelings and the instances of his family were urging him to check the excesses of the *Parlement* by an exercise of the royal authority. It is in this sense that M. de Carne writes: 'From the time of the quarrel over the Confession tickets to the destruction of the Society of Jesus, Madame de Pompadour was the ally of whom men said least and thought most.'[14] And we may detect the traces of her and Choiseul's intervention in the alternations of the King's active opposition and passive submission to the measures taken by the *Parlement*.

> Two or three men alone [says d'Alembert], who did not appear to be of the sort destined to create such a revolution, imagined and accomplished this great project, and the impulse given to the entire body of the magistrates was their work and the fruit of their impetuous activity.[15]

In view of this judgment of a discerning contemporary observer it may be helpful to know something of the personalities that played the principal part in the events. Of the Marquise de Pompadour sufficient has been said already, and likewise of Choiseul, who became the principal Minister in 1758. Besides these, there were in the Ministry the Duc de Praslin, a cousin and submissive follower of Choiseul, and Berryer. This latter had been *Intendant de Police* from 1747 to 1757, and in that capacity had placed his services at the disposal of Madame de Pompadour, discovering those who spoke or wrote against her, and contriving to have them put into the Bastille or otherwise punished. When the nation could no longer stand him as head of the police, the favourite caused him to be promoted to the Ministry, in which he and Choiseul were her leading instruments to do her behests. Among the Parlementaires, Rolland, Chauvelin, de Terray, l'Averdy, and Omer Joly de Fleury were the most conspicuous.

Rolland d'Erceville was quite a young man, not thirty years of age, when the attack on the Society began, but he had attained to the degree of a President in the Court of *Enquêtes*. He was from the first

---

[14] *Revue des Deux Mondes*, 15 January 1859, p. 313, 'La Monarchie de Louis XV.'

[15] *Sur la Destruction des Jésuites*, Edinburgh ed. of 1765, p. 127.

a bitter enemy of the Jesuits, and threw himself heart and soul into all the proceedings against them. We shall not have occasion to refer to him much, but he was the Commissioner appointed in several instances to report on their affairs for the *Parlement*. His own idea of the part he played in the proceedings, and of the spirit in which he acted, may be gathered from a letter written some years later, in which he protested against a will which had left away from him some money he had expected; apparently on the ground that he was not considered by his relative to be sufficiently Jansenistic. 'The affair of the Jesuits alone,' he pleaded, as sufficient evidence of the injustice of his relative's suspicions, 'cost me more than six hundred thousand *livres* of my own money, and in truth the labours I have undertaken especially in reference to the Jesuits, who would not have been suppressed if I had not devoted so much time, health, and money to the cause, ought not to have brought down upon me this disinheriting by my uncle.' He meant that he made these sacrifices in the course of his endeavours to influence public Opinion by pamphlets and otherwise – hardly a recommendation in a magistrate whose duty was to approach the case impartially.

The Abbé Chauvelin had been before the public some years, and combined in himself the double character of a *coryphaeus* among the Jansenists and a friend of the Philosophers. As a Jansenist he had been foremost in resisting the Archbishop of Paris when he tried to enforce the obedience due to the Bull *Unigenitus*, and in causing the *Parlement* to persecute the priests who did their duty by refusing sacraments to the Appellants. He had also paid the penalty of this resisting, having been imprisoned by the King in the fortress of St Michel – all which as a matter of course he attributed to the Jesuits. His antagonism to the Jesuits was therefore of long standing, and his sour and fierce temper made it exceptionally bitter. He was in fact just the sort of man who, if the *Parlement* had been animated by any sort of desire to be impartial, would have been told to stand aside, whereas he was allowed to take a part so leading that popular estimation regarded him as the chief author of the ruin of the Society.[16]

If the Abbé Chauvelin was a fiery and fanatical partizan, the Abbé de Terray was a man without any principles at all, or morals either. Like Chauvelin, he was unsightly in person. That indeed was his infirmity, but, says the *Dictionnaire de Biographie Nationale Universelle*:[17]

[16] Hence the couplet in which allusion is made to his personal deformity, for he was a hunchback, as well as to the lameness of St Ignatius:
> Que fragile est ton sort, Société perverse,
> Un boiteux t'a fondée, un bossu te renverse.

[17] *Sub voc.*

He supplied for the want of ease and grace in conversation by a cynicism of speech and action quite in keeping with his satyr-like body, and thereby obtained a character for grotesque originality which, being sustained by considerable genius, was as effective as the opposite qualities could have been in winning for him social success.

In earlier days he had affected the character of a zealous and austere magistrate, but since 1753, when he inherited a fortune, he threw off restraints and became notorious for his loose morals, particularly for his open adulteries, first with Madame de Clercy and afterwards with the Baronne de la Garde. He was a man of undoubted capacity and industry, and with an iron frame on which no excess of work could tell, but the aim and object of all his labours was personal aggrandisement and enrichment, and in the prosecution of these he was absolutely unscrupulous. 'He did not know,' says M. Henri Martin, 'the difference between justice and injustice, though he understood very well the difference between the possible and the impossible.'[18] At the time with which we are concerned, he was a resolute asserter of the privileges of the *Parlement* as against the Crown; a decade later he was to be, in company with de Maupeou, also a Parlementaire and adversary of the Society in 1761, the ready instrument of the Crown in accomplishing the entire suppression of the *Parlement* by royal authority. In between these two dates, that is, in 1763, his friend l'Averdy was appointed Controller of the Finances, and Terray became associated with him, or rather ruled him, in the management of that department of Government, to which also he succeeded in 1769. It was during this period that he acquired the evil reputation as a rapacious and unscrupulous administrator that has made his name infamous in French history.

> When he died at Paris in 1778 [says the *Biographie Universelle*], he carried with him to the grave the hatred of the families his operations had ruined, and the contempt which the scandal of his morals had universally inspired. He may, in fact, be classed with Richelieu, Soubise, La Vrillière, Jarente, etc,. in the number of those courtiers and ecclesiastics who, under Louis XV, contributed the most to the degradation of the Monarchy, by setting up triumphant vice by the side of the throne.

To Clement de l'Averdy we have already referred as having been promoted, in 1763, to the Control of Finances. He showed no capacity in that office and had soon to quit it, amidst the censures of the many who had been ruined by his unjust schemes for raising money.

---

[18] *Histoire de France jusqu'en 1789*, xvi, p. 275.

Probably, however, as has been said, he suffered in this for the iniquity of the Abbé de Terray, who dominated him. He seems to have been a more honest man than the others mentioned as having been associated with him in the campaign against the Society, but probably he was also less influential.

Of Omer Joly de Fleury, less seems to be known. He was *Avocat-Général* to the *Parlement*, and as such was the spokesman of the *Gens du roi*[19] in some of the *comptes-rendus* in which the charges against the Society were contained, but the blame for them may have lain more with others than with him.

It is notorious how, whilst its foes were preparing for an attack on the Society, the misbehaviour of one of its own sons lent them a most convenient pretext. Among its many important missions there was one at Martinique – an island of the Antilles, belonging then as now to France – over which Père Antoine de Lavalette presided as Superior and Procurator. In the first chapter it has been explained how, without in the least incurring the stigma of clerical trading,[20] the Fathers in charge of a mission might have to engage in large transactions of buying and selling on behalf of the natives. Père de Lavalette, however, not only did this but went further. Finding the mission revenues inadequate, and seeing around him vast tracts of new land capable of profitable cultivation, he bought them for this purpose, and by so doing distinctly contravened the Church's prescriptions. He had no authorization to act thus from his superiors in Europe, as we know from his own confession,[21] and the latter seem to have been in ignorance of what he was doing until the catastrophe occurred. Apparently the remoteness of the Antilles and the extent of his legitimate operations afforded a cover for what would not have been permitted if known. On the other hand he enjoyed the cordial approval of the French Governor of the colony, who, in 1753, when some complaints of his conduct reached the Ministry of Marine at Paris, wrote a strong letter in his defence. Nor as long as we view his conduct from the sole standpoint of commercial morality, does it seem to have been censurable, for it was apparently business on a sound footing, and Père de Lavalette certainly enjoyed the confidence of those he dealt with in Europe. In 1755, however,

---

[19] By this name were known the *Procureur-Général*, the *Avocat-Général*, and their respective staffs. Nominally they represented the Crown at the bar of the *Parlement*, but in fact they received the impulse to act from the *Parlement* rather than the Crown.

[20] *See* p. 8.

[21] Crétineau Joly, *Clément XIV et les Jésuites*, p. 120, gives the text of this confession.

war broke out between England and France, and he was the victim of its very first act. Five of his ships were taken by the English privateers and the sum thus lost to him in goods and specie amounted to about two millions of *livres*.[22] He was thus left in a bankrupt condition, and his creditors in Europe were in consequence involved in grave difficulties. Chief among these were the firms of Lioncy and Gouffre at Marseilles, and Grou and Son of Nancy, who called upon Père de Sacy, the Procurator-General of the French Missions, resident in the Professed House at Paris, to honour his colleague's bills of exchange. They also represented the state of affairs to the French Provincial and to the General. The reply given was that Père de Sacy had received no remittances from Martinique from which he could draw, but that they would strive their utmost to meet the debts of that mission, although unable to accept responsibility in the name of their other houses, each house of the Society being financially independent – which they undoubtedly were according to the law of the Society and the terms of their respective deeds of foundation, as ratified by the laws both of Church and State. This last plea has appeared indefensible to the friends as well as to the foes of the Society who have written on the subject, but is not unintelligible even if it was injudicious in view of the circumstances. It must be remembered that with the exception of the Professed Houses which were but three in number throughout France at that time, and subsisted solely on the alms collected day by day, the property of the Society consisted mainly of colleges founded by various benefactors, which were therefore the Society's property only in a limited sense The deeds of foundation assigned certain purposes to which the revenues were to be devoted, such as the education of extern pupils, or in some cases of the Society's own younger members, and the Society, though it had the administration of all, was entitled to apply to its own uses only such sums as were required for the suitable maintenance of the necessary staffs. It is this, doubtless, that the Fathers had in mind in disclaiming responsibility save for the Martinique Mission, but it is certain that, without any pressure on the part of the courts, they would have refused no self-sacrifice, and would eventually have succeeded in paying off the very last item of Père de Lavalette's debts. As it was they set to work earnestly to grapple with the occasion, and, having paid off at once the more necessitous of the creditors out of their funds in hand, proceeded to borrow a sum of two millions of *livres* on a mortgage of their properties in Martinique and St Domingo, properties which, had it not been for the capture of

---

[22] A *livre* was approximately of the same value as a *franc*.

these islands shortly after by the English, would when realized have more than covered the amount of the loan. Divided counsels, however, among the Paris Fathers caused some delay in their proceedings, and soon it was too late for any private arrangement.

Inasmuch as the misfortune which had befallen Père de Lavalette was due to an act of war on the part of an enemy, whose quarrel was not with him but with his country, the Jesuits might have looked for sympathy, and even assistance from their rulers. Unfortunately these were the very men who were plotting their ruin, and were welcoming their present embarassment as a means which might be utilized for that end. Indeed it is said to have been at the secret instances of their foes at the Court or in the *Parlement* that the two firms, who would have profited more in the long run by trusting to the spontaneous efforts of the Fathers, proceeded to take action in the Consular (that is, the Commercial) Courts, the firm of Lionçy and Gouffre in that of Marseilles, the firm of Grou in that of Paris. They claimed that, the Society being a single organized body, the various officers of which were appointed to their respective posts by its superiors, Provincial and General, the entire body in all its parts should be held pecuniarily responsible for the debts of any one of its members or establishments; and they asked for the power, in the event of non-payment, to distrain on the goods of the Society wherever they might find them in the kingdom. Such a ground of claim was absurd, for on the same principle a Bishop should be held responsible for the debts of all his clergy, and the Pope for those of every Bishop and priest under his jurisdiction. None the less it was accepted readily by the Courts, which decided in favour of the claimants, in the Grou case on 30 January 1760, for the sum of thirty thousand *livres*,[23] in the Lionçy case on 29 May 1760, for the much larger sum of a million and a half *livres*. In each instance the leave to distrain was also granted in the event of non-payment.

The Fathers seem at first to have accepted the difficult situation resignedly, and to have busied themselves with the endeavour to collect the money, but, presumably because the creditors showed themselves too exacting in the matter of time, they sought after some months the advice of eminent *avocats*, and being assured by these that the consular judgments of the preceding year were manifestly unsound in law, determined to appeal to the Grand Chamber of the *Parlement* of Paris. For this again they have been blamed even by friendly critics, as for a foolish step, the fierce bias against them of

---

[23] *Recueil par ordre de dates, de tous les Arrêts de Parlement ... concernant les ci-devant soi-disant Jésuites,* vol. i.

this *Parlement* being so well known. But at least they showed confidence in the justice of their cause as well as their desire to take every lawful means not only for their self-preservation, but also to avert disaster from the many good works with which they were entrusted. The decision of the *Parlement* was given on 8 May 1761, on the basis of the Report of M. Lepelletier de Saint-Fargeau, a rigid Jansenist.[24] It was, of course, in confirmation of the judgment of the Consular Court, and was based on the same inadequate ground that has been mentioned above. The condemned Fathers were given a year to take up the still outstanding bills of Père de Lavalette, as well as to pay off the interest that had accumulated during the interval and the expenses of the various prosecutions, both that before the *Parlement* and any others in which the firm of Lioncy might have become involved with their own creditors. If by the end of the year these claims had not been fully satisfied, the restraint might be levied on their goods within the kingdom.[25]

Three things are worthy of notice about this report of M. Lepelletier de Saint-Fargeau and the *arrêt* in which it was adopted. First, it expressly acknowledges that a large portion of the debts due to Lioncy and Gouffre had been already paid off, which fact should be coupled with the further fact that all the debts to Grou and Son must have been paid off, since no further action was brought by that firm. This is evidence that the Fathers did not make their appeal in disregard for the sufferings of their creditors. Secondly, that by this time it had been realized by the courts that others besides the Jesuits had proprietary claims upon their colleges, for the *arrêt* expressly stipulates that the rights of these others shall be respected by the distrainers. Later on it became known that, when these other liens on the Colleges had been deducted, the remainder was quite insufficient to meet the claims of the creditors. Thirdly, that M. Lepelletier de Saint-Fargeau, instead of confining himself to the question of the Society's liabilities for the debts of one of its houses, dilated much on the iniquities of the Jesuit Institute, and the corrupt doctrines and practices of its members, insisting chiefly on their propensity to regicide. This irrelevance, if improper in an *avocat*, was not undesigned. It has already been suggested that the firm of Lioncy, in taking action against the whole Society, may have been influenced not so much by their own judgment as by the intimations received from persons

---

[24] A man is not necessarily responsible for the sins of his sons, but it is of interest to know that the son of this M. Lepelletier de Saint-Fargeau became a fanatical revolutionist, and was very prominent among those who voted for the execution of Louis XVI.

[25] *Recueil par ordre des dates.*

highly placed, who had their own objects to gain by the manoeuvre. It is at least certain that the attack on the Society was planned beforehand, and the various stages in the programme so arranged that each would seem to provoke the one succeeding it, and so lead on to the final catastrophe. On this point it may be well to quote the testimony of a contemporary writer who, though anonymous, is described by M. St Victor, and with evident truth, as a 'man well acquainted with the intrigues of the time.'[26]

> Whilst the supporters of the party were working thus ardently (by inundating the country with anti-Jesuit pamphlets) to create prejudice in the public mind, the magistrates were concerting together in secret the blows they proposed to strike with the hand of authority. Several times a week meetings were held at the house of President Gauthier de Brétigny. MM. Clément, Lambert, Chauvelin, Bèse de Lys, Rolland, Laverdy, and some others, directed all the operation. In all the towns they had their emissaries, charged to send in reports against the Jesuits, and everywhere to spy into their conduct ... everyone saw that the storm was gathering.

It was clearly then by pre-arrangement that M. Lepelletier de Saint-Fargeau went out of his way to comment adversely on the methods of the Society. He was preparing the way for the next stage, in which the existence of the Society was to be directly attacked.

This next stage was initiated on 17 April 1761,[27] by the Abbé Chauvelin, who made a speech before the Grand Chamber in which he took note that the Jesuits were appealing to the Constitutions as establishing the financial independence of the several houses. This, he contended, was the first occasion in which the Constitutions of the Society had been brought within the cognizance of the *Parlement*, a circumstance which he suggested, should force upon the court certain conclusions. If the Constitutions had never yet been officially examined by the State authorities, how could it be said that the Society possessed State recognition in the country, and yet if it had not had that, was its existence more than tolerated, and such as could be terminated whenever it might seem desirable? Then again, why had the Constitutions never been laid by the Society before the State authorities? Was it not because the Society had always made a point of shrouding them in mystery, one of its rules expressly enjoining that they should be kept secret; and if they needed to be thus

---

[26] *Destruction des Jésuites en France, Anecdote politique et intéressant trouvé dans les papiers d'un homme bien instruit des intrigues du temps.* Publ. London 1766; reprinted in M. St Victor's *Documents concernant la Compagnie de Jésus.* Tome Ier, 1827.

[27] *Recueil par ordre des dates.*

shrouded in mystery, must not the reason be that they contained provisions which would shock public opinion? Having raised this suspicion the Abbé Chauvelin next showed that at all events he personally had seen these mysterious Constitutions, for he ventured to quote (and misinterpret) many passages from them, from which he deduced that they 'contained several things contrary to good order, to ecclesiastical discipline, and the maxims of the kingdom.' Hence, he recommended that the *Parlement* should now examine them, and take such measures as the result might show to be requisite.

Impressed by these considerations the court adopted the course recommended, and began that day by ordering the Jesuit Superiors in Paris to send in a copy of the most recent edition of their Constitutions – that published at Prague in 1757 – within three days. If it imagined that the demand would be unpalatable to the Jesuits, it must have been surprised to find Père de Montigny the very next morning at its bar, with the required copy in his hands. There was no reason, however, why the Jesuits should hesitate. It is true, their Constitutions had from the first contained a clause forbidding them to be shown to persons external to the Society – that is, without the Superior's leave. It was a clause which had been customary in the Constitutions of religious orders, and was motived by the feeling that the principles of religious perfection might seem foolishness to the man of the world, and excite his mockery. But there was never any attempt or desire to conceal them from well-disposed persons, still less from the authorities of Church or State, and as a matter of fact, quite contrary to what Chauvelin had represented, they had more than once been submitted to the French Sovereigns and their *Parlements*. Thus it is proved from the text itself of various Edicts and *Arrêts* by the author of *Nouvelles Observations sur les Jugements rendus contre les Jésuites*,[28] that the Jesuit Constitutions were before the *Parlement* on 20 January 1560, at the Council of Poissy in 1561, before Charles IX in July 1565, and Henry III in May 1580, again before the *Parlement* on 23 December 1592,[29] before Henri IV in 1603, before *Parlement* in 1692 and again in 1765. Moreover, if the Society had wished to keep its Constitutions secret, it would not have allowed them to be published in several editions, or to be placed on sale, with the result, as was the case at that time, that almost every well-furnished library in France contained a copy.

---

[28] Published at Bordeaux in 1763.
[29] 'Vu les dites Institutions et Constitutions d'icelle Société, approuvées par les Souverains Pontifes, et nommément par le feu Pape Grégoire XIII', says the *arrêt* of 23 Dec. 1592.

Chauvelin must have known all this, and so must many other members of the Grand Chamber, but the object was to obtain a pretext for destroying the Society, and accordingly the copy of the Constitutions was handed over to the *Gens du Roi* to examine.

They were to report to the *Parlement* the results of their examination on 2 June, but meanwhile the King had been moved by the representations of his family, and bethought himself of making some feeble opposition to a work of destruction the injustice of which he perfectly realized. Accordingly he sent word to the *Parlement* on 30 May,[30] that

> He wished to undertake himself the examination of the Constitutions of the Society of Jesuits, and bade them send to him on the Sunday now following (that is, the very next day) the First President with two presidents, and the *Gens du Roi* who were to bring with them the copy of the said Constitutions deposited by the Jesuits at their bar.

This Royal order was complied with, but another copy of the Constitutions was procured by the *Parlement* and handed over to the *Gens du Roi*, who were also granted an extension of time for their examination of the same. They came before the assembled Chamber of the *Parlement* on 3, 4, 6 and 7 of July 1761[31] when a voluminous *compte-rendu* on the Constitutions of the Society was read by M. Omer Joly de Fleury, who, as the *Avocat-Général,* was their spokesman. It gave an analysis of the two volumes of the Institute, so far as the character of the Constitutions were in view, and argued on the same lines as M. Chauvelin, but at much greater length. The nature of the improprieties it professed to find in the Institute can be gathered from the conclusions in which it terminates. It recommends certain alterations the chief of which are that exemptions shall be done away with; that no member who has taken simple vows shall be sent away by the General except for canonical faults; that the General shall have no control over the finances of the local houses which shall be administered by the communities themselves assembled in Chapter; that the superiors and other officers, both Provincial and Local, shall be elected by the triennial Provincial Congregations, and that these triennial gatherings shall be presided over by Royal Commissioners. It is suggested that the King, having caused Constitutions of this kind to be examined and proved by his *Parlement*, should issue Letters Patents authorizing them in the Kingdom. It must be granted that this *compte-rendu*, though it

[30] *Recueil par ordre des dates.*
[31] *Recueil par ordre des dates.*

absurdly misconstrues the sense of the Constitutions, is far milder in its tone and character than M. Chauvelin's denunciation. It also differs markedly from the latter in its abstention from those suggestions of intrigue on the part of the Jesuits in which M. Chauvelin had been so lavish. It even acknowledges that, while condemning their Constitutions, it has no fault to find with the conduct of the Jesuits themselves.

> There is [it says], properly speaking, no question of reform here; and we may apply to the Jesuits what (on a former occasion) M. Talon said of other Congregations who gave such edification to the public by their manner of living, that they had no need (in this sense) of reformation.

Such a testimony coming from such a source is extremely valuable and we shall have occasion later on to point out its full significance.

The *Parlement* having heard this *compte-rendu* of the *Gens du Roi*, next ordered it to be referred to Commissioners on the basis of whose Report it would deliberate and act. The Commissioners appointed were the Abbé de Terray, M. de l'Averdy, and apparently two others.

On the day following, 8 July,[32] M. Chauvelin came forward again this time to denounce the teaching of the Society on faith and morals. His discourse is a monument of malign industry, for it teems with references and quotations, none of which will bear examination, but which, by being massed together in a number which defies refutation, succeed in conveying the impression that the Jesuit writers, even those among them who enjoy the highest credit among Catholic theologians, are monsters of iniquity in their teaching. As the question will recur presently it need only be said here that quite a half of this invective is concerned with the doctrine of tyrannicide, which it represents the Society as having consistently taught and practised – endeavouring on the flimsiest evidence, and in the teeth of established facts, to fix on them responsibility for all successful and unsuccessful attempts to assassinate the Kings of France, from that of Jacob [Jacques] Clément downwards. M. Chauvelin's second denunciation, like his first was referred in the first instance to the *Gens du roi* who reported on 18 July, and in the second to the same commissioners as had been told off to report on the Constitutions, chief among whom, it will be borne in mind, was the Abbé de Terray. May we not gauge the sincerity of the scandal which these good Parlementaires professed to take at the moral teaching of the Jesuits, when we find them entrusting the office of reporting on it to such a man?

To go back for a moment to the *compte-rendu* on the Constitutions

[32] *Recueil par ordre des dates.*

of M. Omer Joly de Fleury, a large portion of its contents is occupied with the endeavour to show that though the Society had been authorized in France by Henri IV's Edict of 1604 and supplemented by numerous Letters Patent since issued on behalf of its different Foundations, the right of legal existence thus obtained had been throughout conditioned by certain qualifications, and by the non-observance of these had been forfeited. The *Avocat-Général* had an important reason for taking up this position. It was beyond doubt that the *Parlement* could not of its own authority set aside Royal Edicts and Letters Patent, and yet it was felt that if they were to succeed in proscribing and destroying the Society they must rely mainly on the authority of their own *arrêts*, and hope from the King only that he would not intervene to stop them.

It did not, however, escape the notice of Louis XV that by pursuing this policy they were trenching on the rights of his crown, and accordingly he sent them another communication on 2 August,[33] ordering that the Jesuits within the space of six months should send in to the *Conseil du Roi* a full list of the Edicts, Letters Patent, and other title-deeds of their houses and residences, and requiring of the *Parlement* that it should surcease from all further decrees concerning the Society, so as to leave time for the royal inquiry to be completed. Had Louis XIV been still on the throne the *Parlement* would not have ventured to disobey so imperative an order. But, knowing the weakness of Louis XV and the support they could count on from his mistress and his ministers, they felt they could palm off on him a purely formal compliance with his orders, and continue their campaign unaltered save for a few adjustments more nominal than real. Thus they returned answer to the King that they had registered his orders and would refrain for a year's space from *arrêts* of a definitive or provisional character, save only such as

> their oath to the Court, their fidelity and affection for the sacred person of the said Lord King, and their devotedness to the cause of public peace, could not permit them to put off decreeing, should the exigency of cause arising impel them.[34]

At the same time, they ordered – claiming this as their traditional right – that the list of title-deeds, and along with it full statistics of the names, ages, offices, property, &c., of all their members, should be sent by the Jesuits, not direct to the *Conseil*, but to the *Parlement*, which would pass it on to the King.

---

[33] *Recueil par ordre des dates.*
[34] *Recueil par ordre des dates.*

Seeing that the *Parlement*, in full accordance with its Reporters, professed to be taking action against the Society as constituting a serious danger to the State, it was perhaps not so wonderful that they should have deemed 'the exigency of the cases' to have required their prompt attention, even as soon as four days later. Accordingly, on 6 August, after listening to a demand of the Procureur-Général, and hearing the Abbé de Terray's report on the same, they entertained an appeal *comme d'abus* against the various Papal Bulls by which the Society had been approved in the first instance, and afterwards confirmed and enriched with spiritual privileges. Certain arrangements prescribed or grants made to the Society in these Bulls are indicated, and alleged to be abuses not tolerable in the kingdom. These abuses coincide with those represented by M. Omer Joly de Fleury, and bear on the power of the General, the exaction of blind obedience, the non-reciprocity of the simple vows, the extent of the privileges; and are declared to render the Jesuit Institute 'menacing to the authority of the Church, of the General and Particular Councils, of the Holy See and all Ecclesiastical Superiors, as well as to that of Sovereigns.' Bold language this for a *Parlement* which, if it had a distinguishing mark in the whole course of its history, had it precisely in the persistent opposition it was wont to offer to Pope and King, Bishops, and Councils; bold language particularly for the *Parlement* of that generation, which had been so recently engaged in a campaign against the clergy for obeying the Holy See and their Bishops in a matter exclusively spiritual, and by so doing had provoked their King to send them into banishment. Later on we shall see how far the Pope and the clergy took the same or a different view of this supposed menace to their existence; and, meanwhile we may note two things about this Appeal *comme d'abus*, first, that although held to be so urgent, it alleged no 'abuse' in the Society which had not been in it, and been perfectly well known to all classes of the nation, throughout the hundred and fifty years and more of its existence in France; and, secondly, that it imputed no misconduct whatever to individuals, or anything inconsistent with M. Omer Joly de Fleury's admission, that 'they had given such edification to the public as to stand in no need of reformation.'

On the same 6 August, the Court of *Parlement* issued another *arrêt* still more serious in its character, and professing to be called for by the character of the Society's teaching. The Abbé de Terray, to whom M. Chauvelin's denunciation of this teaching, along with the report thereon of the *Gens du Roi*, had been referred for further verification, had within the short intervening space of nineteen days completed his gigantic task and recommended for condemnation, on the ground of their lax doctrine, thirty-three works of Jesuit theologians, among them being writers of high reputation, like Bellarmine, Salmerón, Vazquez, Suárez, Lessius, and Toletus. Accordingly, the *Parlement*, all the Chambers being assembled,

> having [read] the conclusions of the Procureur-Général, and heard the Report of Maitre Joseph-Marie Terray, *conseiller*, all having been considered, ordered twenty-three out of the condemned list [Suárez, it must he allowed, not being among them], to be torn and burnt in the court of the Palace, at the foot of the grand staircase, by the executioner of High Justice, as seditious, destructive of every principle of Christian morality, teaching a murderous and abominable doctrine, opposed not merely to the safety of the lives of the citizens, but even to that of the sacred persons of Sovereigns.

Nor did it stop here. The definitive settlement of the consequences which ought to ensue on the discovery of this evil teaching was to be conjoined with the definitive settlement of the appeal *comme d'abus*, and therefore left to stand over for a while, but it would be too dangerous to allow the King's youthful subjects to be exposed for a day longer than was necessary to the evil influences of masters impregnated with these doctrines, and so it was ordered, under severe penalties, that until the final settlement was pronounced, no more novices should be received or scholastics admitted to take their vows; also that all Jesuits should cease to hold schools, and all pupils should cease to attend Jesuit schools, after 1 October in any town where other schools existed, and after 1 April in towns where no other school existed – in which latter towns the local authorities were enjoined to see that by 1 April other schools were provided.

Among other consequences flowing from this drastic measure was the ruin of Père de Lavalette's creditors, who thus lost all chance of having their claims satisfied. The main source, as has been explained, from which the Jesuits had been trying to pay them, were the savings out of the funds they were entitled to take from their College endowments on the score of suitable maintenance, and this must now cease with the cessation of their educational labours. And, although a show of consideration for these creditors was kept up for some time longer, and on 23 April 1762, the houses of the Jesuits were put in charge of what we should now-a-days call an Official Receiver, the Courts had lost interest in persons who had ceased to be useful to them, and it eventually left them to their fate.

The *arrêts* of 6 August were duly communicated to the King, who, however, responded on 29 August, by Letters Patent, announcing that his own Royal Commissioners had now reported on the Jesuit Constitutions, and he felt that the matter required of him a serious deliberation. In order, therefore, that his deliberation might not be embarrassed, he bade the *Parlement* suspend the execution of their *arrêts* for a whole year. They received these intimations of the royal will in their usual way. They registered the Letters Patent, but with stipulation that the surcease should expire in less than a year, namely on 1 April 1762; and while they consented out of deference to the King's wishes to leave the Jesuit professors in possession of their schools, they held to their *veto* against receiving new novices or advancing those already received to their vows. Finally they remonstrated with the King for putting obstacles in the path of a course of action which they assured him was imperatively required 'for the safety of the persons of Sovereigns, the tranquillity of States, the principles of morals, the education of youth, the welfare and honour of religion.'

Louis XV does not seem to have resented at the time this abatement of his full orders, but on 26 March 1762, he sent them an Edict based on the results of his deliberations. It authorized the continued existence of the Society, but subjected its members to the laws of the Kingdom, to the authority of the King, and the jurisdiction of the ordinaries, regulated the manner in which the General should exercise his authority in France, and on the other hand cancelled all that had been decreed against them by the *Parlement* since 1 August 1761. An Edict thus innovating on the terms of their Constitutions was not acceptable to the Jesuits, but neither was it acceptable to the *Parlement*, which this time flatly refused to register it. They declared in a dignified way that they could not register the Edict, nor did they think it necessary to offer a reason for their refusal, as the King himself would feel that such an Edict was undesirable, if he would be good enough to read the document they were venturing respectfully to send him.

The accompanying document which had been sent also to every Bishop and magistrate throughout the Kingdom, was the famous *Extraits des Assertions*, a quarto volume, purporting to contain extracts from Jesuit writers, illustrative of their pernicious and dangerous moral teaching. It was put forth as a fuller demonstration, by exact citation of the passages, of the charges against Jesuit teaching, which the Abbé Chauvelin had stated more compendiously in his *compte-rendu* of 8 July 1761. It was drawn up by the command of the *Parlement*, and its authors are supposed to have been M. Roussel de la Tour, of whom we can find nothing save that he was a *Conseiller du Parlement*; the Abbé Goujet, a learned but violent Jansenist writer, who had been prominent among the Appellants, and supposed himself to have been cured of stone by the intercession of the Deacon Paris; the Abbé Minard, who for his Jansenist opinions, had been suspended by Archbishop de Beaumont, who in later years became a Constitutionalist priest, and who when the Terror was over, agitated for the perpetuation of that schism by the consecration of a successor to Bishop Gobel; and, lastly but chiefly, as being the presiding spirit of the work, Dom C. Clémencet, of the Congregation of St Maur. It is sad, if it be true, that a writer of such merit as the author of the *Art de vérifier les dates,* should have had part in so discreditable a compilation; but, like the other two ecclesiastics, he was noted for his pro-Jansenist bias, being one of the biographers of Port-Royal, and the author of some spiteful and utterly unfounded anti-Jesuit tracts.[35]

These *Extraits des Assertions* are not likely to have moved Louis XV, but his fits of activity were soon spent, and the *Parlement* was again left to continue its work of destruction. When 1 April came, the Jesuits were turned out of their eighty-four Colleges within the jurisdiction of the *Parlement* of Paris, and the great educational crisis commenced which had no small share in de-Christianizing France and preparing the Revolution. For it was impossible at such short notice to supply the place of the ejected teachers in these eighty-four Colleges, and we can realize the straits to which the authorities were put when we find that some of the leading Philosophers were asked to name some fit persons for the office. We can imagine what kind of teachers such men would deem fit.

On 6 August 1762, that is, exactly a year from the lodgment of the appeal *comme d'abus*, it was heard and judged. The judgment – which, in the estimation of its authors, was intended to be the final suppression of the Society of Jesus in the French dominions – runs in the King's name, but that is only a formality. It was not signed by the King, nor did it in any sense emanate from him, but from his Court of *Parlement* whose *arrêt* he is made to recite. The *arrêt* is an enormous document which begins by enumerating a vast mass of historical and other documents, steps taken by Kings and *Parlements*, by Popes and Bishops, by Universities and others, in the whole course of the two hundred years of the Society's existence, all tending to discredit it; but among them an entire absence of the vastly larger mass which could have been enumerated, of utterances and actions by all these personages and classes in its favour. Also, though so voluminous and issued in the name of an eminent judicial body, it

---

[35] See the notice of him in the *Biographie Universelle*, s.v. Clémencet, Charles.

is quite unscientific and wholly partizan in its character, as an intelligent reader cannot fail to perceive even after a short inspection. Two points may be selected as illustrating the truth of this. First, in one place Benedict XIV is cited as having on 20 December 1741, 'forbidden the *soi-disant* Jesuits to venture any more in future to reduce the said Indians to slavery, to sell them, &c.' This quotation is inserted, of course, to suggest that among their other crimes the Jesuits had been notable as cruel slave masters. It will hardly be credited, but can be seen at once on reference to the Bull, that the prohibition is addressed *universis et singulis personis*, 'to each and every person, of whatever state, sex, grade, condition, dignity, &c.,' and that the mention of the Jesuits occurs in the midst of an enumeration of the various religious orders, where it stands merely for completeness' sake. Moreover, as a matter of fact the attitude of the Jesuit missionaries to the Bull was that they had solicited it as a protection for their converts against the surrounding Europeans. Secondly, the *arrêt* incorporates and makes important use of a so-called Edict of Henri IV against the Society, dated 1595, of which then no one had ever heard, of which the supposititious character is demonstrated by every possible species of argument,[36] and as evidence for which they can only cite an 'expedition (that is a 'copy') deposited at the bar of our Court and (copies?) of the *arrêts d'enregistrement* of the said Edict at the Courts of *Parlement* of Rouen and Dijon.' They should have been able to cite better evidence than this, and when one reads at the head of this judgment of 1762 the compromising words, 'Having heard the Report of Maître Joseph-Marie Terray, Conseiller', one can but reflect how very likely a person he was to perpetrate a fraud of this description.

Still, the decision of the court was in favour of the Appeal. The abuses detailed in it as inherent in the Society's Institute were declared to be established, and together with these the pernicious character of its teaching; the vows of the Jesuits were declared null and void from the commencement, as having been taken in an Order so stained with abuses: the members were bidden to vacate the colleges, to lay aside the Society's dress, and cease to hold communications with its *ci-devant* superiors: none of them were permitted to continue to teach in any college whatever, or obtain degrees in any University, or have charge of souls, &c., unless they had first taken an oath promising to hold and profess 'the Liberties of the Gallican Church,' the four Articles of the Declaration of 1682, the canons and

---

[36] See 'L'Edit de Henri IV', in *Les Documents concernant la Compagnie du Jésus*, vol. i.

maxims received in the Kingdom; promising also not to have communications with the General or superiors of the Society or any of its foreign members, to combat the pernicious doctrines contained in the *Extraits des Assertions,* and to renounce all subjection to the Institute and Constitutions of the Society.

The *Parlement* of Paris thus took the lead in this work of destruction, and the provincial *Parlements* were expected to co-operate. With four exceptions, those of Alsace, Franche-Comté, Flanders, and Lorraine, all did as they were ordered. In three instances the *comptes-rendus* of the *Avocats-Généraux* to these Provincial *Parlements* have been preserved, and that of M. Caradeuc de la Chalotais, the *Avocat-Général* at Rennes, if remarkable for its unfairness, is, it must be admitted, remarkable also for its literary distinction, in which it contrasts greatly with the heavy and wearisome *comptes-rendus* sent in at Paris. It is on this account that it has come to be the most widely read of them all, and to be taken as the standard statement of the case against the Jesuits in France. As regards its character, it must be remarked that M. Caradeuc de la Chalotais was more in league with the Philosophers than with the Jansenists, and that the traces of this affinity may be seen in the more general character of his denunciation. All kinds of monks, he decides, are bad for the country, and there is not much to choose among them, but as the Jesuits are the most powerful, let them be removed first. We may thank, however, this writer for one passage in his *compte-rendu,* that in which he distinguishes between the Society and its individual members.

> I declare [he says] that so far from accusing the entire Order of Jesuits, that is, all the members, of fanaticism, I exonerate almost all, and especially the French Jesuits ... I would exonerate them as willingly, were it possible, as regards principles of morality which in truth they have only adopted, and which they seem to disavow by their regular conduct.[37]

Nor must it be overlooked that in the voting of these Provincial *Parlements* there was nowhere anything like the unanimity which marked the action of the *Parlement* of Paris. Thus (for the figures have been preserved) at Rennes 32 were for the suppression, 29 against; at Rouen 20 were for, 13 against; Toulouse 41 were for, 39 against; at Perpignan 5 were for, 4 against; at Bordeaux 23 were for, 18 against; at Aix 24 were for, 22 against. Nor was it wonderful there should be these imposing minorities, if, as at Aix, the *Parlement* was expected by the majority to assume the truth of the quotations made by the *Parlement* of Paris.

---

[37] *Compte-rendu des Constitutions des Jésuites*, 1762, pp. 75, 76. Edition of 1762.

Although Louis XV, practised upon as he was by La Pompadour, Choiseul, and Berryer, proved himself too feeble to offer effectual resistance to his *Parlements* in their campaign of destruction, and to carry out the alternative conclusions which his own better judgment recommended, the few steps he did take to transfer the investigation to his own tribunal had the result of eliciting numerous protests from the Bishops and clergy; and these, especially when conjoined with the Letters of Clement XIII, offer a mass of most respectable testimony to the calumnious character of the charges contained in the *comptes-rendus*. In the next section we shall avail ourselves of the powerful argument thence derivable, and we may terminate the present one by calling attention to a few salient features in the foregoing narrative and referring them to the judgment of any candid reader.

1. The charges which the *Parlement* professed to have found established, and to which they appealed as demanding so remorseless and far-reaching a punishment of some thousands of people, are those contained in the various *comptes-rendus*, or rather in those of the Abbé Chauvelin and M. Omer Joly de Fleury – for the rest, including those of MM. Chalotais and Ripert de Monclar, were based on these, and professed to add little or nothing on the authority of independent investigation.
2. These *comptes-rendus* bring charges which fall into two categories, one condemning what they allege to have found in the Jesuit Constitutions, the other what they allege to have found in the Jesuit writers on Dogma and Moral Theology. In other words, no charges are brought against the personal conduct of the Jesuits. Chauvelin indeed brings a number of general charges of intriguing, of cruelty, of idolatry, &c., but all on the basis of inference from their alleged rules and teaching, none on the basis of any direct testimony he can invoke; whilst M. Omer Joly de Fleury and M. Chalotais unite in using language about the Jesuits as individuals which are only intelligible on the supposition that nothing was seen in them as they then were, to correspond with the horrible vices which their Constitutions and writings were declared calculated to engender. And here it is very noticeable that the denouncers of the Society in France took an exactly opposite line to their denouncers in Portugal. In Portugal their Constitutions were pronounced by Pombal[38] to be good and holy,

---

[38] See Pombal's letter to d'Almada, the Portuguese representative at the Vatican, *ap.* Père de Ravignan's *Clément XIII et Clément XIV*, p. 97.

the misfortune being that the Jesuits themselves did not observe them in letter or spirit; in France the Constitutions were pronounced pernicious in their character and tendency, but the Jesuits themselves men of blameless lives. On which contrast we believe it was Voltaire who remarked that the whole matter seemed capable of a simple solution. Let the French Jesuits be sent to Portugal to keep their Rule, and the Portuguese Jesuits be sent to France to break their Rule.

3. If the offensive features in the Society were alleged to be in its Constitutions, the answer which at once suggests itself is two-fold – first, that if it be really so, not the Jesuits but the Holy See, indeed the Universal Church, was responsible, for these Rules were not private but public documents, and had received the approval of nineteen Popes, a vast number of Bishops, and many Sovereigns; secondly, that it could not be really so, or else the members would infallibly become, what according even to this hostile testimony they were not.

4. A similar argument applies to the allegations concerning the teaching of the Society. Men who could in their writings inculcate the scandalous opinions of the *Extrait des Assertions,* must reflect those opinions in their lives, and the lives of those who came under their influence, whereas as we have seen, it was practically, by the failure to invoke any direct testimony, and even formally acknowledged, that neither the Jesuits nor their friends and pupils were of such a character. Perhaps, therefore, it may seem more reasonable for those who cannot study for themselves the Jesuit works from which these extracts profess to be taken, to conclude that they are extracts unfairly made – all the more so when they find even a writer like Döllinger saying that,

> the entire fabrication was such a downright fraud, that one did not know whether to marvel most at the audacity or the dishonesty of these men. In some places the Latin text was falsified, in others the French translations garbled; and by means of interpolations and omissions, changes of words or of punctuation, the writers of the Society were made to say things of which they had never thought, indeed were frequently made to uphold the very opinions which they were rejecting or refuting.[39]

Theiner, too, another writer whose bias was far from friendly to

---

[39] Döllinger, *Fortsetzung der Handbuchs der Christlichen Kirchengeschichte von Hortig.* II, Bd. 2 Abth. p. 794. We take this quotation from Father Duhr's, S.J., valuable *Jesuiten-Fabeln,* p. 437 ('Die verruchte Jesuiten Moral.').

the Society, speaks of this work in similar terms of condemnation:[40]

> All France was flooded with malicious lampoons against the Society, of which the notorious *Extraits des Assertions* surpassed all the rest. In this work malice and untruthfulness vied together in a common emulation which should outbid the other. There was no iniquity which the Jesuits were not made to teach, or of which they were not accused; never was bad faith carried to more outrageous lengths. This book, a veritable cesspool of lies, was sent by an *arrêt* of *Parlement* of 5 March 1762, to all the Bishops and magistrates of the kingdom – a detestable device for ascertaining who were friends and who foes of the Jesuits, and for joining all together in a common crusade against the Order. This object was fully attained.

5. Lastly, we may leave it for the reader to consider whether in a matter in which so much depends on the care taken by the compiler to see that his extracts are not only verbally correct, but convey, even when apart from their context, the true meaning of the author, especially to persons unfamiliar with the circumstances in which these moral problems arise – in other words, whether in a matter where an ordinary reader has to depend so much on the honesty and competence of the compiler – implicit credit can be given to such authorities as Chauvelin, de Terray, Clémency, Goujet, and Minard.

III.[41] [Case for the defence]

So far nothing has been said about any legal defence entered on behalf of the Society before the Court of the *Parlement*. Did they then allow so grave an indictment to go by default? The answer is that they were not given an opportunity of legal defence, and that this is one of the iniquities with which their destroyers are chargeable. It is true that the *arrêt* of 6 August 1761, which found fault with the Constitutions of the Society, was technically provisional, and contained a clause expressly citing the Jesuits to appear in their defence before the time came round for the definitive sentence. 'Permission (so ran the text of the *arrêt*) is given to the Procureur-Général du Roi to notify the General and the Society of the said *soi-disant* Jesuits, that the said Appeal *comme d'abus* has been received, on which the parties will have audience on the first day.' It is true, too, that on 7 January next following, the Procureur-Général

[40] *Histoire du Pontificat de Clément XIV*, I, i, §15.
[41] **The Month, 99 (1902), 497–517.**

claimed that the accused should be declared defaulters, their General not having answered to the citation. But none the less it is true also to say that they were not given a *bona fide* opportunity to plead their cause before the Court. It will be remembered that there was another *arrêt* decreed on 6 August 1761, that namely which condemned the alleged teaching of the Society, and this was so far definitive in character that the Jesuits were forbidden to receive new members, or to continue their schools, to take the place of which new schools were ordered to be at once provided where not already in existence. That at least was to break up their work and take away their character before any opportunity of self defence had been given. And even as regards the Appeal *comme d'abus*[42] itself, the citation was unreal, and the Jesuits were never expected to attend to it. The person notified in the clause just quoted as to appear on behalf of the Society was the General of the Order, who was not a subject of the French Crown and could not becomingly have presented himself before a Court to whose jurisdiction he was not amenable. It was the Provincials of the six French Provinces who would have been cited, had there been any genuine desire to hear their defence.[43] There were also other reasons why the authorities of the Society in France must have felt it difficult to put in their legal defence. In the first place, the King having on 2 August ordered the *Parlement* to surcease from the inquiry, it was acting in flagrant violation of the principles of the monarchy by continuing to pursue it, and the Jesuits might naturally feel that their duty under the circumstances was to obey the King rather than his rebellious magistrates. Again, the whole idea of an investigation charging the Popes with having, by their various Bulls on behalf of the Society, sanctioned a system dangerous to the security of kings and the morals of their people, amounted to monstrous outrage on the Holy See, which no loyal son of the Church could recognize without impropriety. And then there was personal reason for not appearing before the *Parlements*, the temper of which was well understood, and foreboded that any attempt to question the truthfulness of the *comptes-rendus* would be visited with instant arrest, to be followed in all probability by a death sentence.

What then did the Jesuits do in self-defence? According to the anonymous writer of the *Premier Appel à la Raison*, who was certainly a member of the Society, for some time they did nothing, the Superiors even going so far as to forbid under a precept of obedi-

---

[42] *Appel comme d'abus* was the technical name for an appeal to the civil courts from the acts of the Holy See or the ecclesiastics, whenever it was alleged that the latter had been guilty of abuse by overstepping their rights.

[43] See on this point *Il est temps de parler*, ii, p. 231.

ence any publication whatever on the subject. This abstention did not, however, last long. The *Premier Appel à la Raison* was published in the autumn of 1761 by the writer just mentioned, who tells us he had by that time left the Society, and the *Nouvel Appel à la Raison,* which appeared shortly after, is attributed to the Abbé Caveirac, who was not a Jesuit. But by the spring of 1762 a series of treatises began to appear, all necessarily anonymous, – as the *Parlement* would have put to death any person convicted of writing against decrees, – but some of which were certainly from Jesuit pens. Of these the principal were the *Rédacteur Véridique,* the *Apologie Générale de l'Institut,* and *Mes Doutes sur la mort des Jésuites*. In the next year were added to the list the *Réponse au livre intituleé, 'Extraits des Assertions'* (the official answer to the book in question), and the *Nouvelles Observations sur les jugements rendus contre les Jésuites;* and in 1764 *Il est temps de parler.* These apologetic treatises were not all of the same merit, but as a whole they offered a refutation of the allegations of the *comptes-rendus* by which no candid mind can fail to be impressed. Particularly must this be said of the *Apologie Générale*[44] and *Réponse au livre intitulé 'Extrait des Assertions'*, both of which are most ably written and argued out. One would have liked to justify this estimate by an account of how they meet some of the charges of the *comptes-rendus,* but this would be impossible within the compass of the present work, in which it is better to rest satisfied with the verdicts of competent contemporary judges, such as were the Bishops whose words we shall be quoting presently. One feature, however, in these defences of the Society must not be passed over, and that is the courteous and respectful tone which pervades them all. They assume throughout, with a directness bordering on insincerity, that the *Parlements* have misinterpreted the Jesuit Constitutions and theological writings, not wilfully, but only through inadequate acquaintance with the subject-matter. None the less the *Parlements* raged against these moderately written treatises, ordering them to be publicly burnt, and their authors, publishers, and distributors to be searched for, and if found, visited with the severest penalties. Could there have been clearer proof that the passion of revenge and not a zeal for justice was the motive impelling them?

---

[44] A melancholy interest attaches to the authorship of this excellent treatise. The materials for it are said to have been provided by Père Griffet and Père de Menoux, two Jesuits of ripe age and experience, but they appear to have availed themselves of the literary talent of a young scholastic of much promise, Cerutti by name, and it was he who actually wrote the book. Five years later, however, he abandoned the Society, not having the needful fortitude to face its persecutions, and he ended by becoming an advanced Revolutionist and secretary to Mirabeau.

It will be remembered that on 30 May 1761, Louis XV sent for the copy of the Jesuit Constitutions which had been deposited with the *Parlement*, and transferred from the latter body to his own tribunal the task of examining into their character. He had been moved thereto by the representations of his family, and his resolution was perhaps strengthened by a letter of Clement XIII which reached him a few days later.[45] It will be remembered, also, that as the *Parlement* procured another copy of the Constitutions, and still continued its proceedings, the King sent a further and stronger message on 2 August, requiring it to surcease from all proceedings for the term of a year, during which interval his own inquiries would be carried to a completion. In the meanwhile he had appointed a Commission composed of members of the Royal Council, who were to examine and report to him. The Secretary of this Commission was M. de Flesselles, and from his collection of the papers of the Commission, which is still extant, Père de Ravignan has transcribed several important documents.[46] From these we find that the Commission drew up the text of two declarations which they called upon the Jesuits to adopt as their own – one being a Decree interpretative of the decree issued by Father Aquaviva in 1610, and confirming its prohibition to teach the permissibility of tyrannicide under any circumstances whatever: the other a Declaration containing Four Articles, of which the *first* disavowed on the part of the French Jesuits this same doctrine of the permissibility of tyrannicide under certain circumstances; the *second* declared that they held and professed, and would continue to hold and profess the principles enunciated in the famous Declaration of the French clergy in 1682; the *third,* that they would submit in all respects to the laws and ordinances of the kingdom, and to its rules of ecclesiastical law and discipline, and refrain from the use of any privilege contrary to the maxims of the kingdom; the *fourth,* that, if ever they should be ordered either by their General or any other Superiors of whatsoever degree, to do anything opposed to the above declarations or their duty to their Sovereign, to the laws of the State or the public tranquillity, they would treat such orders as null and void, and would refuse obedience to them.

These two texts having been drawn up by the Commission, M. de Flesselles was instructed to communicate with the Jesuits and signify to them the desires of the Commission. Accordingly, we learn from the 'Report, relative to the events relating to the Decree and the

---

[45] The text of this letter is not extant, but it is referred to, as having been written in June, 1761, in another letter from Clement to the King, dated 28 January of the following year.

[46] *Clement XIII and Clement XIV,* i, pp. 137, 517, and ii, pp. 181-193.

Declaration, made by M. de Flesselles in presence of all the Ministers assembled at the Chancelier's house at Versailles', that M. de Flesselles sent for the Père Griffet, and, at his request, also for the Provincial of Paris, who was then Père de la Croix. To these he delivered the said Decree and the Declaration, the former to be sent to the Father General for him to accept and transform into a Decree under his own authority, the latter to be at once signed by the Jesuits of France, and then sent on to the General, that their signatures to it might be sanctioned by his approbation. M. de Flesselles tells us that Père de la Croix urged many difficulties against the project, and that he told him in reply, to write out and send in his observations promptly, as the budget must be despatched to Rome by the first *courrier*. The very next day, which was 30 September, came a letter from the Provincial, taking objection to the word 'held' (*sentire*) which occurred in the texts formulated by the Commission, on the ground – which displeased the Royal Commissioners, but to a Catholic theologian is perfectly intelligible – that no authority less than that of the Holy See, and therefore not the General of a Religious Order, has power to dictate or restrain a man's internal opinions, but only the external expression of them. The Provincial of Paris urged one other objection of detail to the wording of the two documents, on which, however, it is not necessary to dwell. Eventually the Paris Jesuits drew up and signed a Declaration of their own, which they sent on to Rome for the General's approval, together with a text similarly composed by themselves of a draft decree for the General to accept and enjoin. We know that the Province of Guienne did the same, and probably the other Jesuit Provinces of France followed suit. These revised texts avoided the particular defects to which exception had been taken in the text of the Commission, but in other respects were on the same lines as the latter.

When they reached the General, who was then Father Ricci, he refused to adopt the Decree on Tyrannicide, on the ground, as M. de Flesselles tells us, that Father Aquaviva's Decree of 1610 was sufficient, and besides, he had already, on 28 October, written to the King a letter in which he had very distinctly disavowed for himself and his subjects the doctrine of which they were suspected. Father Ricci might perhaps have been more yielding on this point, but presumably felt that by signing a formula thus drawn up for him by others, and presented for compulsory signature, he might seem to acknowledge that the suspicions entertained of the Society were not wholly without foundation. It was the Declaration, however, which encountered the more serious opposition. The General, as was natural, sought for guidance from the Pope, and Clement XIII was most indignant that the French Jesuits 'should have made so solemn a profession of opinions contrary to the rights and authority of the Holy See.' Nor can we be surprised at the Pontiff's displeasure. The Four Articles of 1682 had for their scope to sanction certain infringements by the French Crown on the rights of the Holy See and to subordinate the authority of the latter to the authority of General Councils. Although the French Jesuits do not seem to have been called upon to sign these Articles and conform their teaching to them at the time when they were originally drawn up, still even then certain members of the Society, and notably Père de la Chaise, took an unenviable part in the proceedings leading to their enactment. And it was to add another page to this, the saddest chapter in the history of the French Jesuits, when, in 1761, they allowed themselves to be forced into a formal and official act so inconsistent with their traditional adhesion to the Holy See. Nor did this act of weakness avail in any way to stem the torrent of their misfortunes. How far the Royal Commissioners participated in the King's own desire to save the Society from the *Parlements*, and had this end in view when they proposed to the Provincials the Decree and the Declaration, we cannot tell, but the result was to increase its danger by affording them a pretext for leaving it to its fate. M. de Flesselles finishes his narrative by recording that, when the Council of Ministers heard of the answers received from the authorities of the Society, the Duc de Choiseul could not help exclaiming, 'The Jesuits may become what they will; they are unworthy of the good offices of the King.'

In another respect, however, the appointment of the Royal Commission, and its negotiations with the Jesuits, had a more useful issue. M. de Flesselles tells us that, after having seen Pères de la Croix and Griffet, he sent for Père de Neuville, at that time Superior of the Professed House at Paris. Among other matters, he mentioned to this Father that Mgr Christopher de Beaumont, Archbishop of Paris, 'the modern Athanasius', as he was called, had been intending to publish forthwith a *mandement* in favour of the Jesuits, and that he had been trying to restrain him. The Archbishop had acceded to his request, but on condition that the Bishops should be consulted by the King, and he had promised on the part of the Commission to recommend this course to his Majesty. Père de Neuville, he adds, had on leaving, earnestly exhorted him to accelerate this consultation, and had said, 'Should the Advice of the Bishops be in our favour, it will at least make for us a fine epitaph.' It was in this way that the consultation of the Bishops originated, and though the testimony it elicited from the prelates was not influential enough with the King to make him give effect to his own sound judgment, it did, as we have now to see, form a 'fine epitaph' for the grave of the persecuted religious.

On 25 November, the Comte de Florentin, the Minister of the Royal Household, wrote to Cardinal de Luynes, the Archbishop of Sens, bidding him convoke the Bishops then at Paris, and confer with them on the following points:

1. The use which the Jesuits can be in France, and the advantages or evils which may be expected to attend their discharge of the different functions committed to them.
2. The manner in which, in their teaching and practice, the Jesuits conduct themselves in regard to opinions dangerous to the personal safety of sovereigns, to the doctrine of the French clergy contained in the Declaration of 1682, and in regard to the Ultramontane opinions generally.
3. The conduct of the Jesuits in regard to the subordination due to Bishops and ecclesiastical superiors, and as to whether they do not infringe on the rights and functions of the parish priests.
4. What restriction can be placed on the authority of the General of the Jesuits, so far as it is exercised in France.

For eliciting the judgment of the ecclesiastics of the kingdom on the action of the *Parlement*, no questions could be more suitable, and the Bishops convoked – who numbered three Cardinals, nine Archbishops, and thirty-nine Bishops, that is fifty-one in all – met together to consider them on 30 November. They appointed a Commission consisting of twelve of their number, who were given a month for their task, and reported duly on 30 December, having, it should be mentioned, received during the interval, that is on 19 December, a Declaration of their sentiments from the Jesuits of Paris, which was verbally the same as that above referred to as having been signed and sent to the General.[47]

Of these fifty-one Bishops forty-four addressed a letter to the King, dated 30 December 1761, in which they answered all the four questions in a sense favourable to the Society, and gave under each head a clear statement of their reasons. It is a document which we should like to quote in *extenso*, but it is of some length, and we must content ourselves with a brief abstract of its contents.[48]

---

[47] As it is not likely that they would have presented this Declaration to the Bishops, after having received the news of its condemnatiom at Rome, we may gather that that news did not arrive till later, and this agrees with the General's reference, in his reply to the French Provincials, to his previous letter to the King of 28 Oct.

[48] See, for the text, *Documents concernant la Compagnie de Jésus*, i, p. 51.

To the first question the Bishops reply that the Institute of the Jesuits '... is conspicuously consecrated to the good of religion and the profit of States.' They begin by noting how a succession of Popes, St Charles Borromeo, and the Ambassadors of Princes who with him were present at the Council of Trent, together with the Fathers of that Council in their collective capacity, had pronounced in favour of the Society after an experience of the services it could render; how, though in the first instance there was prejudice against it in France on account of certain novelties in its Constitutions, the Sovereign, Bishops, clergy, and people had, on coming to know it, become firmly attached to it, as was witnessed by the demand of the States-General in 1614 and 1615, and of the Assembly of the Clergy in 1617, both which bodies wished for Jesuit Colleges in Paris and the provinces as 'the means best adapted to plant religion and faith in the hearts of the people.' They refer also to the language of many Letters Patent by which the Kings of France had authorized the various Jesuit Colleges, in particular that of Clermont at Paris, which Louis XIV had wished should bear his own name, and which had come to be known as the College of Louis-le-Grand. Then, coming to their own personal experience, they bear witness that 'the Jesuits are very useful for our dioceses, for preaching, for the guidance of souls, for implanting, preserving, and renewing faith and piety, by their missions, congregations, retreats, which they carry on with our approbation, and under our authority.' Whence they conclude that, 'to forbid them to teach would be to do a serious injury to (their) dioceses,' and that 'it would be difficult to replace them without a loss, especially in the provincial towns, where there is no University.'

To the second question the Bishops reply that, if there were any reality in the accusation that the Jesuit teaching was a menace to the lives of sovereigns, the Bishops would long since have taken measures to restrain it, instead of entrusting the Society with the most important functions of the sacred ministry. They also indicate the source from which this and similar accusations against the Society had their origin. 'The Calvinists,' they say, 'tried their utmost to destroy in its cradle a Society whose principal object was to combat their errors, ... and disseminated many publications in which they singled out the Jesuits, as professing a doctrine which menaced the lives of sovereigns, because to accuse them of a crime so capital was the surest means to destroy them; and the prejudices against them thus aroused had ever since been seized upon greedily by all who had had any interested motives for objecting to the Society's existence (in the country).' The Bishops add that 'the charges against the Jesuits which were being made at that time in so many writings with which the country was flooded, were but rehashes of what had been spoken and written against them throughout the preceding century and a half.' The Bishops further suggest that the true test by which to estimate Jesuit teaching is by interrogating their pupils and others.

> The teaching of the Jesuits [they say] in our dioceses is public. Persons of all states and conditions are witnesses of what they teach. We venture to assure your Majesty that they have never been accused before us, of holding the doctrine now imputed to them. Let those be interrogated who have been pupils in their colleges, who have attended their missions, their sodalities, their retreats; we are persuaded that not a single one of all these will testify that he has ever heard them teach any doctrine dangerous to the lives of sovereigns.

To the third question they reply that the Jesuits have no doubt received numerous privileges from the Holy See, many of which, however, and those the most extensive, have accrued to them by communication with the other orders to which they had been primarily granted; but that the Society has been accustomed to use its privileges with moderation and prudence.

The fourth and last of the questions on which the advice of the Bishops was sought, foreshadowed an idea in the King's mind of which this is the first intimation. The *Parlement* had set down the power of the General, with the corresponding exaction of blind obedience from the members, as the most dangerous of all the features in the Society's Institute, and had drawn the same blood-curdling picture of the consequences likely to ensue from its exercise which is considered authentic by the ordinary English Protestant. Louis XV accordingly, with the fondness for temporizing natural to a weak character, had thought to divert the crisis by obtaining from the Holy See a modification of the Institute in this respect. A similar attempt had been made some eighty years earlier by Louis XIV, when, sad to relate, a party among the French Jesuits had themselves advocated this scheme. The King was hopeful, therefore, that the Bishops would give advice to the same effect, and thus strengthen his hand in his application to Rome. But it fell out otherwise. The forty-four Bishops pointed out that the General's power was not arbitrary, inasmuch as he could exact no obedience save to commands contained within the scope of the Constitutions, whilst the Constitutions had provided most effectual remedies for the contingency of a General disregarding these limits. They then note that change to the Constitutions of the Society in what regards the power of the General would be to overturn the entire Institute, whilst, on the other hand, this authority of the General, throughout the space of more than a century and a half, had been used to the disadvantage of the State on one occasion only, when the French Jesuits had refused to submit to it. The occasion to which the prelates here refer, was the occasion above mentioned. In 1684 Louis XIV, having conquered Belgium, desired the Jesuits of those parts to be transferred from the German to the French Assistancy, and, the General not seeing his way to accede to this royal desire, Louis XIV had forbidden the French Jesuits to hold any intercourse with their General until the latter had given in. They complied with the King's order, and sought to have a Vicar General for France appointed, who was, however, to hold under the General. Such an instance easily recommended itself to these French prelates of 1761, who, though excellent men, were somewhat infected with the Gallican maxims; but by members of the Society it cannot be considered a happy illustration of their loyalty to their temporal sovereign. Father de Noyelle, the General who refused to accede to the King's demand, had other sovereigns besides Louis XIV to consider, and the claims of other nationalities besides that of France. It was Louis XIV, in short, who was overstepping his limits. Still the principle which the Bishops asserted is sound and recognized by the Jesuits – the principle, namely, that by his vow of obedience to a religious superior a man cannot divest himself of the prior obligation to obey his temporal sovereign, in matters lying within the sphere of the latter's authority.

To the forty-four prelates who signed this *Avis* must be added the Archbishop of Paris, who was one of the assembled Bishops, but on some ground of precedence preferred not to sign it, but to adhere to it in a separate letter which he addressed to the King. Nor were these the only French prelates who at that time spoke out in defence of the Society against the wanton accusations of its enemies. During the closing months of 1761 many other prelates, from their dioceses where they were residing, wrote as individuals, some direct to the King, others to the Chancelier, M. de Lamoignon, protesting against the *arrêt* of the *Parlement* of 6 August 1761, and testifying to their sense of the injustice of the accusations made against the Jesuits, and of the loss which their dioceses would sustain by their suppression. Père de Ravignan gives the names of twenty-seven such Bishops, copies of whose letters he found among the MSS. of M. de Flesselles, who had included them among the *acta* of his Commission. We have thus seventy-two Bishops in all who vindicated the Society against its accusers during the first half-year after the publication of the *comptes-rendus* of the *Parlement* of Paris; and we may ask if, seeing what they were in respect of their public character, their theological training, and their intimate experience with the spiritual affairs of their dioceses, the judgment of these prelates ought not to be preferred to that of the *Parlement* or its Reporters.

So much on the opinions expressed by the forty-five Bishops whom the King consulted, and the twenty-seven others who wrote to him from the Provinces. But what about the six minority Bishops? So small a minority might, perhaps, be passed over as inappreciable, and yet five out of the six rendered a collective answer, which, as long as the conduct and teaching of the Jesuits is the one thing in question, did not differ from that of the majority. These five Bishops were the Cardinal de Choiseul, brother of the statesman, Mgr de Rochefoucauld, Archbishop of Rouen, and Mgrs Tinseau of Nevers, Choiseul-Beaupré of Chalons, and Champion de Cicé of Auxerre. The text of their *Avis* is given by Père de Ravignan;[49] it declares that 'the confidence reposed in the Jesuits by the Bishops of the kingdom, all of whom approve them in their dioceses, is evidence that they are found useful in France,' and that in consequence they, the writers, 'supplicate the King to grant his Royal protection, and keep for the Church of France a Society recommendable for the services it renders to Church and State, and which the vigilance of the Bishop may be trusted to preserve free of the evils which it is feared might come to infect it.' To the second and third of the King's questions they answer that occasionally individual Jesuits have taught blameworthy doctrines, or invaded the jurisdiction of the Bishops, but that neither fault has been general enough to affect the body as a whole. To the fourth question they answer that 'the authority of the General, as it is wont to be and should be exercised in France, appears to need no modification; nor do they see anything objectionable in the Jesuit vows.' Nevertheless, these five prelates conclude, and it is in this that they differ from the prelates of the majority, that 'to take away all difficulties for the future it would it well to solicit the Holy See to issue a Brief fixing precisely those limits to the exercise of the General's authority in France which the maxims of the kingdom require.'

Bishop Fitzjames, of Soissons, was the only Bishop, out of the fifty-one, who did not assent to one or other of these *Avis,* and it must be acknowledged that his own *Avis,* the text of which Père de Ravignan also gives,[50] was one calculated to satisfy the *Parlement* in every respect. As regards the conduct of the Jesuits, he makes the same valuable acknowledgment as M. Omer Joly de Fleury and M.

[49] ii, p. 259.
[50] ii, p. 264.

Caradeuc de la Chalotais. 'Their morals (he wrote) are pure. One willingly does them the justice to recognize that there is perhaps no Order in the Church the members of which are more regular or austere in their habits.' At the same time, he thinks them worldly, and points as evidence of this, to their presence and credit in all the Courts of Europe, and the great influence they thus enjoy. Their Constitutions, he considers vicious, and their doctrine abominable – though that of a few individual Jesuits may be good – and he cites the recent action of the King of Portugal as proof decisive that they can engage in schemes of assassination. As for their relations with the Bishops and clergy, he pronounces them to form one long history of aggression and quarrels. His remedy is that the bond uniting the French Jesuits with their brethren in other countries, and subjecting them to a Superior in Rome, should be sundered. They should be transformed into a religious congregation exclusively French, ruled by a General whose power should be strictly limited by chapters held in each house or province. Such was this one Bishop's recommendation, in estimating the value of which we must remember that he was one of the recognized Jansenist leaders of the day – though it is only just to remember also that he was a prelate distinguished for many excellent qualities.

As Louis XV had sought the advice of the Bishops, and had obtained from them so decided an opinion in favour of leaving the Society in France just as it was, it might have been expected that he would exercise his authority in that sense. But we have seen what were the influences by which he was ruled, and noted the motives which probably induced him to frame the fourth of the questions addressed to the Bishops. He would have liked to shelter the execution of his own previously-formed intention under the advice of a number of his Bishops, but as these failed him, he was constrained to go on unsupported save by the counsel of the one Bishop who had stood out against his fellows. Accordingly we find that on 26 January 1762, the Duc de Choiseul wrote to Cardinal Rochechouart, then French Ambassador at the Papal Court, bidding him send for the General of the Jesuits, and explain to him that the only chance of saving his Order in France, was for him to renounce an authority found to be incompatible with the laws of that kingdom, and appoint a vicar of French nationality, who should be charged to govern the Jesuits of France in conformity with the said laws. The message was couched in the form of an imperative demand, and Father Ricci was given to understand that he must act at once, or the King would withdraw his protection, and leave the French Jesuits to the tender mercies of the *Parlement*. The General called together his Assistants, and discussed the matter with them. The evils of the proposed scheme were patent. The French Provinces, thus cut off from the rest of the Society, would sooner or later contract a spirit of their own, very different from that of the parent Society; indeed, might become infected with Jansenistic or other heresies. Then, too, there was the likelihood that other sovereigns might demand a similar disruption for the Jesuits in their dominions, and then the Society – which in its unity, and with the unimpaired organization its Founder had impressed on it, had been recognized as able to do important work for our Lord and His Church – would be dissolved into a number of disconnected fragments, assimilated hardly more than by name with the body to which they had formerly belonged. Was it not better that the Society should cease to be altogether, rather than enter upon this disastrous future? It was, however, for the Pope to decide on so fundamental a question, and Clement XIII, on the matter being referred to him, used the well-known words: *'Sint ut sunt, aut non sint.'* Clement also wrote to the French King in terms of pathetic remonstrance:

> We have learnt [he said] that the Cardinal de Rocheouart, the Ambassador of your Majesty, has in your name requested the General of the Society to name a Vicar General for the Jesuits of France. Such a measure does not lie within his competence, and we ourselves, with all our power, cannot authorize it. To do so would be to introduce too substantial a change into the Institute of the Society, an Institute approved by so many Constitutions of our predecessors, and even by the Holy Council of Trent. Such a precedent would draw after it disastrous consequences, among which the least evil one could expect would be the dissolution of a body which for two centuries has been so useful to the Church, principally because of its union and entire dependence on its head. This union, Sire, and this dependence, whatever may be said by evil-minded persons, has never disturbed public tranquillity, either in your kingdom or any other. What is, however, true about it, is that, in the past as well as at the present day, it has caused infinite difficulty to the enemies of religion and to the disobedient, who see themselves attacked in every place by a numerous body of religious whose occupation is to cultivate progress in piety and in the sciences, and who, being filled with zeal and imbued with one spirit, do not cease to combat error and disobedience. This is why they make every imaginable effort to destroy it, using imposture and calumny as their weapons, because they find that truthfulness will not serve them. And now, when all the means they have so far employed have failed them, they have devised one more, namely, to break the bonds which unite the members of the Society together, well knowing that if these are once broken, ruin will necessarily follow.

These earnest exhortations were unfortunately wasted upon the weak King and his imperious Council, who resolved, if they could not obtain their wish from the General or the Pope, to effect it by a mere exercise of Royal authority. Hence it was that some six weeks after the reception of the Papal letter, that is to say, towards the end of March,[51] appeared a Royal Edict authorizing the continued existence of the Jesuits in France, but modifying their Constitutions in several particulars. The Edict contained eighteen articles, which subjected the Society to the laws of the kingdom (whatever that might mean), the authority of the King, and the jurisdiction of the Ordinaries. It also regulated the manner in which the General's authority was to be exercised, and enjoined various rules for the local government of the houses and colleges. And finally, that the ground might be left clear for this new system, it annulled all the measures of the *Parlements* in regard to the Society, from 2 August 1761, onwards.

Such an attempt to alter the institute of a religious order, and the obligation of the vows of its members, by civil authority only, might, if persisted in, have led to a sharp conflict between the King and the Holy See. This, however, was prevented, as has been recorded above,[52] by the refusal of the *Parlement* to register an Edict which fell far short of satisfying its designs upon its victims.

At this point we may place the commencement of a fresh chapter in the painful story. Though the Royal Edict of March 1762, remained without effect, the concordant testimony of so many Bishops on behalf of the incriminated Society could not fail to produce a deep impression on the fair-minded portion of the community, and to counteract the moral effect of the *comptes-rendus*. Something further must be done if the *Parlement* wished to pose, not as the persecutor of the innocent, but as the scourge of iniquity; and it was with this object that about this time the *Extraits des Assertions* were made public. A copy, it will be remembered from an earlier section,[53] was sent to the King, as the justification of the *Parlement* for not registering his Edict and, in conformity with an *arrêt* of 5 March, a copy was likewise sent to each of the Bishops whose sees lay within the jurisdiction of the *Parlement* of Paris – with a message to the effect that, 'seeing the zeal with which (the prelates) were animated for the welfare of religion, the purity of Christian moral teaching, the maintenance of good morals, the preservation of public tranquillity, and

---

[51] The Royal Edicts of the French Kings were dated by the months only, without mention of the day of issue.
[52] See above p. 48.
[53] See above pp. 48–49.

the safety of the sacred person of the Sovereign, the *Parlement* expected of them that they would take all such measures for the attainment of these ends as their pastoral solicitude demanded of them.' Copies of these *Extraits* were also printed off in large numbers and circulated simultaneously throughout the kingdom.

This publication formed a thick quarto volume, full of quotations, professedly giving the exact words of many Jesuit authors, and in that case convicting them of a mass of opinions on moral matters flagrantly opposed to every dictate of a right conscience. And all these shameful opinions are set forth as held and taught not merely by the writers from whose works they were respectively taken, but by each individual Jesuit – the compilers of the Collection arguing fantastically to this conclusion from a clause in the Jesuit Constitutions which exhorts to unity of sentiment, as the best means of avoiding quarrels and dissensions.

It was to influence the general public that this collection of *Extraits* had been made, and whatever may be thought of the morality of the proceeding, it was certainly well adapted to that end. The laity were incapable of verifying the numerous references, and discovering how many of them were unreal or garbled, and, even in the few cases where the quotations were correctly given, they would be prone to misconceive the state of the question. What then could be the result save to assist the campaign against the Society by divesting its members of the good name they had hitherto borne in the country? The object for which copies were sent to the Bishops was similarly malignant. The *Parlement* entertained a spite against them for the signal manner in which they had spoken in favour of the Society, and it was hoped to place them in the dilemma of either having to condemn those whom they had so recently commended, or of being regarded by the public as partners in their guilt. Nevertheless, it was a good thing that the *Extraits* should be brought thus pointedly under the notice of the Bishops, for it gave them an excellent opportunity for denouncing the fraud. Not indeed that they were able to speak out at once on the appearance of the libel. It required time to master its contents, and compare the citations with the originals. But gradually the episcopal replies to the *Parlement* began to appear, some of which have been preserved. First in importance among them was the long Pastoral Letter of Archbishop de Beaumont, dated 28 October 1763.[54] It was a magnificent exposure of the fraudulent character of the *Extraits*, and in view of its systematic character, and of the saintly character of the writer, may he regarded as the classical

---

[54] *Documents concernant la Compagnie de Jésus,* iii, 2,1.

document on the subject; and it was as such that it received the adhesion of several of the other prelates. But many Bishops wrote separate letters, among them being those of the Bishop of Uzés, dated 13 August 1762;[55] of the Bishop of Castres, written about the same time,[56] and like the other addressed to the *Procureur-Général* of the *Parlement* of Toulouse; and of the Bishop of Lavaur, under the form of a Pastoral to his flock, dated 1 November 1762.[57] Père de Ravignan also mentions similar letters as having been written by the Bishops of Amiens, Le Puy, Langres, Saint-Pons, Grenoble, and Sarlat, and the Archbishops of Auch and Aix. All these letters were to the same effect as Archbishop de Beaumont's, nor do there appear to have been any dissentient voices among the Bishops, with three notable exceptions, which, by the protests they excited, served only to accentuate the general agreement. These three were the Bishops of Angers, of Alais, of Soissons. As the Bishop of Angers subsequently withdrew his letter, and adhered to the judgment of the general body of the Bishops, the three became reduced to two, one of whom was the Jansenist leader, FitzJames, of whom we have already heard, and the other, Mgr de Beauteville, a prelate who, though a good man, was also notorious for his Jansenistic sympathies. Both these two received letters of remonstrance from Clement XIII for what they had written, and FitzJames's Pastoral was even condemned by the Pope for setting forth as *de fide*, and to be accepted by all, 'propositions not only rejected, but also combated by the Catholic world.'[58]

With these judgments of the Bishops we may class the *Réponse aux Extraits des Assertions*, which was brought out by the Jesuits early in 1763, and was evidently much used by the Bishops whose denunciations of the *Extraits* appeared subsequently. Its authors had great difficulty in compiling it, owing to the disorder into which their affairs had been thrown and the confiscation of their libraries, but when it was completed it was thorough. Every quotation in the *Extraits* was examined, and reproduced in the correct form, the omissions being supplied, and the defects indicated; and the same was done for the French translation. The total result showed in the Latin text of the *Extraits* 41 errors of omission or interpolation, or alterations of words or punctuation; 261 suppressions of phrases in the original text; 61 mutilations of the text, most of which have the effect of ascribing to an author a meaning which he does not express or even which he is refuting; 94 unfaithful expositions of the authors'

[55] *Ibid.* ii,13.
[56] *Ibid.*
[57] De Ravignan, op. cit., ii, p. 264.
[58] *Ap.* De Ravignan, i, p. 130.

meanings; and in the French translation, 301 instances similarly classified, in which the sense of the original, even as this is given in the same Collection, is misrepresented. Thus, in all, 758 misrepresentations are detected and catalogued in this *Réponse*.

We must repeat here what has been said already in regard to the many vindications of the Society. Within the compass of such an exposition as the present, it is impossible to give illustrations of the mode in which the *Réponse* meets the misrepresentations of the *Extraits*; we must be content to invite those who have the needful qualifications to read the two works together, and refer others, as in the last section, to such verdicts as Döllinger's and Theiner's. Even as regards the utterances of the Bishops, we must be content to notice two general but conclusive points on which they lay stress, and to give one brief extract from a letter in which Clement XIII, writing back to one of them, speaks of the unanimous censure of the *Extraits* which they had sent him. The two general points are these, that if the Jesuits were really guilty of such abominable teaching, both they themselves and the Jesuit pupils would have observed it, the pupils either to protest against it or be infected by it, the prelates to denounce it and cause it to be stopped. Clement's words to the Bishop of Sarlat, in his letter of 14 November 1764, as given by Père de Ravignan, are these:

> We were engaged in writing to you this reply when another of your letters reached us, dated the 14th of last October. In it you speak at length of the famous book of *Assertions* which, like you, a large number of your colleagues declare to be a work of bad faith and Jansenistic fraud. They declare unanimously that the Collection contains many propositions of which some are common to all the schools, others are taught by a vast number of theologians and doctors, both of canon and civil law, and several are regarded as incontestably true by all theologians.

What remains of the story of the Suppression in France must be told in the briefest manner. In June 1762, another Assembly of the Clergy of France met in Paris. It was a more imposing gathering than that of the previous autumn, being a General Assembly in which all the ecclesiastical provinces of the kingdom were represented, each by four elected deputies, of whom two were Bishops, two clergy of the second order. They were called to vote additional supplies for the conduct of the war then raging, but they used the opportunity – as Clement XIII had invited them to do in a special letter – to approach the throne with a respectful protest against the doings of the *Parlements*, which they characterized as 'contrary to the rules of justice, of the Church, and of civil law,' and with a demand for the retention of the Jesuits, which they declare to be the 'unanimous desire of all the ecclesiastical provinces of the kingdom.' They obtained, indeed, from the King nothing beyond the characteristic answer, that 'it would be best for the clergy not to go beyond what they had already done, lest otherwise they should prejudice the steps he proposed to take in favour of the Jesuits.' Still their eloquent protest, coming as it did after the publication of the *Extraits*, contributed forcibly to the 'fine epitaph' of which Père de Neuville spoke. Indeed, as one looks back on the painful history, it seems a marvel that there should have been such unanimity of clerical testimony on behalf of the Society. But the explanation is doubtless to be sought in the flagrancy of the injustice which the *Parlement* was committing.

From the King himself, though given in his own peculiar way, came the next testimony to the innocence of the Society. He had allowed the *Parlement* to contemn his injunctions and carry out their own schemes, but it was not till the end of 1764 that he co-operated himself in the work of destruction. By that time the troubles of the Jesuits had only increased. Not only were they turned out of all their houses, and deprived of all their means, by the *arrêt* of 6 August 1762; but by a further *arrêt* of 9 March 1764, they were placed in the alternative of either being banished from the kingdom or else taking an oath by which they would renounce the obligation of their vows, and acknowledge the justice of the condemnation by the *Parlement* of their Constitutions and of the doctrines of their theologians. It was an oath which none could conscientiously take, and it is to their credit that it was refused by all save just three priests and a handful of scholastics and lay brothers. Some, however, of the provincial *Parlements* declined to go to these extreme lengths, whilst those of Douai, Besançon, and Alsace had all along refused to join in the proceedings of the *Parlement* of Paris. It was on the plea of putting a stop to this diversity of treatment and enforcing uniformity throughout the kingdom that Choiseul – who continued his hostility to the Jesuits, though the Marquise de Pompadour had died in the previous April – at length succeeded in persuading the King to suppress the Society by Royal Edict. This Edict was published in November 1764, and what is remarkable about it is its brevity and baldness. No motives for the new measure are recited in the text of the Edict, save that the King had informed himself of all that related to the Society of Jesuits, and had determined to exercise his rights. It then decrees that the Society as such is no longer to exist in his dominions, but that its members may remain in the country as private individuals under the jurisdiction of the Bishops; and it annuls whatever criminal proceedings had been undertaken against their Institute, their writers, or their own persons.

An Edict so reticent of the causes which had impelled it was most unusual, but an autograph letter of Louis XV addressed to the Duc de Choiseul, from whose MSS. it was first published by M. de Saint-Priest,[59] explains the mystery. It seems that the original draft of the Edict was long and circumstantial, reciting all the steps taken by the *Parlements*, but this the King refused to adopt, ordering that in place of it should be set down, that 'the Society having excited a great fermentation in the kingdom, he ordered all to leave it, and that he would accord them a maintenance wherever they went.' The King also objected to the word 'punish', which 'said a great deal too much'. He did not, he writes, cordially love the Jesuits, but felt it was their triumph that all heresies detested them; if he banished them for the sake of the peace of his kingdom, yielding therein to the advice of others, he did not wish it to be thought that he assented to all that the *Parlements* had said or done against them; and he concludes by saying, 'I hold my tongue or I might say too much.'

In sending this Edict to Rome, on 3 December 1764, the Duc de Praslin, Choiseul's cousin, wrote to the Marquis d'Aubeterre, the French Ambassador to the Holy See, saying that 'the King believed the Jesuits to be useful both to Church and State, in view of their edifying work and teaching, but that he had felt bound to suppress them for reasons of a higher order bearing on the public peace.' The Duc coolly added that 'the Holy See, in its zeal for religion and regard for the Jesuits, would do well to observe the same silence (in respect to what had been done) which the King had ordered to be observed in his own States.' It was not thus, however, that Clement XIII conceived of his duty. He had already written several letters to the King and to those who might have influence with him, as well as to the Bishops of France; but so far all in vain. On the other hand, he had received letters from Bishops not in France only, but in all parts of the world, to the number of some two hundred, beseeching him to issue some solemn protest against the injustice done to the Society, and assuring him of the immense loss its destruction would be to their dioceses; reminding him too that the honour of the Holy See itself was impeached when an Institute which it had approved in so many ways was declared 'impious and irreligious'. Such was the origin of the Bull *Apostolicum* issued on 9 January 1765, which follows exactly these lines of subject. It has been suggested that it was extorted from this Pope, and, if the term applies to the constrain-

---

[59] *La Chute des Jésuites*, p. 298; see also de Ravignan, i, p. 157.

ing force of the demands of two hundred Bishops, the suggestion is well founded. But that the Bull represented also the spontaneous feeling of its author cannot be doubted by any one who studies the character of the man, and the unwearied solicitude with which all through his Pontificate he struggled against the schemes of the Society's foes. As soon, too, as the Bull reached the Bishops, another series of letters from all parts came pouring into Rome, thanking the Holy Father for what he had done – so that one is entitled to urge this last solemn testimony on behalf of the Society before its Suppression as a document of exceptional authority, representing not the Pope only, but the Episcopate of the Catholic world.

And here we may terminate this account of the downfall of the French Provinces in the eighteenth century. It has been but an outline, but it may serve to give our readers some idea of the character of the forces at that time arrayed against the Society, and of those arrayed in its defence; and it may enable them to form a judgment as to whether the Suppression in France any more than in Portugal deserves to be cited as an instance in support of the facile argument which in this work we are trying to examine, – the argument, namely, which deduces the iniquitous character of the Society from the bare fact that in the course of its history it has been proscribed in so many countries.

Chapter Three

In Spain

I.[1] [The process of expulsion]

When we compare together the three great suppressions of the Society by civil authority during the Pontificate of Clement XIII, we cannot but observe that each has its own peculiar physiognomy. In France there was at all events a trial in a Court of Justice to investigate the charges brought against the Jesuits – though it was an investigation carried on in defiance of, rather than in compliance with, the rules of equity. In Portugal there was no trial, at least no trial of which the proceedings were published, but at all events there was a public statement of the offences charged. In Spain, on the other hand, the Jesuits were not even permitted to know what was the crime for their supposed commission of which they were visited with a punishment more drastic than that which befel them in either France or Portugal. They were told merely that the King reserved the secret within his royal breast. Let us help ourselves with a comparison. Suppose that without a word of previous warning, suddenly, and in the dead of night, all the Nonconformist ministers of England were arrested by the police, and before morning dawned were on their way to exile in some distant country; suppose that neither they nor their country were told a word about their pretended offence, except that the King and Government knew of it only too well, but to prevent scandal had resolved never to disclose its character to a single soul; suppose further that the victims of this mysterious deportation were told that all their property was confiscated to the Crown, but that they would be allowed a shilling a day for their maintenance, which however would be stopped if they should ever venture to write a word in self-defence or even utter a complaint of the harshness of their treatment – suppose that all this were to occur now-a-days, what should we all think of it? And yet this is exactly what did occur to the

[1] *The Month*, **99** (1902), 626–650.

Spanish Jesuits in the spring of 1767, as we are now about to see.

We are referring to the action of the Spanish Sovereign, whose hostility to the Jesuits of his kingdom was unsuspected by them up to the moment when he caused them to be expelled, and whose motives for so punishing them were never proclaimed, and are to this day only matter for conjecture. That they had enemies in the country who had watched with delight their discomfiture in Portugal and France, and were working for a similar result at home, was only too manifest and gave them much anxiety. As far back as 1757 Pombal had caused copies of the *Short Relation*[2] to be spread broadcast over Spain as well as other countries. It was intended to justify him in the eyes of the world for the measures he was taking, and gave his version of the doings of the Jesuit missionaries of Paraguay, a version which, as our readers have seen, represented them as the deliberate organizers of a rebellion against their European rulers. Another volume published about the same time and widely circulated was that entitled *Nicholas I, King of Paraguay and Emperor of the Mamelukes*. It professed to hail from a Jesuit press at San Pablo, in South America, and to give their own account of a kingdom they were setting up, the sovereignty of which was to be always in the hands of a nominee of their General; but its real place of publication was somewhere in Europe, and the author some agent of Pombal's. It was a work the absurdity of which was easy to test, but it is wonderful how widely it succeeded in imposing on the minds of people in Europe. When in 1758 General Cevallo was sent out to Buenos Ayres, his fleet, before venturing to cast anchor, asked anxiously if the town was in the hands of this mythical sovereign. And Padre Juan Escandon – who was sent to Rome as Procurator for the Paraguay Mission, in 1758, and wished on the way to solicit from King Ferdinand VI the needful maintenance for an increase in the supply of missionaries – tells us he could get no access to the Court of Madrid, all there having been taken in by this curious imposture. Nor was it only these two works the circulation of which in Spain was due to an impulse from Pombal. The ex-Jesuit Bernardo Ibañez, who had been cast out of the Society in Paraguay, and the more famous ex-Capuchin, Père Norbert Platel, who had wandered restlessly over India, America, and half Europe, were both engaged, the one in Spain, the other in Portugal (where his services had been formally hired by Pombal), in retailing with tongue and pen their supposed experiences of the scandals caused by Jesuit unscrupulousness. These publications made it their business, at least mainly and directly, to attack the methods and

---

[2] See above, ch. 1, p. 11.

76   *The Suppression of the Society of Jesus*

conduct of the Jesuit missionaries in distant countries. It was the European side of their activity, the fundamental character of their Institute, and the nature of their theological teaching, which, as we have seen, were taken in hand by the multitudinous books which had more recently been published in France and were now flowing in to swell the torrent of misrepresentation in Spain. Padre Navarette, in his Life of Padre Idiáquez,[3] makes special mention of one which he calls *Annales Jesuitarum,* and which must be the *Annales de la Société des soi-disants Jésuites,* for he describes it as raking up all the false charges brought against the Society, from the time of its first entrance into France, by such writers as Dumoulin and Étienne Pasquier. We have not been able to discover any express references to the *Comptes Rendus,* or to the *Extraits des Assertions,* as circulating in Spain at this time, but it may be taken for granted that neither these nor indeed any of the numerous anti-Jesuit publications issued from the Paris press were left unused by the men in Spain who shared the aims of the French and Portuguese Jansenists and Encyclopaedists, and saw that, if they would succeed in their efforts to destroy the Spanish Jesuits, they must first of all seek to destroy the good name they had hitherto enjoyed in the country.

The idea of the Society, of its framework, its objects, and its methods, which was set before the Spanish people in the literature thus introduced among them, was well calculated to attain this object, for there they found it represented, not, as they had hitherto imagined, as a Religious Order devoted to spiritual work of the kind which all Catholics value, but as a corporation possessed with the ambition to impose itself on the entire Church as a dominant power, and having methods and constitutions framed by the most cunning artifices to serve this purpose. There they were taught that Jesuits recognized no rule save that of expediency, and that they did not deem murder itself an improper weapon for removing obstacles from their path, even the persons of anointed kings not being sacred in their eyes. There they were taught that the Society devoted itself to education and the confessional, not in order to guide disciples and penitents along the paths of piety, but to acquire and fashion to a suitable shape submissive tools to be used for the furtherance of their pursuit of power. There they were taught that Jesuit morality was but a system of subtle sophisms to soothe sinners who would consent to aid the Society only on condition that they might cherish their vices, and at the same time nurse themselves in the delusion that they were virtuous. There they were taught that the Jesuits were acquiring enor-

---

[3] See his *De viris illustribus in Castella Veteri Societatem ingressis.*

mous wealth by pillaging the weak and foolish at home, and by carrying on vast commercial enterprizes in their missionary settlements. There they were taught that across the Atlantic these Religious had already succeeded in setting up an independent kingdom, under a King owning the suzerainty of their General, and were prepared to resort even to arms to shake off the rule of their lawful Sovereign.

It must not be thought that all this malignant literature circulated with the free consent of the authorities. On the contrary, several of the libels, such as the *Short Relation* of Pombal and the *Annales des soi-disants Jésuites,* were proscribed by the Supreme Council of Castile, presided over at the time by D. Rojas y Contreras, Bishop of Cartagena. But these official proscriptions, as is usual, only served to whet appetites and add the savour of forbidden fruit, and the publications continued to circulate clandestinely. Nor, recommended as their allegations were by proofs which, if unsound, were at all events clever and specious, could they fail to make a powerful impression on many who read them, and to work their way to persuasion, first among those predisposed against the Society, then among those who had little personal intercourse with its members, and at length even among some of its friends. And what made matters worse was that, in that autocratically-governed country, it was difficult for the Jesuits to defend themselves by publishing replies. Padre Pignatelli, at Saragossa, where he was much esteemed, ventured to provide translations of some of the Apologies for the Society which had appeared in France, and to cause copies to be distributed gratis in the town, but he incurred the resentment of the authorities, who confiscated many of the copies; and we shall have an illustration presently of a similar difficulty which arose over the publication of one of these Apologies at Valladolid.

At the same time there was another side to the picture. If they had clever and determined foes able to malign them in this way, the Jesuits had also many friends to take their part. There were, in the first place, the multitudes who were or had been their pupils or penitents, the mass of whom cherished for them a strong regard and affection. Then there were the Bishops, so many of whom not only used their services in their dioceses, but had quite recently written to the Holy See, protesting very energetically against the treatment meted out to their brethren in France. 'We rejoice,' wrote back Clement XIII in 1765, to one of these, namely, the Bishop of Urgel,[4] 'that to the *Avis* of the Bishops of France ... a quite remarkable assent has been added by the Bishops of Spain, most of whom

---

[4] De Ravignan, *Clément XIII et Clément XIV,* i, p. 542.

(*plerique*) have written to thank Us for our Bull (the *Apostolicum*), and, whilst recalling the numberless services rendered by the Clerks Regular of the Society of Jesus to religion and souls, to congratulate Us on our endeavour to console and defend this venerable Order, now when it is falsely accused of the most atrocious crimes and overwhelmed with the weight of vexations and injustices.' The Spanish Jesuits were aware, too, that they had a powerful friend in the Queen-Mother, Elizabeth Farnese, who had great influence at Court, now that her son, Carlos III, had succeeded, as he did in 1759, his half-brother, Ferdinand VI. It was to her strenuous action that Don Carlos owed the Neapolitan sovereignty which he himself had formerly held, and which he had now passed on to his younger son. He was grateful to her, and devoted to her; nor was it conceivable that he would displease her by taking the kind of measures against the Society for which its enemies were asking. And that its enemies realized this to be the political situation is attested by the words which one of them, Manuel de Roda, used a few years before the Spanish Suppression, when he was Spanish Ambassador to the Holy See. He had around him then a little circle of persons all anxious like himself for the destruction of the Society, but when at times they expressed impatience that the years were running on yet nothing was being done in Spain to follow up the example of Portugal and France, he would reply: 'The time is not yet ripe. Wait till the old woman is dead.'

Elizabeth Farnese was indeed old, and she died in the early summer of 1766, after having, as it was believed, warded off one or two intended assaults on the condemned Order. Still, the King himself was well affected towards it, and anxious to be its protector. Carlos III, unlike Joseph I of Portugal and Louis XV of France, was a man of irreproachable life and deep religious feeling. He thoroughly realized, too, and accepted his responsibility as a King to study the welfare of his people, and had a will as strong as that of his French cousin was weak, to see that his conceptions of what was right and just should be carried out – although, as the result showed, he had not Louis XV's discernment to see through the schemes of his *entourage*. By such a King the Spanish Jesuits might surely count on being treated with equity, and, should an accusation against them be at any time laid before him, on being heard in their own defence, which was the utmost that they claimed. He had, moreover, on various occasions, given them distinct marks of his approbation. Before leaving Naples, he had entrusted the education of his youthful son Ferdinand, who was succeeding him there, to two members of the Society, and he had similarly attached a Jesuit tutor to his elder son Carlos, who was to be his successor in Spain. Again, before leaving Naples, one of his last acts was to assure Father Ricci, their General, who had come to visit him, of his intention to extend to the Jesuits in Spain the same protection and favour as he had shown to those of his Neapolitan Kingdom, adding that he was fully aware of the many services they had rendered to the Crown of Spain. And on his arrival in Spain, one of his first acts was on their behalf. Reference has already been made to the prejudice against them at Madrid when Padre Escandon sought from Ferdinand VI the means of taking some fresh missionaries back to Paraguay. By the time Don Carlos arrived, a reaction of opinion in their favour had been caused by a published account by Father Escandon of the true facts about the missions and the Jesuits' conduct in regard to the carrying out of the Treaty of Limits, confirmed as it soon was by the arrival at Madrid of the report by the new Governor of Buenos Ayres, Don Cevallo. The new King hastened, therefore, to make amends to them for the past by supplying out of the Royal Exchequer the means for taking out not sixty, as was asked, but eighty additional missionaries for the evangelization of those vast regions. Moreover, in 1764 another event happened which drew from him a mark of appreciation. At that time the Royal Ministers had tried a scheme for extracting a much larger revenue than hitherto from the American colonies. According to Archdeacon Coxe's account,[5] the trade in Mexico, Peru, Chili, and Tierra Firma was monopolized by the magistracy, the military, the monks, and the secular clergy, and the idea was to gain over two of these bodies by means of intrigue, and then use their influence to crush the other two, and it was hoped in this way to increase the revenue from Mexico alone by 200,000 *livres*. Such a scheme was of the sort to excite insurrections, as in fact it did, and in Peru arose one which might have had serious results, had it not been that the Jesuit missionaries used their great influence with the people, and appeased them. For this service to their Sovereign they received his warm thanks in a letter written back to the Provincial of Peru.

If, however, the King was favourable, there were Ministers surrounding him who, if the Jesuits had been aware of their real character, would have added immensely to their anxiety. From the spring of 1766 there was at the head of the Council of Castile the Conde de Aranda, a friend of Pombal's, who had been Spanish Minister at Lisbon when their brethren were being expelled from Portugal. At the head of Foreign Affairs was the Marqués de Grimaldi, an intimate friend of Choiseul's, with whom he was in close correspondence, and who had been Spanish Minister at Paris at

[5] *History of the Bourbon Courts*, vol. iv, p. 331.

the time of the expulsion from France. There were also the Duque de Alva, their sworn enemy; D. Manuel de Roda, the one who when at Rome said, 'Wait till the old woman is dead,' and whom Cordara, who had excellent means of observing, considered to be the prime mover in the affair of the Spanish suppression; and D. Rodriguez de Campomanes, the Fiscal to the Supreme Council, another of their secret enemies.

Amidst these hopes and fears the Spanish Jesuits had to live, and one desiderates at this point a means of insight into the nature and spirit of their lives and work. Was it an activity such as their enemies imputed to them, a life of incessant plotting and intriguing, tending to keep the minds of the people in a state of unrest and of discontent with their rulers? or was it the kind of activity which becomes priests and Religious, in teaching youth and writing on useful subjects, in preaching and administering sacraments? Fortunately we have some means for such an insight in two or three biographical works, the authors of which were in complete touch with the events they record. First, there is Padre Caballero's *Bibliothecae Scriptorum Societatis Supplementum,* published in 1814, which contains brief accounts of many Jesuits of that time, most of them being Spaniards who had been expelled by the orders of Carlos III, and Padre Caballero himself being one of these – for at the time of the expulsion he was Master of Rhetoric in the Imperial College of Madrid. Then there is Padre Navarette's *De viris illustribus in Castella Veteri Societatem Jesu ingressis,* published in 1799.[6] He also was one of the expelled Spanish Jesuits, having been Professor of Theology at the English College of Valladolid at the same time. He has preserved biographical accounts, much fuller than Padre Caballero's, of twenty-six Jesuits belonging to the Province of Castile. These are particularly valuable, and bear throughout unmistakable signs of having been written in the first instance by eye-witnesses of the facts, as indeed, in his Preface, Padre Navarette assures us was the case. Then there is the Life of the Venerable Padre Pignatelli, written by Padre Monzón, who was a novice of the Province of Aragon at the time of the expulsion, but became afterwards the constant companion of Padre Pignatelli, and gathered his materials from the most authentic sources. And, finally, as the expulsion included the Jesuit missionaries in the Spanish colonies, we are fortunate in having Padre Peramas's *De vita et moribus sex (et undecim) virorum Paraguaycorum,* all of whom, and he himself among them, were expelled from Peru and Paraguay by the orders of Carlos III. Of the

---

[6] [Sommervogel mentions an edition in 1793. *Ed. N.*]

subjects of these biographies the following are perhaps the most conspicuous.

In the Province of Toledo there were Padre Mourin – born in 1707, and head of his Province in 1767 – the quiet student who never left the house unless for business, the clear thinker whose expositions of difficult subjects were found so illuminating, the obliging friend who would spare no labour to do a service, the fervent preacher who drew crowds to his pulpit, the Jesuit for whom, that he might keep him always at his side, Ferdinand VI sought to create a special office at Rome, desisting only out of regard for the Father's distressed humility; and Padre Navarro, born in 1705, and Rector of the Imperial College at Madrid in 1767, a man whose theological advice was approved and regularly sought by the Council of Castile. In the Province of Aragon there was the Venerable Padre José Pignatelli, born in 1737, a scion of one of the first families in Spain. He discarded brilliant prospects to enter the Society, where he was remarked from the first for that holiness of life the eminence of which has been so far recognized by the Church as to permit of the cause of his beatification being introduced.[7] It was at Saragossa that he was born, and on joining the Society, after a season spent elsewhere for his novitiate and philosophical studies, he was brought back to his native town in 1759. His work was to teach boys in the College, a work in which he had singular success, but he employed the time he could spare from his boys for preaching in public places. He was often in the confessional, was fond of visiting the sick in the hospitals, and the prisoners in the condemned cell. He was a man whose counsels were valued and sought by the leading people of the town, and as a proof of the high estimation in which he was held it may be mentioned that, when in the Easter week of 1766, a bread riot broke out at Saragossa, and assumed dimensions sufficient to alarm the Governor, it was to Padre Pignatelli he had recourse, asking him to use his influence with the people who had so often listened to his sermons. Padre Pignatelli, aided by some of his brethren, answered to the appeal, and at the risk of their lives ran into the midst of the excited rioters, whom, not without grave difficulty, they succeeded eventually in appeasing. The service thus rendered to the town elicited from the King a special letter of thanks addressed to the Jesuits of Saragossa.

In the Province of Castile there was Padre Calatayud, an octogenarian when called to go into exile. His work had been to give parochial missions, and he had been engaged in it for forty-eight

---

[7] [After this was written the cause advanced rapidly: Pignatelli was beatified by Pius XI in 1933, and canonized by Pius XII in 1954. *Ed. N.*]

years. Not a district throughout Spain or Portugal had been unvisited by him for this object, and Bishops, and even Princes, contested with one another as to which should have the preference in securing his ministrations. When he entered a town the populace went out in crowds to meet him, and when he left it, the effects of his labours were invariably seen in the amendment of lives. Thus he had come to be venerated throughout the country, and was even called familiarly the Apostle of Spain. In the Province of Castile there was also Padre Francesco Idiáquez, born in 1711, and perhaps the most conspicuous Spanish Jesuit of any at that time. He was the eldest son of the Duque de Granada de Ega, one of the highest grandees of Spain, but had surrendered titles and estates to his younger brother, preferring himself to join the Society and give his life to the work of God. Like Padre Calatayud, he was known and respected throughout Spain. During the earlier years of his priestly life he was noted as a zealous preacher among the goatherds on the mountains near Valladolid. But his talents caused him eventually to be used chiefly for government, and he held one rectorship after another, until in the eventful years preceding the expulsion he ruled as the Provincial of Castile. In his youth he had been the personal friend and companion of Ferdinand VI, then an Infante of Spain, and in his later years he enjoyed also the esteem of Carlos III, an esteem which was expressed by that monarch as late as a few months before the crisis came on. Padre Idiáquez's Life is the fullest of all in Padre Navarette's collection, and, as the latter tells us, was originally written in Spanish by Padre Gonzales, the friend and companion of Idiáquez for many years. We shall have to draw from it presently for some precious details of the efforts made by this Father to stay off the threatening calamity.

We must be content with a simple mention of some other notable Fathers of the Spanish Provinces of those days. Such were Padre Osorio, like Padre Idiáquez, esteemed at Court for his high birth and his virtues, and appointed to be his successor as Provincial, just when the expulsion was decreed; Padre Menduru, the Apostle of the Basques, another great mission preacher; Padre Colmenarez, so remarkable for his love of the poor, and for a lavishness in alms-giving, during the years of his rectorship at Villagarcia, which many thought imprudent, but which God signally blessed; of Padre Salgado, so loved by the people of Oviedo; of Padre Aimerich, the student who had just come to Madrid to employ his old age in editing an important work on the Catalonian language, when the message of exile found him there; or, as the American Jesuits were involved in the common ruin, of Padre Escandón, already mentioned, who spent thirty-four years of zealous labour on the Paraguay and Peruvian missions; and Padre Chomé, a scholar and a linguist, whom it was proposed to turn into a Bollandist, but who begged for the foreign missions instead, and was sent to Paraguay in 1729. He had thus been nearly forty years on the mission when the King's orders for his deportation to Europe arrived, and found him worn out with his toils and almost bedridden. What those toils were can be gathered from a letter written in 1738, in which he speaks of 2,132 leagues traversed since he left Buenos Ayres, his way having lain across high mountains, through trackless forests, and oftentimes through the haunts of barbarous tribes. Nor did he, amidst these fatigues, neglect the interests of learning, but used his opportunities for studying and writing on the native languages, and communicated his discoveries to the scholars in Europe with whom he kept up a correspondence.

These are but outlines of the lives of twelve out of the fifty and more whose biographical notices are found in the works mentioned. It is impossible to give more in a brief overview of the evidence, and impossible to give particulars of the personal and spiritual lives even of these few. Still, if any one has access to the works of Caballero, Navarette, or Peramas, all of which are to found in the British Museum Library, he will bear us out when we claim that these twelve, and with them many others of various ages, there commemorated, were men of virtuous and even of saintly lives, whole-hearted in their loyalty to God and King, and in their devotedness to the welfare of the people, men in short whom the Society may be proud to know that she possessed in that anxious hour of her existence. They formed, it is true, but a fraction of the 2,500 Jesuits who were touched by the King's edict, nor would it be reasonable to infer that all or most of their brethren attained to the same high level of spirituality as themselves. Still it is reasonable to take them as a measure by which to estimate the character of the general body. Oil does not mix with water, and had the prevailing character of the Spanish Jesuits of the period been such as to justify their inclusion in one wholesale proscription as persons unfit to live in a well-ordered State, it is inconceivable that the holy men to whom we are referring should not have been conscious of the divergence of aims and sentiments between themselves and their fellows, and have been urgent for the purgation of their Society from such scandals, if not for its entire suppression. And yet what we do find in them is an intense affection for the Society, which they regard as the mother to whose spiritual training they owe everything, and an absolute confidence that their superiors and brethren are of like mind with themselves.

It is most necessary to insist on this point. When there is irrefragable testimony and demonstrated proof against a body of men, as guilty of a great crime, presumptions to the contrary must give way. But when, instead of the evidence of such testimony and proofs, there are but vague suspicions, or the allegations of men whose own trustworthiness is doubtful, particularly when they wrap up all their investigations and proofs in inscrutable mystery, it is on the general character of the accused persons that we fall back. Who, for instance, would credit a charge of conspiracy against the life of a sovereign, if brought against the present bench of Anglican Bishops, and supported merely by the result of a secret trial conducted by persons of doubtful honesty? We should say that the known character of these prelates made the charge brought against them simply incredible.

But we are anticipating, and must return to the history, in tracing which through the months of the last year before the Decree of Expulsion, we have, as has been said, a valuable aid in the Life of Padre Idiáquez. This Father was made Provincial of Castile in 1764. In his first year of office he busied himself with providing for the French exiles who had taken refuge in Spain, a work for which he succeeded in obtaining the sanction of the Court, notwithstanding an adverse report by the Fiscal of Castile, Don Rodriguez de Campomanes, who disclosed the feelings with which he was animated by arguing that these French exiles were unworthy of Spanish hospitality, inasmuch as they had refused to take the oath imposed on them by their native *Parlement* – an oath, be it remembered, which involved a renunciation of their vows, and an untruthful declaration that the account given by the *Parlement* of the teaching of the Jesuit theologians was just. It was with the advent of the year 1766 that Padre Idiáquez's anxieties began to be intense. It was a year of insurrections, says his biographer. In various towns there were riots all apparently due to the same general cause – the rise in the price of bread and other necessaries of life, due partly to the bad harvests of the preceding summer, but still more, as rightly or wrongly the people thought, to the conduct of the King's Ministers; particularly of the Minister of Finance, the Marqués de Squillace, who was endeavouring to relieve the deficiencies of the Treasury by creating monopolies. As we have seen, one of these riots broke out at Saragossa, and was suppressed largely through the intervention of Padre Pignatelli. Nevertheless the Society's enemies, who were on the watch for any and every opportunity to defame it, suggested everywhere that the Jesuits were the actual promoters of these troubles, and that, if in one case or another they posed as subduing them, no wonder that they should be able to stop what they themselves had begun. How easy it was for the Society to become, in spite of itself, mixed up in these disturbances and afford material for misrepresentation may be understood from the following incident which occurred within Padre Idiáquez's jurisdiction. The College of Loyola lies in the middle between the two small towns of Azcoitia to the west and Azpeitia to the east. At Azcoitia one of these bread riots broke out in 1766, and the civil authorities were most anxious that it should not spread to Azpeitia. It did, and among those who caught the contagion were certain workmen at that time engaged in some building operations at Loyola. The authorities had sought, though in vain, to arrest them there. The community does not seem itself to have offered any opposition at the time. But Loyola enjoyed the right of sanctuary, which was regarded by the neighbourhood as a privilege belonging to itself. Accordingly there was an outcry against the violation of so sacred a right, and the Governor wrote to Padre Idiáquez a somewhat sharp letter of remonstrance, in which he maintained that the place of arrest lay outside the sanctuary bounds. Padre Idiáquez wrote back suggesting that the question of the boundary line had better be referred to arbitrators, but that, if the Governor would indicate who were the guilty persons, he would direct that they should be given up. On this the Governor wrote back a cordial letter of thanks, and the affair was ended. None the less an unknown foe published the Governor's first letter, while suppressing the rest of the correspondence, and sent it all over the country, and even to the Court, where, until Padre Idiáquez explained matters, it produced an impression unfavourable to the Jesuits.

We must now relate the history of a more serious insurrection which took place at Madrid a few days before that at Saragossa, and became memorable for the way in which it was used to work the destruction of the Jesuits. Reference has already been made to the Marqués de Squillace. He was an Italian high in favour with Carlos III, whom the latter had brought over with him from Naples and set over the finances. Incidentally it may be mentioned that he was friendly to the Jesuits, and not therefore one whose removal from office they were likely to desire, but he was much disliked by the Spanish people, partly because he was a foreigner and partly because of his somewhat drastic and inconsiderate reforms. What, however, finally led to the insurrection was a regulation forbidding henceforth the use of the long cloaks and long-flapped hats which the Spanish men were accustomed to wear. The prohibition was well intended, for these hats and cloaks enabled criminals to conceal their faces and escape detection, and in this way are said to have encouraged street murders. But the people resented the arbitrary interference with their liberty, the more so as the royal orders were enforced in a violent and tactless way. Accordingly the populace of Madrid broke out on the evening before Palm Sunday, 1766 [not 1767 as originally printed, *Ed. N.*], and attacked both Squillace's house and the King's palace. The Walloon guards sent to subdue them were subdued themselves, and many were massacred. Cries of 'Long live the King' were heard, but mingled with other cries of 'Death to Squillace!' Matters became at length so serious that a compromise was thought necessary, and the King appearing on a balcony, accompanied by a band of friars bearing a crucifix and some candles, solemnly promised that Squillace should be dismissed and a Spaniard put in his place, and that the rioters should not be punished for their offence, provided they would now go back quietly to their homes.

So ended the disturbance for the time, but in the night the King fled in secret to Aranjuéz, to his palace on the Tagus, taking Squillace with him. This was regarded by the populace of Madrid as a sign that he meant to break his engagement, and they rose once more, but on learning that Squillace had already been despatched on his journey back to Italy, and that a further amnesty was granted them, they subsided again, and this time finally.

The King, however, felt humiliated and indignant at the outrage he had sustained, and had reasons, whether well or ill-founded, for believing that the rising had not been entirely spontaneous, but had been deliberately excited in the interest of some political intrigue. It was suggested to him by his Ministers that the intriguers in question were the Jesuits, and although probably he did not at first believe it of a body of Religious of whom he had hitherto entertained a very different opinion, he allowed a secret inquiry to be instituted into the causes of the recent insurrection, as well as of the others which had broken out in the provinces in the same year. This was resolved in April, 1766, and in the following month an Extraordinary Tribunal was erected to which the secret inquiry was committed.[8] We shall have to investigate in another section the proceedings of this Secret Tribunal, but for the present it will be more instructive to treat the history from the standpoint of the Spanish Jesuits, who, though they knew that their enemies were charging them with complicity in the riot, knew nothing so far of the Extraordinary Tribunal and the secret inquiry, nor had any grounds for believing that the King and his Ministers disbelieved in their innocence. And as regards this last point they had in August of 1766, that is, five months after the

---

[8] See the *Exposición y dictamen del fiscal del consejo y cámara de Francisco Gutiérrez de la Huerta*. This is an official document drawn up in 1811, when there was question of the Society being recalled to Spain. We shall need to refer to it again in the next section.

Madrid outbreak, what they might well deem to be a clear proof that they need be in no anxiety.

It was somewhere in the spring or early summer that the Azcoitia disturbance took place, and the publication of the Governor's letter which, thus wrested from its context, conveyed so false an impression. As it was rumoured that this letter was being misused at Court, Padre Idiáquez made a journey to La Granja, where the Court then was, on the pretext of paying his respects to the King on the feast of St Louis, which, D. Carlos being a Bourbon prince, was an important annual solemnity. He went round to each one of the Ministers, and to many members of the Royal Household, to most of whom on account of his family connections he was well known. They all received him with the utmost cordiality, and expressed astonishment at the abominable trick. One and all promised him that they would use their influence to let the King see how he and his brethren had been misrepresented. Among those who were especially fervent in their promises to disabuse the King's mind of any false impression he might have derived, was the King's confessor, D. Joachim de Eleta. Eventually Padre Idiáquez had an audience of the King himself. He kissed hands and received in return expressions of kindly feeling and respect from his Majesty; who said afterwards to his chamberlain, 'This poor Religious who just now came to me, gave up the Dukedom of Granada de Ega that he might become a Jesuit;' after which he frequently, through his confessor, wrote to ldiáquez to recommend himself to his prayers.[9] After leaving the King he remained two days at La Granja, during which he received from the Ministers and magnates the most pressing invitations to dinner, and accepted that of Don Miguel Músquiz, 'the Minister of the Royal Exchequer' – a man who, though Idiáquez did not know it, was probably at that very time, but certainly a few months later, preparing in company with the others to extract from the King the decree of expulsion.

Naturally Idiáquez returned to Valladolid, the head-quarters of the Castilian Provincial, much relieved, and prepared to console his brethren. His anxieties, however, did not cease, for the adversaries, engaged in destroying the good name of the Society, were growing more active than ever. Agents were going about from place to place, trying to induce towns or individuals to revive against the Society grievances which had long since been buried; their sermons, their conversations, their actions were sharply watched, and, if a Jesuit was caught saying or doing anything in the least imprudent, it was

---

[9] Navarette, op. cit.

treasured up, magnified, and generalized into a charge against the whole body, whilst even perfectly innocent language or conduct was oftentimes perversely twisted. Padre Idiáquez was considerably exercised about this, and was urgent and frequent in his admonitions to his subjects to give no cause whatever for offence. He even ordered certain Rectors to forego some perfectly just claims, lest their assertion of them should offer opportunity for misconstruction. And he punished severely one Rector who, availing himself of a hint given him by the public Press Censor, published without license the translation of one of the French Apologies for the Society. This last-mentioned incident seemed to him so serious that he thought it necessary to write to the King's confessor and to the Marqués de Grimaldi, to ask them to explain its exact nature to the King, and got back a reply from the confessor assuring him that the King, on hearing his letter read, had declared that 'he was fully persuaded of the integrity of Idiáquez, and never had and never would believe him capable of doing anything inconsistent with his virtue and the nobility of his blood; and that, as for the matter about which he had written, when he heard the opinions of his ministers of justice he would decide what seemed most advisable.' Grimaldi wrote back in the same sense, and Padre González, the biographer of Idiáquez, testifies that he had seen both letters.

This solicitude of the Provincial of Castile to prevent his subjects from offering the slightest cause of offence, or even handle for misconstruction, is particularly to be noticed, for Theiner in the Introduction to his *Histoire du Pontificat de Clément XIV,* gives a very different account of the behaviour of the Spanish Jesuits during the time when their fate hung in the balance. There is no doubt that a large crop of political pamphlets had been published anonymously and clandestinely, attacking the Government of the country, particularly the measures of the Marqués de Squillace. Theiner writes on this point with the studied vagueness he sometimes assumes – apparently when he does not wish his statements to be too closely inquired into – but his suggestion is that some of them came from Jesuit sources. In the absence of allegations definite enough to be tested, we may ask if it is likely that the Spanish Jesuits were acting in this rash manner, at the time when, as the Life of Padre Idiáquez shows, they were in a state of extreme anxiety, and even excessively solicitous to avoid the least thing that might endanger them?

The episode of the unlicensed publication of an Apology must have occurred somewhere in the autumn. In October another event happened which, though no reference to it is found in Padre González's Life of Idiáquez, must have occasioned him and his brethren much anxiety. On 20 October, Padre Isidro López was ordered to leave Madrid and withdraw to Monforte in Galicia, whilst three others, not Jesuits, were suddenly arrested, and sent each to a separate and remote place of confinement. The whole matter was wrapped up in the utmost secrecy, but the rumour spread that they were charged with being implicated in the Madrid insurrection. In the next section we shall find that this was the case, and shall see how trumpery were the allegations on which the suspicion was based. For the present it is enough to say that Padre Isidro López – who was well known at Court, being the Procurator there for the Province of Castile – was never, apparently, subjected to any trial, and certainly to no other punishment save that of the banishment he shared with his brethren – whereas, if he had been found guilty of so serious a crime, we may be sure that his punishment would have been exemplary.

But we must hasten on. At the beginning of the New Year Padre Osorio succeeded Padre Idiáquez as Provincial, and the latter received orders from the General to proceed at once to Madrid, and endeavour to see the King. He started on 7 January, making a rough winter's journey, during which his chaise stuck in the snows of the Sierra Guadarrama. On arriving, he found it no longer possible to get an audience of the King. The atmosphere seemed changed from what it had been in October, and he was told for the first time of an Extraordinary Council which had been appointed to investigate the Madrid insurrection, and which was understood to be deliberating also about the Society. Idiáquez at once betook himself to Aranda, who had always counted as one of the friends of his family. From him he asked the names of the members of this Extraordinary Council, and begged that if it were really true that they had any cause of complaint against the Society it might be heard in its defence. But Aranda seemed confused by his presence, and evaded all his questions. On the other hand, he spoke him very fair, and even withdrew a certain prohibition on Spiritual Retreats at Loyola, which had been laid on the Jesuits shortly before, so that he went away in some sort contented.

But this apparent mark of favour was delusive. No wonder the Conde de Aranda looked confused when Idiáquez sought to obtain from him leave for the Jesuits to know of any charges brought against them and an opportunity for submitting their defence. Even while Idiáquez was with him the die was being cast. The Extraordinary Tribunal established by Carlos III in the preceding May had been converted into an Extraordinary Council. It was a significant change, for it meant that the King had consented to decide the matter by an administrative act, instead of, as was originally proposed, by a judicial sentence. Had the latter course been followed, and it was surely the natural course under the circumstances, it would have been necessary to acquaint the accused with their alleged crimes, to hear their defence, and to test the arguments on both sides with judicial strictness. This necessity was avoided by having recourse to the King's administrative power. Did it not look as if no evidence of sufficient solidity could be produced to justify the severe and wholesale measures it was decided to take?

It was on 29 January 1767, that the Extraordinary Council came to its final decision, and recommended the King to expel every member of the Society from his dominions. They drew up a scheme for the wording of the Royal Decree and for the detailed measures to be taken for its execution. It was not at once laid before the King, but was submitted first to a Special Junta appointed for the purpose, and after that to three ecclesiastics. The Junta consisted of the Duque de Alva, D. Jaime Masones, the Marqués de Grimaldi, the Father Confessor, D. Miguel de Musquiz, D. Juan Gregorio Muniacín, and D. Manuel de Roda; and the ecclesiastics were the Archbishop of Burgos and the Bishop of Avila, and the Padre Maestro Pinelli, of the Order of Augustinians, all three recently appointed to their offices on the nomination of Aranda. By both these sets of revisers the recommendations of the Extraordinary Council were endorsed, and one can imagine how the two-fold process of revision may have helped to make the King believe that the charges against the Society were fully made out, and the expulsion imperatively called for; still, some of their names, and perhaps all, are highly suspicious. However, the King was gained over, and accepted the recommendation of his Council in all respects. Accordingly, on 27 February, he issued a Decree addressed to the Conde de Aranda, as the President of the Council of Castile, in which be announced his resolution to expel all the Jesuits from his dominions, and commissioned the Conde to see to the execution. The wording of this Decree is very noticeable for the studied vagueness with which it glosses over the motives which had dictated it:

> Conforming myself [the King says] to the advice of my Extraordinary Council, assembled for the sake of what was passed on the subject at the meeting of 29 January last, as well as that of several persons of the most distinguished character [he refers here to the Special Junta and the three ecclesiastics], determined likewise by the gravest causes, affecting the obligation in which I find myself of maintaining subordination, tranquillity, and justice among my people, as well as for other pressing, just, and necessary reasons which I reserve in my Royal breast, using the supreme

administrative power which the Almighty has placed in my hands for the protection of my subjects, and for the maintenance of the honour of my Crown, I have decided to order that all the Religious of the Society of Jesus, both priests and coadjutors, or lay-brothers, who have taken their first vows, and the novices who desire to follow them, be expelled from every land of my dominions in Spain, in the Indies, in the Philippines, and other adjacent places; and that the temporal goods which the Society possesses in my dominions be seized; and, in order that this decree may be executed in a uniform manner throughout my States, I give you, for this effect, a full and particular authority ...[10]

Thus empowered Aranda, on 20 March, sent to all the Alcaldes, or Judges Ordinary, of the towns throughout Spain a sealed packet, and an accompanying circular letter. The circular letter explained that the sealed packet was to be kept closed till 2 April, on the evening of which day it was to be opened in all places simultaneously, and its directions promptly carried out. The circular added that any disclosure of the fact of the message having been sent to an Alcalde, if attributable in any way whatever to his conduct, would be taken as an act of negligence in an important matter affecting the King's service, and would be severely visited. To the Alcaldes of Madrid a similar packet and circular was sent, except that there the sealed packet was directed to be opened two days earlier. These stringent measures had their effect, and the secret was well kept.

When the time for unsealing the packet arrived it was found to contain an order to the Alcalde to proceed that very night to expel the Jesuits from their houses within his jurisdiction, together with a list of minute directions as to the mode in which he was to proceed. All was carried out with perfect accuracy in every instance. At Madrid the Alcalde, as the night drew on, provided himself with a troop of soldiers held in readiness, with which he proceeded to guard all the entrances to the Jesuit houses. Exactly at twelve o'clock he knocked at the gate of each College; asked for the Rector, who at once came and received his orders to summon the community by the sound of the bell. They had retired to rest in absolute unconsciousness that anything was about to happen, and they must have been filled with consternation when the bell awoke them. Still, they dressed in haste, and were soon assembled in the refectory. Then they were bidden to stand up, and the Royal Decree of 27 February was read to them. Next their names and *status* in the Society were entered in a register, and they were told that they were to depart at once on their painful

---

[10] See *Colección general de las providencias ... sobre el estrañiento ... de la Compañía*. Madrid, 1767.

journey, leaving everything behind, even the MSS. on which some had spent the labour of a lifetime, everything save the clothes in which they stood up, their breviaries, and a single prayer-book, and, which was spoken of as a signal act of royal considerateness, any snuff and chocolate or small change which it was supposed they might have at the time in their possession. When under strict surveillance these few articles were obtained, all the rooms were locked and sealed up, and the Fathers and Brothers were transferred to a number of vehicles which had been got ready, four being placed in some, two in others. Behind each carriage was a mounted soldier, and before the night was over all were on their way to Getafe, a little town to the south-east of Madrid, which had been chosen as the first port on their way to Cartagena.

In the morning, when there were no longer any Jesuits in Madrid, a Pragmatic Sanction – or Royal Edict of a specially solemn kind – was promulgated in the usual public places to the sound of trumpets and drums. It made further provision for the carrying out of the royal will, but threw little further light on the motives which had dictated it. It began with a paragraph conceived in substantially the same terms as those of the Decree of 29 February, but added four other paragraphs. Of these, the *first* declared that the other religious orders continued to enjoy his Majesty's confidence, by reason of their fidelity and their doctrines, their attachment to the rules of morality, the edification they gave in the service of the Church, and the care with which, as lying outside the sphere of ascetic and monastic life, they abstained from the affairs of Government; the *second* desired all Bishops, Congregations, and corporations ecclesiastical and civil, to be informed 'that the King reserved in his royal breast the just and grave motives which had obliged him to take this measure, in which he was using merely his administrative power, without having recourse to other means, following therein the impulse of his royal clemency as the father and protector of his people'; the *third, fourth, and fifth,* declared that from the proceeds of the goods the Jesuits had possessed in the kingdom, portions on the scale of 100 piastres for each priest, and 90 for each lay Religious, would be paid regularly as a yearly maintenance to each of the expelled Religious as long as he lived, but that no such portions would be paid to foreign Jesuits then in Spain, or to the novices who might choose to follow the fortunes of the Fathers, as these latter were able to return to their homes if they wished; the *sixth* declared that the pensions would cease at once to any individual who should give just motives for the resentment of the Court by his words or writings; and that if any one of them should venture to write anything contrary to the respect and submission due to the royal will, under the pretext of writing an apology or defence tending to trouble the peace of his kingdom, the pensions should cease, not for that one only, but for all the rest. Other paragraphs of this Draconian law forbade the King's subjects to have any intercourse, whether by word or letter, with any Jesuit, whether those expelled, or any others; or to write or declaim in any way whatever concerning the present measure, either for or against it; the King desiring that his subjects should observe silence on the subject, and enjoining that all who did otherwise should be treated as guilty of the crime of treason.

In all the provincial towns, as at Madrid, the Royal commands were carried out strictly to the letter, except that, as may be imagined, the provisions intended to secure a degree of humanity for the victims during their painful journey to the place of their destination, were often frustrated by the roughness of the officials, or the inadequacy of the means at their disposal. Thus it happened, that the exiles had in many cases terrible hardships to undergo; as for instance, at Santander, when 300 were for several days, whilst waiting for the boats, crowded into a college built to house only 30; and in the boats, where a similar overcrowding had almost in every case to be undergone. For each Province a place of embarkation was assigned – for the Castilians, Santander, for the Andalusians, Jeréz de la Frontera, for those of Toledo, Cartagena, for those of Aragon, Tarragona.

Many touching incidents have been preserved to us of the spirit in which these Religious, deemed too dangerous for their country to suffer in its midst, met their hard and unexpected fate. Padre Navarro, the Rector of the Imperial College at Madrid, on being asked after the reading of the decree whether he and his community submitted to it, replied with an old-world loyalty which drew tears from the eyes of the officials, 'We are prepared to suffer not only exile, but even harder things still, to prove our respect and submission to the King.' It is Padre Caballero, who was present, who tells the story, and he it is who adds presently of Padre Mateo Aimerich that 'when, on that saddest of nights, he was put into the same cart with Xavier Ablitas and Gabriel Bousemart, an old man of eighty, it was our dear Mateo who strove to assuage the sharpness of our grief by his frequent and holy words, bidding us to pray for the safety and prosperity of the King, which we all did heartily:' Then there was Padre Calatayud at Valladolid, who on hearing the Edict, cried *Te Deum laudamus,* and when out of regard for his age the officials offered to let him stay, refused and went forth, with his staff and his crucifix, as if on one of his missions, and through the rows of people who ran to meet him in each town he passed through, and asked his blessing; and Padre Idiáquez, who when told that the Conde de Aranda was trying to get him excepted from the decree, replied indignantly: 'No, let me go with my brethren;' and Padre Pignatelli, who made the same reply to a letter, forwarded to him through Aranda, from his brother the Conde de Fuentes, who was by a curious coincidence the Spanish Ambassador at the time at the Court of France. Again, there was Padre Salgado, who had so endeared himself to the town of Oviedo that, when the decree came, the town authorities wished to petition the King that at least he might be left with them; and the young Juan Cosío, who was in a dying state at Salamanca, and was inadvertently passed over by the Alcalde, until he cried out, 'Do not leave me behind,' and then struggled along the way and bore up so bravely, that though compelled to sleep on the bare ground and in the open air, he was so bright that he cheered up the rest, and seemed to have lived only for that object – for he died a few days after the landing at Corsica. Nor was it the priests only who gave these pathetic illustrations of their virtue under trying conditions. There was, for instance, the lay-brother Juan Zubiria, who with eyes dimmed with age, ulcerated legs, and exhausted strength hobbled along with the aid of his stick, saying partly to himself, partly for the encouragement of others, 'All things must be borne for Christ'; and the novices of Villagarcía who resisted such grave attempts to separate them from their vocation, and found their way in spite of all difficulties to the Fathers at Santander. To which particular instances ought certainly to be added the general fact of the patience and resignation these poor exiles all showed, for it must have been striking to impress as it did the various classes they encountered on their way – King's officials, sailors, Corsican leaders, Franciscan friars, an Anglican chaplain.

Their final destination was Città Vecchia, Carlos III imagining that he was doing a kind action by the exiles in sending them to the Papal dominions. But it was an outrage on a neighbouring Sovereign to send him without warning a large body of Spanish subjects to plant themselves on his territory, and Clement, kindly disposed as he was, saw that great evils might arise from such an influx. Bad harvests had raised prices as it was, and this increase of mouths would tend to raise them still more, and perhaps stir up the people and excite disturbance. It was evident too, that the pensions might be stopped at any moment, and the entire support of these 2,500 Religious made dependent on the Pontifical Exchequer. Accordingly he sent word to the King of Spain that the exiles would not be allowed to land. It was a reasonable step, but it was hard on the exiles, who had to continue their wanderings just when they were hoping that their troubles were in some degree over. They were taken to Corsica, an island wholly insufficient at any time to accommodate so large a number, and at this time torn by a civil war between the French, acting on behalf of the Genoese, and the native Corsicans. There it was that the Religious of four Provinces were destined to remain for the next year and a half, and it passes comprehension how they managed amidst almost insuperable difficulties and almost intolerable hardships to settle down into their ordinary life of religious observance, and even of regular studies in the case of the younger men.

We have not yet spoken of the fate of the missionaries in the Spanish colonies. It might have been expected that these at least would be left unmolested, seeing how impossible it would be to replace them. But the King was inexorable. The same order was sent out to the Governors, and the same procedure followed as in Spain, so far as the circumstances would allow. For instance, Padre Chomé, of whom mention has been made, was found, on the day appointed for the expulsion in those regions, far away among the Chiquitos in the very centre of South America. He was worn out with his trials, bed-ridden, and looking for the near approach of death. But though the officials would have liked to leave him in peace, the royal order left them no alternative, and he was carried on the backs of Indians through valleys and over mountains, even over the lofty ranges of the Cochobamba Andes, towards the Pacific coast, until life could endure it no longer, and he died at Oruro, a town situated ten thousand feet above the sea level. Thus, too, were the Peruvian and Paraguayan Fathers all torn from their flocks, which never recovered from their loss, and carried to Corsica, where, having joined their brethren, they were with them at length transported to Genoa, and thence to the Papal States, the Pope's political prudence being no longer able to hold out against the impulse of his great compassion.

In the next section we shall try to investigate the causes which had such an effect on the mind of Carlos III as to impel him to this harsh and inconsiderate act. But whatever they may prove to have been, this at least we can at once claim – that it could not be right to condemn so many men of good reputation without a fair trial in which both sides were heard; and that, even if some Jesuits, fewer or more numerous, had been guilty of a great crime, it was still unjustifiable to involve so many who were palpably and confessedly innocent in so terrible a punishment.

II.[11] [The accusations]

We have seen under what mysterious circumstances the Spanish Jeuits were taken from their homes and sent into life-long banishment. We have seen how this cruel punishment was awarded to them, not by a judicial sentence following on an equitable trial, but by what was euphemistically styled an 'administrative act', that is to say, by a procedure which allowed for their being sentenced without a previous hearing or even a notification of their supposed offence. The same inexplicable reserve was adopted in communicating the fact of their expulsion to the Holy See. As Spain was a Catholic country, and Carlos III prided himself on being *par excellence* the Catholic King, he might have been expected to show some anxiety to vindicate himself in the eyes of the Sovereign Pontiff, and for that purpose to send to Rome a complete and convincing statement of his reasons for a measure so seriously affecting religious interests. On the contrary, particular pains were taken to keep this knowledge from the Pope's ears. The Nuncio at Madrid, Cardinal Pallavicini, was left in entire ignorance of what was preparing, until he learnt it like the rest of the world from the actual carrying out of the expulsion. Nor were the usages of common courtesy observed by sending to the Pope a special envoy to be the bearer of this important message, but, as if to intimate to him that it was no concern of his whether the measure were just or unjust, the Royal letter was sent by the ordinary courier to Mgr Azpuru, the Spanish Minister at the Vatican, who was at the same time instructed that he must simply deliver it to the Pope, and decline all invitations to explain or negociate as to its contents.

We know, too, that this unusual and discourteous treatment of the Holy See was intentional. In the last section mention was made of the *Consulta* of 29 January 1767; in which the Extraordinary Council gave, as the result of its inquiries, the advice which induced the King to decree the expulsion. The text of this *Consulta*, so far as he was able to obtain it, was incorporated by Don Gutiérrez de la Huerta, at the time Fiscal to the Supreme Council of Castile, in his *Dictamen* of October 1815.[12] In this *Consulta* the Extraordinary Council recommended that

> the Royal Decree should be conceived in terms of an administrative decree providing for the peace of the monarchy, without touching in any way the question of the examination of the Institute, or of the qualification

---

[11] *The Month*, 100 (1902), 20–34.
[12] The full text of this *Dictamen* may he found in the Mexican periodical, *El Observador Católico* (1849, tom. iii), where it is printed as an Appendix – BM. press mark, PP. 909, c.2.

[i.e. the censure] demanded by the conduct and morals of the Jesuits ... and that the communication of this measure to Rome should not be made through a special envoy, but by the ordinary way of the courier from Naples, and by the first who shall go after the execution of the Decree, and that it shall be signified to the Holy Father that what has been done was requisite to preserve the tranquillity of the State, on which account it was to be hoped that his Holiness would approve of it as having been necessary, and as having been done with the greatest circumspection and after serious inquiry.

Continuing, the Council gives its motives for advising this course:

In this manner, embarrassments and unpleasantnesses in dealing with the Court of Rome will be avoided, and there will be no need to treat of the matter with the Nuncio. The despatch will be addressed to his Majesty's Minister at Rome, who will be told to refuse all explanations, and confine himself to the simple delivery of the Royal letter. By acting thus it will also be possible to avoid entering into the question of the recommendation which, as is well known to the Council, the Spanish Jesuits have solicited, and are expecting from the Pope through the medium of Cardinal Pallavicini, the present Nuncio to these kingdoms, whom it will be necessary to treat with the most profound disregard until the publication is over; and when that is accomplished, it will be enough to reply to him that the matter has been communicated to his Holiness, so far as seemed necessary or desirable.

The terms in which Carlos III carried out this recommendation, in his letter of 31 March, were these:

Most Holy Father, Your Holiness knows well that the first duty of a Sovereign is to guard the security and tranquillity of his State and the well-being and peace of his subjects. In the fulfilment of this duty I have found myself in the urgent necessity of promptly expelling from my kingdom and dominions the Jesuits who have been resident within them, and of sending them to the States of the Church, where they may be under the wise and holy direction of your Holiness, the worthy Father and Teacher of all the faithful. I should be acting without due regard for the Apostolic *Camara* if I were to oblige it to burden itself with the maintenance of those Jesuits who are my born subjects, but I have made provision so that each may have a sufficient subsistence as long as he lives. I trust that your Holiness may take this my determination simply for what it is, namely, as an indispensable administrative decree, made after previous inquiry and deep reflection; and that whilst doing me this justice you will not hesitate to send me, as I supplicate you, your holy and apostolic blessing, both on this and all others of my actions which are similarly directed to the greater honour and glory of God.

This letter was delivered to Clement XIII on the morning of 13 April, and he was overwhelmed with grief and astonishment at the fresh calamity, coming as it did from so unexpected a quarter. Three days later he wrote back the following letter of earnest expostulation.

> Of all the blows by which we have been struck during the nine years of our Pontificate, the cruellest of all to our paternal heart is undoubtedly that which has come to us from your Majesty ... Is it you too, my son (*Tu quoque, fili mi*), who act thus? Is it the most religious and pious King of Spain, Carlos III, who must lend the support of his arm – that powerful arm which God gave him to sustain and advance His glory as well as that of the Church, and the salvation of souls, – to the enemies of this same Church and of God, so as to destroy right down to its foundations a Religious Order so useful and dear to the Church itself, an Order which owes its origin and its splendour to those saintly heroes whom God deigned to choose from the Spanish nation that He might spread His glory throughout the earth? Is it thus that he wishes to deprive his kingdom for ever, and his people for ever, of the many spiritual aids and succours which the Religious of this Society for two centuries and more have imparted so abundantly by their preaching, administration of the sacraments, and instruction of youth in piety, letters, worship, and the honour of the Church?
>
> Ah Sire, our heart cannot bear the thought of such a ruin. But what pierces it more deeply is to see the wise and just King Carlos III, the prince whose conscience is so delicate and whose intentions are so upright, and who would never allow that the very last of his subjects should suffer the very smallest injury to his private interests without first having had his cause legally discussed and all those formalities observed which the laws prescribe in order to safeguard to each his rights – that this same prince should have thought himself permitted to condemn to a total extinction, taking away from it its honour, its country, its lawfully acquired property and its lawfully possessed foundations, an entire body of Religious dedicated and consecrated to the service of God and of others, without having been previously examined, heard, or permitted to defend themselves ...
>
> You say, Sire, that your Majesty has been provoked to this step by the obligation of maintaining peace and tranquillity in your States, wishing thereby to give us to understand that some trouble which you have encountered in the government of your people has been excited and fomented by some individuals belonging to the Society of Jesus. But even if that be true, why, Sire, did you not inflict a punishment on the guilty, without making it fall on the innocent as well? The body, the Institute, and the spirit of the Society of Jesus, we say it in the presence of God and man, are absolutely innocent of all crime, and not only innocent, but pious, useful, and holy in their ends, their laws, and their principles; and whatever endeavours their enemies may have made to prove the contrary

they have not succeeded; they have produced no other effect on minds that are calm and impartial save to cause themselves to be discredited and abhorred as liars on account of the contradictions on which they have professed to base their false pretentions ...

But, say the politicians, it is a *fait accompli*. The project has been adopted, the royal ordinance has been promulgated. What would the world think, if it saw the measure revoked or its execution suspended? What will the world say, Sire? Why not rather ask what will God say? ... Let then this matter be regularly discussed; let justice and truth be brought to bear on it, that they may disperse the clouds that have been raised by prejudice and suspicion; hear the counsels and warnings of those who are doctors in Israel, of the Bishops, of the Religious, in a cause which concerns the good estate and honour of the Church, the salvation of souls, your own conscience, and your eternal salvation.

It is unnecessary to add anything in praise or defence of this pathetic letter. It will be acknowledged that it breathes a tone of wisdom and justice, as well as of the tenderest affection for the monarch to whom it was sent. How then was it received?

It reached Madrid on 28 April, being in due course entrusted to the Nuncio to deliver; but as Cardinal Pallavicini was ill at the time, he commissioned the Conte Ippolito Vincente, the priest who was auditor to the Nunciature, to deliver it to the King. Vincente at once applied for an audience, which, according to the etiquette of the diplomatic service, he had a right to obtain. His request was none the less refused, the pretext of pressing occupations being alleged. He then set off at once for Aranjuez, where the Court was. He asked for and saw the Marqués de Grimaldi, who told him the King was well aware why he had come, but, as he had no intention of changing his mind, declined to see him. Vincente protested against this unusual course, but in vain, and then announced the Holy Father's intention to resist the entrance of the exiles into his dominions. Grimaldi went back in haste to communicate this unexpected news to the King, whom he found in company with de Roda and Padre Joachim, the confessor. They discussed it together, and Grimaldi returned to say that the King still declined to see him, but would write an answer to his Holiness. Such was the disdain with which the expostulations of the Father of Christendom were received, expressed though they were in terms of the most perfect justice, propriety, and friendliness. It must be remembered too, that in another letter sent at the same time to the King's confessor, in which the Holy Father exhorted him to show the King the injustice of his proceedings, Clement XIII offered expressly to cooperate in punishing adequately any individual Jesuits who might have been convicted of seditious or otherwise improper conduct; nor can we doubt but that he would have been prepared to suppress the entire Spanish Province, or even the entire Order, could evidence be laid before him which convicted them of a general and ineradicable criminality. Why then this determination to withhold from him the motives of the King's action?

On 29 April, that is, the day after he received the letter Carlos III sent it through Don Manuel de Roda to the Conde de Aranda, that it might be laid before the Extraordinary Council. The *Consulta,* in which they replied to the King's demand for advice, was signed on 30 April, and the text has been published. It is a further illustration of the spirit in which it was thought becoming to treat the Holy See, and as such throws important light on the character of the men who were the authors of the Suppression. The Council begins by remarking that the Papal Brief was 'deficient in that courtesy and moderation which was due to a Sovereign like the King of Spain and the Indies', and that 'inasmuch as it intruded on matters belonging to the temporal order, ... it might well have been refused admittance into the country, were it not that it was desirable to take from the Court of Rome every pretext for resentment.' It goes on to complain of 'the deplorable tone of the Brief, so inconsistent with Apostolic mildness', and counts this inconsistency the more significant as the Papal Secretary of State, Cardinal Torregiani, was the intimate friend and fellow-countryman of Fr Ricci, who was his confessor and director.[13] It then criticizes, one by one, the points of the Brief, and gives an insight into the pretended motives for the expulsion which may be passed over here, as the question will recur presently. Finally, it rejects the Pope's entreaty for a proper trial, on the ground that 'in cases of banishment and confiscation it was not usual to proceed by the method of contentious jurisdiction, but by an exercise of tutelary and administrative authority.'

None, however, of these criticisms of the Brief were intended to appear in the King's reply. His Majesty was recommended to make his letter short and evasive.

> It is, Sire [they say], the unanimous opinion both of the Fiscals and of the Extraordinary Council that your Majesty should cause the reply to his Holiness's Brief to be drawn up in the most concise terms, so as not to let it enter into the substance of the question, either by way of answering (what the Pope has urged) or admitting of any negotiations, or of giving heed to further representations, since it would be to act contrary to the law of silence enjoined in the Pragmatic Sanction of the 2nd inst., if [your

---

[13] Torregiani was a friend to the Jesuits, but there was no ground for saying that he was dominated by them.

Majesty] were to accept the sophistical discussions founded on exaggerations and generalities such as the Brief contains, and such as have nothing else to recommend them save that they come in the name of his Holiness.

They finish by saying that the Council is submitting a draft letter for his Majesty's consideration, which, however, is not included in the text of the *Consulta*. Don Carlos adhered in substance to the advice given him, but it is presumable that he disregarded this draft letter, for he wrote back in a tone differing much from that of the *Consulta*, and more worthy of the occasion and of his own personal character. His letter is dated 2 May, and in it he says that his filial heart is filled with sorrow and bitterness at finding what afflictions and tears he has caused to a Father whom he reveres and loves. He adds that his sorrow is the greater because his word is not trusted, but that he begs to repeat his previous assurances that he had abundant and superabundant justification for the step he had felt bound to take.

The impression conveyed by the above-cited documents is that the reasons which had moved the King to decree the expulsion were to be kept absolutely secret by himself and the few Ministers whose services he had used in detecting the guilt of the Jesuits. They were to be 'preserved in the Royal breast,' and, as nothing was ever officially published, it was inferred that the imputed offence must have been one which of its own nature required to be kept secret. Hence speculation became active on the subject, and the theory which acquired a certain verisimilitude supposed that the Jesuits were credited with throwing doubts on the legitimacy of the King's birth, and writing a book in support of this contention – all with the object of prejudicing the people against him and causing him to be set aside in favour of his younger brother, Don Luis.[14] It is necessary to refer to this conjecture, but although writers such as Coxe, Schoell, and Ranke have accepted it, it does not seem to have a firm basis, whilst, as we shall see, the motive of the King's secret can be otherwise explained.

Meanwhile, it is to be noted that to some persons the motives of the Decree were freely communicated. Thus in the *Consulta* of 30 April 1767 – the *Consulta* already referred to in which the Papal Brief of 16 April was discussed – there is, following immediately on the clause recommending that the Pope should be told nothing, a clause recommending that the substance of the motives should be

---

[14] See on this point the story of the packet left with Padre Navarro at the Imperial College at Madrid in Christopher Murr's *Journal zur Kunstgeschichte* (ix. 213), and the story of the packet entrusted to Padres Larraín and Recio to be delivered at Rome in Boero's *Vita del V.P. Pignatelli* (pp. 135, 587).

communicated to Mgr Azpuru, that he might know better how to deal with the situation. A similar statement of reasons was sent to the Marchese Tanucci, the chief Minister to the young King Ferdinand of Naples. This letter is a document of great value,[15] but may be omitted here, because another document of a more radical character, and of similar purport, will have to be quoted later in this section.

After all, in these two cases the disclosure from his Royal breast was made by Carlos III to trusted servants who were working in his interest. In another case he gave his confidence to the Ambassador of France, and under circumstances which permitted the latter to send on the news to his chief in Paris, where they were read to the whole Council, and forthwith became public property. A summary of this letter from the Marqués d'Ossun to the Duc de Choiseul is given by the Comte de Saint-Priest in his *Chute des Jésuites*. According to it, Carlos III gave an audience to d'Ossun, in which he made the following statement:

> He swore that he had no personal feeling against the Jesuits, and until the most recent plot, had declined on several occasions to adopt counsels adverse to their interests. He had in this way disregarded the warnings of faithful servants, who had told him how since 1759 these Religious had not ceased to revile his Government, to defame his character, and even to question the sincerity of his religious faith; and had replied (to these faithful servants) that he believed them to be prejudiced and misinformed. The insurrection of 1766 had, however, opened his eyes, for he was certain that the Jesuits had fomented it, and had proofs that it was so, since several members of the Society had been arrested while distributing money to groups (of rioters). They had been corrupting the *bourgeoisie* by calumnious insinuations against his Government, and had only been waiting for a signal. This first opportunity had sufficed them, and they were content to concoct a pretext out of the most puerile trifles, the form of a hat here and a cloak there, the malversations of some superintendent, the knaveries of some *corregidor*. Their enterprize had failed because the tumult broke out on Palm Sunday. It was on Holy Thursday during the Stations that he was to have been surprised and surrounded at the foot of the Cross. The rebels pretended no doubt that they were only resorting to violence that they might extort conditions. Continuing his narrative, the King protested twice over that his words were true, and cited the testimony of the most upright judges and incorruptible magistrates of his kingdom, and added that, if he had anything to reproach himself for, it was that he had been too lenient with this dangerous body. Then heaving a deep sigh, he said, 'I have learnt too much.'

---

[15] See the text in S. Manuel Danvila's *Reinado de Carlos III*, vol. iii. App.

Saint-Priest gives no date for this despatch from d'Ossun, but it must have been written about a month after the date of the expulsion, for on 8 May the Conde de Fuentes writes back to the Marqués de Grimaldi announcing its arrival, and expressing his astonishment that such things should have happened without his being informed of them.[16] Lord Rochford, too, wrote a similar letter to the Earl of Shelburne, which is dated 6 April.[17] Lord Rochford also adds some further details which d'Ossun had given, but which Saint-Priest omits from his summary. Thus we learn that the proofs of Jesuit complicity in the riot were said to have been drawn from an examination of the papers which had been taken from them; that the entire Royal Family was to have been extirpated had the plot succeeded, and that a further attempt was to have been made in the current year, had not Aranda's vigilance forestalled it.

This despatch of d'Ossun's is of special interest, not so much because it acquaints us with the principal crime imputed to the Jesuits, for of that we shall hear again from other sources, but because its account comes to us fresh from the lips of Carlos III, and gives a sure insight into the state of his mind. He was incapable of doing an intentional injustice, and from his words to d'Ossun we can safely infer that he was thoroughly convinced of the guilt of his Jesuit subjects, and sincerely believed it to have been established by irresistible proofs that they were bent on taking his life; as likewise, that in banishing them from his kingdom he thought he was discharging a painful but necessary duty. To acknowledge this, however, is by no means the same as acknowledging that the King's belief was well-grounded, or, in other words, that he was not the victim of a deception practised on him by Ministers who were by no means as conscientious as himself.

Can we, then, get behind the scenes, and ascertain anything more full and definite about the supposed plot and the proofs on the strength of which it was deemed to be ascribable, not merely to a little party of Spanish Jesuits, but to the entire body? The answer is that in these days we can find, if not all that is required to dispel the mystery, at least enough to explain and extend the account given by the King to d'Ossun. In 1815, Ferdinand VII, the grandson of Carlos III, wished to restore the Society in his dominions, in response to a multitude of petitions from Bishops, municipalities, and others, and accordingly he consulted his Supreme Council. It was then that the Fiscal to the Council, Don Francisco Gutiérrez de la Huerta, was

---

[16] Nonell, *Vida del V. P. Pignatalli*, p. 156. It will be remembered that the Conde de Fuentes was Padre Pignatelli's brother.

[17] Coxe, *Spain Under the Bourbon Kings*, iv. 361.

commissioned to examine and report on the value of the motives which were laid upon Carlos III as necessitating the Suppression. The *Dictamen,* to which allusion has already been made, is an elaborate document, based on such papers as Don Gutiérrez could obtain from the State Archives. This collection of papers was, however, very imperfect as is wont to happen in such cases, and Gutiérrez derived the impression that many papers had been purposely destroyed. In 1857 appeared Sr Antonio Ferrer del Río's *Historia del Reinado de Carlos III en España,* a work of anti-Jesuit tendency, but based on elaborate research which greatly increased our knowledge of the proceedings of the Extraordinary Council. In 1893 appeared Sr Danvila y Collado's *Reinado de Carlos III,*[18] a thoroughly critical work, containing further valuable and till then unpublished documents. It is on these three works that we shall mainly rely for what remains to be said about the Spanish Suppression.

There can be no doubt that by 1766, the Government of Carlos III had become unpopular, and this unpopularity found vent not only in the popular risings in Madrid and certain of the provincial towns, but, as is wont to happen in despotically governed countries, in a multitude of clandestine publications which, whilst speaking with formal respect of the King, violently attacked his Ministers, and turned their measures into ridicule. From the character and quality of these pasquinades it was inferred, rightly or wrongly, that the simple people who were conspicuous in the insurrections were but tools in the hands of some more educated persons who were working in the background for purposes of their own. Accordingly, in April 1766, the Conde de Aranda was commissioned to institute the Secret Inquiry, and strive to discover these real authors of the disorders with a view to their prosecution. To aid him in his investigations he was empowered to choose one member of the Supreme Council and one of its Fiscals. His choice fell on Don Miguel María de Nava, and on Don P. Rodríguez de Campomanes, and the three formed the Extraordinary Council in its first commencements. Later on, other members were aggregated, namely, Don Pedro Ric y Egea, and Don Luís del Valle Salazar, together with Don Pedro Colón de Larreátegui, Don Andrés de Maraver y Vera, and Don Bernardo Caballero, the last three for matters relating to the Society in the Indies.[19]

On 8 June 1766, this Extraordinary Council agreed on its first *Consulta,* and in this nothing was said of the Jesuits, though in vague

[18] In six volumes, forming part of Sr Cánovas de Castillo's splendid *Historia General de España*.
[19] Ferrer del Río, op. cit. ii p. 126.

and general terms the rioters were said to have been stirred up by ecclesiastics holding and propagating opinions depreciatory of the Royal Power. But on 22 September, another *Consulta* was passed, which adopted a report laid before the Council by Campomanes, and in this the Jesuits were formally incriminated, though still only in vague terms. 'The Fiscal discerns,' says Campomanes of himself, 'throughout all the branches of this vast and complicated episode [viz., the Madrid outbreak], a religious body which, even whilst this inquiry has been going on, has not ceased to circulate publications intended to impose on and attract to itself ecclesiastics and other bodies, with the object of inspiring a general aversion for the Government, and for the principles needful to be applied in reforming the abuses under which this country is labouring – it being easy for them to gain over to their side persons who need to be reformed.'[20]

There were some further intermediate stages of this kind, through which the indictment of the Society was gradually developed; but we may pass at once to the *Consulta* of 29 January 1767, in which the expulsion was finally determined on. Don Francisco Gutiérrez tells us in his *Dictamen* that he could only find a mutilated copy of this *Consulta,* the part preserved being that which arranges for the carrying out of the expulsion, and the part lost that which should give the motives we are searching for. Sr Ferrer del Río, on the other hand, says that the document was lost precisely in 1815, during its transport from the State Archives to the study of Don Gutiérrez. From information privately received, I understand that both these authorities are mistaken, that the Motives were not found by Gutiérrez because, in conformity with the usual custom, they were on a separate paper, and that this is to be found still in its proper place at Simancas. It is not, however, accessible to us at present, and we may therefore take with Sr Ferrer del Río, as its equivalent, another paper which, with fair probability, he considers to have been based on it. This other paper is the *Memoria Ministerial* drawn up by Moñino, and adopted by the Extraordinary Council on 30 November 1768, as a statement suitable to be sent on to Clement XIV. It is a document too long to transcribe,[21] but the following is an abstract of its contents.

It starts by observing that at the time of the accession of Carlos III to the throne of Spain the Jesuits manifested an aversion for his person and system of government. What enraged them was that the

---

[20] *Ibid.,* p. 129.
[21] The full text is given both by Ferrer del Río (*ibid.* p.137), and by Danvila (vol. iii. Appendix).

King, seeing that the influence they exercised in the country was too preponderating, strove to reduce it to more becoming proportions. They were deprived of the office of Royal Confessor, which till recently had been held by one of their body, and, whereas the high offices in Church and State had hitherto been given mainly to their nominees, the King made himself a rule to distribute these honours more equitably. He still maintained the Jesuits in the confidential office of educators to his children, thereby showing that he had no personal animosity against them; but that was insufficient for their ambition, to gratify which they were prepared to go to all lengths, even that of disturbing the country and risking a civil war.

This enterprize they inaugurated by a campaign of calumny and seditious suggestions, which they carried on by means partly of private conversations and correspondences, partly of warnings and denunciations uttered from the pulpit, and still more by virulent writings clandestinely published and widely disseminated. The objects of these attacks were the King and his Ministers, whom they represented as heretics at heart, engaged in undermining the faith of the country; and they trumped up prophecies that the reign would be short, and predicted the advent of insurrections and mutinies.

When in this way minds seemed to them sufficiently prepared, some of their chiefs and leading intriguers met together in conference at Pardo, in the beginning of 1766, and organized the insurrection which broke out at Madrid on Palm Sunday of that year. They induced some simple-minded people to get up a riot by appealing to their dislike for the Marqués de Squillace and his measures for repressing the *somberos* and long cloaks, so that on the surface it appeared as if the sole object of the riot was to cause these measures to be revoked and their author dismissed. Soon, however, it became clear that the Jesuits were working behind the scenes, and using the overt rioters as instruments for advancing aims of their own. This appeared particularly in the demands for the restoration to office of the Marqués de la Ensenada, a tool of the Jesuits, and for the substitution of one of their cloth in the place of Padre Joachim Eleta; as also in the appellation assumed by some of the rioters of 'soldiers of the faith', who were to restore sound faith to its proper position in the country. Failing to secure their secret objects at the time, through the collapse of the conspiracy, the Jesuits tried means to revive it, continuing their campaign of calumny, lauding as an heroic movement the Madrid insurrection, and exciting others of a similar kind in many provincial towns. The fanaticism thus excited led to many crimes, such as that of Salazar, one of their pupils, who was put to death for his insulting and threatening language about the King; and it was noted how they bewailed his fate, as likewise the arrest and imprisonment of certain others of their friends.

As time ran on they had recourse to other expedients, and beset the Ministers with anonymous letters threatening further disasters to them or to the Sovereign unless some Jesuit partizans were introduced into the Ministry. At length, however, they began to discern, or presume, that their conduct had caused them to be made the subjects of a secret inquiry. Then they began to change their tactics. They stopped their correspondences and burnt many of their papers, and, what was worse, in order to divert the object of the inquiry from themselves to others, they resorted to calumny and induced their agents to bear false witness, laying what were really their own misdoings at the door of innocent persons.

While they were found to be acting thus in Spain serious reports of their misconduct in the Indies began to reach the Ministers. It was found that they had been tyrannizing over the natives in the Reductions, acquiring for themselves enormous wealth, drawing into their hands a supreme power, both in spirituals and temporals; and more even than that, for they had actually been proved guilty, by letters seized on the bodies of their agents, of negotiating for the handing over of Spanish colonies to the English, who were to guarantee them certain trading rights in return.

The *Memoria Ministerial* adds a further section, in which it considers the remedy needful to be applied. Obviously the country must be rid of its cruel enemies, but by what course should this be done? It would be possible to put the culprits on their trial and inflict on them an appropriate punishment. But to this the King's clemency (!) was opposed, and besides, it would be a dangerous thing to allow their baneful principles to be publicly discussed. It was better, therefore, to leave the guilty unpunished and provide merely for the protection of the country, by an administrative measure which would remove the disturbers of its tranquillity beyond its borders. It might indeed be urged that all the Jesuits were not guilty, and it would be better therefore to reform this Society by removing its unsound members than by expelling them all. But, although it was fully conceded that many, indeed most of its members, were innocent and upright men, wholly uninitiated into the secret of its conspiracies, still it was impossible to distinguish between the innocent and the guilty, and besides, in a sense the innocent were the more dangerous of the two, as they were trained to obey implicitly all the orders of their Superiors, and their innocence became a cloak to the misdeeds in which they were the irresponsible agents. They were to be treated, therefore, like madmen, who could not expect to have their hands left free.

Here, then, is the case against the Spanish Jesuits, which was framed by the Extraordinary Council, and laid before Carlos III. Undoubtedly it sets them before us as a most mischievous body, and one well worthy to be expelled from any civilized country. But it will be noted that it is an indictment only, and unaccompanied by any proofs of its justice. Even as an indictment we will venture to contend that it bears the appearance of an ingenious web spun by twisting deeds and words which may possibly have had a very innocent significance in themselves, and imputing motives by which the accused may possibly not have been actuated. Still, what we particularly desiderate are the proofs on which the Extraordinary Council based these serious charges, and in a following section we shall show how infinitesimal they are – if indeed that is not a term conceding too much.

Meanwhile there is a question, smaller in itself, but leading on to the solution of the other, which we may determine now. What was the King's secret which he declared his intention to reserve so strictly within his Royal breast? There can, it seems to us, be no longer any doubt but that the contents of the indictment just given were what formed, and all that formed, the matter of this Royal secret. In the Pragmatic Sanction, and in the first letter to Clement XIII, it is the motives for the expulsion which the King declares his intention to keep secret, and these, as we have inferred, were the reasons given in the *Memoria Ministerial;* nor is there a suggestion in this *Memoria* of any further reasons lying behind, and incapable of disclosure. Moreover, we have found in the *Consulta* itself, of 29 January, in the part published by Don Gutiérrez, as well as in the *Consulta* of 30 April, the recommendation given precisely in reference to the reasons set forth in the former *Consulta,* that they were to be kept from the Pope and the Bishops, who were to be told that the King reserved them in his breast.

Here, however, a difficulty arises. The reasons given in the *Memoria Ministerial* have about them nothing of a private character, nothing save what, as it would seem, required to be made public as widely as possible. Why then was there such stress laid on keeping them strictly secret? But again the answer is clear, being in fact given in the two *Consultas* just referred to. It was not desired that the Pope should have any say in the question of the expulsion, whereas if its motives had been communicated to him he would have had grounds on which to base a reasoned representation.

Still, why should the Pope be kept thus entirely out of a matter which so closely affected the interests of religion? After all he was the Father of the faithful. This also is a point on which the

Extraordinary Council did not omit to deliver itself. In the *Consulta* of 30 April it is stated that the Pope, through his Secretary of State, is entirely in the hands of the Jesuits, who would not allow his judgment in their case to be other than what they were pleased to dictate to him, whilst even the Bishops of Spain, through his authority over them, were amenable to Jesuit influence. Let the reader judge if such a reason was of much value. The pretext was an ingenious one, but if the courts, whether of Church or State, had been thrown open to an honest and searching inquiry, no Jesuit influence could have stayed its course. May it not rather be that the Ministers of Spain and their Extraordinary Council felt that the motives by which they were justifying to themselves a measure which they had quite other reasons for devising, were motives which would not bear the light of too searching an examination? This is an explanation which would fit the facts, but let us hang it up in suspense till we have seen what proofs of their indictment the Ministers were able to obtain.

III.[22] [The evidence]

We have seen what kind of a case against the Spanish Jesuits was formulated in the *Memoria Ministerial*, and have inferred that it was an indictment substantially the same which was laid before the King in the *Consulta* of 29 January 1767, and induced him to expel them from his dominions. If it was a true portrait of the incriminated Religious we must admit that they were a most disturbing force to have in a country, but, as was pointed out in the previous section, this *Memoria Ministerial* is an accusation only, conceived in the most indefinite terms and unaccompanied by any proofs, whereas it is the proofs which we require to have, before we can judge of the justice or injustice of the expulsion. Our task, therefore, in the present section must be to ascertain what proofs underlay the accusation, and to judge of their sufficiency.

It is a task not free from difficulty for two reasons. One is that we have not had personal access to the numerous papers bearing on the subject which are to be found in the Spanish Archives, and must depend on the published works of others, namely, of the three authors mentioned above, Don Gutiérrez de la Huerta, Sr Ferrer del Río, and Sr Danvila y Collado. The impression produced on one by reading even the latest and most thorough of these three is that there is much material still unpublished which will some day yield rich results. Still they were competent investigators, and we may assume

[22] *The Month*, 100 (1902), 126-52.

without risk that what they have given fairly represents the whole, so that we shall not be seriously astray in resting our judgment upon it. The other reason which makes our present task difficult is of a more radical kind. The Extraordinary Council over which the Conde de Aranda presided was invested by the King with the most ample powers to choose its methods of procedure, and it seems to have considered itself free to neglect the ordinary forms of justice whenever it thought fit. Thanks to the device of dealing with the Jesuits by an administrative measure instead of by judicial procedure not a single Jesuit was put on his trial, or allowed to make a deposition – which means to say that in no case have we their version of the deeds imputed to them, and, what is more, in no case probably was their version laid before the King. Nor in the instance or two that we have of the judicial proceedings against persons accused of having been their instruments and accomplices is there that completeness which leaves a satisfied feeling in the mind. In short we can obtain a few further details of the charges than we could get from a document like the *Memoria Ministerial,* but still only charges the substantiation of which is concealed from us. What this means is that in forming our judgment we are thrown back on the character of the judges, all of whom were the specially selected agents of an Extraordinary Council which, to put it mildly, was not without a strong prejudice against the accused. In England, the England at all events of the present day, an investigation thus conducted would have no chance whatever of commanding public confidence, and we might perhaps content ourselves with taking refuge in this consideration. We desire, however, to carry as far as the documents will allow an investigation so closely affecting the reputation of the Society.

The *Memoria Ministerial* places in the foreground the alleged complicity of the Jesuits in the Madrid Insurrection of 1766. What precedes in this document assigns a motive as explaining why the Jesuits should wish to cause commotions in the country, and describes a supposed campaign of calumny by which they prepared the minds of the people for a revolt against their rulers; whilst what follows in the same document is of the nature of a generalization, charging them with similar offences in the provincial towns, and likewise in South America; all being intended to lead up to the conclusion that it would be an insufficient remedy to punish merely the few individuals who might be convicted of definite offences, but that it was necessary to put an end to the entire body. We may observe here incidentally, that in the *Consulta* of 30 April 1767, this generalization is carried further, the Madrid Insurrection being in fact treated as a somewhat minor link in the chain of offences, for constituting which the whole past history of the Society in the various countries of the earth is exploited.

It is obvious that we must pass over now this extensive generalization, though in some degree it will be necessary to return to it when we come to an examination of the Brief of Suppression of Clement XIV. Still in passing it over we may cite the judgment of Gutiérrez de la Huerta, who in his *Dictamen* notes the skill with which the effect has been produced, by omitting all in the history of the Society which was to its credit and had gained for it the appreciation of rulers and people, and painting in the strongest colours, to the exclusion of all shades and half-tones, the comparatively fewer episodes which might be made to tell against it.

On the question of the motives which the Jesuits are alleged to have had for disturbing the country, it will be enough to say that the dismissal of Padre Rábago, the Jesuit confessor to Ferdinand VI, and the dismissal of the Marqués de la Ensenada from the leading post in the Ministry, were the result of a Court intrigue. There were at that time two parties among the courtiers of King Ferdinand VI, one desiring an alliance with England and Portugal against France, and the other an alliance with France against England and Portugal. Richard Wall, a Spanish statesman of Irish nationality, was leader of the pro-English party, with which naturally Sir Benjamin Keene, the English Ambassador, was in league; and Ensenada was leader of the pro-French party. The pro-English party were in favour of the Treaty of Limits which proved so disastrous to the Paraguayan Missions as well as to the interests of Spain, and in this way Padre Rábago became involved along with Ensenada, both of whom offered a strenuous opposition to the treaty and its consequences. Wall was moreover a strong anti-Jesuit, as his letters bear witness, and, when his party became the stronger, they managed to contrive the dismissal of both Ensenada and Rábago.

Padre Rábago was the last Jesuit confessor at the Spanish Court, and his dismissal was followed by a gradual leavening of the high offices of Church and State with incumbents adverse to the Society – a process which continued and became enlarged when Carlos III succeeded his brother on the throne. It was but natural that the Jesuits should be mortified at this change, and should use language in word or writing expressive of their wounded feelings – in criticism, for instance, of the unpalatable appointments – some of which language was unreasonable and indefensible, and some perhaps really scandalous. We are not aware of any extant evidence that this happened, but there may be, and as Jesuits being human have among them at all times their fair share of imperfect and imprudent characters, it is likely that such things happened then, and it may be assumed that they did. But to be guilty of this kind of intemperate action is one thing, to be guilty of an organized effort to regain lost power and influence by resorting to the most evil means, striving to fill the country with seditions, forming plots against its rulers, and even attempts to assassinate its Sovereign – that is quite another thing, and a kind of guilt which ought not to be imputed to any class of men whatever, still less to a body of men dedicated to the service of God, except on the most convincing array of positive evidence. And yet where is there a trace of such evidence to be found? Certainly there is none in the *Memoria Ministerial* nor in any *Consulta* out of the many which the campaign against the Society called forth, nor does Sr Ferrer del Río produce any, though he certainly would have done so if he could. On the other hand, it is easy to see why this assignment of motive finds its place in the *Memoria Ministerial*. As we shall find, Aranda and his colleagues had no positive evidence worthy of the name to connect the Jesuits with the Madrid Insurrection. Their proof, such as it was, was inferential – the Insurrection must have been due to the Jesuits because they were the people who had a motive for wishing it. In other words, these documents, by which the King was persuaded to take the severest action against a multitude of his subjects, argued in a vicious circle. They proved the supposed guilty conduct of the Jesuits from the motives by which they were supposed to be animated; and they proved the supposed motives from the supposed conduct.

It may seem premature to suggest at the present stage this judgment on the reasoning of the *Memoria Ministerial,* but it will be helpful to keep it in mind whilst we study the evidence they could produce for connecting the Jesuits with the Insurrection – to which study we have now to pass.

We may take as a basis the report of Don Gutiérrez, supplementing it where required from our two other authorities. It is towards the end of his *Dictamen* that he comes to the question of the Insurrection. After briefly narrating the history of this event, he tells us that 'ever since the time of Ferdinand VI the enemies of the Society had been on the look-out for an opportunity to destroy it, and they seized upon the Madrid Insurrection as one made ready to their hands.' They persuaded the King that this rising 'could not have been the work of the wretched mob which cried out in the streets, but must be due to the Jesuits, who were accustomed to tumults, rebellions, and regicides, and had infected the nation with the fanaticism they were wont to infuse into their friends and adherents; that a large number of these adherents were to he found at the Court itself; astute, intriguing, and daring persons, who were prepared for any enterprize; and that the person of the King himself was not safe from danger should it suit the Jesuits to make an attempt upon it – in the hope of being able to overturn the Government, divide its offices among their friends, regain their former absolute and despotic power, recover the Royal confessorship, and destroy by fire and bloodshed those good and loyal subjects whom they regarded as their enemies.'

It will be noted how closely this account of the indictment laid before the King corresponds with what we have found in the *Memoria Ministerial*. But it is the proofs of this indictment that we are seeking, and Don Gutiérrez, after describing the appointment of the Extraordinary Council, tells us how the Ministers of Carlos III set to work to obtain them. The Alcalde *de Casa y Corte,* whose name was Cevallos, was commissioned to make inquiries as to the Jesuits at Madrid, and his companions, Leiza and Ávila, were to make inquiries as to certain other persons, whilst similar commissions were set up in the country towns to make inquiries there, all being bound to observe the utmost secrecy.

> No sooner [says Gutiérrez] were these appointments made, than secret spies were disseminated throughout the kingdom; complaints, denunciations, and false testimonies or every kind were encouraged; and favour was shown to all who spoke ill of the Jesuits, and such offices as fell vacant were used to reward friends and multiply partizans.

This corresponds with what we have already heard from Padre González, who, in his Life of Idiáquez,[23] has related how the Fathers became conscious about that time of an increased disposition to watch all their utterances, making the most of the smallest indiscretions, and even twisting into a scandalous sense assertions which in themselves were perfectly innocent. But what was the result?

Don Gutiérrez tells us that the mass of the witnesses whose testimony was received belonged to the class of those who were the habitual defamers of the Society, and that these, 'not knowing of anything bearing on the alleged crime, thought it sufficient to make depositions reciting all the false principles with which the Jesuits have been credited by their adversaries in all time, and on this ground to denounce them as ambitious, mischievous, relaxed in their morals, seditious and malevolent.' But

---

[23] See above, p. 87 [the Life seems to be one included in Navarette's collection: see pp. 80, 82. *Ed. N.*]

in regard to the Insurrection none mentioned any occurrences save what were useless or of no account, because resting on mere popular rumour instead of personal knowledge. Some said Jesuits in their sermons uttered seditious words; others that in their discourses and conversations they talked against members of the Government; others that in the College (at Madrid) they gave manifestations of joy while the riot was going on; and that from this College first went forth the cries that were afterwards heard in the street, when the people demanded to have the Marqués de la Ensenada back as Minister; and there were even some who said that on the night of the riot a man was seen walking about concealed among the rioters who looked like Padre Isidro López.

This is really all that Don Gutiérrez has to say about denunciations directly charging the Jesuits with having a hand in the Insurrection, and apparently nothing was done to test these rumours, as indeed they could not be properly tested without an examination of Padre López and his colleagues. And as neither Ferrer del Río nor Danvila seem to have found anything more definite, Don Cevallos, the person entrusted with the inquiry into the offences of the Jesuits themselves, must have had an easy time.

But they also sought to reach the Jesuits through prosecution of men whom they took to be their friends. Foremost among these were three well-known persons, one a cleric, the other two laymen, namely, Don Miguel de la Gándara, the Archdeacon of Murcia, Don Lorenzo Hermoso, and the Marqués de Villaflores, all of whom were residents at the Court These are the three to whom the *Memoria Ministerial* refers when it speaks of the Jesuits betraying their guilt by the sorrow with which they 'bewailed .... the arrest and imprisonment of certain others of their friends'.[24] Sr Ferrer del Río tells us that they were 'known to be the leaders of the rioters, and were punished as such, it being impossible for Aranda to spare them.' We find too the Nuncio, writing to the Cardinal Secretary of State, just after the publication of the Pragmatic Sanction, and stating that 'Campomanes had said that "the Abate Gándara was more guilty than Damiens in France", which seemed to imply that he was considered to be a regicide, and it is believed that he will very soon be conducted to the Court Prison, and visited with an appropriate punishment.' Here then we have three very important cases which fortunately we can pursue further, as Don Gutiérrez has given us a connected account of the interrogatories to which these three supposed leaders of the riot were subjected. We must be content to summarize his account, but shall try to lose nothing of its contents,

[24] See above pp.106–107.

for so good an opportunity must not be lost of an insight into the character of Aranda's methods, and the quality of Sr Ferrer del Río's judgments.

On the night of 20 October 1766, the three men were arrested all at the same time, and their papers confiscated. Villaflores was placed in solitary confinement in the Castle of Alicante, Hermoso in that of Pamplona, whilst the Abate Gándara was taken to the Castle of Batres. At the same time Padre López was not indeed arrested, but ordered to retire to Monforte in Galicia. In this way the suspected persons were separated from one another by the whole breadth of the kingdom, the professed object being of course to prevent them from acting in collusion, but the real object being in all probability – as the reader may be inclined to think after hearing what there was to bring against them – to keep away from the Court, where all four had till then been resident, a set of men whose discernment, courage, and high character might have been employed in detecting and explaining to the King the nature of the injustice into which he was being entrapped.

> In spite of their arrest [Gutiérrez tells us], nothing in any way suspicious was found in their papers, but, on the contrary, much that demonstrated that both they and the Jesuits were entirely innocent of the Madrid Insurrection. Hence, after taking from Gándara, Hermoso, and the Marqués de Villaflores simple depositions stating what they had to say about the charges brought against them, it was found necessary to stop the prosecution, there being simply no evidence on which to convict them.

This break-down left the Extraordinary Council in an unpleasant position, for the King was all expectation, having been assured that abundant evidence against the Jesuits would be forthcoming. It was then, thinks Gutiérrez, that the expedient of proceeding against them by an administrative act instead of a judicial sentence, suggested itself to the Council. But however that may be, the three men were still kept in confinement and perhaps were accused of the crime in a guarded manner in the *Consulta* of 29 January, as we have seen that they were in the *Memoria Ministerial*. They were also subjected to a further examination in the following autumn, which resulted in some sort of a verdict against them. Let us hear then from Gutiérrez the sequel of their case, which he gives with some detail for each person separately.

Hermoso was brought from his prison at Pamplona to the Court prison at Madrid, in December 1767, but it was not till the following March that they were prepared to administer to him any interrogatories. In the previous spring, when called upon to name the Jesuits with whom he had dealings, he had replied, 'With none', and that he had never counted among their friends. During the interval they had got hold of four witnesses, of whom one was said to have been a personal attendant on Padre López. This man deposed that previously to the Insurrection Hermoso used to frequent the room of Padre López for secret conferences. The other three witnesses were said to be servants at the Jesuit College, and merely testified to the credibility of the personal attendant. On the strength of this testimony the Commission sent for Hermoso to appear again before them. First, they charged him with having been, in collusion with Gándara and the Jesuits, an author and leader of the conspiracy against the King and the State. He replied that this was absolutely false, and that there was not even a foundation for the charge, as the rising explained itself, being directed against the measures of Squillace, and the *alguacils* who had proceeded to carry them out so tactlessly. And as for his having conspired with Gándara and Villaflores, the former was not one of his friends, any more than López, and the latter was not even known to him by sight. Then they told him that he had been seen mingling with the rioters and directing them. He replied saying that as a matter of fact he had been the whole time in the Court, and brought twelve persons of the Royal Household, all men of position, to testify that they had seen him there. Thirdly, they told him that it had been proved against him by witnesses that on the Monday after the riot he had gone, in company with the Cardinal Patriarch, from Madrid to Aranjuez by the Bridge of Toledo, and had been able to pass both himself and the Cardinal through the insurgent guards, who had been overheard saying that it was Don Hermoso, one of their leaders, who of course must be allowed to pass.[25] To this his answer was that the witness had evidently not told the truth, as he went out by the Bridge of Segovia, and, though it was true that the Cardinal and himself had been allowed by the insurgents to pass, it was because he had given them money on behalf of the Cardinal. And he brought members of the Cardinal's household to corroborate him. Finally, the servant of Padre López came forward again to say that he had made a mistake about the person, that he had never seen Hermoso before, and that it was the Abate Suárez whom he had mistaken for him. This, according to Gutiérrez, is all that the papers contain with regard to Hermoso.

The Abate Gándara, being an ecclesiastic, was sent to be tried by his Ordinary, the Archbishop of Burgos, himself at that time a

[25] When the King fled by night after the riot to Aranjuez, the insurgents were indignant at what they took to be an indication that he did not mean to keep his word in regard to the terms extracted from him. Hence they watched all the exits from the city to prevent the Court from rejoining the King. This explains the third charge against Hermoso.

member of the Extraordinary Council, who, however, delegated another to examine him. In the summer of 1766, Aranda had issued an order that all ecclesiastics who held no appointment in Madrid should leave the city, and return to their dioceses. The first offence with which Gándara was charged was disregard of this order, but his reply was that he had acted on his Majesty's expressed permission, and even command, to remain at the Court. Next he was charged with being on terms of friendship with Padre López, and this he freely admitted. Thirdly, he was charged with having, during the weeks preceding the Insurrection, received many suspicious visits from Padre López, for whom he had regularly sent his own carriage, and that the manifest topic of their conferences was the plot against the King and the public tranquillity. To this he replied that not only was this charge of plotting quite unfounded and false, but that as a matter of fact the priest who paid him those regular visits was not Padre López but the Augustinian Padre Ferrer, and that the reason of so many visits was the illness from which he was then suffering, Padre Ferrer being his doctor. And Padre Ferrer being called confirmed his statement. As they had nothing else to urge, the ecclesiastical judge reported that Gándara was an innocent man who had been aggrieved by an unjust prosecution. Under these circumstances it might have been expected that he would be restored to liberty, but, on the contrary, the Fiscals Campomanes and Moñino demanded his retention as a dangerous person, and likewise that he should be condemned to pay the costs of the prosecution. This was granted by the King on the advice of the Extraordinary Council, and the result was that the Abate was left to end his days in a rigorous and solitary confinement. Don Gutiérrez observes that such an outrage would have been impossible, but for the dense secrecy in which the inquiry was shrouded, but points out how necessary it was for the interests of the Ministers of the Council. Ever since the arrest of Gándara in October, 1766, it had been told the King, and circulated among the people, that this man had been guilty of an attempt on the King's life. If, therefore, he were released now, the whole proceedings of the Council would be discredited, and perhaps the King, becoming suspicious of them, might take to himself other advisers.

Against the Marqués de Villaflores they had still less to bring. He was charged with being a friend of the Jesuits, a frequent visitor to their rooms, and hence a plotter with them against the State. His answer was, that his friends among the Jesuits were their men of letters, and literature was the ordinary subject of their interviews. He was also charged with having been among the rioters, which he denied, and with having been the author of a satirical tract against the

Government published shortly after the Insurrection, but this too he denied, and, according to Don Gutiérrez, conclusively proved to be false. Nor was there more to bring against him.

After what they did in the Gándara case we cannot be surprised to hear that the Fiscals expressed no wish for the acquittal of Hermoso and Villaflores, but it is surely matter of astonishment that they should have asked that they should be condemned to death, after having been first put to the torture to ascertain their accomplices. That, indeed, seems to have been too much even for Aranda and his Council. Still, what they did was to condemn Villaflores to ten years' detention in a fortress, which was afterwards commuted into an internment on his property at Granada. Hermoso's case they found more difficult to deal with, as he demanded not merely to be released but to have his character vindicated by a public statement of his innocence, signed, according to the terms of the ordinary law, by the two Fiscals. This demand, reasonable though it was, in the interests of their own reputation they were bound to refuse, so they sent him back to his prison with strict orders to say nothing to any one about the proceedings against him or his own answers.

Even if the prosecutions of these three men had been concluded before the date of the expulsion, which they were not, it can hardly be maintained that they contribute much towards justifying that measure; but let us see what other cases were relied upon. We know of but two only, of which let us take first that of Don Benito Navarro, which though in chronological order it comes last, takes precedence as being the one instance of a legal inquiry in which the Society was directly accused. Sr Ferrer del Río has *more suo* a brief account, in which he says off-hand that the Jesuits were convicted by the testimony of many witnesses of having been the principal authors of the Insurrection of March 1766, and of the attempt made in the following year. Sr Danvila gives a detailed summary of the proceedings in the case, taken from the official *Memoria,* signed by the Relator, Don José Maldonado, and published at Madrid by Joaquín Ibarra in 1768. It is from Sr Danvila therefore that we must borrow, leaving the reader to judge how far the facts fit in with Sr Ferrer del Río's statement. Dr Navarro was an advocate of some repute, who on 28 October 1766, laid before the Conde de Aranda a written denunciation of Don Juan Balanchán. In it he deposed that Balanchán had told him of his complicity in the Insurrection; that he had written letters warning certain persons to keep away from the places to be attacked, in composing which letters, that he might elude detection, he had imitated the style of the Marqués de Villaflores; that he had bought the faggots of wood for burning the house of Sr Hermosilla;

that he had taken part in the massacres in the Calle de Bordadores; that he had given seditious papers to some women to distribute; that he had written the Counter-Proclamation which was set up in the place of the Proclamation that had been pulled down; that he had made a false deposition before Don Felipe Codallos in support of one in which Don Silvestro Palamares denounced Padre Isidro López, saying of him that on the day of the Insurrection he (Padre Isidro) was to be seen at the door of the Jesuit College, surrounded by several others, all disguised, and engaged in starting the cry for the dismissal of Squillace, and the recall to office of the Marqués de la Ensenada. In regard to this last point Navarro, in reply to a question by Don Codallos, deposed that Palamares was an anti-Jesuit, was not a man to be trusted, and was moved to make this charge against Padre Isidro, only in order that he might establish on his own behalf an *alibi* which would relieve him from the suspicion of having himself taken part in the Insurrection.

Aranda, on receiving this denunciation from Navarro, passed him on to Campomanes, who, on 23 December, caused him to be arrested and confronted with Balanchán. What happened at this confrontation, or during the following month, Danvila does not tell us, but suddenly, on 29 January 1767, Navarro turned round, and declared that all his charges against Balanchán were false, and that it was the Jesuits who had put him up to make them. Padres Miguel de Benevente and Ignacio Gonzalez, he said, had told him they believed Balanchán and Palamares had been denouncing their Fathers to the President, and he would be doing a charitable act if be would undermine their credibility by bringing an accusation against them. He resisted the suggestion in the first instance, feeling it to be an unlawful act, but they had assured him that, on the contrary, it would be highly meritorious; and, as his family had been from childhood upwards under Jesuit influence, and he himself had sucked in their teaching as it were like milk from the breast, he eventually succumbed to their seductions.

On hearing this the Fiscal was only too glad to drop the prosecution of Balanchán and institute one against Navarro himself, which, however, was held over till 19 September 1767. Navarro then repeated his former confession, and also enlarged it. He declared that Padre Benevente himself must have been the author of the Counter-Proclamation, as was clear from various statements that he had made to him; that the Jesuit Fathers were the undoubted authors of the Insurrection, and likewise of an attempt to excite another on its first anniversary – to prepare for which they had spread the unfounded rumour that decrees were about to be issued against the head-dress of the women and the whiskers of the men. The Court, as might be anticipated, accepted the case as made out against the Jesuits, but did not leave Navarro unpunished. They sentenced him to four years' imprisonment, and various disabilities to follow.

Inasmuch as Navarro's 'confession' was not made till 29 January 1767, the very day when the expulsion was decreed, it cannot, any more than the 'convictions' of Gándara, Hermoso, and Villaflores, have counted among the motives for the expulsion, and yet it is made to do so in the *Memoria Ministerial* which says the Jesuits 'resorted to calumny and induced their agents to bear false-witness, laying what were really their own misdoings at the door of innocent persons.' There can be no doubt that this passage refers to the Navarro case.

But, though too late to have been among the motives for the expulsion, was this man's final testimony that of truth? The passage quoted shows that the Council accepted it as such, but that does not decide the question, nor, we submit, do the circumstances point to such a conclusion. Why was he not confronted with the accused Fathers, and their depositions opposed to his? In the autumn of 1767 they were, indeed, far away, but the confrontation could have taken place during February, and no doubt would have been were it not for the resolution taken to put no Jesuit Father on his trial, or even to take from him a deposition of any kind. Nor are we told of other witnesses by whom this man's testimony was confirmed. All then depends on his personal character, and what is the value of that when we find, according to his own account, that up to the last moment he had been telling the grossest falsehoods, and reflect that he had a distinct motive for turning round, the times having become such that evidence favourable to the Jesuits would be most distasteful to the Court, but evidence against them most grateful. True, he was punished, as he deserved to be, but he may not have foreseen that, or may have felt that even so he would get off cheaper than by persisting in his original tale. To these considerations must be added, that the testimony of a contemporary writer is extant, according to which Navarro's behaviour before the Court was not his only misdemeanour. This contemporary writer is Padre Fernando Cevallos, a monk of the Order of San Geronimo, and a member of their community at Madrid, who wrote a *Memoria* on the Expulsion of the Jesuits, in which he gives some interesting side-lights on matters that came within his cognizance. Of Navarro, when discussing his case, he tells us that some years previously he had been found guilty of alluring a girl-child (*una tierna señorita*) into a clandestine marriage with him, by the use of forged papers. Further, though Dr Benito Navarro was

no more worthy of credit as regards Balanchán than as regards the
Jesuits, we learn from Sr Danvila that Balanchán had other accusers,
and Padre Cevallos, who had been a personal witness of the
Insurrection, tells us that this man, when arrested on Navarro's
denunciation, had confessed to several acts of participation in the
Insurrection, as that he had written and distributed satirical papers,
that he had been among the rioters all day on Monday, that he had
been one of those who called for the King to show himself to the
people, and told the rioters to listen to him and not to a preacher.
Palamares, too, who, it seems, was an apostate monk, was, according to Cevallos, among the rioters.

One further point must be noticed before we leave the Navarro
case, for it reveals to us the kind of evidence on the faith of which
the Council inferred that Padre López and other Jesuits had been
among the rioters, directing and encouraging them.

Next we come to the case of Don Juan de Salazar Calvete, the
person of whom it is said in the *Memoria Ministerial* that he 'was put
to death for his insulting and threatening language against the King,
having been excited thereto by the fanaticism of his Jesuit instructors.' The *proceso* in this case, according to Danvila, is not at
Simancas, but he gathers from the correspondence between Aranda
and Roda enough to acquaint us with all that we need concerning it.
Salazar was arrested at the end of May 1766, and was tried before
the Alcalde *de Corte,* D. Pedro Davila. He was convicted, says
Aranda, of having used injurious expressions about the King; and the
Consulta of 30 November 1767, explains more at length that he had
gone about dressed as a woman, apparently during the Insurrection,
declaring that they must not stop till the King's brains had been spilt
on the ground. This, so far as we know from our authorities, was the
sole instance in which the idea of regicide appears in the examinations, although, as we have seen, it figured so largely in the account
of the conspiracy given by Carlos III to d'Ossun.[26] By what evidence
Salazar was convicted does not appear, but he was sentenced to
undergo the torture to see if he had had accomplices, to have his
tongue cut out, and then to be hanged. No names of accomplices
were elicited by the torture, but the rest of the sentence was duly
carried out on the 28 June 1766. If the man was guilty of the alleged
offence his punishment was not unintelligible, or, according to the
conceptions of those times, excessive, but in what way, it will be
asked, were the Jesuits implicated in his crime? The *Memoria
Ministerial* has told us. In his childhood Salazar had been at a Jesuit

[26] See above, p. 102.

school, and he sent for two Jesuit Fathers, one being his old master, to hear his confession before his execution, and in an intercepted correspondence they bewailed his fate. That is all. And what does it come to? Voltaire, Diderot, and even Tanucci, who as we shall see presently, was the prime mover in the affair of the expulsion, had all been pupils of the Jesuits. Were the Fathers, then, responsible for all the anti-Christian sentiments and acts – including the persecution of the Society – with which the names of these men became afterwards associated?

These are all the prosecutions for the Madrid Insurrection of which our authorities know, as having been used to connect the Society with the crime; but we may class with them the banishment of Ensenada, which was ordered a few weeks after the event, namely, 18 April 1766. Nothing was published as to the reason of this banishment, and rumours were accordingly rife on the subject. Ferrer del Río says it was generally believed that the millions of *reals* which circulated among the rioters had been provided by Ensenada, or rather given out by him, who in his turn had received them from the Jesuits. But at least there was no proof of this, as Lafuente – a hostile authority cited by Danvila – acknowledges. Besides which Danvila is able to give a letter from Roda to Ensenada, written at the time of the latter's banishment from Court, in which he assures him that the King, though compelled for good reasons to send him away from Court, had no cause of complaint against him, and retained the same high opinion of him as before. All which goes to show that the sole reason for Ensenada's banishment was that the people had asked for his return to office, and that he was known to be friendly with the Jesuits.

These are absolutely all the prosecutions recorded by our three authorities, which even in the remotest degree bear on the question of Jesuit complicity in the Insurrection. It would be too absurd to ask if they sufficed to inculpate the whole Order and justify its suppression, but surely no one will claim that they amount to a solid suspicion, much less demonstration of guilt, against a single member of the Society. The utmost result in this direction which they yield is that one fanatical person who had used culpable language against the King, had in his childhood been at a Jesuit school, and one man of bad character brought a serious charge against two Jesuit Fathers, at a time when he had a strong personal motive for so doing. And, if it should be said that Navarro's testimony at least constituted a suspicion, why was it not followed up, and why were the incriminated Jesuits not examined? We have heard, indeed, the diplomatic reply to this last question, but it is too great a tax on our credulity to expect us to believe that they would have dispensed with a judicial inquiry in the case of Jesuits directly accused, had they foreseen the slightest chance of obtaining a conviction. Nor is it possible to fall back on the immunity of the Religious from prosecution in the secular courts for, in the first place, there was the Court of the Nunciature; in the second, there was the leave recently obtained from the Holy See to override the immunity of the ecclesiastics in this particular investigation; and thirdly, there was the claim of the Spanish Sovereigns to regard treason as among the 'privileged' offences, with which the secular courts were entitled to deal even when ecclesiastics were the offenders.

But let us come to the more indirect charge against the Society of having sought to excite public opinion against the Crown and the Ministers by inflammatory pamphlets, sermons, conversations, and correspondences. In view of the suddenness with which the expulsion was carried out, and the consequent completeness of the raid on whatever papers were to be found in the various houses, the Government had certainly excellent means of discovering any evidence of this kind which existed. It was likely enough, too, that they would find much which could be made to subserve their purpose. The Jesuits may have been, as we believe them to have been, absolutely innocent of the more serious offences imputed to them; but, as we have already granted, it was likely that they should feel sore at much that was being done by the Government, both in its general dealing with Church questions, and in its treatment of the Society in particular. And if they felt sore it was to be expected that their sore feelings would find expression, not so much in public utterances – for an earlier section has shown to what a state of anxiety and even fright they were reduced – but at least in their private correspondence and conversations with trusted friends. There is a famous letter of Padre Calatayud, dated 18 September 1765, and addressed to his Provincial, Padre Idiáquez, which illustrates this. He was distressed at the unrestrained publication in gazettes and pamphlets of the multitudinous calumnies against the Society, which had come in from Portugal and elsewhere, whilst there was the greatest difficulty in obtaining leave to publish any reply. 'The times are perverse,' he wrote, 'and some of those who are about the Court are ill-disposed.' What he desired was that Padre Idiáquez, on behalf of his Province, seconded by his brother, the Duque de Granada de Ega, and the Cardinal Archbishop of Seville, should present themselves before the King, and ask that his Majesty would in some way express his displeasure at the conduct of *El Mercurio*. No exception can be taken to this mode of action, but other Jesuits who felt as keenly may have been less prudent in their expressions, and these, when they fell into the hands of the Extraordinary Council, might have been twisted into matter of serious accusation.

What then did they find? To be accurate, we ought rather to ask what they found in the time precedent to the expulsion, since it is for the motives of the expulsion we are looking. If the question were thus to be limited, we are not aware what justification of the suspicions of the Council could be brought forward. But we may take the broader view, especially as the vindication of the good name of the Jesuits is of more importance than a criticism of the dispositions of their judges.

Even thus extended, the question is hard to answer. If, indeed, we must go by general statements, we should have to suppose that a great deal, and that of the most alarming and astonishing character, was found in the Jesuit houses. The King himself, writing to Tanucci on 23 June 1767,[27] speaks of 'all that is being discovered daily in the papers that have been taken from their Colleges', and says that he has told Roda to send him the particulars. But we must judge of the value of these general accusations from the particular instances which we find alleged as typical specimens of the rest, and of these we can only find the following.

On 23 June 1767, that is, on the same day as the King's letter just referred to, Roda obeyed the Royal orders, and gave Tanucci the desired particulars. But the only papers he can name as having been found in a Jesuit house are 'certain *secret instructions* full of impiety, irreligion, and perverse politics.' On 21 July Tanucci wrote back, thanking him, and saying that 'he had already seen these *secret instructions* in other books, particularly in *I Lupi Smascherati,* which was attributed to Toggini.[28] On turning to *I Lupi Smascherati* we ascertain – as indeed the name intimated – that the *secret instructions* in question were the *Monita Secreta,* the well known anti-Jesuit forgery. The Jesuit College had a copy in its well-stocked library, as has the house in which this is written. What harm in that?

In the Rector's room of the Madrid College was found a copy of certain *Constitutions or Ordinances drawn up for the use of a new league which has been established to defend the King and the country and to put an end to oppression.* This was no doubt in itself a seditious pamphlet, and one that emanated from the leaders of the Madrid insurrection, for copies were circulated in the streets a few days before the outbreak. But the fact of its being in the Rector's room,

---

[27] Danvila, iii. p. 70.
[28] Danvila, iii. p. 78.

'among the Forbidden Books', is sufficiently explained by its being, like the *Monita Secreta,* an historical document, a copy of which the College naturally wished to preserve; nor do Ferrer del Río or Danvila refer to its discovery as at all compromising.

The *Consulta* of 30 November 1767, after speaking of the Salazar case, says his doctrine of Tyrannicide is defended in the *Answers to the Assertions* which Padre Adriano Croze translated at Vitoria, and which was found on the person of Padre Crispin Poyanos at Calatayud. The *Consulta* adds that an original manuscript on Tyrannicide, written by Padre Diego Rivera, Provost of the Professed House at Madrid, was found in that house. Here the *Answer to the Assertions* is the *Réponse aux Assertions,* that is, to the celebrated *Extraits des Assertions,* of which mention has been made in a former chapter. It is the chief of the replies by the French Jesuits to the charges of the Parliament. This work we can read for ourselves and see that the description given of it as defending Tyrannicide is untruthful, and doubtless, if we could see Padre Rivera's treatise, we should find that it is quite as incorrectly described by the *Consulta*.

This same *Consulta,* which is the most detailed of those emanating from the Extraordinary Council, also brings a general complaint against the Jesuits for translating and circulating answers to the attacks made upon them in the neighbouring countries. By so doing, it suggests, they were showing disrespect for the judges who had condemned them, and tending to bring royal and magisterial authority into contempt everywhere. It was a contention to some extent in keeping with the ideas of eighteenth century Absolutism, but in these days we lay more stress on a man's right to defend himself when accused.

As regards the other modes of utterance in which the Jesuits are alleged to have sinned, we find it laid to their charge (i) that 'in their Missions at Barbastro (a town in the north-east of Spain) they had said that the sceptre would soon depart from the House of Bourbon';[29] (2) that Padre Domingo Navarro, a Jesuit missionary in South America, had in an intercepted letter to his Provincial, Padre Vergara, dated 3 June 1767, 'hoped that there might either be a change of King, or that Señor Cevallos might be sent back to Buenos Ayres as Captain-General';[30] that at some date, not specified, Jesuit preachers at Murcia had spoken of a comet, then visible, as betokening the approaching death of the King; that elsewhere they had announced the near advent of Antichrist, and his descent from the

---

[29] Consulta of 30 November.
[30] Letter of Bucareli, then Governor of Buenos Ayres, to the Conde de Aranda, dated 16 September 1767. Given by Sr Ferrer del Río.

House of Bourbon. These are nearly all, and typical of all, the definite instances of disloyal speech which the various reports of the Fiscals and decrees of the Extraordinary Council cite in substantiation of their sweeping charges. Without further details it is impossible to pronounce on their justice, and the two instances where we do get a bit of further detail serve only to increase our suspicions of the rest. Thus it appears from the *Consulta* of 30 November 1767, that the remark about Antichrist coming from the House of Bourbon was made, not by a Jesuit, but by a secular priest who had come from the Philippines,[31] made too in August 1767, when the Jesuits were no longer in Spain. This man was a defender of the Jesuits, which was apparently the extent of their connexion with his remark about Antichrist. As for Padre Domingo Navarro's remark, of which we know only on the authority of an enemy like Bucareli, it was the simple truth that nothing short of what he stated would save the hitherto flourishing South American Missions, and the fact that he wrote it in a letter to such a saintly man as Padre Vergara[32] is a guarantee that there was nothing scandalous in the tone of the remark. We repeat it, however; we are not contending that no Jesuits made culpable remarks from the pulpit or in private channels of communication. We claim only that the few words which were made matter of accusation against them shall not be accepted as such without evidence, which is not forthcoming, and still more that they shall not be taken, as they were taken, as incriminating the entire Order. In an earlier section we showed how earnestly and in how loyal a spirit Padre Idiáquez had laboured to check even the smallest imprudences in speech, and Theiner[33] gives a letter addressed to the Nuncio at Madrid by Cardinal Torregiani, the Pope's Secretary of State, in which letter the Cardinal tells us of the repeated exhortations in the same sense which had been sent to his Spanish subjects by Padre Ricci, the General of the Society.

Our readers have now some means of judging how far the Spanish expulsion can be taken as decisive proof of the guilt of the Society, but they may feel an outstanding difficulty, and say, if the Spanish Jesuits were so innocent and so untouched by the researches of the Secret Inquiry, what inducement could a King like Carlos III or his Ministers have had for their severe measures?

Let the answer be given in the words of Sr Danvila:

---

[31] Danvila, iii. p. 65, 66.
[32] See his life in P. Peramas's *De vita et moribus sex virorum Paraguaycorum*.
[33] *Histoire du Pontificat du Clément XIV*. Tableau, sect. xxx.

The question whether the Society of Jesus participated in the rising at Madrid has been sufficiently discussed to permit of a definitive judgment. From the commencement some individuals belonging to the Institute were recognized as intervening in the tumult, and were punished in consequence by the Padre Provincial Idiáquez;[34] but this same Religious, who laid his vindication before the King and obtained a personal satisfaction, distinguished certainly between the fault and the responsibility of the entire body, and what was due to a few individuals for their personal acts. This also was the point of view discussed between Clement XIII and Carlos III, and although the former denied (the general responsibility), the Extraordinary Council of the latter could not, either then or afterwards, present any decisive proof that the rising at Madrid in 1766 was instigated or directed by the Society. The foreign nationality of the King's Ministers, and their bold attempt to attack the national dress and popular customs, was quite sufficient to produce the tumult, and impartiality forces us to acknowledge that the Jesuits must have been pleased to witness it,[35] seeing that the foreigners who had excited the people's indignation had declared a war to the knife against the Jesuits and all that they represented in the world of ideas, since the accession of Carlos III to the throne of Spain. The Jesuits, in the space of two centuries, aided by the protection of the Holy See, had extended their doctrine and its influence over the whole known world; education was in their hands, and with it the future of the youth of the country, the organization of the State, and even the conscience of the Kings. This network, which had been the characteristic of the ancient Spain, was incompatible with the Regalist absolutism of the Spanish monarchs, and still less with the reforming tendencies of the Encyclopaedist Ministers of Carlos III. The shock was bound to come, and did come on the collision of the two powerful forces. This is why the motives assigned for the expulsion were drawn chiefly from the ideas, the politics, and the spirit of the Society of Jesus. This is why the Spanish monarch reserved the causes of the expulsion in his royal breast. This is why we hold that the sole cause which produced it was an essential change of royal policy, a true Reason of State, such as on some occasions covers grave acts of injustice – for it must always be a grave injustice to charge a religious society with having conspired against the fundamental institutions of its country, and yet not be able to point out in any way the object and plan of so dark a conspiracy.

---

[34] We insert this sentence, as it is part of the passage quoted, but Sr Danvila is here the victim of a clerical error. Padre Idiáquez was not Provincial of Toledo (in which Province lay Madrid) but of Castile, and the misconduct of one of his subjects which is referred to consisted not in taking part in the rising, but in publishing some months later, a translation of one of the French Apologies for the Society, without having obtained permission from the Royal Censors. (See above, p. 88.)

[35] This hardly follows, nor is there evidence that it was so.

This, we submit, is the true explanation of the fall of the Society not merely in Spain, but in Portugal, and to a large extent in France too; and the explanation likewise, as will be seen, of the general suppression by Clement XIV. Divided out as the rule of mankind has been by God between the spiritual and temporal powers, whilst the very best results have followed when these two powers have worked together in harmony, history has seen them more often in conflict as to the borderline of their respective territories. In these conflicts it is the fashion to represent the Church as always the usurper, the civil power as always the much-enduring victim constrained at last to vindicate its just rights. Still an opposite view is at least intelligible, and perhaps nearer the truth, though it would be an error to suppose that either of the two powers has been consistently, in the right. We require, however, to notice chiefly, not the isolated cases of conflict, but the principles which each side embraced. By the eighteenth century the principles of those who exaggerated the rights of the Crown had become systematized, in which form they are known by the name of Regalism. Opposed to these were the principles maintained by the Holy See; and on each side there were not only statesmen to carry their system into practice, but lawyers and theologians to expound and champion it.

It was here that the Society of Jesus came in. By the law of her being she was – taking her as a whole – on the side of the Holy See. The direct rule, whether of states or churches, was never in her hands, but indirectly her influence was considerable, inasmuch as influential persons often used the spiritual advice of her confessors, or studied the works of her theologians, so many of whom were conspicuous for their advocacy of the Church's claims. Such was the character of the Society, as it existed in the second half of the eighteenth century; and, as at that time Regalist theories in their extreme form were tenaciously held by the Bourbon Sovereigns, who were prepared to enforce them with all the strength of their despotic power, and without much heed to the justice or injustice of their methods, it followed, by the logic of events, that the existence of the Jesuits should become critical. As Sr Danvila says, an old order in which the Church had been more or less free was passing away and a new one in which she was to be enslaved was coming in. A sharp encounter between the two forces was at hand, and the Society must be a chief sufferer from the shock.

It is with Spain that we are at present concerned, and there is plenty of evidence to show the extent to which Regalist principles prevailed in the Court of Carlos III. His Ministers were the more attracted to them, inasmuch as they were all more or less captivated by the opinions of Voltaire and his *confrères,* with whom, moreover, some of them were in regular correspondence. The King himself was unquestionably a devout Catholic, with a genuine reverence for the Holy See, and a genuine anxiety to act in all respects conscientiously. But he had also infirmities of character which, notwithstanding his strength of will, caused him to become a nose of wax in the hands of his chosen advisers. He had the Bourbon incapacity to tolerate any exercise of power which was not under his own control, and this was admirable material for receiving the impression of Regalist notions. Moreover, his intelligence was not of a high order, as his letters show, and he was incapable of independent judgments. He leant on the judgments of others, on which account it was the more unfortunate that he realized so little the importance of hearing both sides. It is not only his ecclesiastical policy which illustrates these defects. They are equally visible in the misguided action which provoked the Madrid Insurrection. A Sovereign of real intelligence would have perceived at once the consequences likely to follow from entrusting the principal posts in his Ministry and his Household to foreign place-hunters. But the latter had their personal interests to serve, and plied him with sophistical arguments, which he was powerless to see through, and too stubborn to abandon until taught by the stern experience of insurrection.

Among the various advisers on whom he leant Tanucci was the leading spirit, and may be justly called his evil genius. This man was originally a Professor of Jurisprudence at the University of Pisa, and had rendered Carlos III some service when he was as yet a young man, and establishing his sovereignty over the Neapolitan territory. It was this which first led to Tanucci's entering the King's service, and from that time he became his most trusted Minister and political educator. Carlos III simply took over his political opinions from Tanucci, and as the latter was a pronounced Regalist, and even, to use a modern word, anti-clerical, the result was that, in spite of his piety, the King himself caught the contagion. Even before Don Carlos left Naples he had been thus led into measures adverse to the Holy See, and, as regards the Society of Jesus, although in his external acts he showed himself a friend, and was believed by it to be such, he was in reality, as some of his letters show, even then strongly prejudiced against them.

When Carlos III passed to the throne of Spain, and abandoned that of Naples to his son Ferdinand, it was into Tanucci's hands that he left the guardianship of the latter's youth. Still, Tanucci's influence over Don Carlos did not cease. The correspondence thence ensuing is most instructive, and it is one of the valuable features of Sr Danvila's book that it has incorporated so much of it. It may be said that through these letters Tanucci dictated the policy of the reign, and what was to be its ecclesiastical policy is revealed in the following extracts. On 6 October 1761, Richard Wall, then in office at Madrid, writes to Tanucci that the separation of what belonged to dogma from what was matter of money or jurisdiction, was the principle with which they must keep the Court of Rome under control. That meant to say that all ecclesiastical appointments, and the free disposal of all benefices, appertained to the Crown, and was outside the competence of the Holy See. This limitation of the Church's rights was sufficiently sweeping, but it was not sweeping enough for Tanucci, who wrote back, on 13 October, that even Papal acts relating to dogma must be submitted to the King for his approval, as he is the head of the house. Consistently with this opinion of Tanucci's, Carlos III issued a Pragmatic Sanction on 20 November, forbidding the introduction of any Papal document into the country until it had first been submitted to the King for his approval and had obtained his *exequatur*. Then Tanucci, in a letter to the Duque de Losada, one of his party – who, as chamberlain, was in daily intercourse with Carlos III – expressed his pleasure at what had been done, but added a warning that the Court of Rome must be constantly watched, as it was always striving to usurp jurisdiction and get money. On 2 January 1762, Wall writes back, that the King is much pleased to know that Tanucci approves of what he has done in issuing the Pragmatic and insisting on the *exequatur,* and then, on 26 January, Tanucci replies by sounding a further note of anti-clericalism. 'The influence of the Royal confessors', he says, 'and especially of those who take a Fourth Vow to the Pope [i.e., of the Jesuits], ... have frustrated all useful projects, but have had the advantage of giving Spain a King who will make his reign remarkable by this (relating to the *exequatur*) and other useful measures for the good of the people.'

Here is sufficient evidence that under the guidance of Tanucci, Carlos III and his Ministers were set upon a campaign of anti-clericalism, in which the destruction, more or less complete, of the Society would hold a conspicuous place. The correspondence between Madrid and Naples in 1766 reveals to us how they came gradually to realize that the Madrid Insurrection afforded a pretext for such a measure, too handy to be missed. As Danvila puts it:[36]

> The correspondence of Tanucci with the Ministers of the King of Spain in 1766 is a mirror in which is reflected all that was thought or done in

[36] Op. cit. iii, 16.

Madrid against the Jesuits, and no one can doubt but that the idea of the expulsion, the form in which it was carried out, even to the confiscation of all their goods, took birth in the brain of the Freethinker who, for the space of a quarter of a century, had conducted the political education of Carlos III.

It is on the following facts that Sr Danvila relies for this judgment.

In the first instance Aranda, as we know from his Report of 9 April 1766, had no thought of connecting the ecclesiastics with the Insurrection. This is the more important as his chief lieutenant, the *corregidor* of Madrid, had been able, in conducting his investigation into the causes of the rising, to secure the services of three of the leading rioters; and yet in the secret correspondence which this *corregidor* had with the Ministers, during the first six weeks after the rising, there is not a single suggestion adverse to the Jesuits or other clergy. But on 6 May Tanucci, who till then in his letters had merely inveighed against 'the stupid populace', writes to the King 'that the more he thinks of the ingratitude of the people, the more he is persuaded that it is due to bad education and the suggestions of the ecclesiastics.' On 13 May, in a letter to Catanti, one of the Neapolitan envoys, he translates this conjecture into a categorical statement. 'The ecclesiastics,' he says, 'and certain Ministers who were offended at the restrictions set by his Majesty on their robberies [he means Ensenada] had applied the spark to the popular fury.' On 20 May he writes to the Principe de la Cattolica, the Neapolitan Minister at Madrid, 'that the populace would never be submissive and quiet until the King had begun to expurgate the friars, there being no doubt that it was their influence which had stimulated this sedition,' and on 20 June, he writes again to Losada that 'he is persuaded that the ecclesiastics were the secret authors of the disturbance.' It is surely not mere coincidence that at this stage the Extraordinary Council issued its second *Consulta,* that of 8 June, in which nothing is as yet said of the Jesuits, but the people are vaguely said to have been stirred up by the ecclesiastics.

On 1 July Tanucci begins to speak more definitely about the Jesuits, and writes to another envoy, Centomani, that the anonymous satires against the King were evidently a Jesuit poison, and that 'such a fact of itself alone should suffice to make a Sovereign expel the Jesuits from his dominions'. On 9 August he writes to Azara, the Spanish agent at Rome, 'that he is convinced the sedition originated with the ministers of the Church,' and that 'the King had a natural right to expel the Jesuits from his kingdom;' and on 15 August, again writing to Azara, he tells him that 'the Jesuits are always the same, being everywhere seditious, hostile to monarchs and nationalities, public robbers, full of vices, and mostly atheists,' and 'he wonders why the King allows the College at Loyola still to stand.' And yet that in making these confident imputations he has no ascertained facts to rest upon, is clear from his letter to Losada on 29 August, in which he tells him that 'if they (the King and his Ministers) have not yet discovered the authors of the tumult they never will.' Nonetheless, on 2 September he formally suggests the expulsion, whilst expressing his fears lest the King should find his Ministers without the needful courage to carry it out on the same grand scale as in Portugal and France. He did not realize, it seems, what apt pupils of his teachings he had got in the Ministers of Carlos III, whose Extraordinary Council on 22 September, following out the lines of his suggestions, though, as we have seen, they had certainly not proved anything against the Society, were able to discern its impulse 'working throughout all the branches of the vast and complicated episode.'[37]

Meanwhile, Tanucci still continued developing his malign suggestions to his docile correspondents. On 14 October, he writes to Losada that the purging of the country from the Jesuits should be thought out with much care as, 'once resolved on, it should be carried out thoroughly, and at one and the same moment throughout the kingdom,' whilst on 9 December he tells the King, through the same correspondent, that his desire would be that the Jesuits should be cleared out of Madrid before the King returned thence, and be expelled from Spain altogether at the earliest date possible, ... that their property should be confiscated and a sum of one hundred ducats given to each for his subsistence.' And these were just the further details of the expulsion in which the *Consulta* of 29 January 1767, went beyond the indefinite *Consulta* of 22 September 1766.

Here then we may end our account of the Spanish Suppression, for the reader now knows how much evidence the King's Ministers had on which to convict the Jesuits of the imputed crimes, and knows also what motives, apart from a demonstration of guilt, they had for desiring the Suppression of the Society.

---

[37] See above p. 105.

Chapter Four

The Harassing of Clement XIII

I.[1] [The build-up of pressure by the Courts]

The expulsion of the Jesuits from Spain was quickly followed by their expulsion from the Kingdom of the Two Sicilies and from the Duchy of Parma. It was inevitable that this should be; for King Ferdinand of Naples was, as we have seen, the youthful son of Carlos III of Spain, and Duke Ferdinand of Parma was his youthful nephew. The King of Spain, in fact, treated these two young Sovereigns as his feudatories, and regulated their policy in all respects – a practice which it was the more easy for him to pursue, as they looked up to him as the protector of their weakness, and besides were bound to him by their accession to the Family Compact.[2] Moreover, Tanucci, the statesman by whom Carlos III was so entirely dominated, was the all-powerful Minister at Naples, and Dutillot, Marchese de Felino, another statesman of Regalist and Voltairian sympathies, was all-powerful at Parma.

We know from the correspondence of Carlos III and his Ministers with Tanucci, from which Sr Danvila quotes extensively, that no distinct offence was ever alleged as having been committed by the Neapolitan Jesuits. Their one offence was that they belonged to the same Order as their brethren in Spain, and must therefore have the

---

[1] *The Month*, **100** (1902), 258–73.
[2] The Family Compact was a secret agreement made on 15 August 1761, between France and Spain, who afterwards admitted into it the Sovereigns of Naples and Parma. By it these Bourbon princes bound themselves to act together, and support one another in all matters of foreign policy. The end they had originally in view was to counteract and destroy the influence of England in the Mediterranean and on the American Continent, but in that respect it proved a failure, chiefly because of the vigilance of the Earl of Bristol, then British Minister at Madrid, who discovered it at once and denounced it. Thus its one success, if such it is to be termed, was in uniting these Bourbon princes in their campaign against the Society.

same antipathy for their Bourbon King, whose life, his father assured him, was not safe as long as they were near his person. It is to the credit of the boy-King that in the first instance he resisted the proposition that he should expel so cruelly 'the Religious who had taught him his first lessons of Catholic Faith, and were so much venerated by his people.' Nor can we blame him,[3] if at his tender age he yielded eventually to the assurances and exhortations of his father, of his Minister, Tanucci, and of his confessor, the Bishop Latila. The expulsion was carried out in the Neapolitan dominions on 3 November 1767, the same course being followed as in Spain; and the condemned Religious were conducted across the Papal frontiers; and threatened with a death sentence if they should venture to return.

Under any circumstances we may be sure the Duke of Parma, like the King of Naples, would have been ordered by his relative, Carlos III, to expel the Jesuits from his dominions. But as it happened, their case there was complicated by the quarrel between the Duke and the Holy See over a series of anti-Papal decrees which, under the influence of Felino, the young Duke had been publishing during the previous four years. The Pope during that time had been engaged in remonstrances and negotiations, and to these some pretence of yielding had been shown; but on 16 January 1768, a fresh edict had been unexpectedly published, which Clement XIII described as 'filled with outrages and calumnies, and with a pernicious doctrine of schismatic tendency which sought to separate the faithful from the Head of the Church, the sheep from their pastors; and has resulted in oppressing the ecclesiastic jurisdiction, overturning the hierarchy, diminishing the rights and prerogatives of the Holy See, and subjecting his authority to the civil power, and reducing to a state of servitude the Church of God which is free.'

These words are from the *Monitorium* which Clement XIII issued on 30 January 1768, and in which, 'relying on the decrees of General Councils and on the dispositions of the Sacred Canons against the violators of ecclesiastical liberty,' he declares the Duke's anti-Papal Legislation to be by the provisions of the said Councils and Canons null and void, and its author involved in their censures. It was the

---

[3] Ferdinand IV lived to discover how he had been misled, and, in 1804, when he was restored to his throne, solicited from Pius VII permission for the Society, then restored only for the Russian Empire, to return to his kingdom of Naples, promising to give them back as much of their former possessions as was still in his hands. [Relying on verbal permission from Pius VII the English Jesuit Province was refounded in 1803, even if this was not recognized by the Vicars Apostolic until much later: cf. T. M. McCoog, S.J., *'Promising Hope'*, 2003, pp. 274–279. *Ed. N.*]

kind of decree in protection of the spiritual domain by which a Pope might have responded to similar legislation in any other country, but the Duchy of Parma had been constituted a fief of the Holy See by Paul III.[4] The Holy See held this relation of subjection to be still subsisting, on which account, in his *Monitorium* Clement XIII spoke of the Duke's dominions as 'our Duchy of Parma and Piacenza'. On the other hand, this implied claim to suzerainty made the *Monitorium* doubly obnoxious to the Bourbon Courts, whose aid and support the Duke at once sought. They readily responded, and on 16 April next following, presented to the Holy Father, through the Spanish Ambassador, Mgr Azpuru, a joint memorial in which they demanded the revocation of the Brief and a solemn reparation to be made to the outraged Duke, threatening that if this were refused they would not hesitate to make reprisals – France annexing to her sovereignty the Papal possessions around Avignon (which had belonged to the Holy See since 1348, when they were purchased from the Countess of Provence), and Naples annexing the Duchy of Benevento (a district on the southern confines of the Ecclesiastical States, which the Roman Church had possessed since 1052, when it was given to it by the Emperor Henry III). Clement's reply was, as might have been expected, that if they chose to lay violent hands on the sacred territory of the Holy See he should offer no forcible resistance, but that no such aggression should induce him to swerve from the path of duty and fidelity in vindicating the Church's rights. The threat was accordingly carried out in that same year, but meanwhile a more prompt response to the *Monitorium* was made by the Duke of Parma, in deporting the Jesuits from his dominions into those of the Holy See, which he did on 5 February, following the same plan as had been set him by Madrid and Naples. The Jesuits had had nothing to

---

[4] The Duchies of Parma and Piacenza had been originally part of the Exarchate of Ravenna, along with which they passed into possession of the Popes in 590. During the intervening time they were governed by Cardinal Legates, but Paul III, who was of the Farnese family, constituted them into a fief of the Holy See, and gave them to his son Antonio, born before he entered the ecclesiastical state. By the terms of this gift they were to pass in succession to the heirs male of Duke Antonio, who was to pay the Holy See a yearly tribute of nine thousand crowns. The male line of the Farnese lapsed with Duke Antonio, the grandfather of Carlos III, and he himself then claimed the Duchies by right of his mother, Elizabeth Farnese. This right was recognized by the Treaty of Aix-la-Chapelle in 1748, and Don Carlos actually held the Dukedom till he became King of Naples, when he passed it on, according to the terms of that treaty, to his brother, Don Philip, the father of Duke Ferdinand. The Holy See never recognized this provision of the Treaty of Aix-la-Chapelle, and every year, on the vigil of SS. Peter and Paul, protested against the violation of its right.

do with the issue of the *Monitorium,* nor was anything else laid to their charge, but Felino was glad to have so easy an opportunity of retaliation on the Holy See.

The Jesuits thus expelled from Naples numbered about one hundred and eighty, and those expelled from Parma about the same. To these must be added a small number driven out of the island of Malta, on 22 April 1768, by the Grand Master, acting under the commands of Ferdinand IV of Naples, of whose sovereignty the island was a fief. These numbers, though serious enough in themselves, were small by the side of the five thousand expelled from Spain and the Spanish colonies, or the two thousand expelled eight years previously from the Portuguese dominions. But meanwhile, the Spanish expulsion had also had its effect in France, where the enemies of the Society represented it as due to the honour of their country, that it should not be outdone in the severity of its measures by a neighbouring kingdom. Accordingly, the Abbé Chauvelin, on 9 May 1767, obtained the registration of an *arrêt,* requiring that all Jesuits who had not taken the prescribed oath – which involved a sacrilegious repudiation of their vows and a mendacious admission of the justice of their condemnation – should quit the country forthwith. An *arrêt* to the same effect, it will be remembered, had been passed by the *Parlement* on 9 March 1764, but its harshness had been tempered by the Royal Edict of November 1764, in which, whilst suppressing the corporate existence of the Society within his dominions, Louis XV had allowed the individuals to remain under the jurisdiction of the Bishops, and had provided them with a maintenance. Now, however, the King gave in to the *Parlement* and another five thousand or more members of the proscribed Order were compelled to tread the paths of exile.

Such, then, was the situation created within the space of eight short years by the despotic action of Royal authority, whilst wielded by Regalist and Encyclopaedist Ministers in Portugal, France, and Spain, and the dependent States of Naples and Parma. A Religious Order of men who had given their lives to the work of God under a rule approved and recommended in the Catholic Church, one which had existed for a century and a half in each of the five countries named, and had during that long period rendered services spiritual and educational which had been conspicuously and widely appreciated alike by sovereigns and subjects, is suddenly declared to be, and to have been throughout, so pernicious in its principles that no civilized rulers ought to tolerate its existence in their dominion. The accused are nowhere put on their trial, or allowed a hearing of any kind in their defence, whilst in one country the very nature of their supposed offence is concealed both from them and from the public, and in another it is inferred from books and formularies which had been known all along to Bishops and statesmen, without ever having been taken in the sense now assigned to them. In one country their Constitutions are declared to be holy, but the conduct of the present generation in conflict with them; in another the conduct of 'almost all' the individuals is declared to be blameless, but their Constitutions immoral; whilst in a third 'most of its members are declared to be innocent and upright men', but the central government to be seditious. Yet all, without discrimination, to the number of some twelve thousand, are turned out of their homes, robbed of their possessions, even of the fruits of their own pens, and deported into foreign lands, the Portuguese without the provision of any means of subsistence at all, the rest with a precarious promise of a scanty dole. And finally the large majority of these exiles were crowded together on the confined Papal territory, giving edification everywhere by the manner of their lives, but causing a great economic difficulty, the solution of which was hard to discover. It was an appalling spectacle, but even yet the fury of their persecutors was not satiated.

We have now to investigate the history and causes of the suppression by Papal authority, and must begin by redirecting attention to the standpoint from which it should be studied. Eventually we shall have to examine the character of the Brief of Suppression itself, and to consider how far its language amounts to a condemnation of the Society, or is consistent with belief in its innocence. But our previous task must be to gather from the antecedent and surrounding conditions how far the author of the Brief was moved to issue it by his own unfettered judgment on facts duly authenticated, or was merely yielding to force applied by the Bourbon Courts, who created for him the necessity of either suppressing the Society or permitting a still graver evil to befall the Church. The importance of this question is manifest if all that the Powers did was to lay before the Holy See a full and complete array of the evidence that had dictated their own action against the Society, and to exhort him to have it impartially and searchingly examined, in an inquiry to terminate in a solemn and unfettered Papal judgment – then, if the result had been a judgment confirmatory of the proposal of the five Courts, the moral value of that judgment would have been immense, nor could the reputation of the Society have easily recovered from the stigma. It would then have mattered little whether it were suppressed by a formal decree or left to itself, for even if left to itself it must speedily have lost its hold on the sympathies of good men, and must have ceased to attract into its ranks the devotedness of generous hearts. On the other hand, if the action of the Courts took the form of coercing the Holy See; if instead of supplying it with the motives on which they had themselves relied, they sought rather to conceal from it their true motives for wishing the suppression, and palmed off upon it an array of motives confessedly trumped up for the purpose; if instead of trusting to its free and unfettered judgment they consciously and intentionally strove to force it into suppressing the Society, without regard to its own judgment and solely in deference to their demands; and if to attain this end they did not hesitate to employ threats of an armed invasion of the Pontifical territories, of schisms to be forced upon their own subjects, and other assaults on the spiritual liberties of the Church – then, especially if the Brief of Suppression should show a tendency to avoid rather than to employ the language of condemnation, though it was still a valid exercise of Papal authority to which obedience was due, it ceases to have any moral value as a judgment on the Society's conduct, and leaves the reputation of the latter just where it was. Such is the aspect under which it will be necessary to study the history to which we now pass.

After having banished the Society from their own possessions it was to be expected that the five Sovereigns should wish to see the work of destruction completed, and, as this could only be accomplished through a Papal Suppression, that they should begin to work for that end. It is noteworthy, however, that long before the Spanish expulsion the idea of a general Suppression had been entertained by some of the Ministers to whom Carlos III gave his confidence. Thus, on 14 April 1762 – that is, at the time when the *Parlement* of Paris was in the midst of its campaign against the French Jesuits, and had turned them out of their houses – Tanucci wrote to the notorious Voltairian Abbé Galliani, saying: 'It will be necessary either to extinguish entirely this Order of Jesus, or else caress those gentlemen very effusively; for, if the Order is not extinguished, it will grow stronger every day, since misfortune teaches people to reflect and to increase their vigilance.' Moreover, he and Richard Wall were in correspondence on the subject as early as 1761, as Sr Danvila proves by his citations from their letters. And if these two minds were occupied by the idea, it might be presumed that they would seek to instil it into the mind of a King who attached so much importance to their views.

Still, these earlier exchanges of opinion kept within the sphere of desires and aims. The first indication of a serious intention to realize the idea of a Papal Suppression is, so far as we are aware, in a letter of the Duc de Choiseul's, written on 21 April 1767[5] – that is to say,

---

[5] Danvila, *Reinado de Carlos III*, iii. p. 234.

three weeks after the date of the Spanish expulsion. It is addressed to the Duc d'Aubeterre, the French Ambassador to the Holy See, and says that, 'If the Pope is wise, unbiased, and firm, he will be able of his own accord to take the course of completely dissolving the Society by a Bull, so that it may cease to have any existence whatever.' He is sure, indeed, that the Pope will not act thus, nor will Torregiani let him, as he gets money from the Jesuits, but 'if he (the Pope) had but one single political idea in his head, he would see that, for the glory and interest of the Holy See, the abolition of the Society is necessary, and that, as long as the Sovereigns send their Jesuit subjects to Rome, and the Pope supports them there, the cause of these Religious will be identified with that of the Court of Rome.' Choiseul goes on to authorize d'Aubeterre to speak to the Pope in this sense, that he may at least be made aware that France is far-seeing enough to anticipate the evils likely to result if the Pope declines this course. And yet in another letter, dated 30 May,[6] this same statesman lets us see clearly, that if he sought for the suppression of the Jesuits it was not because he believed them guilty of the crimes imputed to them. 'It is most desirable,' he writes to d'Aubeterre, 'for the sake of the Jesuits themselves, that they should all without exception be secularized. I do not inquire whether the charges brought against their doctrines and morals are well founded or not, but I know that an almost universally prevailing opinion and an established truth come to almost the same thing so far as regards the effect they produce. Thus these Religious, united in a Society, will always appear suspect and dangerous, whereas, if restored to the secular state, they might exercise their talents and virtues with advantage to themselves and the public.'

Meanwhile, on 27 May 1767, d'Aubeterre wrote[7] back re-echoing the sentiments of his chief, and agreeing that to suppress the entire Society was the only prudent course for the Pope to take, but they must not flatter themselves they would bring him to see it, surrounded as he was by persons much opposed to the idea, who put scruples into his head which he could not solve. He says M. Rezzonico (apparently not the Cardinal) had urged the idea on the Pope several times, but he had always been badly received. To this letter Choiseul replied on 1 June,[8] suggesting that Torregiani should be gained over to the side of the Courts by means of a bribe, and authorizing d'Aubeterre to go to the sum of one hundred thousand

---

[6] Theiner, *Pontificat de Clément XIV*, i.110.
[7] *Ibid.*
[8] Danvila, p. 237.

crowns. And on 8 July,[9] d'Aubeterre wrote back that Torregiani has a private secretary, named the Abbate Fantini, and a chamberlain named Benedetti, but that they are both fanatical adherents of the Jesuits, and he cannot manage to suborn either of them. In other words, money was of no avail to gain over Torregiani. D'Aubeterre then opines that if the Pope is to he induced to decree the Suppression, it must be by threats; it is now for the first time that we hear of the brutal proposal which was eventually carried out. D'Aubeterre's suggestion is that, as the Pope will not otherwise secularize the Jesuits, it would be best for France to occupy the Comtat of Avignon, which might be done on the plea that it was bad policy to allow so small a State to exist in the midst of a large one, whose tranquillity it disturbed by harbouring its enemies, the Jesuits. When the King had occupied the territory, he might send the Pope three or four millions of Crowns out of which he would be able to pay his debts.

In this way France appears to have taken the initiative, but Spain soon began to move. On 19 June, Carlos III wrote to Louis XV,[10] 'I think it would be most useful if the Pope would be willing to dissolve the Society entirely,' and he then proposes that France and Spain should concert plans together – as the scheme would encounter much opposition at Rome. Louis XV wrote back a month later (19 July) quite falling in with his Royal cousin's proposal. And Carlos III had already taken action, for on 20 June 1767,[11] Tanucci wrote to Azara, telling him that he had Grimaldi's orders for Azpuru and Azara to act under him in starting negotiations for a Papal Suppression; he then impresses on them the necessity of keeping the matter a dead secret, lest the Jesuits should come to hear of it and intrigue to prevent it. Another letter, written by Roda to Tanucci on 4 August,[12] explains to us what kind of intrigues on the part of the Jesuits were to be feared. The Jesuits' usual method, he says, is to get what is disagreeable to them deferred. 'They are friends of time, with the aid of which they have successfully passed through many difficulties and dangers. All the policy of Torregiani has been of this kind. He has, through the Nuncio, asked to have sent to the Pope a statement of the offences committed by the Jesuits in Spain, promising that if it comes His Holiness will take measures which should be satisfactory to the King, and would correct the vices and defects of the Jesuits. But,' says Roda, 'if the King had listened to this proposal, they would have

[9] *Ibid.* p. 243.
[10] *Ibid.* p. 239.
[11] *Ibid.* p. 240.
[12] *Ibid.* p. 246.

made sport of him.' Apparently by this last phrase Don Roda meant that they would defeat his Majesty's object, which was to extort the Suppression; and that is not unlikely, for the Holy Father would at once have referred the statement sent to him to a proper court of inquiry; nor would such a course, even though it had occasioned some delay, have been unreasonable under the circumstances. But Don Roda's letter is valuable evidence just because it shows so clearly that the endeavour of the Powers was not to procure that justice should be done, but that their own wishes should be enforced without reference to their justice or injustice.

One more letter belonging to this period must be cited as evidencing the spirit in which the rulers of Spain thought it proper to treat the Holy See. On 9 September 1767, d'Aubeterre, writing to Choiseul,[13] tells him that the Spanish agents have been making researches into the history of the two States of Castro and Ronciglione, which were anciently dependencies of the Duchy of Parma. It has been explained above under what tenure the Duchy of Parma was originally granted by Paul III to the Farnese family. The Duchies of Castro and Ronciglione had been included in that grant, but having become involved in debt by the misgovernment of the Dukes, they were taken back by the Holy See in the days of Duke Ranuccio II, in 1649. There was indeed a right of redemption within the space of eight years preserved to the Dukes, but as the redemption money was never offered till the eight years were up or even afterwards, the right accruing to the Holy See from its purchase became absolute, and had not been disputed since. What d'Aubeterre's allusion means is that the Spanish Ministers were excogitating a pretext of coercing the Pope by a threat that the Duke of Parma would otherwise claim the restoration of those two Duchies. As the territory involved had its frontiers not more than thirty miles from the city of Rome, such a claim would have been as harassing to the Popes as it would have been unscrupulous in the aggressors. And this idea of aggression, be it remarked, was conceived several months before the issue of the *Monitorium*.

Portugal was also beginning to work for the same end, though, having broken off relations with the Holy See for some years, it was only possible for her to act through the other Powers. A letter, dated 14 July 1767,[14] from M. de Semonis, the French Minister at Lisbon, informs Choiseul of the policy which d'Oeyras (i.e. Pombal) wished to see adopted. De Semonis had had a conversation with him, and

---

[13] Theiner, *Ibid*. p. 121.
[14] Danvila, *Ibid*. p. 245.

reports that he desired an accord between France, Spain, and Portugal, in demanding the abolition of the Society and the substitution of another Secretary of State in place of Torregiani, and proposed that the Pope should be told that if he refused these demands, the three Powers would convoke a General Council, in arranging for which they would address their communications, not to Clement XIII, but to the Holy See – that is, they were to depose Clement XIII. The more polished Frenchman did not take to d'Oeyras's brutal methods, and replied that the affair was one of great delicacy, and, as the reigning Pope was so aged, it might be better for Portugal to have recourse to a National Council for the determination of occurrent ecclesiastical questions, and hope that the next Pope would prove more satisfactory. To this d'Oeyras objected that he had no trust in the Bishops of his country – an interesting admission that his measures were disapproved of.

These citations prove plainly enough that at that early date after the Spanish expulsion the three Courts were bent on obtaining a Papal Suppression, and that it was by the force of their threats rather than of their proofs that they hoped to get the Pope to comply with their desires. But with the autumn of 1767, their campaign entered on a new stage, and produced documents which afford us a further insight into the character of their strategy. On 23 September Don Aires de la Mello, the Portuguese Minister at Madrid, made a formal communication to Grimaldi, at the time Minister of Foreign Affairs at Madrid, assuring him that his Faithful Majesty felt the importance of their working together in their endeavour to obtain a Papal Suppression, and proposing a plan of action. This plan of action was explained in a despatch from d'Oeyras to Aires de la Mello, in which it is described as being that which the Portuguese Procurator General had recommended. A copy of the despatch was communicated to Grimaldi by Aires de la Mello along with his own covering letter.

The despatch had two parts, of which the first formulated the reasons[15] which should constrain the Courts to apply for a Papal Suppression. These reasons were four in number: (1) the disquietude caused by the Society in the kingdoms entrusted to the charge of the three Powers; (2) the despotism it exercised over the Curia, whilst it barred the access to the Holy Father of those who would give him sound advice and information; (3) the shocking principles of the Society in regard to Tyrannicide, so incompatible with the security of the lives of Royal personages, and the singular skill it showed in hallucinating ill-instructed persons, and converting them into

---

[15] Danvila, iii. Apendix. Doc. 117, p. 638.

The Harassing of Clement XIII 143

adherents and instruments; (4) the favourable opportunity for common action then offered to the Powers who were at peace with one another.

The second part of the despatch discusses the best method of dealing with the Holy See. It shows some advance on the crude plans broached by d'Oeyras to de Semonis three months previously, but still bears the stamp of its author's brutality. Three plans are proposed, of which the first is for the Powers to withdraw their Ambassadors from Rome, to forbid their subjects all intercourse with the Holy See, and in this manner to cut off the pecuniary supplies on which the Holy See depended. It was the plan which Portugal had been following since 1759, and amounted to a state of schism. Pombal probably did not object much to that, but he had come to realize that the withdrawal of Almada from the Vatican cut both ways. Hence he now decides against the first proposition on the ground that it deprives the Pope of the one means he had of obtaining sound information and advice.

The second proposition of the despatch was that a General Council should be summoned by the three Sovereigns, who in so doing would be supported by the examples of Theodosius, Otho, Louis of Bavaria, and others. This is what d'Oeyras had suggested to Choiseul through M. de Semonis, but reflection had apparently convinced him that it might have an effect quite contrary to his wishes. Hence he now decides against the proposition on the ground that it would involve too long delays, and besides would be unsuitable, as the suppression of a Religious Order was a matter not for a General Council, but for the Pope, who should be ready to decree it even on less grounds than were afforded by three powerful Sovereigns each declaring the Society to be a danger to the security of his Royal person, his kingdom, and his subjects.

If, however, the Pope refused to yield to these reasonable considerations, there remained only the 'way of fact' (*via facti*), which was the third proposition of the despatch. War must be declared against the Pope as a temporal prince, and his territories invaded. This had been done on former occasions, and theologians like Melchior Cano had maintained its lawfulness. The *casus belli* would be that the Pope was allowing the General of the Jesuits and his colleagues to use the Pontifical territory as a basis for their machinations against the complaining Sovereigns, and he should be told that, by invading his States to put a stop to the evil they were not failing in respect to his august dignity, but merely recalling him to the observance of his duty.

Carlos III referred these propositions from Lisbon to his extraordinary Council on 18 October, and the Council received and adopted the report of its Fiscals, Campomanes and Moñino, on 30 November, in a *Consulta,* which is the longest and most elaborate of those published by Danvila.

The Fiscals thoroughly fell in with the idea of a combined movement on the part of the three Crowns, in advising which they followed the same main divisions as d'Oeyras, giving reasons for demanding a Papal Suppression and proposals as to the means by which it should be extorted from the Pope. In giving these reasons, they make what we must take to be a compromising admission. They say, 'It is to be supposed that many of the causes which have obliged the three Sovereigns to expel the members of that Society from their dominions will have no cogency whatever at Rome,' and they enumerate the following as instances – that the Jesuits have stirred up discords on ecclesiastical questions with the object of disputing the native authority of the Bishops; have disturbed the cloisters of nuns, with the object of withdrawing them from the obedience of their religious Superiors; have invaded and usurped sovereignties (they mean, in the colonies) with the object of accumulating riches to aid them in withstanding their own Princes; have accumulated privileges with the object of making themselves independent in all States; have contrived plots with the object of establishing their domination over civil Governments; have introduced new devotions with the object of alienating the faithful from their active pastors; have maintained the indirect temporal power of the Pope over Kings and his right to depose them, to absolve subjects from their allegiance, and to authorize other Sovereigns to invade their territories; and have derived from this supposed power of the Pope over Kings their pernicious doctrine of Tyrannicide. All these Jesuit methods and principles, the Fiscals urge, are viewed with favour by the Curia, and they name particularly the case of the Indirect Temporal Sovereignty which, they allege, was employed at the instigation of the Jesuits against James I of England by Paul V, against French Sovereigns by other Popes, and is even tolerated by the present Pontifical Government, notwithstanding the assassination of the King of Portugal and the recent tumults in Spain, both of which were excited by the Jesuits, and yet have not aroused the indignation of the Holy See against them. From all which the Fiscals conclude that these Jesuit principles, though abominated by every political Government and responsible for so many disturbances and so much bloodshed throughout Christendom, are viewed with only too much approval by the people who surround the Pope; and that the Sovereigns must in consequence, look not to him, but to themselves, to root out all these crying abuses.

There are those, no doubt, who will readily take this severe indictment for unvarnished truth, but saner minds will reflect that a Pope's counsellors are not always or of necessity irredeemable villains, and will conclude that the *Consulta* is only giving a highly-coloured *ex parte* representation of matters possibly susceptible of a much more innocent interpretation. Particularly may they conclude thus, if they recollect the terms of praise in which the moral influence of the Society was appreciated in that very decade by the French Bishops in their Assemblies, and by so many other Bishops from various countries, Spain included, before and after the publication of the *Apostolicum*; when, too, they note, on the other hand, how distrustful d'Oeyras felt as to the possible verdict of a General Council. Another conclusion, to which this *Consulta* points, bears still more closely on the subject of the present chapter. Seeing, the Fiscals contend, that the Pope and his Curia are in sympathy with the teaching and practice of the Jesuits, the Sovereigns must rely, not on him, but on themselves for the removal of such abominable abuses. In other words, the Fiscals and the Extraordinary Council here make a formal acknowledgment that they have no intention of letting the Jesuit question be judged by the Pope, but mean to coerce him into lending his spiritual authority to execute what they themselves have decided.

Let us now return to the text of the *Consulta* of 30 November. Having concluded that the Sovereigns must themselves deal with the Jesuit question, it sets down five reasons as requiring them to force on a total Suppression. These are (1) the unity in action of the Jesuit body, which in all parts holds the same language and evinces the same propensities; (2) their impenitence and obstinacy, evidenced by persistence in courses once taken up; (3) their incorrigibility; (4) their hopes of returning to the countries from which they have been expelled, which keep alive the dissensions between their friends and foes; (5) the favourable nature of the present opportunity, when the Courts are united and their people have had recent experience of the harm the Jesuits can do. We need not dwell on these reasons, which offer nothing fresh for our consideration, and can pass at once to the practical means for obtaining the Suppression which the Fiscals recommend.

First, they agree with the Court of Lisbon, in rejecting the idea of a General Council. There are, they say, so many Cardinals and Bishops under Jesuit influence, and these would be able to control a General Council; moreover, a General Council could not extinguish the Society without having first instituted a formal process of inquiry into its conduct, and such a process would be dangerous (apparently because it would probably end in a verdict of acquittal). Secondly, they reject also the idea of National or Provincial Councils, because these also might terminate undesirably, as happened over the question of the dissolution of the Templars, when the National Councils in England and Spain reported in their favour.

Having rejected these two proposals, they next make three positive suggestions. Although Local Councils are undesirable, they think it would be an excellent thing if the Kings of Spain and Portugal would order the Bishops of their respective kingdoms to address to the Pope united solicitations for the extinction of the Society, as being prejudicial to their own authority and the public tranquillity. And it is naïvely suggested that each Bishop could thus make his own reflections separately (on the probable consequences to himself if he resisted the royal order?), and the danger would be obviated of allowing them to talk the matter over in common. Secondly, they recommend that some men of learning and reputation should be set to write treatises in exposition and approval of the motives for the Suppression, and that the Governments should provide them with facts suited to this purpose. Thirdly, they recommend that the endeavour should be made to induce as many as possible of the other Sovereigns to lend their influence. They anticipate that the Holy See could not possibly stand out against so universal a demand, but they foresee that in many countries the Bishops will use their influence to dissuade their Sovereigns from so acting. They suggest, however, that the Sovereigns should be told that their active interposition was not required, only their passive support, and that they should be allured by a reminder of the large sums of money applicable to pious purposes which the confiscation of the Jesuit possessions might place in their hands. Fourthly, they consider the Portuguese proposal to resort to the 'way of fact'. This they reject as inadvisable, as it might stir up an Italian war, as it would be undignified for three great Sovereigns to wage war on the ruler of a petty sovereignty like the Pope's, as it would scandalize their subjects to see them marching armies against the Father of the Faithful; and finally, because it did not seem needful, in view of Clement XIII's advanced age. It would be better, they say, to await his death, and then impress upon the Cardinals the risk they would run by electing a new Pope who would not consent in good faith to the extinction of the Society.

The *Consulta* also reports on two more points which, though not expressly contained in the Portuguese despatch, were being considered by the Courts at the time. One was that the Pope should be called upon to punish the heads of the Society as being chiefly responsible for the abuses which required its suppression. The Fiscals withdraw their subjects from his communion. We have now [contin]inue this scandalous history.

[On 3] December 1767, Cardinal Torregiani wrote to Mgr Luciani,[17] [who h]ad succeeded Mgr Pallavicini as Nuncio at Madrid, directing [him to] protest on the part of the Holy Father against the sudden [deport]ation of the Sicilian Jesuits into his territory, which had been [carrie]d out without any previous intimation, and which he called ['calcu]lating on the Holy Father's humanity'. Luciani wrote back on [21 D]ecember. He had had an audience with Grimaldi, who told him [that t]he Court of Naples had 'for a long time back' been resolved that [they] would tolerate the Jesuits in their midst no longer. Grimaldi then [made] this important statement, which forms another decisive proof [that] their intention was not to invoke the Pope's judgment, but to [for]ce his action. 'Monsignore,' he said, 'the fire is now lighted; the [Cath]olic Courts have made the Suppression of the Society their *mot [d'or]dre*, and if the Holy Father does not accede to this, tell your [Cou]rt further steps will be taken, and that the loss of several of the [Pon]tifical possessions is inevitable. But if His Holiness consents to [sati]sfy the Catholic Courts by suppressing the Society, he will [reco]ver what he has already lost and will avert new disasters. [Ot]herwise I fear lest what the Courts now use as a means will in [fu]ture be enforced as a principle.' Luciani further tells us that either [on] the same or another occasion, the Portuguese Minister at Madrid [as]sured him that 'his King was ready to restore relations with the [H]oly See to their former state' – that is to say, to put a stop to the [sc]hism in which the King of Portugal had then involved his country – [i]f the Pope would only consent to suppress the Society.' The assur[a]nce was given in Grimaldi's presence, who remarked that 'it was a [s]trange thing for the Pope to sacrifice to his blind predilection for [t]hese Religious the sacred interests of religion in such a country as Portugal.'

On 26 January 1768, Luciani[18] in another despatch mentions discovery of two ancient consultations on the lawfulness of a Catholic prince making war on the Pope, one being by Melchior Cano, the other by a Jesuit Father attached to the Imperial College at Madrid, who had been consulted on the subject by Louis XIV of France, then engaged in a quarrel with Innocent XI.[19] The Minister caused the text of these two consultations to be published, to which Luciani referring

---

[17] Theiner, op. cit. i. p. 107.
[18] *Ibid.* p. 121.
[19] We have not been able to discover the name of this Jesuit Father, but Luciani felt sure that much surprise would be caused at Rome by the knowledge that any member of the Society should have perpetrated such a work.

decided, very discerningly, that this woul[d]
would give the Pope a pretext for claimi[ng]
tribunals, which might result in their obta[ining]
accompanied by declarations strongly in th[e]
for consideration was whether the Pope
appoint another Cardinal in place of Torreg[iani]
tiations with the Powers. This proposal a[lso]
inadmissible. There were plenty of Cardinal[s]
ities at Rome, and they might easily get one
less instead of better than Torregiani. Henc[e]
failure of Choiseul's similar attempt in th[e]
suggest that the Cardinal should be plied wit[h]
must see that with the death of the Pope, his
cease, and that he would provide better for his
ing a lost cause whilst he has so good a cha[nce]
himself for the loss of the supplies he at prese[nt]
Jesuits. The Fiscals piously add their regrets that
Roman Curia should have fallen so low as to be
mundane inducements, but conclude that as such i[t]
must be dealt with. The integrity of Torregiani s[hould]
have been too much for their base artifice.

Such are the contents of the important *Consulta*
1767, in which the intention of coercing the Po[pe]
avowed, and the best mode of carrying out th[e]
discussed. It resulted in a draft-scheme of procedure
follow, which Grimaldi drew up for presentation
Lisbon. This draft was referred back to the Extraor[dinary]
and the *Consulta* thence resulting suggested some mod[ifications]
instructive character. However, that *Consulta* was not
following March, and is best considered in the next sec[tion]

II.[16] [Final days of Clement XIII]

The last section brought the history of the negotiaions
five Courts on the Jesuit question up to the date of 3[0]
1767, that is to say, nine months after the Spanish exp[ulsion]
have seen how they resolved among themselves to work [for]
Suppression, and how the means on which they relied
Clement XIII to fulfil their desire was not the force of any
Jesuit misconduct they were prepared to lay before him, but
of their threats to deprive him of his territory, and as the la[st]

---

[16] *The Month*, 100 (1902), 366–376.

says: 'Your Eminence will see what is aimed at by the publication of such writngs.' It should be observed, moreover, that Luciani's letter is dated two days before the publication of Clement XIII's *Monitorium* against the Duke of Parma. Theiner's reflections on this order of dates is very just and deserves to be quoted.[20]

> These facts prove sufficiently that the King of Spain had for some time past entertained the idea of compelling the Pope to a total extinction of the Society, and of threatening him that, in case he did not comply, he would take from him the States of Benevento and Corvo, and of Castro and Ronciglione, besides urging the King of France to do the same with Avignon and the Comtat de Venaussin. The affair of Parma [that is, of the *Monitorium*] appeared to the Courts to have occurred the more opportunely as it supplied them with a pretext for carrying out the usurpation with some semblance of right, namely, of a pretension to avenge the outrage offered to their relative ... But neither Spain nor Naples, and much less France, ever thought seriously of occupying those States solely because of the Parma affair. They wished to have in their hands a pledge, the restoration of which would be the price for the Suppression of the Society of Jesus. The outcome of the affair furnishes incontestable evidence of this; for the revocation of the decree against Parma which the Sovereigns demanded, was in fact nothing more than a pretext for wresting from the Pope the desired Suppression, since it was well understood that he would never consent to that other humiliating concession.

We can now come to the *Consulta* of 21 March 1768, which, it will be remembered,[21] had to report on the draft of Grimaldi's plan for extorting the Suppression from the Pope. The King had directed that the five episcopal members of the Extraordinary Council - namely, the Archbishops and Bishops of Saragossa, Burgos, Orihuela, Albarracín, and Tarragona - should in this instance be specially consulted. We can trace their clerical influence in the resulting *Consulta,* and gather from it that they were, as might have been expected, all good Regalists. The Council, whilst acknowledging Grimaldi's draft to be 'firm, solid, and clear' in its language, thought it desirable that the *Supplica* to the Pope 'should be conceived in terms which, far from awakening mistrust in the Curia, or indignation at an attack made on their cherished doctrines and interests, would depict the body they were asked to dissolve in the colours of a true enemy to the Apostolic See.' This was certainly a prudent suggestion. Though the Pope was to be made the victim of coercion, it was clearly desirable that he should be enabled to keep up appear-

---

[20] *Ibid.*
[21] See above p. 147.

ances, the more so as the Suppression could only be effected by a Bull or Brief, in which it would be necessary to incorporate some statement of reasons for so stringent a measure.

What they suggest is that the *Supplica* should 'cite the history of Pius IV, Clement VIII, Paul V, Alexander VII, Innocent XI, Clement XI, Benedict XIII, Innocent XIII, Benedict XIV; and further allege in proof the obstinacy of the Society in resisting the Pontifical Constitutions regarding missions in the East, and the scandal occasioned to Christianity by the consequent loss of missions; the war of heretics against the See of Peter precisely because of its toleration of men who had laboured constantly to destroy Christianity down to its roots by means of idolatrous rites and cults; and finally the insuperable difficulty opposed to the return of the Protestants to the bosom of the Church, as long as they were treated to the spectacle of the Holy See seeming, by its protection of the Jesuits, to regard with favour their anti-monarchical and seditious system'.

This ecclesiastically-leavened *Consulta* made also another suggestion which does credit to their discernment, if not honour to their sense of equity. They recommend that the Pope should at once be called upon, not only to suppress the Society, but to do it by way of an administrative act, without entering on any formal discussion, or invoking the aid of any consultative Congregation. And they urge that this demand should be accompanied by a threat that in case of non-compliance, 'Spain would feel compelled to suppress the Tribunal of the Nunciature, and stop all recourse to Rome on the part of its subjects, save in those matters which were explicitly reserved to the Holy See by the ancient discipline of the Church, the Bishops thus regaining their original and native authority according to that ancient discipline.'

We see sufficiently from the foregoing facts what were the plans recommended for coercing Clement XIII. In the sequel we shall find that in their substantials they were adhered to by the allied Courts, although in some particulars they were set aside. We must, however, pass very summarily over the remaining history, so far as it lay within the reign of Clement XIII.

On 16 April, as has been told already, the Joint Note of France, Spain, and Naples, in reference to the affairs of Parma, was delivered to the Pope by d'Aubeterre. It threatened reprisals in the event of the Pope refusing to revoke his *Montorium,* and to make reparation to the outraged Duke. As Clement refused, Avignon and the Comtat de Venaissin were occupied on 11 June, and Benevento and Corvo on 12 June. On 15 June,[22] in an audience in which Clement

---

[22] Theiner, op. cit. p. 130.

XIII complained of the occupation of Benevento, the news of which had just arrived, d'Aubeterre asked for the supersession of Torregiani by another Cardinal, with whom the Powers could better negotiate. Clement, after some protests against the impropriety of such a proposal, asked him whom he desired to see appointed. D'Aubeterre then asked for Clement's major-domo, a man whom he had described in a letter, dated 27 April 1768,[23] as the one anti-Jesuit member of the Papal household. This was preposterous, as the major-domo was not even a Cardinal, and eventually the Pope appointed Negroni, thereby justifying the anticipations of the Fiscals, for Negroni was not at all the kind of man they wanted.

On 13 August, as the result of another *Consulta* given two days previously by the Extraordinary Council, Carlos III sent secret instructions to Azpuru[24] to demand five things of the Pope which must be granted at once. They were (1) the withdrawal of the *Monitorium* of 30 January; (2) the recognition of the independent sovereignty of the Duke of Parma; (3) the recognition that the territories recently annexed by France and Naples were to remain incorporated in those two kingdoms respectively; (4) the exile of Torregiani from Rome; (5) the instant suppression of the Society and secularization of all its members, together with the perpetual exile from Rome of its General, Padre Ricci. Only on these conditions, he was to say, could good relations be established between the Holy See and Spain. The King of Spain also induced the King of France to make a similar demand, and Tanucci,[25] on 28 September, sent 4,000 Neapolitan troops to Orbitelli, a port situated a few miles north of Cività Vecchia, that they might be ready to occupy Ronciglione and Castro on the first opportunity. He had even the insolence to lodge a thousand troops in the Villa Madama, King Ferdinand's villa at Rome, which stood right opposite the Castle of Sant' Angelo, and to say that he was thus acting under the orders of Choiseul – a representation which Choiseul, whose refined habits revolted against the coarser methods of his fellow-workers in the South, indignantly repudiated. Carlos III, on the other hand, wrote to Tanucci urging him to carry into effect at once the occupation of the two Duchies.

Let us now turn for a moment to consider the attitude of Clement XIII in the face of all these endeavours to force his hand. The most resolute foes of his policy have recognized his saintly character. Thus the Abbé Clément, who was sent to Rome about this time by the Jansenists to watch over their interests, tells us that at Padua, before

[23] *Ibid.* p. 128.
[24] *Ibid.* p. 134.
[25] *Ibid.* p. 139.

his elevation to the Papacy, 'he was called the Saint; and was an exemplary man, who, notwithstanding the immense revenues of his diocese and his private estate, was always without money, owing to the lavishness of his almsdeeds, and would give away even his linen'; and even this hostile writer allows that 'he had no other dependence on the Jesuits than that with which he was inspired by his esteem for the regularity of their lives and their zeal for the ministry.'[26] He was also, by general acknowledgment, a most lovable man, grave, but exquisitely gentle and winning in his manners. He was not a strong character and perhaps was too prone to lean on others. But his extreme conscientiousness made it impossible for him to be the creature of any man. Moreover, he was inflexibly just and incapable of yielding when a principle was at stake.[27] It was a defect, perhaps, in him that he was so unable to restrain his tears, or the disclosure of the spiritual motives by which he was fortifying himself interiorly, but he was always reasonable, courteous, and conciliatory in his language with the Courts, and invariably took up sound positions. In the matter of the campaign against the Society his position was sound and edifying throughout. When the first notification of the coming Portuguese expulsion reached him, he wrote back to Joseph I, on 2 August 1759,[28] saying that 'if among the persons who wear the habit (of the Society) there are some or several who are guilty of some offence or other, it is just that these should be made to suffer a proportionate punishment, and God forbid that we should ever think

[26] *Journal d'un voyage et correspondence en Italie et en Espagne.* Ap. Ravignan, i. p. 30.

[27] It is charged against him that he was dominated by Cardinal Torregiani, his Secretary of State, who in turn was dominated by his Jesuit confessor, Fr Ricci. That he paid much attention to Torregiani's counsels is doubtless true, but he was not open to reproach for that, for Torregiani was himself a man of genuine piety, sincere motives, and good judgment. Even a writer so hostile as Theiner is fain to say of him that 'he was a noble-minded, firm, and upright man, energetic and capable of vigorous action and thoughts;' and can only censure him for regarding the great ecclesiastical questions which then agitated the Christian world, more with the eye of a theologian who discusses them, than with the masterly insight of a statesman who judges, dominates, and directs them' – fine words which, being interpreted, mean that Torregiani regarded such questions too much in the light of conscience, and too little in the light of expediency.

And as for the latter's supposed dependence on Fr Ricci, who was another excellent man, there is no ground for it save the bare fact that Fr Ricci was his confessor, and that, needless to say, did not mean that he undertook to accept Fr Ricci's dictation, even if the latter had been prepared to offer it, in regard to the exercise of his secretarial office. Besides, Torregiani was a far stronger character than the timid and retiring Ricci, and far more capable of dominating him than likely to be dominated by him.

[28] De Ravignan, op. cit. vol. i. p. 77.

of protecting the guilty and so authorizing disorders ... But we should be false to our conscience if we did not counsel your Majesty to beware of confounding the innocent with the guilty and making the former suffer penalties due only to the latter.' We have seen, too, how he spoke in like sense to the King of Spain, in April 1767, and have heard from Don Roda how he was still holding to the same position in the August of that year.

When the Courts began to press him with their threats he at once realized the situation, but refused to be influenced by such unworthy motives, and kept on till the end with quiet though sorrowful determination, opposing a passive resistance to each fresh attempt to terrorize him and vindicating the cause of right in a succession of dignified protests. Thus on 14 June 1768, when the news of the occupation of Benevento had just arrived, he said to d'Aubeterre, as the latter states in his despatch of next day,[29] 'The last time you came to me with menaces, today you come with arms in your hands ... Benevento has been occupied by the Neapolitan troops, but I place these reprisals with the menaces that preceded them, at the foot of the Crucifix ... He it is who must judge between us.' And on 27 October, through Cardinal Torregiani, in a message acquainting the Nuncios at the various Courts with the five demands made on him in the previous month: 'The Holy Father, thanks be to God, although exteriorly so agitated, is not discouraged in his heart; these adversities only confirm him the more and encourage him to suffer the greatest possible reverses for the cause of God and His Church. Violence will never hinder him from speaking out with an Apostolic liberty, and recalling the Kings, his sons, to their duty.'

Still, if his soul was strengthened, his body was enfeebled under the stress of the sufferings which 'the Kings, his sons', inflicted on him, and the limits of its endurance were well-nigh reached when the tragic year 1768 drew to its close. Nor had the new year fulfilled many of its days when the last crushing blow fell on his head. Louis XV felt small personal interest in the cruel campaign, and his light-minded Minister, Choiseul, was wearied out by Clement XIII's persistent refusals. The French Court had, however; made a rule for itself to follow the lead of the Court of Spain, and Carlos III with his bull-dog tenacity thought not of withdrawing but of driving his fangs deeper into the heart of the afflicted Pontiff. His new move was another and sterner joint representation from the three Bourbon Courts, whose Ministers by pre-arrangement, in the third week of January, 1769, presented each a *Memoria* demanding the instanta-

---

[29] Theiner, *ibid.* p. 130.

neous suppression of the obnoxious Order. The text of the Spanish *Memoria* – or rather a summary of it – is given by Sr Ferrer del Rio,[30] and runs as follows:

> The disorders caused by the Religious of the Society in the Spanish dominions, and their repeated and persistent opposition to every lawful authority deemed to be disaffected towards their interests, have obliged the Catholic King, in the exercise of his God-given power, to chasten and repress their crimes, and to destroy throughout his States so abiding a focus of disturbance. But, if he has thus fulfilled his obligation as Father of his people, much still remains for him to do as a Son of the Church, as its protector, and the protector of religion and sound doctrine. There can now-a-days be no doubt as to the corrupt character of the speculative and moral teaching of these Religious, or of its downright opposition to that of Jesus Christ, nor is there any one who remains unconvinced that the tumults and attempts of which they are accused, are due to the demoralization which their government has undergone since the time when, having lost sight of the aims proposed to them by their saintly Founder, they embraced a political and mundane system adverse to all the authorities established by God on earth; and so became hostile to the persons of Sovereigns, bold in inventing and sustaining murderous opinions, and persecutors of prelates and virtuous men. Nor has the Holy See itself been exempted from their persecutions, calumnies, threats, and insubordination, and the history of many Sovereign Pontiffs yields abundant evidence of what they have had to suffer through the Society's misdeeds, and of what they have to fear should they venture to oppose its ideas of domination, its interests, or its opinions. Its persistency in exciting disorders, and its absolute incorrigibility, are equally proved by many examples which can be drawn from the countries where they still exist, and the impossibility of its ever becoming useful in the future is deducible from the discredit into which it has everywhere fallen, now that the mask of imposture, with which it deceived the world, has been torn from it. As long, too, as the Jesuits exist, there can be no hope of drawing into the Church the dissident princes, who, seeing the disturbances these Religious create in Catholic States, how they insult the sacred persons of Kings, and stir up the people to resist public authority, will keep away from the Church that they may avoid the danger of introducing such calamities into their own kingdoms.
>
> Moved by these reasons which are most notorious; penetrated with a filial love for the Church, and filled with zeal for its exaltation, as well as for the advancement and glory of the legitimate authority of the Holy See, and the tranquillity of Catholic kingdoms; intimately persuaded that public prosperity cannot be secured as long as this institute survives; desiring, finally, to fulfil his duty to religion, to the Holy Father, to himself, and to his subjects, the Catholic King begs of His Holiness, with the utmost

---

[30] *Reinado de Carlos III*, ii. p. 250.

urgency, that he will entirely and totally dissolve the Society called that of Jesus, and secularize all its members, forbidding them to form any other congregation or community, under any title of reform or new institute, or to be subject to any other superiors save the Bishops of the dioceses where they reside after secularization.

It must not be forgotten that the various *Consultas* and other documents appertaining to the Secret Inquiry into the Jesuit question, some of which are now accessible, and have been used in this account, were at the time carefully concealed from the Pope, Jesuits, and the public generally, all of whom were in absolute ignorance of the mysterious causes of the Spanish expulsion. The true significance, therefore, of this *Memoria* presented to Clement XIII on 18 January 1769, is that it was the first and only communication of the reasons which in the judgment of the Spanish Court had justified their action towards the Society up to date, and ought now to induce the Pope to grant a total suppression of the Order. On other hand, we can see how utterly inadequate these reasons were for the purpose. They could hardly be more vague and impalpable, and we know from the two *Consultas* of 30 November 1767, and 23 March 1768 – the effect of whose recommendations is chiefly traceable to the language of this *Memoria* – that their vagueness was intentional. Moreover, the portion touching on the dealings with the Society of various Popes, the behaviour of the Society in regard to missions, and the nature of Jesuit writings on Tyrannicide, was such as could not possibly take in the Holy See, to whom the real truth underlying these malignant insinuations was perfectly well known. On what feature then in this *Memoria* did the Spanish Court count as calculated to impress the Holy See with the urgent necessity of suppressing the Society, and doing it at once? It is but too clear that they counted solely on the force of the threat – not indeed explicitly mentioned in the text, but none the less clearly intimated by the circumstances of its delivery – that in the case of non-compliance, or even further delay the Powers would not hesitate to resort to fresh and more far reaching deeds of aggression.

The Neapolitan *Memoria* traverses the same ground as the Spanish, which was to be expected, since it was composed, or at least supervised, at Madrid, as we learn from a letter of Grimaldi's to Tanucci, dated 27 December 1768. There is thus the less need to transcribe it at length, but the following short extract from it must be given just to illustrate the ridiculous style it employs, perhaps under the impression that it was a style suitable to put into the mouth of a youthful Sovereign.

> Considering that ... the fortunate moment should not be lost when the Eternal Wisdom has made manifest the loss which both Church and State ... have sustained through the way in which the ... Society of Jesus has abused the piety and patience of Sovereigns, Bishops, and people, his Majesty has not been able to resist the impulse of his charity for the human race, for religion, peace, justice and discipline, and has resolved that Cardinal Orsini shall, in his name, beseech His Holiness to have compassion on the faithful of Jesus Christ placed by the Holy Spirit under his protection ...[31]

The French *Memoria* was expressed in simpler and less turgid language, besides which it abstained from all reference to the moral and speculative teaching of the Society. This abstention was designed, as we know from Choiseul's letter to d'Aubeterre of 27 December 1768.[32] He gives as his reason that he did not wish his Court to be involved in discussions on this point, but perhaps it was also because he could see through the absurdity of the charges brought against this teaching, and did not want to make his King ridiculous by adopting them.

Azpuru presented the Spanish *Memoria* on 18 January 1769; Orsini the Neapolitan on 20 January; d'Aubeterre the French on 22 January. Clement received them and dismissed them sadly and courteously, saying but few words, and promising to read their communications. A few days later (on 28 January) Torregiani, on his behalf, wrote to the Nuncios words of protest the justice of which will hardly be denied.[33]

> His Holiness cannot understand how the Courts have had the deplorable courage to add this new grief to all those which afflict the Church, and for no other end save to torment still further the conscience of His Holiness, and his afflicted soul. An impartial posterity will judge and will say if such actions can be considered new proofs of the filial love which these Sovereigns boast of cherishing towards His Holiness, or gages of that attachment which they pretend to profess towards the Holy See.

It was thus he protested, but, according to Theiner, he was brought by the three Joint Notes to realize the necessity of suppressing the Society, and convoked a Consistory for 16 February to discuss the question. There seems no proof, but it is possible his thoughts may have turned in that direction. A condemnation of the Society in the absolute dearth of any proof to justify it, and in the presence of such

---

[31] See Danvila, *ibid.* p. 274.
[32] Theiner, op. cit., p. 142.
[33] *Ibid.* i. 145.

manifest proof that the Powers were working a crooked policy, it is not likely that he could ever have brooked; but suppression was a different matter, and he might perhaps have concluded that in view of the intense and growing conspiracy against the Society it would be better for all concerned to grant it. But he was not called upon to decide this anxious question. Cardinal Negroni, in giving audience to the Ambassadors on 28 January, said to them: 'This last move of the Courts will open the Holy Father's grave.'[34] And so it was. On 2 February, he sang Mass with his usual devotion, and blessed and distributed the candles. During the day he visited the Blessed Sacrament, exposed for the *Quarant' Ore*, and when the day was over retired to rest without showing signs of illness. But in the night he had an attack of the heart which proved fatal before his nephew, Cardinal Rezzonico, or the Cardinal Secretary, Torregiani, though both were sleeping in neighbouring bedrooms, could be summoned to his side. He had fought a good fight; he had offered a noble spectacle of moral force contending against physical violence, and, although his reign was one long chronicle of calamities, he must always count among the great Popes.

[34] *Ibid.*

Chapter Five

The Conclave of 1769

I.[1] [Preparations and deferred commencement]

The adversaries of the Society hardly concealed their satisfaction on hearing that the Holy See had become vacant. They had failed to bend the gentle firmness of Clement XIII, but now there was the possibility of a more compliant Pontiff, and every nerve must be strained to convert the possibility into a reality. Our task in this chapter must be to study their conduct under these changed conditions, and judge how far it was consistent with belief in the justice of their cause, or loyalty to the supreme spiritual authority they professed to venerate, and that we may be aided in this task by a definite criterion we had better commence by adverting to the proper spirit in which a Papal Election should be conducted, and the legislation by which the Church has sought to secure its observance.

Of the many Bulls for the regulation of Papal Elections there are four we need to bear in mind – the *Cum tam divino* of Julius II (14 January, 1505), the *In eligendis* of Pius IV (9 October 1562), the *Aeterni Patris* of Gregory XV (15 November 1621), and the *Apostolatus Officium* of Clement XII (5 October 1732). All insist on the importance of the charge entrusted to the members of the Sacred College, as for instance does Clement XII, in the following impressive passage:

> Under threat of the Divine judgment we command and enjoin the said Cardinals to see that in giving their votes, and all else which in any way appertains to the Election, they keep God before their eyes, and, seeking not their own but the things of Jesus Christ, religiously, sincerely, and freely conduct themselves in electing him whom, in the Lord, they judge fit to rule the Universal Church with fruit and advantage – setting aside all mundane arts, factions, and party aims, all carnal affections, private

---

[1] *The Month*, 100 (1902), 517–36.

The Conclave of 1769 159

aims and desires, all intercessions made by Secular Princes and other worldly inducements, even considerations of gratitude or any similar ties being altogether subordinated and disregarded. (We also enjoin and command them), mindful of the above Constitutions [which had been previously enumerated], and of the penalties imposed by them, not to venture or presume to do, permit, or countenance, anything opposed to this aim [of electing a suitable Pope], or anything by which the Election might be retarded, or the liberty of suffrage infringed, whether by themselves, or through another, directly or indirectly, under any colour, pretext, or artifice.

Gregory XV had also previously specified some particular abuses from which the electors must abstain.

Let the Cardinals abstain from all compacts, agreements, promises, understandings, pledges, treaties, and whatsoever engagements, threats, signs or countersigns of their votes or voting-papers, or any other intimations given by word or in writing, with the intention of including or excluding either a particular person, or several persons, or a certain class whether of creations or anything similar, or with the object of indicating that a vote will be given or not given ... Conferences (*tractatus*) however, in reference to the Election we are far from meaning to forbid.

And Julius II had even invalidated any and every Election in which a simoniacal gift, or contract, or promise had been made or accepted.

It was to preclude, as far as possible, the entrance of these abuses, and to keep steadily before the minds of the elector the true methods to be pursued, that the Conclave was devised and enforced; for its purpose is to isolate the electors from outside influences by shutting and barring them in, and strictly forbidding any interchange of speech or letters between them and any outside persons whatever.

With the same salutary object precautions were taken to preclude the delays during which intrigues might have time to gather, and during which the Church might suffer from the want of its supreme ruler.

When ten days have elapsed from the death of the Pope [says Pius IV], the entrance into Conclave must no longer be delayed or deferred, but on the day following, when the Mass of the Holy Ghost has been sung, whether the absent Cardinals have arrived or not, those present must at once enter the Conclave, and having entered must without delay, and without occupying themselves with the *capitula* wont to be made during the first days, proceed to the business of election, a scrutiny being taken each day, and after the first scrutiny an accession[2] being permitted, ... and when, after the lapse of ten days, the Cardinals present have made the Election, ... even if they may not have awaited the arrival of other Cardinals, even though these others should be Legates despatched a *latere* or for any other public cause whatever, and even though they be absent by the permission of the Supreme Pontiff, the Election thus made shall not be impeached under the pretext that the absent Cardinals have a journey to make, or are prevented by any other probable or notorious impediment – since the public advantage accruing from a prompt Election ought to he preferred to any other reason whatever.

Another regulation for the prevention of delays was that which limited somewhat drastically the diet of the electors. Each must have his meals by himself in his own cell, and must be contented with a single dish at each meal; nor must even this single dish be provided for him from the stores of any other Cardinal save himself.

Finally it was prescribed that the Constitutions regulating Papal Elections should be twice read to the electors, once on the death of the preceding Pope, and again after the solemn entry into the Conclave. Having thus heard it read each Cardinal must bind himself publicly and by oath to its observance. Moreover, the gravest penalties, including the major excommunication to be incurred *ipso facto,* were enacted by these same constitutions against all those who violated them.

Such are the prescriptions by their fidelity or infidelity to which we are to judge of the conduct of those who on either side took part in the Conclave of 1769, and we can now pass on to the history.

The object of the allied Courts was to obtain a Pope who would comply with their demands. Clement XIII, say the Instructions given to the French Cardinals on their departure for Rome,[3] although of the purest morals and most upright intentions, 'had only proved that these are insufficient qualifications for a good Pope; and had done more harm to the Roman Church than several of his predecessors who had been less regular and less religious', all 'because he had no profound acquaintance with the character of Courts, or with political affairs, and did not understand the consideration due to the persons and independent authority of other sovereigns' – a respectable euphemism which we, in the light of their conduct, may take to mean, that Clement did not see that he ought to countenance the

---

[2] To save time, when the votes of the morning scrutiny have been made known another scrutiny follows in which votes must not be given to any fresh candidate, but may be given to any who has secured one or more votes in the previous scrutiny. This is called 'accession'.

[3] See de Ravignan's *Clément XIII et Clément XIV*, ii. p. 363.

claim of the secular Courts to subordinate to their own sweet wills the consideration due to religion and equity. The new Pope must be of a different kind, and above all things must be one who would forthwith, and apart from any judicial inquiry or independent judgment, suppress the Society of Jesus.

This was their object, but there were serious difficulties in the way of its attainment. The electors were, as usual, divisible into three classes, those who were zealous for the spiritual independence and sacred traditions of the Papacy, those whose chief solicitude was to advance the interests of the secular sovereigns, and an intermediate class who held or were thought to hold less decided views. Of these classes the first were called the *Zelanti;* the second the *Crown Cardinals,* the third the *Indifferents* (that is, the Neutrals). In the Conclave of 1769 these distinctions were especially marked, and the difficulty for the Crown party was that they were much less numerous than the Zelanti, whilst the Neutrals, on whose co-operation they must rely if they were to succeed, were an unknown quantity to them.

Indeed, at the beginning of the Conclave the Crown Cardinals were quite an insignificant number. The Duc d'Aubeterre, the French Ambassador to the Vatican, in a letter to Choiseul, dated February 6 1769,[4] sets them down as consisting only of Orsini, who was also the Neapolitan Ambassador; Sersale, the Archbishop of Naples; Branciforte, the Archbishop of Palermo; Migazzi, the Archbishop of Vienna; Lante, the Archbishop of Turin; and the Cardinal of York; but there were some, namely, Migazzi and Lante, even among these few of whom he could not have felt certain. On the other hand, there was a goodly company of Zelanti, men of the highest reputation, whose virtues and talents even their adversaries recognized; for it must be borne in mind that the one charge brought against them by their adversaries was the charge of fanaticism – another dexterous phrase, which on their lips did not bear its usual signification, but meant only that the Cardinals thus characterized refused to render a blind obedience to the Courts, and asked for the evidence of Jesuit guilt. To this class of Zelanti belonged Cardinals Torregiani, Castelli, Rezzonico (the nephew of the late Pope), Boschi, Chigi, and Buffalini, and some fifteen others, of whom d'Aubeterre in his letter of 6 February recommends that, at all events, the six named should be resolutely excluded by the Courts, as being too favourable to the Society.

We have said that the Neutrals were an unknown quantity to

---

[4] Theiner, *Histoire du Pontificat de Clément XIV,* i. p. 181. French Edition.

d'Aubeterre and his fellow-Ministers, and he complains of it in the same letter.

> As for the rest [he writes] not one has as yet discovered himself, like the six just named, whose election, we think, must be opposed. It is not that we feel more secure of the others for what with these secret affiliations, it is impossible to judge of their true sentiments in regard to the Society, ... so difficult is it to arrive at conclusions now-a-days with any sort of certitude about any Cardinal in the Sacred College. During the last Pontificate, which has lasted ten years and a half, the Jesuits have been masters of all 'graces' [i.e., appointments, privileges, etc.], whence one can judge what a number of creatures they have made,[5] who take great care to conceal themselves and cannot be detected. Moreover, a Cardinal when he becomes Pope changes his mode of thinking so much that one can count on no one.

Two days later, writing again,[6] he revises his judgment about Chigi, and classes him with Fantuzzi, Stoppani, Serbelloni, Pozzobonelli, and Sersale, as 'the only members of the Sacred College from among whom a wise and felicitous choice could be made.' This observation is of interest, as illustrating the state of uncertainty in which he still was as to the sentiments of the Cardinals. His next sentence in the same letter is even more interesting, as containing the first appreciation of Ganganelli as a possible candidate. 'There is one other,' writes the Ambassador, 'who would suit us better than any of those last named, the Cardinal Ganganelli; but there is a considerable party against him, and therefore no ground for thinking of him as possible. If one were to propose him, the only result would be to get him rejected.'

It was in the face of this situation that the Ambassadors of the Crowns, d'Aubeterre, Azpuru, and Orsini, found themselves when Clement XIII expired on the night of 2 February 1769. As his death was so sudden they were without definite instructions from their Courts, though, as the event had been anticipated and discussed in their diplomatic correspondences during the previous five years,[7]

---

[5] This is what d'Aubeterre imagined, and what persons like him not unfrequently imagine of the Rome of the present day. But there is a vast difference between such imaginations and the reality of facts, both as regards the present day and as regards the period we are considering. No one, for instance, can read Padre Cordara's *Commentarii* (cited below), without perceiving that during the two preceding reigns of Benedict XIV and Clement XIII the Jesuits were very far indeed from having everything their own way. But d'Aubeterre's mistake is that he classed as a Jesuit adherent every ecclesiastical dignitary who refused to be the servile agent of the Bourbons, and claimed to exercise an independent judgment on questions affecting ecclesiastical liberty or justice to individuals.

[6] *Ibid.* p. 182.

[7] *Ibid.* pp. 169, etc.

they were sufficiently aware of the course they would be expected to take. They reported at once to their respective Courts the death of Clement XIII and the state of feeling, so far as they understood it, which prevailed among the Cardinals; and they explained the common policy they had agreed to pursue till they received further orders. They resolved to say to all who asked them, that 'their Courts had no idea of making a Pope, or giving him the law, but that they did not want one made without their knowledge, and that as soon as a worthy and proper subject was proposed they would give assent at once, and there was no need to fear lest they should put difficulties in the way.'[8] This was a most becoming attitude for them to preserve, and had they a *bona fide* intention to preserve it, no one would have reasonably reproached them. Unfortunately, their whole conduct, as we shall see, proved that to make the Pope was the precise object for which they intended to strive, and these protestations to the contrary were only a blind.[9] They were thoroughly suspected by the Zelanti, and knew that, if they proposed a candidate openly, they would be taking the course most calculated to impede his election. They were intending, therefore, to work in secret and cause their candidate's name to be brought forward first through the voting-papers which they hoped secretly to influence. But a prior step must be to discover a candidate who would suit – and we have seen how as yet they were unprovided. Hence the need of delaying the Election till they had collected more certain information as to the real sentiments of the Cardinals. Accordingly, they resolved to pay visits to each of the Cardinals then in Rome, and insinuate a delicate threat that if a candidate were elected before the foreign Cardinals, that is, the French and Spanish Cardinals, had arrived, the indignation of the Courts would be excited, and the candidate elected might be refused recognition. We know from a previous correspondence between d'Aubeterre and Choiseul that the former's original suggestion, in the letter of 12 February 1766,[10] was to put this brutally to the electors,

[8] Theiner, *ibid*. p. 179 (in the letter of 6 February).
[9] De Ravigan (op. cit. i. p.246) points out that at times in their confidential communications the adherents of the Court party did not even stick at the phrase. 'All that I see here,' wrote de Bernis, on 30 March, that is, very shortly after his entry into the Conclave, 'makes me think that we shall not be strong enough *to make the Pope*'. And d'Aubeterre himself wrote on 14 April, 'Here is a thing to fear, for in that case *we could not make* either the Pope, or the Secretary of State, and should be put to shame.'
[10] 'We are determined to make a united and public protest against any election made prematurely, and to annonnce that, being subreptitious and schismatic, our Courts would never recognize a Pope thus elected; we mean also to signify this to the Conclave, and have it placarded throughout Rome.' (Theiner, *ibid*. p.174.)

but Louis XV's sense of propriety was outraged by the idea, which besides would have committed him to a policy[11] he might find inconvenient. Accordingly, Choiseul wrote back that he must on no account utter any such threat, and so now when the moment contemplated had arrived, d'Aubeterre and his colleagues excogitated a more subtle course. They would assure the Cardinals whom they visited, that 'they knew them to be too prudent and attached to the interests of the Church to think of any such premature Election', but, at the same time, they would make them feel that if such a thing did happen, they would be obliged to withdraw at once from Rome to Frascati, withholding their recognition of the Pope-elect, until they had received instructions how to act from their Courts, 'who could not have foreseen such an eventuality.'

From d'Aubeterre's next letter to Choiseul, dated 15 February, we learn,[12] so far as his information was correct, what was being done by the Jesuits to ward off the danger. Their General like the Ambassadors, had paid visits to all the Cardinals about to enter the Conclave – though Orsini had refused to see him.

> He had wept and groaned, and recommended his Society to each Cardinal separately, reminding them of the services it had rendered to the Church and religion, the Saints which had sprung from it, and the persecution it was enduring at the present time, for no other reason save its constant attachment to the Holy See; and finally begging them not to forget that this Institute had been confirmed and approved by a General Council. Such are in substance the words he used, without naming any of the Powers or any person in particular.
>
> I am informed that he does all in his power in a secret way to stimulate the Cardinals of his party and induce them to hasten the Election so as to make a Pope who would be devoted to them. I know for certain that this party is making every possible move to attain that result.

As M. d'Aubeterre, and after him Theiner, are fond of speaking of the manoeuvres of the Jesuits during the Conclave and of the Zelanti Cardinals as dominated by them, it may be well to add here the Duc de Choiseul's comment on the paragraphs just quoted. It is given in his reply to d'Aubeterre, dated 14 March,[13] which is introduced by Theiner as follows:

> Returning to the panic-stricken fear of Jesuits, by which his Ambassador was incessantly pursued, Choiseul ... strives to reassure him by saying,

---

[11] Theiner, *ibid.* p. 175.
[12] Theiner, *ibid.* p. 183.
[13] *Ibid.* p. 202.

'It is hardly probable, Monsieur, that the Jesuits have retained at Rome, especially since the death of Pope Rezzonico, and after the formal requisition for the extinction of their Society, a credit and consideration sufficient to counteract efficaciously the wise and salutary views which we have to lay before the Conclave for the good of religion and the honour of the Holy See, and for the peace of the Church and of the States which profess the same faith. The step taken by Père Ricci, the General of these Religious, in his visits to the Cardinals, has been confined within limits which do not merit either complaint or censure.'

Choiseul, says Theiner,[14] gave a general approval to the action which d'Aubeterre, in concert with Azpuru and Orsini, proposed to take during the Conclave, but impressed on him the necessity of being very cautious not to commit the Courts to any measure which would compromise them. He told him that of the five French Cardinals only two were going to Rome, the others being impeded for reasons of age and health. Both de Luynes and de Bernis, the two who would go, had orders 'to come to an understanding with him as regards all points connected with the Conclave and the Election, and were to receive from him the necessary communications and instructions both before and during their sojourn in the Conclave' – in other words, were deliberately to violate the solemn engagements to secrecy and isolation to which on entering they would bind themselves under oath. As regards the expediency of openly insisting in the Conclave on the suppression of the Society, Choiseul did not feel so sure as d'Aubeterre, and feared lest by so doing they should overshoot the mark, and lose rather than gain their influence on the Election. As regards the selection of the candidate, in a second letter of 28 February, he writes that the King of France had no special person in view, and his desires were dictated only by a zeal for the Catholic religion, the honour of the Holy See, and the public tranquillity. If a good candidate were chosen to govern the Church with intelligence, wisdom, and circumspection, they would applaud him; if, like the late Pope, he embraced false principles and took unjust measures, they would know how to restrain him. Perhaps between the lines of this letter we may read something of Louis XV's better nature and judgment, but altogether the tone of the French Minister, as distinguished from that of their Roman Ambassador, is milder and more reasonable than that of the Spaniards, and reflects the undoubted feeling of the French King – who had no wish of his own for the suppression of the Society, but desired only to give a sop to the Parlement in the interests of peace, and by pleasing the Spaniards, to consolidate the Spanish Alliance on which he relied for resisting the assaults of the English. The

---

[14] *Ibid.* p. 184. Theiner does not give the date of this letter.

one thing which Louis XV had really at heart was probably the retention of Avignon as a part of his dominions, and on this Choiseul insists in these instructions to d'Aubeterre. At the same time it must not be thought that, because the French Court felt less spontaneous interest in the personality of the new Pope, they were the less determined that he should be one who would suppress the Society; for it was their Ambassador, d'Aubeterre, who was the leading spirit of all in coercing the Conclave to such a choice.

Theiner has nothing about the replies sent by the Spanish Court to the reports of its agent at Rome. Neither is Danvila very lavish in his information, but we learn from him[15] that Grimaldi, in a letter to the Conde de Fuentes, the Spanish Ambassador at Paris, dated 23 February 1769, told the latter that the King of Spain approved of the course agreed upon between Mgr Azpuru, d'Aubeterre, and Cardinal Orsini; and considered that advantage should be taken of so fortunate an opportunity to demand the extinction of the Jesuit Order, 'as it was better that the new Pope should find the question already raised, and receive his Tiara with the knowledge (that he must deal with it), than that he should have it first brought before him at the commencement of his reign.' In this same letter Grimaldi writes also that the Spanish Court 'only wants a Pope who will be a lover of peace, learned, and virtuous, and, as a consequence (!) of these three qualities, favourable to the Crowns.' From Danvila too we learn that the reports received from Azpuru and Azara, about the characteristics of the different Cardinals, had been referred to Don M. de Roda, who in turn reported that Cardinal de Sersale, the Archbishop of Naples, would be the best candidate to support – but says of Ganganelli: 'He used to enjoy a high reputation which, however, has diminished since he became Cardinal. He is a mere scholastic, but thinks more soundly than the mass of those who have spent their lives in such studies. I had much to do with him, and it appears to me that he would make an industrious Pope and a lover of the sovereigns, and would be in no way opposed to the *regalia* and other principles of the Secular Courts. Still, as being a Regular and sixty-four years of age, I fear he will not succeed (in becoming Pope), the Cardinals do not like government by a Regular; especial when it is likely to last a long time.'

The Neapolitan Court of course acceded to the ideas of Spain and France, and it was agreed that d'Aubeterre should lead the Court party from outside the Conclave and Orsini from within, and that the rest should take their directions from these. As for the Empress Maria

---

[15] *Historia del Reinado de Carlos III*, iii. p. 297.

Theresa and her son the Emperor Joseph, they had no grievance of their own against the Society, and declared so on several occasions, but the Bourbon Courts, as we have seen in a former chapter, realized the desirability of securing their support, and had sought to gain them over by various matrimonial alliances. Thus Leopold, Duke of Tuscany, the Empress's second son was married, in 1765, to the King of Spain's third daughter; and of the Empress's daughters, Marie Amélie Josephine was married in 1769 to Duke Ferdinand of Parma, and Marie Caroline Louise Jeanne in 1768 to King Ferdinand of Naples; whilst Marie Antoinette's marriage with the Dauphin, afterwards Louis XVI of France, was being negotiated, and was destined to come off in 1770. The Empress had succumbed to these influences, and by the time of the Conclave, although she could not be brought to participate in the intrigues of the Bourbon sovereigns, had engaged to offer to them no opposition. During his mother's lifetime the Emperor Joseph's power was limited, but the ideas which a few years later made his reign so disastrous to the Church, were already forming in his mind. In company with his brother, Leopold, he paid a visit to the Conclave in the middle of March, and interchanged some civilities with the Cardinals. As regards the election he preserved the same neutral attitude as his mother, but in a private conversation with d'Aubeterre, according to the latter's account,[16] told him that although not wishing to intervene personally, he would welcome a Pope who would suppress the Jesuits.

Now that we understand in some measure the character and plans of the arrayed forces, we can pass on to the Conclave itself. The Cardinals made their solemn entry on 15 February, and from that time forth we ought, had the above cited Papal Constitutions been observed, to hear no more of communications between the Crown Cardinals and their allies without. Nevertheless, Orsini[17] held a regular correspondence with d'Aubeterre from the time of his entry into the Conclave until 16 May, which was just before its close – Orsini giving the most detailed information of all that was passing within the Conclave, including the results of each scrutiny and each accession, and d'Aubeterre, after repeating all to his colleagues and his chiefs in Paris, sending back to Orsini instructions for the Crown Cardinals to follow. Obviously this was a gross violation of the Conclave oath which Orsini had taken, and it is not too much to say that in so acting he perjured himself twice a day. Theiner[18] indeed tries to defend him on the ground that he may have thought himself justified by the necessity of the case, being an ambassador as well as an elector, and the occasion being one which he

---

[16] Theiner, *ibid.* p. 208.
[17] Theiner, *ibid.* p. 155.
[18] Theiner, *ibid.* pp. 165, 166.

held to be of vital importance to the welfare of the Church; but it is hard to see how a serious writer could set up such a defence. Nor is Theiner more convincing when he adds that the Zelanti Cardinals were acting in like disregard of the Bulls. What he refers to is some interviews and letters between Cardinal J. F. Albani, one of the Zelanti leaders, and D. Nicholas Azara, the Spanish agent. We shall come to this presently, but whether Albani broke his oath or not, the conduct of Orsini and his allies without and within the Conclave (for de Bernis, when he arrived, carried on a similar correspondence with d'Aubettrre) remains indefensible.

If, however, these Cardinals stand condemned for betraying the secrets of the Conclave to the outside agents who were thus enabled to pull the wires of their electoral action, the correspondence thence resulting is most valuable material, and Theiner has done a service to history in publishing so much of it. There is bias in it, of course, which requires to be discounted, but it is the report of singularly able observers whose interest it was to be accurate, and it reveals in all their nakedness the intrigues of the Court party.

From these sources we learn that in the third scrutiny, which took place on the evening of 17 February, the Zelanti party were able to count twelve to fourteen votes,[19] whilst the Crown party found itself represented as yet only by Orsini, York, the two Corsini, and Sersale – Carraccioli, Cavalchini, Conti, and Malvezzi, on whose votes they had counted, being detained by sickness. This was most discouraging for Orsini, as a majority of two-thirds of those present was required for an election, and the consequent object of the Crown party, as we know from d'Aubeterre's correspondence, was to get together a body of sixteen votes. As the electors were never likely to number as many as forty-eight this would give them what was called an *exclusiva*, that is, the power to exclude any candidate they chose,[20] and they meant

---

[19] Theiner, *ibid*. p. 188. Cardinal Neri Corsini, aged eighty-four, was uncle to Cardinal Andrea Corsini, aged thirty-four.

[20] 'All our object should he to secure to ourselves an exclusive influence, so that it may be impossible to make a Pope without our consent.' (d'Aubeterre to the Duc de Praslin, 23 August 1765, ap. Theiner, *ibid*., p. 169.) 'The enterprize of getting a Pope who will suppress the Society of Jesus is very difficult, as the Jesuits have inundated Rome with their creatures ... If we could form a strong and reliable party sufficiently numerous to give an exclusive vote, the opportunity of imposing conditions would arise, but the difficulty is to get such a party. Orsini flatters himself that he will obtain it, if Pirelli and Perelli unite with him in good faith, but I doubt if he will succeed, unless in the name of his Sovereign he makes them understand that they will fall into his disfavour if they form any different party, or join with those who are clearly opposed to this idea.' (Grimaldi to Tanucci, 14 March 1769, ap. Danvila, op. cit. iii. 305.)

The Conclave of 1769   169

to use the leverage thus gained by standing out against all candidates till one was reached on whom they could count for suppressing the Society. It was no concern of theirs if this involved a lengthy Conclave, with serious consequent loss to the welfare of the Church and the Roman States.

The discovery, however, so early in the Conclave that the Zelanti could count on twelve or fourteen votes, presaged not only the improbability of the Crown party obtaining an *exclusiva,* but also the probability of the Zelanti obtaining an *inclusiva,* that is a sufficiency of the votes of the Neutrals to secure the election of their own candidate.[21] Thus at least it appeared to Orsini, who reports to his chief that Rezzonico and Albani, relying on their present advantageous position – for as yet there were but twenty-nine Cardinals in Conclave – were trying every means to hasten the Election, so that it might be an accomplished fact before the Crown Cardinals had time to arrive. He adds that fortunately the Cardinals Lante and Perelli, although partisans of the Jesuits, had, in a conference of the Zelanti leaders on 19 February, pointed out the danger of such a course, which far from restoring peace to the Church, might, on the contrary, render it for ever impossible, and increase the discord, by making the Catholic sovereigns still more hostile to the Holy See. The Cardinals Stuart of York and Orsini had spoken to Rezzonico in the same sense, though in guarded language, so as not to reveal in any way the schismatic action the Ambassadors were contemplating.

Rezzonico and Albani realized that the advice was sound, as no doubt it was, but Theiner fails to point out that if these Cardinals thought of electing a Pope at once, they were only carrying out the spirit and the letter of the Papal Constitutions; which, as we have seen, expressly direct that the foreign Cardinals are not to be waited for, the importance to the Church of a speedy Election being superior to that of allowing absent Cardinals to record their votes. Indeed, it was only by a stratagem quite at variance with the intention of the Bulls, that the real business of election could be postponed. Twice each day direct scrutinies had to be, and were, taken, each followed by a scrutiny of accessions; but day by day for nearly three months they were rendered nugatory through the Cardinals dividing up their votes among impossible candidates, or else giving them to 'No One'.[22] There is, too, another point to be considered in this connection. There were a few Cardinals resident in Italy whose arrival was delayed by illness, but it would have been too absurd to ask that the

---

[21] Theiner, *ibid.* p. 189.
[22] Theiner, *ibid.* p. 193.

Election should be postponed for them. It sounded more intelligible that the German, French, and Spanish Cardinals should be allowed the time needed for their long journeys, and it was on this that Orsini and his friends rested their appeal for delay. Of these Cardinals, however, who were but five in number – that is, those who were to come, were only five – the French Cardinals, de Luynes and de Bernis, had not both arrived till 26 March, six weeks after the opening of the Conclave, and the Spanish Cardinals did not arrive till 24 April. They could surely have reached Rome before that, and one asks the reason of their procrastination, nor is it possible not to feel that it was deliberately arranged by the Courts, that they might have time to ascertain which candidate, if elected, would best serve their purpose. The evidence for this we shall see presently – but a word must be said first on what Orsini in his correspondence represented as the intrigues of the Zelanti leaders.

When their plan of hastening the Election failed, according to Orsini,[23] the Zelanti Cardinals next sought to excite a prejudice against the Crown Cardinals by spreading the rumour that the sovereigns intended to make the Pope, and were working actively for the candidature of Sersale. 'To belie this rumour', writes Orsini, 'I reply constantly that the sovereigns do not want to make the Pope, but do not wish to have one contrary to their interests, and that they are ready to give their assent to the election of any worthy and suitable person on whom the choice of the electors may fall. As for the candidature of Sersale I reply by a fit of laughter, without saying whether he pleases me or not – and I do not show myself favourable or unfavourable to any person.' This was very clever of Orsini, and illustrates his remarkable skill as a diplomatist, but none the less the rumour he combated was perfectly correct. The sovereignis did want to make the Pope, and they had fixed their eyes on Sersale as the candidate who would suit them best. As soon as the breath was out of the body of Clement XIII, the Augustinian General, Vasquez, a leader of the opposition to the Society, had written to de Roda, recommending this prelate.[24] He had knowledge, he said, 'of his humble, docile, and well-intentioned character, and was sure that through him the causes of contention could be peacefully settled, and the Society extinguished with all due solemnity in a Bull which would cite the execrable principles of the Jesuits and their diabolical operations as the reason which made their suppression necessary,' and Roda in turn had recommended him to his Sovereign.[25] Tanucci also

[23] Orsini to d'Aubeterre on 19 Feb., ap. Theiner, p. 190.
[24] Danvila, op. cit. iii.p. 291. Vasquez's letter is dated 4 February.
[25] *Ibid.* p. 297.

supported his candidature, and the instructions addressed to the French Cardinals by their Court, after stating that 'the King of Spain and the Court of Naples are most anxious for his elevation', say that 'his Majesty desires Cardinals de Luynes and de Bernis to unite with the Cardinals of Spain and Naples, in carrying, as far as lies in their power, the election of Cardinal Sersale to the Pontificate'.[26]

To enable us to judge of the conduct of the Court party we have the invaluable evidence of their own words contained in the diplomatic correspondence from which Theiner draws so largely. It would be well if we could have evidence equally direct by which to judge of the conduct of the Zelanti Cardinals, whom Theiner assures us were as intriguing and regardless of their oaths of secrecy as the others. Unfortunately Theiner, although as Vatican librarian he had exceptional opportunities for research, has not been able to produce any correspondence in which these Zelanti Cardinals have recorded with their own pens their plans and purposes with reference to the Election. Doubtless this is due to no fault of his, but simply to the fact that no such correspondence exists. Still it is necessary to bear this fact in mind when we read his pages, for it means that when he reports the doings of the Zelanti Cardinals, and tells us of their motives, he is relying only on the impressions and inferences of their adversaries – men, who although observers of great acuteness and anxious for their own sakes to be accurate, were after all but outside observers, and not free from the bias which predisposes intriguers to assume that their opponents must be pursuing the same sort of aims and methods as themselves. It is in the light of this consideration that we must estimate the two facts, the only two facts, alleged by Theiner in his account of this early stage of the Conclave, as convicting the Zelanti leaders of improper intrigues and violations of their Conclave oaths. The first of these facts is that Torregiani and J. F. Albani wrote from the Conclave to Cardinals Paracciani, Buffalini, and Oddi, telling them how serious was the position of affairs and exhorting them to make haste and come.[27] But Theiner does not give us particulars of the communications thus sent, or indicate the source from which he derives his information; nor is it hard to imagine ways in which an exhortation to come into the Conclave could have been lawfully conveyed. The other and more important breach of secrecy with which J. F. Albani is charged is that of having opened communications with Azara the Spanish agent, for the sake of exploiting the 'secret of

[26] De Ravignan, op. cit. ii. p. 367.
[27] Theiner, *ibid.* p. 191.

Spain'; that is, the desire of the Spanish Court about exclusions and inclusions. Here again Theiner is unduly sparing in his details and in the indication of his sources. He quotes from a letter of Orsini's to d'Aubeterre, under the date of 21 February[28] – that is, six days after the solemn entry – a passage from which we learn that these communications between Albani and Azara were chiefly held before the Conclave began. Orsini, however, complains of their continuance up to that date through an intermediary named Ximenez, but without saying whether this man was a Conclavist or not, and for all the rest Theiner gives no authority at all, and evidently could have had no better authority than this Ximenez or Azara, who were both untrustworthy. Let us suppose, however, that Albani was guilty in this case of a breach of secrecy, – on which hypothesis we have no wish to defend him, – at all events the matter of his negotiation was not, as in the case of the Crown Cardinals, of an unbecoming nature. As Orsini kept reiterating that the sovereigns and their adherents had no thought whatever of making a Pope, and would accept any candidate the Cardinals might choose, provided he were not one marked out by his hostility to their interests, it was surely a proper thing that Albani, on behalf of the Zelanti, should ask to have the names of the candidates whom the sovereigns wished to bar, and, if this were not obtainable from Orsini, should seek it from another who was understood to enjoy the confidence of the Spanish Court. Orsini, indeed, both on this occasion and again a month later when Albani came to him direct on a similar errand,[29] resisted the application, which in his report to d'Aubeterre he professed to attribute to the desire of the Zelanti to insist on precisely those candidates whom the Courts wished to exclude. But Cordara,[30] in a passage which will be quoted in full below,[31] tells us he heard from the lips of several of the Zelanti Cardinals that they had fully realized the inadvisability of electing a Pope who would be personally displeasing to the Courts, and that they had been solicitous only to find a candidate who would please the Courts and yet not lack the personal qualities requisite in a worthy Pope. This was a very intelligible policy to follow, and in its light we may interpret the purpose of J. F. Albani on the occasion we are discussing. On the other hand, Orsini's solicitude that

---

[28] Theiner, *ibid.* p. 193.
[29] Theiner, *ibid.* p. 213.
[30] *Commentarii de suis et suorum rebus usque ad occasum Societatis Jesu.* Published as the First Part of the Third Volume of Döllinger's *Beiträge zur politischen, kirchlichen und Cultur-Geschichte.* See pp. 40–42.
[31] See p. 195.

Albani should not obtain the information he sought bears a much less satisfactory interpretation, as we already know from his own acknowledgments. He wished the other side to be kept in absolute ignorance of the names which the Courts would bar, because, in spite of their protestations to the contrary, the Courts wished to make the Pope, but had not been able to fix definitely on their candidate; and even when they had, wished to get him proposed by others, in order that their attachment to him might not be publicly suspected.

Repelled in their endeavours to find a meeting-ground between themselves and the Court party, the Zelanti Cardinals, whilst awaiting the arrival of the foreign Cardinals, could only continue the daily farce of marking time by unreal scrutinies. Meanwhile the Court party were utilizing the long interval thus secured in a much more efficacious way. 'The instructions,' says Theiner,[32] 'from the Court of Madrid, indicating the Cardinals approved by the Courts, had been anxiously awaited by Orsini, and arrived in Rome in the first half of the month of March. They were accompanied by a brief estimate of the character of the Cardinals then present in the Conclave, who numbered forty-four. These two documents had been drawn up at Madrid, and then sent on at once by the Marqués de Grimaldi, under the orders of the King, to the Courts of Versailles and Naples. It appears, however, that the cunning Azara, together with the able lawyer Centomani – who was a priest and *chargé d'affaires* for Naples at Rome, and the intimate friend of Tanucci – had first of all drafted these documents at Rome and thence sent them on to Madrid to receive there such changes and additions as that Court might please.' The Table, which forms the second of these documents, is transcribed by Danvila from the Simancas Archives.[33]

The points to notice in this Table are the following: (1) All the Cardinals on whom the choice of the elector could by any possibility fall – for non-Italian Cardinals and Cardinal ambassadors were ineligible – are arranged in four classes, of which the first gives those among whom the Spanish Court wished the choice to lie, the second those whom it wished to exclude altogether, the third those whom it wished to avoid as uncertain, the fourth those whom it regarded as impossible on personal grounds. Attached to the name of each Cardinal is his age; in the third column is the judgment of the Spanish Court concerning him; in the second column that of Tanucci; in the fourth that of Choiseul.(2) Twenty-one out of forty-three are

---

[32] Theiner, *ibid.* p. 198.
[33] *Estado. Legajo,* 4,570. Theiner, *ibid.* p. 310.

LIST OF CARDINALS

	Age	Notes by Naples	by Spain	by France
		1st Class		
Sersale	67	...	very good	...
Cavalchini,	86	...	good	very old
Negroni	59	...	good	very young
Durini	76	...	good	rejects
Corsini, Neri	84	...	good	impossible
Conti	80	...	good	impossible
Branciforte	58	...	good	like very much
Caracciolo	54	Tanucci thinks bad	good	very good, but too young
Corsini, Andrea	34	...	good	very good, but too young
Ganganelli	64	a Jesuit ?	good	very good
Pirelli	61	Tanucci thinks bad	good	good
		2nd Class		
Tonegiani	72	...	very bad	very bad
Castelli	64	...	very bad	very bad
Buonacorsi	61	...	very bad	very bad
Chigi	58	...	very bad	very bad
Boschi	54	...	very bad	very bad
Rezzonico	45	...	very bad	very bad
Oddi	90	...	very bad	very bad
Albani, Alexander	77	...	very bad	very bad
De Rossi	73	...	very bad	very bad
Calini	73	...	very bad	very bad
Veterani	66	...	very bad	very bad
Molino	64	...	very bad	very bad
Priuli	62	...	very bad	very bad
Buffalini	60	...	very bad	very bad
Des Lances	57	...	very bad	very bad
Spinola	56	...	very bad	very bad
Paracciani	54	...	very bad	very bad
Albani, J. F.	49	...	very bad	very bad
Borromeo	49	...	very bad	very bad
Colonna	45	...	very bad	very bad
Fantuzzi	61	...	very bad	very bad
		3rd Class		
Lante	74	...	doubtful	
Stoppani	74	...	doubtful	with Stoppani or Serbollini Pope then Pallavicini
Serbelloni	74	...	doubtful	Secretary of State
		4th Class		
		(Null or indifferent)		
Guglielmi	74	...	...	...
Canali	74	...	...	...
Pozzobonelli	73	...	...	...
Perelli	73	Tanucci thinks bad	...	good
Malvezzi	54	...	...	...
Pallavicini	50	...	...	Secretary of State
York	44	...	...	...
Pamphili	44	...	...	...

set down as to be excluded absolutely by the secular Courts, whereas the right of *Veto* recognized as belonging to the Courts of France, Spain, and Austria, allowed these Courts to exclude but one each; moreover, the names placed in the second division are, in substance, the names of those who bore the highest reputation in the Sacred College for talents and piety. (3) Of the eleven placed in the first class, three were too old for promotion, and three were too young, as Choiseul himself observes in the fourth column. Thus, practically, the list restricts the choice of the electors to five out of the forty-three, and of these five Sersale is singled out as the favourite candidate, although Orsini's feigned laughter at the idea of his candidature is significant testimony to his incompetency, and hence to the fact that a readiness to destroy the Society, such as they ascribed to him, was deemed to be the one qualification needful in the new Pontiff, to whom the destinies of the entire Catholic world were to be entrusted.[34] (4) The notes on Ganganelli are interesting. The Spaniards set him down as good, Choiseul as very good, while Tanucci notes that 'there are letters which say he is a Jesuit'. There was a secretiveness about this Cardinal which perplexed those who had to do with him. We shall see later how it exhibited itself during his Pontificate in his preparations for the Suppression, and it made him a sad puzzle to several of his fellow-electors in the Conclave.[35] Azara and Centomani had written to say that there were letters in existence which showed him to be a Jesuit, and Tanucci was so strikingly impressed by the news that he stood out against Ganganelli to the last; de Bernis, too, as will appear in due course, became very suspicious of him towards the end of the Conclave, whilst Rezzonico in its early days suspected him of being an anti-Jesuit so strongly that, according to Theiner, he said out before all the Cardinals, on 19 February that he would sooner vote for any one else of the Cardinals than for him.[36] On the other hand, we have heard how Roda thought well of him, which was doubtless the reason of his name appearing among the Papabili in the Spanish table, and d'Aubeterre, whose judgments in his favour have been already given, writes to Choiseul on 15 March, expressing himself as much surprised at Tanucci's

---

[34] Clement XIII in 1768 addressed a letter to Sersale, as, Archbishop of Naples, reproaching him for his silence whilst the Jesuits were being cruelly banished from that country and the rights of the Church in many ways invaded by the State. Probably it was his having been the recipient of this letter which, in the eyes of the Spanish Court, constituted his chief recommendation for the Pontificate.

[35] Theiner, *ibid*. p. 254.

[36] Theiner, *ibid*. p. 191.

adverse opinion. 'If,' he says, 'there is among the Cardinals in the Sacred College one who can be considered little addicted to the Jesuits, it is without contradiction (Ganganelli).'[37] And Azpuru,[38] after a conversation with d'Aubeterre, wrote to the same effect to Grimaldi on 16 March.

The history of this important Conclave has now reached a crucial point. The real business of the Election could not begin till the arrival of the foreign Cardinals, but the record of the previous weeks has sufficed to show how the electoral body was constituted and to what influences it was exposed. In particular it has shown us that the Bourbon Courts, in spite of their protestations to the contrary, were bent on 'making the Pope' – not that they had fixed on any definite person whose election they meant to carry, but that they meant to obtain a Pope who would be certain to suppress the Jesuits, and suppress them simply at the bidding of the Courts, apart from any independent inquiry into their merits or demerits. And it has been shown that the chief motive force on which these Courts counted for securing their end was the thinly-veiled threat of a schism which they were prepared to force on, if a candidate were chosen of whom they disapproved – for the negotiations and manoeuvres of the Crown Cardinals were all based on this underlying threat, apart from which they understood clearly that their negotiations within the Conclave would have been ineffectual.

II.[39] [Negotiations within the Conclave]

We have seen how, contrary to the spirit and even the letter of their Bulls, the Cardinals in Conclave were constrained to defer the Election of the new Pope until after the arrival of the foreign Cardinals. The three Courts had intimated through their Ambassadors, that they would refuse recognition to any candidate elected before that time, and this meant that they would follow the example already set by the King of Portugal, and coerce their subjects into schism. As the Cardinals feared to risk so terrible an eventuality, they condemned themselves to a wearisome period of inaction which lasted for upwards of ten weeks – for the Conclave opened on 15 February, but the Spanish Cardinals did not arrive till the end of April.

Meanwhile the Crown Cardinals were far from idle. They were

---

[37] Danvila, *ibid.* p. 311.
[38] *Ibid.*
[39] *The Month,* **100** (1902), 581–91.

busy corresponding with the French and Spanish Ambassadors, and through them with the Courts of Versailles and Madrid, and were maturing their plans for controlling the Election when the time for it should come. On the general character of their strategy they had already determined. The menace to refuse recognition to a candidate elected before the arrival of the foreign Cardinals was to pass into a menace to refuse recognition to any candidate for whom their approval had not first been secured – in other words, to any candidate on whom they felt unable to rely as certain to suppress the Society. This was a menace which the Crown Cardinals took care to repeat at every opportune moment during the Conclave, using always language of studied delicacy, but at the same time taking pains that their meaning should be understood. Having this powerful force in reserve they could afford to take up a negative attitude in their external dealings with the Conclave, and they kept declaring in a pious vein that they had no commission to force a nominee on the electors, and would themselves therefore propose no candidates at all; but that they would accept any suitable person proposed by the general body of the Cardinals, nor offer opposition of any kind save in the contingency, which was not to be anticipated, of a candidate being proposed who would be hostile to the interests of their Courts. Yet while exteriorly expressing themselves in this correct way, secretly they were negotiating with individual Cardinals and endeavouring to form their *exclusiva* of sixteen votes, by the dexterous use of which they would be able to reject one candidate after another, until by a process of elimination they could force on the proposal by others of some candidate who would suit their purpose.[40]

Here, however, as we have already noted, their chief difficulty arose. If they were to carry out their plan successfully they must first know for certain what candidates would suit them – yet on whom could they rely? They would like Sersale, but his chances of being accepted by the Conclave were very small, and, though there were a few others towards whom they inclined, they felt an absolute confidence in no one. As d'Aubeterre had said in his letter of 6 February, 'so difficult is it now-a-days to arrive at conclusions with any sort of certitude about any Cardinal in the Sacred College ... Moreover, a Cardinal when he becomes Pope changes his mode of thinking so

---

[40] 'Without declaring any exclusion, we draw out and kill off all the candidates disagreeable to the Crowns merely by insinuating that their election might not be recognized by the Ministers of the Sovereigns. This method has seemed to us the most efficacious of all and the least odious; and it is also inexhaustible.' (Bernis to Choiseul, 17 May 1769. Given in fac-simile in Crétineau Joly's *Clément XIV et les Jésuites,* p. 261.)

much that one can count on no one.'[41]

It was to meet this difficulty that an idea suggested itself to the Bourbon agents quite at the beginning of the Conclave. Might it not be possible to engage the future Pope by a formal promise that if elected he would give effect to the desires of the Courts? There were two ways by which such an engagement might be extracted, both of which appear to have been under the consideration of the Spanish Court from the beginning. One was to proceed openly and bring the matter before the Conclave. They were stipulating that the election must fall on a candidate who would not be opposed to the interests of the Courts, and it might be further explained to the Conclave that this meant that they could only recognize a Pope who would give them the satisfaction they had demanded in vain of the Pope just dead, particularly in regard to the Suppression of the Society of Jesus. And it might be claimed of the Conclave that, such being the political situation, the Cardinals before electing a candidate should require of him a formal and public promise that if elected he would comply with these demands of the Powers. The other way of securing their purpose would be for the Crown Cardinals to approach privately the Cardinals towards whom they inclined, and endeavour to extract from them a confidential but written promise to the same effect – assuring them that if they refused the Courts would refuse to recognize their election, but if they assented the entire influence of the Courts would be used on their behalf.

Azpuru, with whom – in collusion with his colleague Azara and with the Marquis d'Aubeterre – the idea of a promise before election originated, communicated it promptly to his chiefs at Madrid. We are not aware of the precise letter in which this was done, but it must have been written early in February for the letters it elicited from Grimaldi were dated 7 March. These were five in number,[42] and included one addressed to Azpuru himself giving him instructions how to deal with the matter; one addressed to the Conde de Fuentes and another to Tanucci, who were to inform the Courts of Versailles and Naples what had been written to Azpuru, and to invite them to send similar instructions to their own representatives at Rome; and

---

[41] Theiner, *Pontificat de Clément XIV*, i. p. 181. Compare also Bernis's estimate of the Cardinals in his letter to Choiseul, of 3 April (ap. Masson's *Le Cardinal de Bernis depuis son Ministère*, p. 104): 'A little more or less fanaticism in favour of Ultramontane principles is the sole nuance which distinguishes the members of the Conclave. And they do not wish as Pope either a young man, or an aged man, or an incapable man. This fixed intention on their part makes the business of electing the Pope very difficult.'

[42] Danvila, *Historia del Reinado de Carlos III*, p. 304.

one each to the two Spanish Cardinals, de Solís and de la Cerda, who were being sent to the Conclave, that they might know what they would be called upon to do. In the Instructions to Azpuru it is said that 'the three Courts are determined to insist on the demands made during the Pontificate of Clement XIII, that they may indeed abate somewhat of the satisfaction to the outraged Duke of Parma which they had required of that Pope, but that as regards the Jesuits nothing short of their absolute suppression would be accepted.' It was, however, 'matter for consideration whether it would do for the Conclave then sitting to pass a decree in virtue of which the future Pope would be bound to consent to one or both of these points.' Such a decree on the part of the Conclave and such an agreement on the part of the Pope would be entirely just and reasonable, and was unquestionably due to the three powerful monarchs on whom the Church had to count as its firmest supports. At the same time it was presumable that a considerable party in the Conclave would oppose the idea, and hence, as it would not be proper to compromise the respectable names of these monarchs by making an overt demand which there would be a risk of not obtaining, it was impossible to prescribe beforehand any fixed course. His Majesty therefore left it to the prudence of the three Ministers acting in concert to decide according to the exigencies of the situation what course would be most prudent, but they must remember that two things were to be considered: one, whether the proposal if made would be likely to succeed and the honour of the Courts would not be risked; the other, whether it was proper to make it.[43]

Azpuru received the above Instructions about the end of March, and some days later d'Aubeterre received a corresponding communication from Choiseul, which was dated 21 March.[44] Choiseul emphasized somewhat more than Grimaldi the dangers that might

---

[43] This last clause may seem to save the consciences of those who penned and issued these Instructions, but how little stress they mentally laid on it is clear from its omission in the companion letter to Tanucci. There we read only that 'the King's desire and his (Grimaldi's) own is that the question of the Suppression should be laid before the Conclave, but (that) the enterprize would be very difficult as Rome is inundated with creatures of the Jesuits, and hence the order to Azpuru has been conditional; if (they) could succeed in forming a firm and reliable party sufficient to give an *exclusive* vote, the case for imposing conditions would arise, but the difficulty is to form such a party ... The King of Spain is consulting Azpuru on the propriety of laying this demand in reference to the Society of Jesus before the Conclave, and is leaving it to the discretion of the Ambassadors (whether to do so or not) as they may see their opportunity, since parties change every day.' (Danvila, *ibid*. p. 305.)

[44] See Theiner, *ibid*. p. 219.

follow from prematurely raising the question of the Suppression, and also gave prominence to a point in which the French took a more direct interest – namely, that the new Pope should formally recognize the incorporation of Avignon into the French monarchy. But the French Foreign Minister finished his communication by directing d'Aubeterre to take the Instructions to Azpuru as addressed also to himself; and to communicate them to the French Cardinals, de Luynes and de Bernis, who had by this time reached their cells in the Conclave.[45]

Notwithstanding the anxieties expressed by Grimaldi and Choiseul lest the attempt to extract a promise should prove too dangerous, Azpuru and d'Aubeterre, with a not unnatural predilection for their own progeny, determined to exercise the discretion allowed them in its behalf, and directed their Cardinals accordingly: Azpuru, to remove the scruples of any doubters they might encounter, also drew up a *dictamen*, or theological opinion, in which he argued for its lawfulness. In this *dictamen* he asks whether, if any one believes the suppression of the Jesuits to be necessary for the peace and welfare of the Church, he can without fearing to incur the guilt of simony demand of a Pope before his election the promise to execute such a measure. He divides the answer according to the two methods above distinguished, and decides that no scruple whatever need deter a man from demanding such a promise publicly from each of the Cardinals, giving as his reason that a promise so made would not open the way to the Pontificate to any one Cardinal more than another. Nor does he consider that a promise privately and confidentially extracted from an individual, in return for a promise to support his candidature, would be less permissible. 'Inasmuch,' he says, 'as learned and conscientious men hold the said Suppression to be necessary for the welfare and peace of the Church, a promise exacted from an individual Cardinal as the condition of support for his candidature would be no more simoniacal, as by taking upon himself such an engagement he would only be binding himself to fulfil his most sacred obligations?'[46]

What is fallacious in this argument is that it confounds a promise to do what is self-evidently and by the consent of all men conducive to the welfare of the Church with a promise to do what a few men only, and in particular those who promise their support to the candidate, may in the exercise of their own private and perhaps biassed judgment take to be for the welfare of the Church. It might and

---

[45] Cardinal de Bernis entered the Conclave on March 25th, and Cardinal de Luynes a few days earlier.

[46] The text of Azpuru's *dictamen* is given (or summarised?) by Ferrer del Río in his *Reinado de Carlos III* (ii. p. 273)

should be unnecessary, but it would certainly not be simoniacal, to extort from one about to be made Pope, even as a condition of obtaining votes, a promise to live a moral life and not subordinate spiritual to temporal interests – for no Cardinal who was not prepared to set this ideal before his eyes could be worthy of elevation to the Papacy. On the other hand, in regard to all questions bearing on the welfare of the Church the answer to which is not self-evident but requires to be determined by the exercise of a prudent judgment – and the question whether the Society of Jesus ought to be suppressed was obviously such – it is the Pope's right and duty to exercise that judgment himself, according to the lights which God may give him at the time, nor may he barter away this his personal responsibility to another. He may indeed, and should, instruct himself by the counsels of others, but if he were to bind himself by a promise to do what afterwards in the exercise of his personal judgment he might deem incompatible with the welfare of the Church, or with the principles of equity, or to be wrong in any other way, his promise would be both unlawful and invalid, whilst if made before his election, and as the price of his election, it would be also simoniacal, and by the Bull of Julius II (*Quum tam divino*) would even render his election invalid.

Now that we have seen and examined the grounds on which these diplomatists justified their methods, we may return to the course of the history. Both Azpuru and d'Aubeterre, soon after the receipt of the Instructions from their Courts, that is, on 10 April,[47] sent in letters to Orsini – d'Aubeterre further asking him to communicate the contents to the French Cardinals and concert with them the necessary steps for obtaining the promises.

When we remember how Orsini was persistently violating his Conclave oath by his systematic correspondence with the Ministers outside, it is impossible to credit him with an excessive delicacy of conscience. Still he had a conscience and his conscience revolted against the unworthy proposal now made to him. He wrote back the very same day both to Azpuru and d'Aubeterre, resolutely declining to do as he was directed.[48] 'I am held back', he said, 'less by the thought that this step would produce no advantageous results than by the conviction that it would cause general consternation among the Cardinals; and most especially by the voice of my conscience, which I do not wish to soil for any consideration whatever. To take part in such an act would be nothing less than to become guilty of an act of simony, and to arrive at an election which would be invalid and,

[47] Theiner, *ibid*. p. 220.
[48] *Ibid*.

what is more, immoral.' And on the day following he wrote again, saying that 'he had told the French Cardinals what had been proposed and they agreed with him altogether, and they all three hoped that d'Aubeterre would not trouble them any more with such a demand, as the resolution they had taken was a matter of conscience from which they would never swerve.' Theiner does not give the letters of the two French Cardinals, but they seem to have written to d'Aubeterre[49] in the same sense as Orsini. That de Luynes should take this right-minded course is not astonishing, for he was an excellent man,[50] but it is with a feeling of agreeable surprise that one finds de Bernis doing the like. We have heard something in a former chapter of this enterprizing little *Abbé de Cour,* who began his career

---

[49] Cf. Masson, op. cit. p. 100.

[50] It was this Cardinal de Luynes whose signature headed the *Avis* in favour of the Society addressed by the forty-four French Bishops to Louis XV on 30 December 1761, and we may be surprised to find him now among the Cardinals pledged to elect a Pope who would suppress it. If we wish, however, to account for the change, we must not fail to observe the similar change in others. Up to the day when the King of Naples expelled the Jesuits from his dominions Cardinal Orsini was one of their firm friends. He had been educated by them in his youth, he was a frequent and almost daily visitor at the Gesù, and had chosen Padre Ricci for his confessor. Cardinal de Solís, too, whom we shall meet with presently as the leading Spanish Cardinal at the Conclave, had been a leader among the Society's friends in Spain, and in 1759 wrote to Clement XIII a splendid letter on their behalf. (See Ravignan's, *Clément XIII et Clément XIV,* ii. p. 132.) He changed only when the Spanish monarch published his severe edicts against them. These were Cardinals; but an exactly similar *volte-face* was to be witnessed in the Spanish Ambassador at Paris, the Conde de Fuentes, who it will be remembered was a brother of the Fathers Pignatelli. And many like cases of prelates and prominent laymen could doubtless be collected. On the other hand, there were indications that the change was external only and did not affect their inner sentiments. Azara felt certain that de Luynes was at heart a Jesuit, and de Fuentes likewise, and d'Aubeterre entertained similar suspicions of de Solís; nor again do we find any of the four named joining in the severe charges against the Jesuits. They laboured for their suppression and for the measures leading up to it – that was all. And if we ask the reason why, we must trace it to the fearful despotism of the Bourbon Courts of those days, together with the demoralizing principle of blind obedience which they exacted from all their servants. There is a kind of blind obedience which is praiseworthy, but it is one which is circumscribed by careful limits. In the obedience which those sovereigns required there were simply no limits at all, and a servant of the Crown was expected to assume the rectitude of every order given to him, and carry it out without reference to his own beliefs and feelings. It is this which explains the extraordinary inconsistency of the Cardinals and others, and if Orsini, de Luynes, and de Bernis drew the line at the simoniacal promise when called upon to exact it, it was only because the immorality in this instance was too glaring. Even here, however, they showed a nervousness at having to resist an order given, which speaks volumes as to the servitude in which they lived.

by paying court to Madame de Pompadour and owed it to her influence that he had been promoted successively to the leading post in the French Ministry, to the archbishopric of Albi, and finally to the Cardinalate. He was even now a man of the world rather than a spiritually-minded prelate. Still he had improved somewhat since his promotion and had his good points, of which, as of his worldly-mindedness, we shall have evidence in the sequel. Moreover, if sometimes flippant and always vain, he had good talents, and could often take sound views of the situations in which he was placed. It is to these better qualities in his nature that we must ascribe his refusal to be mixed up with Azpuru's simoniacal proposal.

The two Ambassadors were not a little annoyed at the resistance of the Cardinals placed under their directions, and d'Aubeterre wrote back to Orsini on 12 April, a letter in which, whilst withdrawing one of the alternative proposals, he continued to insist on the other. 'The Ambassador', he wrote in the third person, 'thinks with your Eminences that it would be dangerous and useless to broach the subject to the Sacred College, but he does not at all agree with the conscientious scruple which makes you opposed to the idea of binding the candidate to be elected by a written promise in regard to the Jesuits.' Orsini, however, and his French colleagues, stood firm, as he told d'Aubeterre in his prompt reply. Neither to the Conclave as a whole, nor to an individual Cardinal, would they ever make so improper a proposal. D'Aubeterre's next letter, on 15 April, manifested his growing vexation by the tartness of its tone. It was true that the French Cardinals agreed with Orsini, and it was equally true that he himself thought otherwise; 'nor could he ever be brought to understand how the proposal could be simoniacal, seeing that it involved no question of temporal advantage, but only of a matter which was purely spiritual, and useful to the Church and the Holy See – one too which had already been demanded of it, and might be demanded of it at any time.[51] D'Aubeterre overlooks, it will be observed, the little detail that the Pontificate was a rich benefice, such as an unworthy candidate might be tempted to ambition, and that the promise was to be set before him as a price by paying which he could have his ambition gratified. However he submits resignedly to the scruples of the Crown Cardinals, though with regret, that 'they should be obliged in consequence to forego the surest means of destroying the Jesuits and securing the peace of the Church.'

So at least he wrote to Orsini, but he wrote also to Choiseul on 18 April,[52] and from the tenour of this letter we see how unwilling he

[51] Theiner, *ibid*. p. 222.
[52] *Ibid*.

was to abandon the project, whilst through the lines we can read his desire that the Courts should try the effect of a little terrorism in reducing these Cardinals to compliance. In this letter he first explains why it would not be feasible to broach the question of the promise to the Cardinals as a body. The Cardinals have no power to impose any such obligation on the candidate they elect, who on becoming Pope would have the right to undo all that had been done. He then affirms his desire for the secret promise, and repeats the defence of it which he had already given to Orsini. He laments the scruples of the Crown Cardinals, and tells how 'he had proposed to them to open their minds in confidence to Cardinal Ganganelli, a celebrated theologian in these parts, who has never had the reputation of relaxed morals.' And he concludes by explaining the immense importance of extracting the desired promise from the candidate whose election they might be able to carry. 'Nothing is more uncertain,' he says, 'than the course which a Pope will take if he has not been previously bound down, whilst on the other hand, although the Bulls authorize him to regard as null any promise made before his Election, he would none the less be obliged to keep it since otherwise he would be publicly dishonoured in the face of the Christian world ... The task, however, is to persuade our Cardinals, and that does not appear to be easy.' And in a further letter, dated 26 April,[53] he harps on the same strain, and states that 'he has secretly consulted many theologians, who have advised him that there is no ground for the excessive delicacy (of the Crown Cardinals), and that Azpuru, who is also of this opinion, is very much annoyed at their refusal to carry out the measure, as it is one for which his Court is most anxious, being of the highest importance and the best calculated to assure the attainment of their principal object.' Cardinal de Bernis had also written to Choiseul a few days earlier,[54] and their letters were crossed by one which shows that the French court had yielded to the remonstrance of de Bernis rather than to the solicitations of d'Aubeterre himself. Choiseul remarks wisely that whether the plan of extorting a promise be defensible or not, of which the Casuists alone could judge – at any rate, it was practically useless, as no Cardinal at all fit to be made Pope would be induced to take it. This letter, however, was not written till 2 May, and could not therefore have arrived in time to influence the result, and meanwhile with the arrival of the Spanish Cardinals the controversy between the Ambassadors and the Crown Cardinals became further complicated.

[53] *Ibid.*
[54] Masson, loc. cit.

Cardinals de Solís and de la Cerda – of whom the former was Archbishop of Seville and the latter Patriarch of the Indies – reached Rome at the end of April, and de la Cerda entered the Conclave on 27 April, de Solís on 30 April.[55] Their first act was to associate themselves with the French and Neapolitan representatives in protesting that they did not aspire to make the Pope, but only to prevent a surprise election; and that they would willingly co-operate in the election of any candidate who should come to the front from among those who were reputed to be prudent, impartial, and virtuous.[56] They kept repeating this protestation on suitable occasions, both before and after their entrance into the Conclave, and for so doing were applauded by the Cardinals of all parties. Unfortunately, in their case as in the case of the other Crown Cardinals, public protestation and private manoeuvrings were at variance.

A meeting of the Crown Cardinals had been called which was to take place on 3 May in the cell of Cardinal Orsini. Its object was that the Spanish Cardinals might explain to the others the further instructions they had brought from Madrid, and it was understood that, in virtue of the agreement between the three Courts, these were also to be received by the French and Neapolitan representatives as their final rule of action. An account of the meeting was sent off to Azpuru by de Solís, in a letter written the same day, and the following is a summary of its contents.[57] De Solís had explained to the other Cardinals that the Spanish Court still wished for Sersale as the new Pope, but, if his candidature proved impossible, before the choice of the Conclave could be allowed to fall on another it would be necessary for him first to promise in writing to suppress the Jesuits. To this, however, de Bernis and de Luynes at once replied that such a compact would be simoniacal, and repugnant to their consciences. They confirmed their opinion by citing that of several theologians and canonists, and protested that if the Spanish Court insisted on their exacting any such promise, they would simply abstain from taking part in the Election, and leave the other Crown Cardinals to vote by themselves. They also urged, as Orsini had previously urged in his letter to d'Aubeterre, that the compact would be useless, as it could have no binding force on the future Pope, should he afterwards see fit to change his mind, besides which the proceeding must ultimately become public, in which case it would scandalize the faithful and cause the heretics to exult. De Solís vainly endeavoured to gain them over to the view of his Court, and suggested by way of compromise

[55] Ferrer del Río, op. cit. ii, p. 277.
[56] *Ibid.*
[57] Ferrer del Río, *ibid.* p. 277; Danvila, *ibid.* p. 320.

that the engagement instead of being written might be made by word of mouth in the presence of the Crown Cardinals. But the French Cardinals replied that this way of doing it would be worse, not better, and when it became known would have the effect of alienating several of the Cardinals on whose votes they were counting, and so destroy all their chances of an *exclusiva*. Orsini again declared his agreement with the French Cardinals, and recommended as by far the safest course that they should work for the success of a candidate on whose character they could rely for his future willingness to favour the pretensions of the three Courts. Externally the Spaniards yielded to this opinion, and de Solís tells Azpuru that, in view of the stubborn resistance of the French and Neapolitans, they felt that the case had arisen which their instructions contemplated, and that it would be risking the honour of their Courts to urge any longer the question of the compact.

Whether the Spanish Cardinals gave up the idea entirely is not quite clear, for from this time forth they drew off to some extent from their colleagues, and began to work apart for the furtherance of their ends. By so doing they excited the suspicions of de Bernis and Orsini, as we shall see in the next section, and it is difficult not to feel that they were engaged in negotiations of which they knew the others would disapprove. If, however, the object of this secrecy was to persist in their endeavour to extract the written promise from one or more of the candidates, it is at least satisfactory to know that they failed to succeed, and we shall hear later from their own lips that they never ventured so far as to propose the promise to a single Cardinal. This is to the credit of the Cardinals whose candidature they favoured, but does not acquit the Courts or their Ambassadors of a readiness to secure their objects even by these base means.

III.[58] [The election of Cardinal Ganganelli: Clement XIV]

We have now reached the final stage of the Conclave, and have to see by what process of transformation and development Ganganelli's election, which at one time seemed hopeless, was carried at length by a unanimous vote. Towards the end of April, and just before the arrival of the Spaniards, there reached the Ambassadors from Madrid a second list[59] in which the names of the Cardinals were tabulated according to the place they held in the estimation of the Spanish

[58] *The Month*, 101 (1903), 48–61.
[59] D'Aubeterre communicated it to his Cardinals on 23 April. Theiner, *Histoire du Pontificat de Clément XIV*, vol. i, p. 225.

Court. This revision was the result of the weekly letters sent to Madrid by Azpuru and Azara. It divided the Cardinals into the same four classes as before, but arranged the names differently in one or two cases.

An accompanying letter explained that the details of the arrangement had been well considered, and that the Crown Cardinals were to strive first for the success of the name placed first on the list; if they failed with this name, then for that next on the list; and so on till the names in the first and second classes were exhausted. On the other hand, should the Conclave show a disposition to elect one whose name was set in the third class, it was to be informed that if such an election were persisted in, the case would arise for the Ambassadors to withdraw to Frascati; whilst if it strove to carry a name in the fourth class, the representative of one of the three Courts was to deliver a formal veto on behalf of his Court. With this explanation we transcribe from Theiner[60] the list in question.

I. FIRST CLASS (Papabiles.)

Sersale, Malvezzi, Cavalchini, Neri Corsini, Conti, Ganganelli, Perelli, Branciforte, Negroni, Carracciolo, Andrea Corsini; (subsidiary), Stoppani.

II. SECOND CLASS (Indifferents)

Pallavicini, Canali, Guglielmi, York, Pamphili.

III. THIRD CLASS (To be avoided.)

Oddi, de Rossi, Pozzobonelli, Serbelloni, Pirelli, Durini, Lante, Calini, Veterani, Molino, Priuli, delle Lanze, Spinola, Borromeo, M. A. Colonna

IV. FOURTH CLASS (To be excluded)

Torregiani, Boschi, Castelli, Buonacorsi, Chigi, Fantuzzi, Buffalini, Rezzonico, Alexander Albani, J. F Albani.

On comparing this list with the previous list, given earlier in this chapter, it will be observed (1) that seven out of the eight Cardinals who then formed the fourth class, and were described as lacking the personal gifts requisite in a Pope, are now exalted to the first or second class; (2) that Malvezzi, one of the seven, is put second on the entire list, an assignment which we shall find readily intelligible later on when we

---

[60] Ibid.

learn how he treated the Jesuits at Bologna; (3) that Cavalchini's place on the list is evidently due to the counsels of Roda, who had recommended[61] him as one who would make no difficulties about at once suppressing the Society, and who, although so aged, might live long enough to alter the balance of opinion in the Sacred College by the creation of new Cardinals pleasing to the Crowns; (4) that, inasmuch as Cavalchini (aged eighty-six), Neri Corsini (aged eighty-four), and Conti (aged eighty, and besides in his dotage),[62] were most unlikely to secure a sufficiency of votes, Ganganelli, though nominally placed sixth, was practically placed third, or rather, he was practically placed first, since he was the first candidate on the list whom the Conclave were in any way likely to accept – Sersale and Malvezzi being quite impossible.

It was with this list in their hands and, as we learn from de Bernis,[63] nineteen or twenty votes at their command, that the Crown Cardinals, now that the serious business of the Election was allowed to commence, began to work the ballots in the interest of their Courts. Theiner has reprinted from the original archives of the Conclave a table giving the results of the evening scrutinies for every day between 27 April and 18 May. It will assist us to understand the tactics of the Crown Cardinals, and is here subjoined.[64]

It appears from this list that, apart from Ganganelli, four names were prominent in the voting-lists during the last three weeks of the Conclave. Of these Fantuzzi, Colonna, and Pozzobonelli were the candidates of the Zelanti Cardinals, and it may be wondered why, when the situation was so critical this party did not concentrate its strength on a single name. Theiner's theory, founded presumably on the conjectures of Orsini, is that they were divided among themselves by personal jealousies, but it is more likely that they were putting forward several candidates with the view of discovering which would be acceptable to the Crown Cardinals – who, it will be remembered,

---

[61] Ferrer del Río, *El reinado de Carlos III*, tom. ii, p. 267.
[62] In the first list Choiseul marks both Conti and Neri Corsini as 'impossible'. See above, p. 174.
[63] De Bernis to Choiseul, of 5 April, ap. Masson, *Le Cardinal de Bernis depuis son Ministère*, p. 98. This number is apparently made up of the votes of the five Crown Cardinals and of those placed in Categories I and II of the revised list.
[64] Theiner, *ibid*. The figures for the scrutiny of 18 May cannot be altogether correct, for there were forty-six Cardinals only in the Conclave at the time of the Election, whereas the aggregate of the votes recorded is, according to Theiner's list, 50. Probably the excess should he deducted from the votes ascribed to Colonna and Pozzobonelli. The votes ascribed to Ganganelli are at all events correct. When in the voting of the previous scrutinies the aggregate is less than 46, we may infer that the remaining votes were either scattered among other candidates, or given to 'No one'.

		Table of Scrutinies in the Conclave of 1769				
		Fantuzzi	Colonna	Pozzobonelli	Stoppani	Ganganelli
April	27	10	9	6	5	5
	28	9	9	7	6	4
	29	8	11	4	5	4
	30	8	11	4	5	4
May	1	9	11	4	4	4
	2	9	11	4	4	4
	3	9	9	4	5	4
	4	9	10	4	5	4
	5	10	9	3	4	4
	6	11	6	4	7	4
	7	7	8	4	6	4
	8	5	9	3	6	4
	9	5	11	4	6	4
	10	4	11	5	7	4
	11	3	11	6	5	5
	12	5	11	6	6	6
	13	5	13	6	7	6
	14	4	11	9	8	10
	15	4	11	9	11	10
	16	4	11	8	8	10
	17	1	12	12	5	10
	18	1	13	11	6	19

whilst threatening a schism in the contingency of an unwelcome candidate being elected, persistently refused to state beforehand what names would be regarded as belonging to this category. And if such was the motive of the Zelanti they were not left long in uncertainty. In the list which the Court party had in their hands Fantuzzi's name was down as one of the eleven who were the most objectionable of all, whilst Colonna's and Pozzobonelli's were in the division of those who were only less unpalatable and such that the election of any one of them, should it come to pass, was to be met by the withdrawal of the Ambassadors to Frascati. Accordingly, on 29 April, when, says Theiner, Fantuzzi's chances were good, d'Aubeterre wrote to Orsini, 'It is certain that if they force us to it by an election disagreeable to the Courts, I shall leave Rome at once. My intention is in that case to go to Frascati, and I imagine that will also be the retreat of your Eminence. If M. Azpuru likes to come with me, I shall offer him hospitality, ... but I always hope that there will be a sufficiency of wise people in the Conclave to stop the fanatics.'[65] And de Bernis, in

---

[65] Theiner, *ibid*. p. 234.

a letter to d'Aubeterre of 8 May, tells us how faithfully the Crown Cardinals had carried out his orders: 'Yesterday evening I took the course of speaking so strongly of the departure of the Ministers from Rome, and of the renewal of the declaration (to that effect) made eight days ago ... that fear has seized our adversaries. Fantuzzi has had but few votes in the scrutiny (to-day). We renewed the declaration all together to John Francis Albani, who holds the office of sub-dean, and who answered us like an angel.'[66] Reference to the voting list shows that Fantuzzi's votes began to fall off from that time, and de Bernis in the same letter tells us that this Cardinal personally intervened and withdrew his candidature. For Colonna and Pozzobonelli votes continued to be given, but it was a foregone conclusion that they could not succeed, as it was well understood that the Courts would not have them; and on 12 May we find d'Aubeterre assuming as much, and already looking forward to the next candidates whom the Zelanti might bring forward. 'We must now see which of his creatures Rezzonico will put forward next. If he thinks to draw us out of our hostility by force of making us reject candidates, he on his side will fall into downright contempt for having let his creatures fall to the ground.'[67]

In the midst of all this unhallowed manoeuvring it is refreshing to hear that there were members of the Conclave who could speak the language of Christian sincerity, and on the following day we find de Bernis writing back to d'Aubeterre and saying: 'Cardinal Rezzonico has told us that our way of thinking would not hinder him from proposing Cardinal Colonna, if he could obtain a sufficiency of votes, and that he would have no regard for the sentiments of the Courts, but much regard for the sentiments of the Sacred College, and his conscience. I had much difficulty in getting rid of him. Nothing would appease him, and he said that it was for us to act as we would, and for him to act as his conscience dictated.'[68] The end however was nearer than either side imagined, and apart from Stoppani and Ganganelli no more names came before the electors.

Of Stoppani it is not necessary to say much. He seems to have been a worthy man, but the fact of his appearing on the Spanish list as a 'subsidiary' to the first division implies that the Court party had some ground for hoping that he would prove an anti-Jesuit Pope. Both de Bernis and Orsini, who, as we shall see, were doubtful about Ganganelli, were attracted towards Stoppani, and probably it was through their action that his name came to figure on the lists.

[66] Ap. Crétineau-Joly, op. cit. p. 357.
[67] Theiner, ibid. p. 234.
[68] *Carayon's Documents inédits sur la Compagnie de Jésus.* Doc. xviii. p.183.

Nevertheless, his candidature did not make much progress, partly because the Zelanti were suspicious of his relations with the French, partly perhaps because d'Aubeterre became dissatisfied with him for refusing to give the written promise,[69] but chiefly (no doubt) because the candidature of Ganganelli was deemed preferable.

Regularly in each scrutiny from the commencement of the Conclave until 27 April this Cardinal received two or three votes and never more. During the next sixteen days this number slightly increased, yet never rose above six. But on 14 May it suddenly rose to ten, and again after remaining at this figure for four more days, took another leap to nineteen, the highest number recorded for any Cardinal so far. We have to see how this sudden change was brought about. The point is one on which Theiner has a theory which he announces in the following magnificent passage:

> Whilst human passions were agitating on either side with the utmost activity, Divine Providence took in hand the man of its choice, and conducted him by wonderful ways of justice to the infallible throne of truth on which he was so soon to sit, and for which he had been predestined since the origin of time.[70]

In a sense every Papal Election, even that of Alexander VI, is ascribable to Divine Providence. But of course what Theiner means is that the selection of Ganganelli for the Papacy was brought about so unexpectedly, and in a manner so much in despite of all human calculations, that it can only be explained by supposing some very special intervention of Divine Providence swaying the hearts of the electors and impelling them to vote contrary to their natural propensities. In other words, Theiner wishes us to understand that Cardinal Ganganelli, though the man destined in the Providence of God to defeat all their schemes for preserving the Society, was the choice not of the Crown Cardinals, but of the Zelanti, and was carried by their votes to the Papal throne.

In proof of his theory Theiner lays special stress on a letter sent from within the Conclave by Orsini to d'Aubeterre on 16 May, the

---

[69] 'None of the Cardinals have gone so far as to propose to any one that the Suppression should be secured by a written or spoken promise, although the French Ambassador has through various channels solicited the same of Stoppani, as he himself (i.e. d'Aubeterre) told me, and I have already informed your Excellency.' (Azpuru to Grimaldi, 18 May, ap. Danvila, *Reinado de Carlos III*, tom. iii. p. 327). It is not said here whether Stoppani refused or not, but it may be presumed that he did, especially as otherwise his candidature would have been more zealously promoted.

[70] Theiner, *ibid*. p. 236.

day when he tells us the election of Ganganelli was first seriously considered. 'I believe', writes Orsini, 'that all the attempts of which I have spoken remaining without effect, Rezzonico is beginning to speak of Ganganelli. I shall be attentive to see if the rumour takes consistency.'[71] And in a postscript he adds, 'After I had written the above letter, Cardinal Albani came to me and made a long discourse on the subject of Ganganelli, saying that he might be elected Pope within two or three days, and that the Crowns made no opposition. I replied that the time had not yet come for us to pronounce on the subject. He then began to expound to me the reasons why the Courts should he satisfied. These reasons were his opposition to the Jesuits, his attachment to Don Manuel de Roda, his quality as Postulator of the Cause of the Venerable Palafox, and different other things to which I answered nothing. Albani added afterwards that nearly all the Old College[72] would vote for him as well as a great portion of the New, to which I replied, "Let Rezzonico propose him."'

This passage shows indeed a certain readiness on the part of the Zelanti to give their votes to Ganganelli, even though they suspected him of anti-Jesuit proclivities,[73] but inasmuch as the Courts by dint of threats and exclusions had rendered so many previous attempts ineffectual and so many other candidatures impracticable, it hardly requires a theory of semi-miraculous intervention to explain why this party should have at last turned their attention to one who may well have appeared to them the best of the few still left to their choice. The Holy See had now been vacant for three months and a half, and it was becoming imperatively necessary to provide it with another occupant without further delay. And that this was the motive which finally determined them to support Cardinal Ganganelli can be established directly from another source, for Cordara in the work quoted lower down tells us J. F. Albani said to him, 'We could not make a good Pope as we wished; and we did not want to make a bad one; so we made the best we could find among the doubtful candidates.'

In fact however, it was not the Zelanti party but the Spaniards who initiated Ganganelli's candidature, as Cardinal de Solís himself tells us in a letter to Azpuru dated 28 June. This was a communication

---

[71] Theiner, *ibid*.
[72] By the Old College were meant the Cardinals created by the predecessors of the late Pope, by the New College those created by himself.
[73] It may, however, be as Orsini evidently suspected, that Albani in putting forward these reasons for Ganganelli's acceptabtilty to the Courts, was merely trying to draw Orsini, and so find out whether it was a fact that Ganganelli had these proclivities and was being put forward by the Spaniards on account of some secret understanding.

evoked by the desire of Carlos III to know exactly what happened during the eventful last two days of the Conclave, and it will be well to give the text in its entirety.

> The Cardinals of the three Crowns had agreed together that it would be impossible for Sersale or Cavalchini ever to become Pope, whilst Fantuzzi and Colonna had been informally[74] excluded, and opposition was offered to Stoppani by the adherents of Rezzonico and J. F. Albani, who were strongly moved thereto by the belief that the French, as they had published, were pledged to obtain his elevation. Under these circumstances Cardinal de Solís, in a meeting of the Crown Cardinals proposed Cardinal Ganganelli as a candidate worthy of the tiara, both because of the combination of suitable qualities which adorned him, and because the way in which he had already expressed himself in private justified a confident expectation that he would fulfil the desires of his (de Solís's) Sovereign, and carry out the measures which his Court wished to see undertaken by the new Pope.
>
> Cardinal de Solís experienced much opposition from Cardinal de Bernis, who, as he protested, was far from wishing to dissociate himself from the instructions received by the Spanish Cardinals, but who – men's judgments being diverse – judged differently from Cardinal de Solís about Cardinal Ganganelli, and suspected that he would not prove so suitable as was anticipated. And Cardinal Orsini, though less decisively, adhered to this opinion.
>
> Cardinal de Solís endeavoured to convince the said Cardinals that they were mistaken, and assured them that the private interview he had had with Cardinal Ganganelli made him feel certain that none would be fitter to occupy the See of St Peter. Cardinal de Solís also pointed out that if they did not propose the said Cardinal, there was a danger of Cardinal Chigi being proposed, who was a man detested by the Crowns, and, as they were aware, placed by them on the list of vitandi. Cardinal de Solís, however, finished by protesting that he wished to take no step in the Election apart from the unanimous consent of the Cardinals who held the voice of the Courts – such being the instructions given them by the Minister, Don Thomas Azpuru.
>
> It was eventually agreed to communicate the proposal (about Ganganelli) to Cardinal Rezzonico – for fear lest he should propose another who would not be acceptable to the Courts – and this having been done confidentially, he (Rezzonico) replied that he would lay it before his adherents, but that it was a matter which must be carefully considered and therefore required time.

[74] A formal exclusion would have been made by the formal *veto* which each of the three Catholic Powers – France, Spain, and Germany – were entitled to exercise *once* during a Conclave. By an 'informal' exclusion de Solís meant the kind of exclusion the Courts were arbitrarily exercising during that particular Conclave through their threats to refuse recognition.

The Rezzonico party knew that the election of Cardinal Ganganelli would be quite acceptable to the Court of Spain, and most satisfactory to it; and this consideration also drew into agreement with that party the party of Cardinal J. F. Albani, who were further influenced by the fact that the French had not obtained their desires in regard to Stoppani. And as for the French themselves, they saw that Stoppani could not be made Pope, and that after Sersale and Cavalchini the Spanish Cardinals preferred Ganganelli to any other, and they had therefore to yield to the insistency with which Cardinal de Solís showed them that it would be advantageous to the three Crowns that Ganganelli and no other should fill the See of St Peter.

The Rezzonico and Albani party remained a day and a half without giving any reply, and the national Cardinals suspected some secret intrigue was going on which might be injurious to their interests. When therefore they came together for their last meeting (in the Conclave) they thought of finding out what the others were arranging so secretly, by obliging them to give a categorical answer. Whilst, however, they were in this state of doubt and were considering de Bernis's continued fears for the result if Ganganelli became Pope, Rezzonico informed them in the name of his own party and that of J. F. Albani, that they were ready to vote for (Ganganelli). Having learnt this and having also obtained the previous consent of Cardinal de Bernis, the Royal Meeting, that is to say, the Cardinals of the three Courts, agreed that Ganganelli should be elevated to the Pontificate, as being the most worthy to occupy the throne of St Peter. And in eight hours the election was brought to pass.[75]

The negotiations described by de Solís in this letter were confined to 17 and 18 May, but they were the outcome of less formal negotiations which had been going on for some days previously. De Solís tells us, in this very letter, of the conferences he had held with Ganganelli; and Azpuru, in a letter to Grimaldi of 25 May,[76] tells us what was their purport. 'Ganganelli', he writes, 'although he neither made the promise nor refused it explained himself in terms which caused Cardinal de Solís to feel certain that he would carry out the Suppression if he were elected to the Pontificate.' And de Solís had also interchanged several previous communications with Cardinal Albani as we learn from d'Aubeterre, who in his letter of 17 May,[77] complains to Choiseul 'of all the secret negotiations of the Spaniards with Albani, carried on without the knowledge of our Cardinals, for promoting the election of Ganganelli.' He adds, 'They made a mystery of it to me too. I had it first from de Bernis ... The proceeding is not straightforward.'

[75] Danvila, *ibid*. pp. 337–9.
[76] Danvila, *ibid*. p. 336.
[77] Danvila, *ibid*. p. 337.

But although d'Aubeterre resented the exclusion of his countrymen from these secret negotiations, he still retained his favourable opinion of Ganganelli, who was besides down on their list as a suitable candidate, and indeed was practically at the head of it. Hence he says in the above letter, 'Provided a good thing is done it does not matter how it is done.' De Bernis was also moved by Ganganelli's place on their list to support his candidature, notwithstanding the suspicious conduct of the Spaniards, but was not without grave suspicions as to the advisability of so doing. 'As Ganganelli,' he writes on the same day to Choiseul, 'is on the list of good candidates we shall promote his election; but as we owe the truth to the King, we cannot conceal from him the suspicions this Cardinal has aroused in us by his mysterious life, and our feeling that it is impossible not only to answer for certain as to his views, but even to conjecture what may prove to be his system of government.'[78]

It must have been this mystery enshrouding the true views of Ganganelli which had a contrary effect on Cardinal Albani and induced him to discuss his candidature sympathetically with de Solís. In Ganganelli's past record there were features which pointed to his being favourable to the Society as well as others which pointed to his being adverse to it; and in the Conclave he seems likewise to have produced contrary impressions on those with whom he spoke. On Cardinal de Solís he had left an impression that he shared the ideas of the Courts, and this was also the impression he produced on d'Aubeterre, who, as we have seen,[79] even supposed that if asked he would give a theological opinion defending the exaction of the written promise. On the other hand, he caused some of the Zelanti to think he would resist the Courts like Clement XIII. It is here that Cordara's testimony comes in usefully. In the *Commentarii*[80] to which reference has already been made, this writer, who wrote indeed somewhat after the date but had access to the first-hand evidence of many of the members of the Conclave, gives us the account he had gathered from the lips of 'Cardinals J. F. Albani, Borromeo, Buonacorsi, Valerani, Buffalini, Serbelloni, Fantuzzi, and other Cardinals'. On this warrant he tells us that 'until just before the end of the Conclave the mass of the electors were distinctly adverse to Ganganelli, but that then the feeling was general that the Election ought not to be deferred any longer. Ganganelli on being asked if he would support Stoppani,

---

[78] Masson, op. cit. p. 106.
[79] See above, p. 184.
[80] *Commentarii de suis et suorum rebus usque ad occasum Societatis Jesu*. In the Third Volume of Döllinger's *Beiträge zur politischen, kirchlichen und Cultur-Geschichte*.

replied, "No, for he would certainly oppress the Jesuits," and said this so decisively and suddenly that he appeared to be speaking direct from his heart.' The news of this remark spread at once through the Conclave, and caused very many to think better of him. Presently the feeling in his favour was greatly promoted by the sudden conversion of Cardinal Castelli, a man who was held in the highest esteem by the Conclave. This Cardinal had been strongly against him, but now turned completely round, and, the support of the Albani party being thus obtained for Ganganelli, Rezzonico declared that he and his friends would not stand out against his elevation. Such is Cordara's account, and though it is hardly likely that a small and isolated incident such as he mentions would have accounted for all that followed, we may safely gather that this incident was but one of many indications which conspired to make the Zelanti, who were now in their days of weariness and desperation, think that in spite of the mystery in which he enveloped himself, Ganganelli's real sentiments were those of which they approved.

We must now return to Cardinal de Bernis, by the aid of whose reports we can bring the story of Cardinal Ganganelli's election to an end, and supply a few further details as to its causes. Although in view of his place on the list de Bernis felt constrained to vote for him, he continued to feel uneasy even after the meeting with the Spanish Cardinals on the 17th, and determined that he would make another attempt to gather Ganganelli's sentiments from his own lips. Theiner knows nothing of this step of de Bernis, but M. Masson has printed[81] a letter he wrote to Choiseul on the 19th, containing a full account of it, of which we can only give the substance. De Bernis, it seems, sent his Conclavist, the Abbé Deshaises, to Ganganelli's cell on the evening of the 17th. Ganganelli greeted him with expressions of gratitude to the three Crowns for their intention to carry through his election, but modestly deprecated the honour and even talked of refusing it. Deshaises, after dissuading him from this course, 'told him,' says de Bernis, 'in my name that the three Crowns, and especially the King, must expect from his gratitude that he would do what would be agreeable to them, and that he would take in hand first of all the work of destroying the Jesuits, and the satisfaction to be given to the Duke of Parma.' He replied that he had a plan for satisfying the House of France in regard to this last matter, and that as for the Jesuits he was convinced that their destruction was necessary, and that he would address himself to that task, employing the necessary forms. The Abbé then asked him what forms these would be, and was

---

[81] Masson, op. cit. p. 108.

told that it would be necessary to ask the consent of the Powers and of their clergy. De Bernis was relieved on hearing the report of his Conclavist, but being anxious to remove all obscurities he sent him back the following night to Ganganelli, this time with a written memorandum, containing definite questions he was to be asked to answer. Some of these referred to the Parma question, the Avignon question, the withdrawal of the Bull Unigenitus, and the supreme importance of Ganganelli recognizing that it was to France he would owe his tiara – to which last point he replied that 'he carried the King (of France) in his heart and the Cardinal de Bernis in his right hand.' 'In regard to the Jesuits,' writes de Bernis in this same letter to Choiseul, 'I made him feel that, if in destroying them he observed the (usual) forms he would run the risk of causing himself to be suspected of wishing to make the affair last on for ever, and so allowing the Society to subsist; and I showed him that it was of consequence for his honour and glory that he should promptly make plain his true dispositions by some striking act. His answer was that he would not confine himself to words, and that the facts should soon justify his intentions.'

De Bernis was now fully satisfied, and having first obtained from Ganganelli some further guarantees as to the persons he would appoint to the principal offices in the Curia, he set off at once to hasten on the Election before there could be time for the opportunity to pass away. He found Rezzonico in the cell of Pozzobonelli, and though it was now one o'clock at night he then sought the Albani adherents, the Spaniards, and Orsini, and induced them to agree to this candidature. After what we know of the occurrences of the previous two or three days we can understand how he found it easy to secure this general agreement, especially as the latest scrutiny had given Ganganelli nineteen votes. It remains only to say that the Cardinals en masse repaired at once to the cell of Ganganelli to kiss his hand, and that on the following morning he was elected by forty-six out of the forty-seven possible votes – the outstanding vote being his own, which was given to Rezzonico.

Such is the history of this eventful Conclave, in bringing which to a close it may seem that we ought to summarize the two chief conclusions which it suggests – as to the conduct of the Bourbon Courts and as to the conduct of Cardinal Ganganelli. On the former, however, of these subjects enough has been said in the course of these studies, and the reader must now judge for himself how far the Crown Cardinals were mindful of their responsibility as electors, and the Bulls they were sworn to observe; how far the Catholic Courts were inspired by a regard for the principles of justice and equity, and for the respect in which they professed to hold the highest authority in the Church; and how far, in consequence, Cardinal Ganganelli's election can be deemed the result of the free deliberations of the electors and not rather the result of an unlawful pressure applied from without, so excessive as to impart a unique character to this Conclave amidst all the Conclaves of the last four centuries. The reader can judge, too, whether such conduct on the part of the Courts harmonizes with the supposition that they believed themselves to possess genuine evidence convicting the Jesuits of the crimes of which they accused them, and not rather with the supposition that they felt that they had no evidence to support their accusations which they could venture to produce, and were in reality fabricating these accusations to serve as a mask, under cover of which they could demand the destruction of a Society they hated for much less commendable causes.

It is this first conclusion on which we would wish the reader to lay most stress. As for the conduct during the Conclave of Cardinal Ganganelli, who now became Clement XIV, although it was not perhaps conformed to the highest standard, it does not appear to have been seriously culpable – that is to say, if we confine our attention to the bare facts, after having washed off the tinge imparted to them by the partizan statements of the French and Spanish agents. He does not seem to have obtruded his personality on any party among the electors, but when they came to inquire about his views he gave them. Although these views were of a nature to satisfy the inquirers, and so undoubtedly furthered his election, there is no reason to suppose that he gave them insincerely, and at all events he involved himself in no stipulations.[82] On the contrary, in his final replies to de Bernis's

---

[82] Crétineau-Joly, in his *Histoire des Jésuites* and more fully in his *Clément XIV et les Jésuites* (p. 260), accused Ganganelli of having given the written promise to suppress the Society, and has been severely blamed for so doing by Theiner and others, including Père de Ravignan, who may be said to have written his *Clément XIII et Clément XIV* at the instigation of Father General Roothaan, precisely to combat this contention of Crétineau-Joly. It is conclusive against Crétineau-Joly's theory that, as we have seen, Azpuru in his despatch of 18 May, told Grimaldi 'none of the Cardinals had gone so far as to propose to any one that the Suppression should be secured by a written or spoken promise.' And, indeed, Crètineau-Joly refutes his own theory when he tells us that in the said writing, which was addressed to the King of Spain, Ganganelli declared 'he recognized that the Sovereign Pontiff had the right, and could in good conscience suppress the Society of Jesus, whilst fully observing the canonical laws; and that it was to be hoped that the future Pope would strive his utmost to accomplish the wish of the Crowns.' Such words do not amount to a stipulation, and it should be noted that the clause about observing the canonical laws involves the same cautious reserve we have found in the words addressed to the Abbé Deshaises. Still it

memorandum, he still preserved that ambiguity of expression which so perplexed the Cardinals of all classes, but was clearly motived by the desire to guard his future liberty of action. It will, however, be necessary to consider further the character of the new Pope in the following chapters.

---

must be confessed that under the circumstances they tended to make the Crown party suppose that Ganganelli was the kind of candidate they wanted, and it is probable, therefore, that the assurance contained in these words, or a renewal of the same to de Solís in a subsequent interview, was what made the latter say (see above, p. 193) to the French and Neapolitan Cardinals that 'the private interview he had had with Ganganelli made him feel certain that none would be fitter to occupy the See of St. Peter.' But it will be asked, did Ganganelli really set down in writing and deliver to the Spaniards the expression of opinion on which we are commenting? Crétineau-Joly professed to have had the original document in his hands (see the Abbé Maynard's *Jacques Crétineau-Joly*, p. 304), but as he never produced it or explained its *provenance*, Theiner had some reason for declining to believe in it. It is not indeed possible to be certain of it, still the collateral evidence implies that some such written declaration existed. Not only is something of the kind needed to explain the confidence in Ganganelli expressed by Cardinal de Solís, but we have Cardinal de Bernis, in a letter to Choiseul dated 28 July, saying that the 'writing which (the Spaniards) made the Pope sign is in no sense obligatory; the Pope has himself explained to me its tenour,' and also a despatch of 20 November 1769, in which he says 'the Spanish Cardinals were contented with a writing in which Cardinal Ganganelli, in his quality as a theologian, said that he thought the Sovereign Pontiff could in conscience suppress the Society of Jesuits, whilst observing the canonical laws, and those of prudence and justice.'

Chapter Six

The Bullying of Clement XIV

I.[1] [First six months of the Pontificate]

Now that the Conclave was over the Bourbon Courts could resume their demands for the suppression of the Society. The situation too looked now more favourable, the new factor which had entered into it being the personal character of the new Pope whom they had set on the throne. The external facts of the previous life of Lorenzo Ganganelli are few and simple to relate. He was born on 31 October 1705, in the little town of Sant' Arcangelo, near Rimini, in the Romagna. His father, Lorenzo Ganganelli, was a surgeon with a small country practice; his mother, whose maiden name was Mazzi, sprang from a family of some distinction at Pesaro. As his father died in 1708, it was to his mother's exclusive care that his early training was due. On attaining to school age he was placed by her at the Jesuit school at Rimini, and there he remained for three years, after which he was transferred to Urbino, to a school kept by the Scuolopian Fathers. It was at Urbino that he got his vocation to the Order of St Francis, and on 17 May 1723, he entered the Novitiate of the Conventual Friars in that City. It was there that he took the name of Lorenzo, by which he is best known – his baptismal name having been Giovanni Vincenzo Antonio. He had talents and application, and in due course, having taken the degree of Doctor of Divinity at Rome, he was set to teach theology and philosophy at Milan, Bologna, and other Italian cities in succession. In 1741 he was recalled to Rome, and placed by the Cardinal Protector of the Franciscans at the head of their great College of St Bonaventure. Whilst he held this position he attracted the attention of Benedict XIV, who came to esteem him highly, who appointed him in 1746 a Consultor of the Holy Office, and who was credited with the inten-

[1] *The Month*, 101 (1903), 179–97.

tion of eventually calling him to the Sacred College; but it was to Clement XIII, in 1759, that his elevation to that dignity was in fact due. In the earlier days of his Cardinalate Clement XIII used his services in various ways, but grew to distrust him, probably because of his intimacy with Don Manuel de Roda, and during the last years of his reign left him practically unemployed. Under what circumstances this Cardinal, who till then was not specially conspicuous among the Cardinals, came to be elected Pope, has been narrated in the last chapter.

It is seldom an easy task to reconstruct the physiognomy of a character belonging to a past age, especially when burning questions and controversies have gathered round the man's personality, and this is particularly the case with Clement XIV. Cordara, the ex-Jesuit, to whose *Commentaries* we have twice had occasion to refer, tells us that 'if one listened to the Jesuits and their friends, no Pope was ever worse, whilst if one listened to their enemies no Pope was ever better.' Cordara himself however, was more discriminating, and together with the spirit of impartiality which is transparent in his treatise, he had excellent materials for judging, in the results both of his personal observations and of those of his many friends who knew Ganganelli when Pope. As described by this witness, the new Pope was, if not so attractive a personality as his great predecessor, still one that was decidedly pleasing. As a simple friar he had always borne the reputation of a good Religious, pure in his morals, fervent in his piety, attached to the poverty of his state, and noted for the strict observance of his rule. In his relations with others he was quiet and unassuming, easy of access, and cordial and hearty in his conversation. Intellectually Cordara credits him with good talents and a sagacious judgment, and he was certainly a lover of books, and a hard worker. After he was raised to the Cardinalate, and even after his accession to the Papacy, he remained unaltered in these respects, and it was particularly noted how he retained his simple habits and his love of poverty, and how far he was from using the opportunity of his own advancement to push on his relatives or make their fortunes. Such is Cordara's account of him, and it tallies with what we can gather from Caraccioli's collection of his letters,[2] and from

---

[2] *Lettres intéressantes de Clément XIV.* Published by the Marchese Caraccioli in 1776. There has been much discussion about these letters. The Marchese Caracciolo in his Preface is suspiciously reticent as to the channels through which he obtained them, and gives them in a French translation instead of in the original Italian. On this account, and because it is difficult to believe that some of the contents could have come from Fra Lorenro, many critics have rejected the entire collection as spurious. But von Reumont's judgment (*Ganganelli* –

de Bernis's despatches in which he describes his many interviews with the Pontiff.

His possession of these virtues and this unstained reputation may well have seemed to the Zelanti electors to mark him out as one who would make a fairly good Pope, and Cordara's criticism, with which it is easy to agree, is that 'he would have made an excellent Pope had his lot fallen on happier times.' But unfortunately the times were not happy for the Pontiff charged with the responsibilities of the Holy See, and by the side of these virtues, there were in Lorenzo Ganganelli certain shortcomings which seriously disqualified him for the critical task confronting him. What the times needed was a strong and fearless Pope, who would not quail before the might of secular sovereigns, nor allow himself to be coerced by their threats into courses of which his own judgment disapproved; a Pope with a ripe political experience, or at least with an inborn faculty of insight into the motives of politicians and the tendency of their actions; above all, a Pope able to convince the diplomatists that he was incapable of resorting to shuffling expedients or concealing his real motives, but was one who would always pursue a straight policy based on the principles of equity and truth, apart from which they must never expect to extort anything from him. Clement XIV unfortunately was the reverse of all this, as may be gathered from the history we have now to relate. He was essentially a weak man and an opportunist, and had what so often accompanies a weak man's opportunism, a deficient sense of the justice due to individuals; he delighted in the good-will of secular princes and quailed before their anger; he had no political experience whatever, and was easily taken in by the artful representations of ambassadors and others; he had a weak man's tendency to secretiveness, which led him, on the one hand, to manage everything himself, refusing the counsels of the experienced Cardinals who were his natural advisers, and, on the other, to attribute his delays to causes which were felt to be unreal and caused him to be suspected by the powers.

In thus assigning the qualifications wanting in the successor of Clement XIII, we must not be supposed to mean that he should have been an admirer of the Jesuits. On the contrary; even from the point of view of their interests, it would have been better to have a Pope,

---

Papst Clement XIV - seine Briefe und seine Zeit, 1847. Preface, pp. 40–42) is that it is in substance a genuine collection, though some of the letters are spurious and others interpolated. Von Reumont argues very justly that it would hardly be possible to fabricate so many letters, addressed to correspondents most of whom were alive at the time of the publication, and yet impart to them the unity, distinctness, and spontaneity of a living character.

like Clement VIII or Benedict XIV, who could be trusted to do nothing that was not equitable, and at the same time would be beyond suspicion of undue leanings towards the Order whose fate was to be determined. Still, as Clement XIV was called upon to deal with the Jesuits, it is of interest to ascertain how he was predisposed towards them. One of the Caraccioli letters is addressed to Cardinal Cavalchini, which, though undated, must from its contents have been written not many weeks before the death of Clement XIII. In this letter, if it be genuine, Cardinal Ganganelli gives in his own words his opinion on the Jesuit question. After emphasizing the importance for the Holy See of preserving good relations with the Catholic Powers, especially in an age when incredulity was so aggressive, he protests against the notion 'that he is hostile to certain religious because he does not wish to sustain them against the Kings'; but adds that 'we must not embroil ourselves with the Catholic Powers for the sake of our predilection for them,' and even if 'we did it would only result in bringing down on them further storms.' Here he denies that he is hostile to the Society, but that need not mean that he was well inclined to them, and his own account of himself in a conversation with Orsini,[3] shortly after his election, was that 'in his youth he had been their tertiary,[4] but had come to realize that they were intriguers'. And this agrees with the facts. Cordara tells us that in former days his relations with the Jesuit Fathers in the various towns where they had been his neighbours had ever been most cordial; and, though it would be hazardous to place entire credence in Cordara's story that Jesuit influence obtained for him his Cardinal's hat, Cordara's witness does suffice to prove that the Jesuit Padre Andreucci had spoken of him to Clement XIII as being their warm friend. But after he was made Cardinal he was drawn into the circle which gathered round Manuel de Roda, at that time Spanish Ambassador, whose house seems to have been the head-quarters of the conspiracy which had its associates and sympathizers in the principal cities of France and the two Peninsulas, and was busily engaged in preparing the general movement against the Society. When Roda was recalled to Madrid and made Minister of Finance, Ganganelli continued to correspond with him, and it was at Roda's suggestion

---

[3] See letter of Tanucci to Grimaldi, ap. Danvila, *Historia del reinado de Carlos III,* iii, 353.

[4] That is, their friend. The Orders of St Dominic and St Francis have Tertiaries attached to them, but the Society of Jesus has never imitated their example. The foes of the Society, however, at the time of which we are speaking, found it convenient to assume that a large body of laity were under the rule of the General, and this was the name by which they chose to designate them.

that he was offered and accepted the office of Promoter of the Cause of the Venerable Palafox. He appears also to have been a regular correspondent, through Friar Castan, a Franciscan resident at Avignon, with Mgr Jarente, the Jansenist Bishop of Orleans, a determined enemy of the Jesuits; and, in von Reumont's judgment,[5] it was through the good opinion of him expressed by Mgr Jarente to his intimate friend, Choiseul, that the latter was induced to recommend him so strongly as a suitable candidate for the Papacy. The future Pope could hardly be in these intimate relations with anti-Jesuit leaders without imbibing largely of their ideas; nor is it necessary, on that account, to think of him as changed from the upright and well-intentioned ecclesiastic, to whom the above-given testimonies bear witness. He can have been and apparently was the dupe of his associates. As the result of their manoeuvring, the Bourbon territories were flooded with books, pamphlets, correspondence, which collected, invented, and circulated every form of charge against the hated Religious. Some of these charges may have been substantially true, others may have had a nucleus of truth enclosed in far-reaching exaggerations and misrepresentations; many must have been downright fabrications; and in like manner, the evidence invoked on their behalf will have ranged through every degree of credibility or incredibility. The kind of anti-Catholic letters which in our own days their foreign correspondents contribute to English papers, or the articles to periodicals signed by anonymous scribes professing to be devout but scandalized Catholics behind the scenes, are parallel instances, which enable us to realize how minds at all prejudiced or uncritical, can be gained over to believe the most incredible things of an unpopular class of people, on the faith of malevolent gossip or third or fourth-hand reports of witnesses ashamed to give their names.

Such was the Pope into whose hands the power was now placed of deciding whether to preserve or destroy an influential body of ecclesiastics whom his predecessors, even those who disliked them, had consistently protected.

His first occupation was to announce his election by autograph letters to the Catholic Sovereigns, and in those addressed to the Bourbon Kings, although he made no direct reference to the Jesuit question, he spoke in fervent terms of the need of restoring peace to the Church, a phrase which under the circumstances of the time indicated not obscurely his readiness to defer to the wishes of the Courts. In his audiences with the ambassadors he was somewhat more explicit. On 31 May, d'Aubeterre writes[6] to his Court that he had

[5] Op. cit. pp. 64, 322 (Letter to P. Valentin).
[6] Theiner, *Histoire du Pontificat de Clément XIV,* vol. i, p. 352.

been with the Holy Father the previous day, when the latter 'again professed his very best intentions to arrange everything to the satisfaction of the House of Bourbon', and 'in regard to the Jesuits said they must grant him some time, as he could not do everything at once, but he assured (d'Aubeterre) that the Courts should have reason to be contented.' The Ambassador adds that the Pope was 'doing everything by himself', that is to say, without employing the advice and co-operation of his Cardinals – a line of conduct which, as will be seen, characterized Clement XIV's dealing with the Jesuit question throughout. From two letters addressed to Grimaldi, one by Orsini and one by Azpuru, both dated 8 June,[7] we learn that the Pope gave to these Ministers similar assurances of his intentions, and we also obtain another insight into the Pope's personal feelings in regard to the Society. With Orsini and the Ambassador of Malta, writes Azpuru, '(the Pope) had entered into frequent explanations, and – referring to certain affairs in which the Jesuits had taken part during the previous Pontificate – said they had ruined every work which they had taken in hand.' He also told Orsini he knew 'what deceivers they were with their astute practices and inventions', and chaffed him for 'having been a penitent of Padre Ricci, conversing with him about the method of the latter, till he drew from the Cardinal an acknowledgment that he had been enlightened to change his own method, and to recognize the delusion under which he had laboured whilst the said Father was directing his conscience.'

Although in these early audiences granted to the ambassadors the Jesuit question was thus made the subject of conversation, there was as yet nothing of an official character in the communications interchanged. Azpuru had indeed urged upon d'Aubeterre, as the latter tells us in his letter of 31 May, that the Ministers should at once deliver to his Holiness a duplicate of the Memorials they had presented to Pope Clement XIII in January. Azpuru said he had been instructed by Grimaldi to take this step, and Grimaldi had also told him that orders to d'Aubeterre to do likewise had been sent him from Versailles, but d'Aubeterre replied that no such orders had reached him as yet, and he could not fall in with the proposal till they did. Choiseul's instructions were not in fact sent till 4 July,[8] by which time d'Aubeterre had been recalled to France, and had been succeeded at the Embassy by the Cardinal de Bernis. It was to the Cardinal, therefore, that Choiseul wrote this letter which expressed the two-fold feeling then animating the French Court – the wish to follow the lead of the Spanish Sovereign (whose alliance was so

[7] Danvila, *ibid*. p. 350.
[8] Theiner, *ibid*. p. 355.

valuable to France as against the rivalry of England), and the repulsion against Spanish methods as wanting in tact and delicacy. The clearness in which the Pope had expressed himself on several occasions in regard to the Jesuits was, thought Choiseul, a sure guarantee that the desired measures would be taken, and that being so it was due to his Holiness that he should be allowed the interval of time for which he asked. If then M. Azpuru continued to press for a joint presentation of the Memorials, Cardinal de Bernis was to accede to the plan. The Duc felt, however, as he knew the Cardinal himself felt, that the success of a negotiation was often retarded by the endeavour to precipitate it. He trusted, therefore, to the enlightened discretion of his Eminence, and hoped that the Spanish and Neapolitan Ministers would allow their action to be regulated by it.

Whilst awaiting these instructions from his chief, de Bernis and his fellow-ambassadors were engaged in devising methods for common action in furtherance of their campaign. But de Bernis was not altogether satisfied with his colleagues, as he tells us in a letter to Choiseul, dated 13 July.[9] Azpuru was not particularly intelligent, and Orsini at times was too imprudently vivacious, whilst Almada, the representative of Portugal (for now that Clement XIII was dead this erratic personage had returned to Rome, and was about to be accredited to the new Pontiff) was both indiscreet and incapable. Still they agreed, as did their Courts, that de Bernis should be their leader, and the Cardinal deemed himself to have found a valuable assistant in Padre Vasquez, the Superior General of the Augustinians, a friend and regular correspondent of Don Manuel de Roda, and with him a leader in the little Roman *coterie* which had been working for the destruction of the Society now for many years past. This Padre Vasquez seems to have impressed on the Cardinal de Bernis the importance of keeping all their proceedings absolutely secret. 'The friends of the Jesuits,' so Theiner summarizes, 'were striving their hardest to find out what was being done, and had set clever spies even about the person of the Pope himself in order to deter him by motives of fear from taking any measure adverse to the Society. They had even begun to circulate threatening prophecies.'[10]

Theiner is continually giving his readers to understand that the Jesuits were as much intriguers as their adversaries throughout all these critical years of their history, and indeed by their intrigues substantially justified the measures taken against them. When, however, we ask him for proofs that they were thus engaged, the proofs offered are as uncertain

---
[9] Theiner, *ibid*. p. 356.
[10] Theiner, *ibid*. p. 356.

as his proofs of the intrigues of the ambassadors are certain. The allegations in the passage just quoted offer a good illustration of this, and as such it may be opportune to inquire into their value. It is true that in his letter of 13 July, de Bernis tells us that prophecies were beginning to be distributed, which declared that 'the suppression of the Society was being projected, but that the Pope would die before he had time to sign the Bull'; and also that 'Vasquez had warned him that among the gentlemen of his household, his chaplains, his valets, and his liveried servants, there were emissaries of the Jesuits, the Government, and the foreign Ministers.' But whilst de Bernis and his colleagues can be trusted implicitly as first-hand witnesses when they tell us of their own conduct and motives, the second and third-hand reports they give us about the conduct and motives of others need to be sifted by criticism. At a time when all Rome was keenly watching the course of the campaign against the Society, it was inevitable that every action of a Pope or an ambassador, or any other leading actor in the drama, the visits they paid or received, the words they uttered, the expressions on their countenances, should be sharply scrutinized by those who had such excellent opportunities of observation as the members of their respective households; it was inevitable that these matters should be discussed, interpreted, and reported from mouth to mouth; and inevitable too that such reports should be gathered up by persons so closely affected as the Jesuits or brought to them in a more or less diluted form by their many friends. But surely neither the Jesuits nor their friends were to be blamed for this, still less to be credited in consequence with commissioning or controlling an organized system of spies. And again as regards the prophecies, when men who put their trust in God see some terrible calamity to religion impending, and to all human appearances inevitable, their natural character comes out and, whilst some bow their heads in blind submissiveness, others catch at straws, and not infrequently some fancy themselves the recipients of heavenly intimation of better things, which they feel impelled to announce to the sufferers for their consolation and support. There may be a credulity in this which deserves to be set down as silly, and there were undeniably Jesuits at the time who incurred that reproach, but it must not be forgotten that there were others to condemn them even among their own brethren; Cordara, for instance, and Thorpe,[11] bewail in no qualified terms the disposition

[11] Fr Thorpe was an English Jesuit who at that time was English Penitentiary at St Peter's. He wrote regular letters at short intervals to his brethren in England, the originals of which are in the Stonyhurst Archives. They form a most valuable chronicle of events from the standpoint of a fair-minded but somewhat optimistic Jesuit observer, and offer conclusive evidence that, so far from being engaged in active intrigues, the Roman Jesuits were like sheep in a thunder-storm, awaiting the issue of events in utter helplessness and uncertainty.

of some of their brethren to believe in these vain predictions. Still if their credulity was foolish there was absolutely nothing in it on which to base the fearful charge which, as we have seen, Theiner adopts from the interested lips of de Bernis, when he suggests that under cover of announcing prophecies the Jesuits and their friends were intimating threats, even of murder, the fulfilment of which they would themselves take means to secure.

Choiseul's letter of 4 July should have reached the Cardinal de Bernis about the 25th of the same month and, had nothing intervened to modify the situation, it might perhaps have enabled him to win over his colleagues to the policy of waiting. But the Holy See had meanwhile performed a simple act of administrative routine the consequences of which it could hardly have been expected to foresee. It was customary to grant to all those of the regular clergy who were in the habit of giving parochial Missions the power to announce a Plenary Indulgence to be gained on the ordinary conditions by all who had taken part in such Missions. The practice was to limit the grant to a period of seven years, at the expiration of which the Procurator-General of the Order was expected to apply for its renewal, in expediting which the officials on whom the duty devolved, regarding it as mere matter of routine, did not deem it necessary to make more than a perfunctory reference to the Holy Father. It was under these conditions that the Procurator General of the Society of Jesus applied for the renewal of the Mission Indulgence shortly after the accession, of Clement XIV, and the Brief *Coelestium munerum,* by which the renewal was granted, bore the date of 12 July. The style of the document was fixed by previous usage,[12] and in its initial paragraph, ran thus:

> We freely bestow the treasures of heavenly gifts ... on those who we know are, in their love towards God and their neighbours, and their zeal for the Christian religion, making every endeavour to procure the salvation of souls. And we regard as of such kind the Religious of the Society of Jesus, especially those whom our beloved son, Lawrence Ricci, General Superior of the said Society of Jesus, decides to send for this purpose in the present and succeeding years to the different provinces of Christendom. We therefore, desiring to foster, and advance by spiritual graces the piety and labour of the said Religious, and likewise the religious spirit and devotion of those to whom they are sent, being moreover induced by the prayers of the same Lawrence Ricci humbly addressed to us for this end, and wishing to promote as far as we can in the Lord his pious resolves, trusting in the mercy of Almighty God ... grant, &c.

[12] See for instance in the *Institutum Soc. Jesu* (Prague edition of 1759, vol. i, p. 250) an identically worded Brief of Benedict XIV, dated 4 June, 1749.

Theiner, in his account of this episode, acknowledges[13] that the renewal of this Brief of Concession was in itself 'an act of the most simple kind', and is sure that 'it would have passed unperceived had not the Fathers of the Society themselves designedly given it a great publicity.' But 'immense numbers of copies were printed off and distributed throughout Rome to show that Clement XIV was a most zealous partizan of the Society of Jesus, and like his predecessor would reject all the demands of the Courts for its suppression'; and he adds that 'this inconsiderate step could not but greatly embarrass the Holy Father in his relations with the Powers, and could only supply them with a fresh and powerful weapon with the aid of which to extort all the more certainly the suppression they desired.' One can readily realize the chagrin with which the Bourbon Ministers viewed this wide circulation of a Brief the conventional language of which, witnessing as it did to the feelings hitherto entertained by the Holy See towards the Society of Jesus, set in unpleasant contrast the policy they were striving to force on the reigning Pontiff. Still when Theiner credits the Jesuits with having promoted the undue circulation of the Brief, he is giving another illustration of his false method of citing the interested allegations of the persecutors as trustworthy proof of the doings of their victims. From Fr Thorpe's letter of 26 July, we find that the Jesuits, foreseeing the difficulties which might arise if the fact of the renewal of the Brief should become publicly known, took special pains to keep it secret. Fr Thorpe tells us that it was a mere chance that the Brief was solicited and obtained at that time – the *septennium* having just then expired, and it being down on the *agenda* list of the Procurator-General that he should apply for the renewals of this and similar privileges on their expiration. 'But the General,' he says, 'prudently observing that some commendation of the Society, which is contained in the *Breve*, might perhaps be too much noticed either by friends or foes, recommended great caution in divulging it, and not to mention it without necessity. The printer had not the same delicacy, and had an interest in making more copies than a scanty hundred, which were all that the Jesuits required. The story was told out of the print-house that the Pope had made a *Breve* in vindication of the Society, every word was aggrandized, people hastened to get copies of it, and the printer made his advantage of them.' On 5 August, Fr Thorpe rrecurs to the subject, and writes: 'Some persons who affect a tone of indifference and impartiality, blame the Jesuits for causing the little *Breve* to be published, and for having it printed at the Pope's print-house; but they do not reflect

---

[13] Theiner, *ibid.* p. 359.

that no such *Breve* can, without a special license from that press, be printed elsewhere, and printed copies are required by the Bishops and other ecclesiastical superiors, to whom the Jesuit missioners must present them.'

Such was the real origin of the stir caused by the issue of the *Coelestium munerum*, but the ambassadors, as we have seen, were determined to set it all down to the intrigues of the Jesuits, by whom they professed to believe that the Pope had been captured. Accordingly they were most irate, and met together to determine how they should deal with the crisis. They decided that there could now be no doubt of the expediency of presenting to the Holy Father the Memorials demanding the suppression which had been presented to Clement XIII just before his death, and they agreed that de Bernis should draw up a further secret Memorial, which might serve as a covering letter to the others, and should run in the names of all three Ministers. It was a long document, but to the following effect: they had not so far renewed to his Holiness the demand of their Courts, which had been made to his predecessor. They had indeed received orders from their respective Courts to take that step, but out of reluctance to disturb him during the first days of his Pontificate, they had in the exercise of their discretion abstained from so acting up to the present – being further influenced by the knowledge that his Holiness had expressed himself so clearly as to his intentions, and even as to the details of the plan he had in mind, and by the feeling that to present the Memorials so soon might seem to imply a want of confidence in his assurances. The recent concession of the Brief of Indulgence had, however, made them feel that they must delay no longer in giving effect to the orders of their Courts. For

> the Jesuits and their partizans were making capital of this Brief, and drawing consequences which fed fanaticism and encouraged the protectors of an Order which had degenerated from its Institute; whose moral teaching had at all times appeared to the most virtuous and learned people to be relaxed and dangerous, and whose theology had always appeared unsound on several essential points; which engaged, contrary to the spirit of the canons, in commerce, in intrigues, in cabals; and which four Sovereigns, respectable not only for the crowns they wore, but also for their attachment to religion and filial respect for the Holy See, had been obliged to proscribe in their States after the most careful reflection.

And the Pope was asked to bear in mind that

> time given to an enemy who believes himself to be lost may become fatal

to him who gives it; and let him open his mind to the sovereigns who had always been the support and ornament of the Pontifical throne; and let him communicate to them his plans and ideas, in which case he would find alike in their affection and their power both consolation and safe resources.

These various Memorials were presented to the Pope on 22 July, and from a letter of de Bernis to Choiseul, dated 26 July,[14] we learn how Clement XIV received them. It is a letter of special interest for the insight it gives us into the mind of the Pope at this stage of the movement. Clement in the first instance resented the delivery of the Memorials, and refused to receive them. He said they implied distrust in his good faith. But, de Bernis pointing out that he would certainly render himself suspect if he declined to receive them, he took them and promised to read them. Then, entering into explanations, he said the Brief was one of a kind such as was given to all missionaries, only that 'the Jesuits had had the insolence (these, says de Bernis, were his very words)[15] to make a parade of them; but he would before very long issue two other Briefs which would beat down considerably the pride of these Reverend Fathers, and make them see that he feared only not to do his duty.' In regard to the suppression of the Society the Pope spoke with great force and clearness, and de Bernis's report of what he said to him had better be quoted textually.

> (The Pope) said he had his conscience and his honour to preserve, the former by adhering to the canons and following the example of his predecessors in similar cases; the other by not sacrificing lightly the consideration he owed to the Emperor, the Empress, the Republic of Poland, the King of Sardinia, the Venetians and the Genovese, and even to the King of Prussia – none of whom demanded the suppression; that, although he had been menaced and made to fear for his life, it would not be fear which would prevent him from giving satisfaction at once to the sovereigns of the House of France, but that he knew his rules and his duties, and that no human respect should induce him to disregard them; that now at once he promised the three Sovereigns that he would approve what they had done in regard to the Jesuits in their own States and in barring for ever their return there; that he would ask for the advice of the clergy of the three kingdoms (and we agreed that he should do nothing in

[14] Theiner, *ibid*. pp. 363-367.
[15] This shows that Clement XIV, like the ambassadors, assumed that the Jesuits had promoted the wide circulation of the Brief. As he kept every Jesuit at a distance from his person, and would listen to no word said on their behalf by their friends, naturally he was without the means of testing the allegations of their enemies.

this way without giving us time to inform the King beforehand);[16] that when he was supported by the advice of the clergy of France, Spain, Naples, and Portugal, he could act with freedom and honour; that their advice could not but be favourable, and would act as the sound of a bell to the other Catholic States; that then all the sovereigns together, or at least the greatest part, would call for the entire abolition of the Jesuits; that meanwhile he would proceed step by step towards this goal, and would prove his good faith more and more each day, acting, however, with prudence and method; that if the General of the Jesuits should die, he would suspend the nomination of his successor; but that he must conclude by insisting that they must give him time and show him consideration.

We shall find that the plan of procedure which Clement XIV thus sketched out to de Bernis is the plan to which he substantially adhered in the sequel, but it must not escape notice that amidst the various requirements of his honour and conscience, he does not include that of making a genuine and independent inquiry into the charges brought against the Order he was prepared to punish. This cannot be because he did not advert to the need of such a step, for we shall find him referring to it, though ineffectively, on subsequent occasions. What then is the reason for an omission which will strike a fair-minded reader as so remarkable? We put the question because it is not impossible that the omission is due, not to Clement, but to de Bernis, who was not incapable of omitting a detail of the conversation which he knew would be much resented by his Court. If, however, the omission was due to Clement himself, it does not seem possible to explain it satisfactorily, but it may have been that he had the need of an equitable inquiry in his mind, and hoped to attend to it, but feared to propose it too bluntly to the Courts, and so relied on other reasons which they were more likely to respect. But on either hypothesis the omission is significant.

De Bernis's letter runs to great length, and includes other matters. Among these we need only notice one or two; namely, his judgment that time alone can manifest for certain whether Clement XIV is really intending to suppress the Society or merely seeking to beguile the Courts and gain time; his anxiety to protect himself against the suspicions entertained by the Court of Spain that he was not serious

---

[16] In making this stipulation de Bernis shows his discretion, but also betrays his consciousness of the hollowness of his case. It would never have done to let the clergy express an unbiassed opinion. Why, they might express it, as the French clergy had done in their *Avis* to Louis XV of December 1761 (see above pp. 67–69) and again in their Assembly of June 1762; or like the Bishops of France and Spain, in union with many Bishops of other countries, when they wrote to Clement XIII in praise of the *Apostolicum*!

and energetic enough in working for the suppression; and his further anxiety to secure his own recognition as the leader of the other ambassadors. In another letter, written a few days later, namely, on 9 August,[17] he refers again to the distrust of him felt by the Spanish Court because he had not pushed the matter on faster, and remarks, not unwisely, that 'it would be dangerous to push the Pope too much – since if one should suspect him, or fill him with fear, one may force him perhaps to come out of his embarrassment by remitting all the business of the Courts to Congregations.' The danger here mentioned is another point worthy of notice in the policy of the Courts. It has been said how, contrary to the time-honoured and reasonable methods of his predecessors, Clement XIV, unversed though he was in the art of diplomacy, and beset though he was by ambassadors bent on extorting a quite unprecedented exercise of Papal power, thought fit to deprive himself of the wisdom and experience of the Cardinals who were his natural counsellors. De Bernis's anxiety, expressed in the words just quoted, shows that it was by the instigation of the Courts Clement XIV had been led to take so infatuated a course, and that they felt it was only thus they could use him as their tool.

The protests of the ambassadors were not the last word Clement XIV was destined to hear of the unfortunate episode of the *Coelestium munerum*. When the news reached Madrid through Azpuru's despatch of 27 July,[18] in which a copy of de Bernis's letter to Choiseul was enclosed, Carlos III appears to have been struck by the proofs which the event had elicited of the Pope's really favourable dispositions, and still more of the zeal and ability with which de Bernis had been furthering the interests of the Courts. Accordingly he made no complaint of the *Coelestium munerum,* but sent back orders to Azpuru that the Holy Father should be left undisturbed during the interval of time for which he had stipulated. At Paris, when the news of the occurrence arrived, much more indignation was felt or simulated, the cause of which, however, lay more in the conduct of the Spanish Court than of the Pope. Although for the moment the reading of de Bernis's despatch had restored that diplomatist to the King of Spain's good graces, he had previously been very suspicious of him, and had sent various letters about him to Paris, complaining that 'he was at heart a friend of the Jesuits, and was endeavouring to shelve the demand (of the Courts) for their suppression.' He had even gone on to entertain suspicions as to the sincerity of the French alliance.

[17] Theiner, *ibid.* p. 367.
[18] Danvila, *ibid.* p. 362.

The effect was to rouse Choiseul out of his indifference. 'In France', he writes on 2 August, in a private letter to de Bernis,[19] 'people are persuaded it was I who caused (the Jesuits) to be expelled; in Spain they publish that I love them, and am sustaining them, and even, I fancy, that I am affiliated to them. Neither side speaks the truth; I swear it in the face of the universe. There is nothing about which all my life through I have felt so indifferent as about the Jesuits; but at present I am getting utterly tired of them, for they have become the mania of the Courts, to such an extent that at Madrid they forget about England and Mr. Pitt, and interests the most important and precious, to dream of the Jesuits and worry me with them. Let all the devils take them, and the Pope too if he does not relieve me of them.'

The reference to Mr Pitt, illustrates what has already been stated in a former chapter, namely, that by Choiseul the suppression of the Jesuits was desired, not for its own sake, but as a means to an end. He had recommended the King to expel them from France as a means of quieting down the turbulance of the *Parlements*; and he was recommending him to co-operate with Spain for their entire suppression in order that the latter power being so obliged might become the more wedded to the alliance against England.

Influenced by this consideration he now felt that he must take some drastic means to remove the suspicions of Carlos III, and concluded that the best course would be to go beyond him in applying pressure to the Pope. Accordingly, he sent for the Nuncio, Mgr Giraud, and – to make the masquerade more effectual – contrived to see him in the presence of the Conde de Fuentes. After first asking and receiving an explanation of the affair of the *Coelestium munerum,* 'he put on', writes Mgr Giraud to Pallavicini, the Cardinal Secretary, 'that ministerial tone with which former experience has made your Eminence familiar, and explained to me that the Kings of France and Spain, and the other princes of the House of Bourbon, were not the sort of persons to be trifled with; that after having led them to hope for the suppression of a Society which disturbed the peace of these Kings, and therefore also compromised the interests of religion, no grant or renewal of a favour ought to have been accorded to it; that his Majesty was weary of all this temporizing, and was sending a sign-manual by the same courier (as carried Giraud's despatch), ordering his Eminence Cardinal de Bernis to renew publicly before the Holy Father his demand for the total suppression of the Society, and if he failed to obtain it within six weeks, to abandon his embassy and make

---

[19] Masson, *Le Cardinal de Bernis depuis son ministère,* p. 126. Letter of d'Ossun to Choiseul, dated 27 July.

an open rupture; and de Bernis was further to add that, even if the other Ministers of the Bourbon Courts, in default of instructions, did not unite with him in this step, he would himself to the letter carry out this order from his Court.'[20]

The official despatch to de Bernis of which Choiseul thus spoke to Giraud, was dated 7 August. It gave 'two months' instead of 'six weeks' as the limit which must not be exceeded, and directed that the memorial to be presented to the Pope should be expressed 'in the most friendly and considerate terms. But it was equally positive in declaring that the King's mind was made up, and foresaw that, if the assigned limit should be overstepped, it would not be possible to hinder the sovereigns of the House of Bourbon from breaking off all communication with a Pope who either prays with us, or is useless to us.'[21] In the accompanying private letter of 2 August, from which a portion has been already cited, Choiseul reveals to us more fully the direction his suspicions were taking: de Bernis believed that a secret correspondence over the head of the Ambassadors was being carried on between the Pope and the King of Spain's Confessor, D. Joachim de Eleta, Roda being the intermediary. Choiseul thinks it may be so, but that if it is, it has originated with the Pope, not the King, and means that the Pope, feeling embarrassed by the circumstances, and fearing to be poisoned by the Jesuits, is dangling a red hat before the eyes of the confessor, in the hope of inducing him to gain over the King of Spain to a reconciliation with the Society. The Courts, however, would set against the Pope's fears other fears of a more substantial nature, and would put an end to his petty Roman tricks.[22]

The Nuncio's account of his interview with Choiseul reached Clement XIV in due course and upset him very much. As de Bernis foresaw this, he withheld his own communication from Paris. He did not even venture to approach the Holy Father at once, but sent the Abbé Deshaises to solicit certain Briefs of an uncontentious character, which were needed in France. What he hoped was that Clement would unburden his mind to Deshaises, and so it happened. He declared himself astonished that they should visit on him the wrongs done to them by his predecessor, when he was endeavouring to right them, and that they should suspect his good faith in regard to the Jesuit question – merely because he had asked for the time which was indispensable for observing the proper canonical rules, and those dictated by duty and decorum and by consideration for the clergy and princes of Christendom who had entrusted their seminaries, their

---

[20] Theiner, *ibid.* p. 369.
[21] Theiner, *ibid.* p. 370.
[22] Theiner, *ibid.* p. 372.

missions, their colleges, and their universities to the Jesuits. The time he asked for could not be limited to two months, as within that space it would not be possible even to draw up the text of a Bull with an adequate array of motives.

Feeling now surer of his ground, de Bernis went himself to the Pope on 29 August, and had a long audience, the report of which was written off to Choiseul on the next day. Clement began by reminding him of what he had already done to arrive at a happy solution of the impending questions.

> Within the three months of his reign he had already done more against the Jesuits than any of his predecessors. Besides the Loretto affair, and that of Frascati, he had just forbidden the Roman Jesuits to preach in their churches during the Jubilee[23] – a thing which had already caused a great sensation. He was preparing a censure of some of their books, and the suppression and reduction of several of their houses. He wished by these preliminaries to give the clergy a means of declaring themselves against this Order, as likewise (to give) the princes who had not yet petitioned him to unite themselves with the House of France. He suggested that France and Spain should assist him by negotiating with Germany, Poland, Genoa, and Venice. He protested that violence and precipitancy should never enter into his principles of conduct; that by force and menaces they would never get him to do anything, but that he would always be docile to the wishes of 'our King' (it is thus he speaks of his Majesty) as long as that prince did not ask him to renounce his duty as Pontiff and common father.[24]

De Bernis here observed that the prince, not knowing his Holiness (as he did) might suppose he sought to gain time in the hopes of saving a Society which he was not accused of favouring, but whose power and attempts on his life he was believed to fear. On this the Pope entered into many details (why does not de Bernis do the same?) as to the new discoveries he had made of the intrigues of the Jesuits. He said that many Jesuits at different times had done good service to the Church and to letters, but the Society itself had always caused trouble. That he knew better than any one how much it was to be feared, but he was cured of all apprehension for his person. He had put himself in the hands of Providence, and fear would not

---

[23] At Loretto the Spanish confessorship had just been taken away from the Jesuits, and given to a Franciscan; at Frascati the episcopal seminary and part of their own college had been taken from them by the Cardinal of York; and whereas in all the Roman churches special services were to be held in connection with the Jubilee for the Pope's accession, the Jesuit churches were forbidden to join with the rest.

[24] Theiner, *ibid.* p. 375.

prevent him from satisfying the princes of the House of France. It was his honour only, his conscience, and his common-sense which prevented him from hurrying through the affair of the suppression, and so failing to observe the rules of Canon Law, those of justice and of a sound and reasonable policy. On Bernis adding that it was not himself, who knew him, but the Kings of France and Spain whom it was necessary to convince, the Pope promised to write an autograph letter to the Kings of France and Spain assuring them of his true sentiments. Bernis, of course, jumped at the offer and arranged that the letter to his own Sovereign should he sent by the next courier. It was not sent so soon as that, and in an audience of 18 September, de Bernis had to press again for its despatch, and it was thus put into his hands on 25 September.[25] In the next section we shall give its text; here it is sufficient to say that it was a very obscure document, conceived in the most vague and general terms, but still such as in the circumstances amounted to a promise to grant the suppression. The letter to the King of Spain, on the other hand, was much more definite, but was not obtained till 30 November.

II.[26] [Playing for time?]

The last section covered a period of only six months from the accession of Clement XIV, but the period was one which seems to be marked off by a distinctive note. The points which it brought out may be thus summarized: (1) The new Pope had declared on several occasions, and with a certain effusiveness, that it was his wish to gratify the offended Powers; and so restore peace to the Church, and that for this reason he was prepared to suppress the Society; he had also gone a step further, and in several confidential communications professed personal dislike for the Order, as given to domineering and intriguing. (2) He asked, however, for time to make the needful preparations, and had represented that time was all the more necessary as, having to encounter the opposition of his Curia, he felt obliged to keep the matter secret and hence must do everything himself. (3) In spite of these repeated professions of willingness on the part of the Pope, the representatives of the Courts distrusted him – de Bernis indeed less than the others, but even he to some extent – and suspected that he was merely playing them off with fictitious assurances, whilst his real object was to procrastinate, in the hope that some change of political conditions would sooner or later deliver

---

[25] Masson, op. cit., p. 154, where the text of the Pope's letter is given.
[26] *The Month*, **101** (1903), 259–77.

him from their tiresome demands. (4) They, on the other hand, were resolved to bring him to the point without delay, and pressed him on by strongly worded Memorials and veiled threats, by which means, at the end of the half-year, they at least succeeded in entangling him in two written engagements, addressed to the French and Spanish Kings, which they could in future always bring up against him.

This was their procedure, and it may have occurred to a reader that they were unreasonable, even from their own point of view, in demanding the act or suppression so soon, and accounting it suspicious that the Pope should require a few months to prepare for it. After all there could not well be a suppression without a Bull, or at least a Brief, and in such a document the decree must be fortified by an array of motives – unless it were to stand self-condemned – whilst the collection of materials for this array and their embodiment in an effective text was a thing that could not be done in a day.

Still this is a consideration which the Courts are not likely to have overlooked, and if in spite of it they suspected Clement XIV of an *arrière pensée,* it must have been because their practised eyes saw something in his manner which inspired distrust. The history of the procrastinations of the next two years will show that their suspicions were not without foundation.

Are we then to infer that the Pope was playing a double game, and playing it under conditions in which only extreme folly could anticipate success? There is no need for such a violent hypothesis. In view of the various reports of de Bernis and the other ambassadors, it is hardly possible to doubt that Clement XIV's dislike for the Society was real and persistent throughout his Pontificate; nor, perhaps, is it possible to deny that, however unwarrantably, he believed the Jesuits to be capable of vindictive schemes against a Pope who should destroy them. Still it would be to judge ill indeed of the Pontiff if one were not to credit him with the endeavour to determine their fate according to higher principles than those of personal dislike or fear, and it is to such an endeavour, as it appears to us, that his remarkable procrastinations must be ascribed. So far as one can pierce the thick veil of secrecy behind which he concealed his thoughts, it looks as if the opinions he held at the time of his accession gradually underwent a change, or at all events a modification. A religious Order is not an essential feature in the structure of the Church, and it had seemed to him the proper and obvious course to sacrifice the Society rather than risk the schism which the offended sovereigns were tendering as the alternative. But as time ran on and he studied the question more deeply he came to realize that it had other aspects which were of the gravest import. Could he disregard the glaring opposition to his predecessors, especially to the author of the quite recent *Apostolicum*, in which he would place himself by destroying as guilty of many crimes an Order whose merits they had so constantly and cordially praised? Could he disregard the wishes of those other sovereigns who had not asked for the suppression, but on the contrary had endowed colleges and entrusted them to the care of these Religious? Could he disregard the wishes of so many Bishops who, when not restrained by Court pressure, had so urgently called upon his predecessor to defend the Society? Was it not clear that the leaders of the movement for suppression were Regalists, Jansenists, and Encyclopaedists, whose real motives for desiring it were quite different from what they professed, and was it not clear that their refusal to supply proofs of the alleged guilt of the Jesuits meant that they had no proofs to give? Then again would he not be destroying a multitude of schools, missions, and other good works, almost indispensable for the well-being of the Church, if in this sudden way he destroyed the Religious in charge of them before there were others duly trained to take their place? Would he not be scandalizing a vast number of fervent Catholics, whom the Holy See had hitherto encouraged to look up to these Religious as trustworthy spiritual guides, if through his lips it now held them up as corrupters of society? And, lastly, would it be just to affix a life-long stigma on so many individual Religious whose entire innocence even the Courts themselves acknowledged? If thoughts like these were passing through the Pontiff's mind, is it not intelligible that he should grow more and more reluctant to take the step required of him, and that under the influence of this reluctance he should procrastinate from month to month, in the vain hope of either out-tiring his tormentors, or at least of excogitating some plan of suppression in which the above-mentioned evils could be mitigated? And is it not intelligible that, whilst his thoughts were in this confusion, and yet he was being harassed by the continual remonstrances of the ambassadors, he should in his endeavour to conciliate them and at the same time obey his conscience, at one moment give an assurance of which he did not foresee the full consequences, and at another qualify it with a reservation which seemed to be an attempt to elude it? It is, of course, only conjecturable that these were the inner thoughts agitating the Pontiff's mind during those four anxious years; but we put it to our readers, whether it is not a conjecture which explains intelligibly the strange history we have now to tell, of promises so often renewed and as often left unfulfilled, and whether it is not the theory which offers the best vindication of the Pontiff's reputation.

At all events in what it has to record of the action of the Pontiff, the history of the two years' period to which we now come is simply the history of these procrastinations, and of the various pretexts under which they were justified, whilst in what it has to record of the action of the Courts it will afford us further evidence of the insincerity with which the campaign against the Society was carried on.

One piece of evidence bearing on this latter point which must not be passed over takes us back for a moment to the summer of 1769. It is contained in a letter dated 26 August, addressed by Choiseul to de Bernis, a letter occasioned by the continued complaints of the Spaniards, who had returned to their suspicions of de Bernis; and it was intended to stimulate de Bernis to more resolute insistency. Possibly the Duc himself had suspicions that de Bernis, being a Churchman, might be really half-hearted over a policy of coercion so oppressive to the Holy See. At all events he thought fit to apply the spur to the Cardinal in the following manner:

> I will finish the history of the Jesuits by setting before your eyes a view which, I think, will impress you. I do not know that we did well in expelling the Jesuits from France and Spain; still it is a fact that they have been expelled from all the dominions of the House of Bourbon. I believe that it was still more ill-done, when these monks had been thus expelled, to make so imposing a demand at Rome for the suppression of the Order, and advertise all Europe that it had been made. Still it has been done, and the result is that the Kings of France, Spain, and Naples are at open war with the Jesuits and their adherents. Are they to be suppressed or are they not? Are the Kings to prevail, or are the Jesuits to gain the victory? That is the question which is now agitating the Cabinets, and is the source of intrigues, annoyances, and embarrassments to all the Catholic Courts. Surely it is impossible to contemplate this scene with indifference, and not see how unbecoming it is; and if I were Ambassador at Rome I should be ashamed to see the Padre Ricci the antagonist of my master.[27]

Is it conceivable that one who could write thus seriously believed the Jesuits to have committed the crimes laid to their charge? And de Bernis' reply suggests a similar reflection.

> I have no *arrière pensée* against the Jesuits. Like yourself, M. le Duc, I do not inquire whether it was right or wrong (*bien ou mal fait*) to expel them from the four kingdoms, or whether, after they had been expelled, it was right or wrong to make a formal demand for the suppression of the Order everywhere. I start from where we are. It is necessary that the Kings of France and Spain should gain the battle in which they are engaged against the General of the Jesuits. Only the Pope can enable them to gain it, and the task is to get him to do so.[28]

[27] Theiner, *Histoire du pontificat de Clément XIV*, i. p. 377.
[28] Ibid. p. 378.

We can now come to the Pope's letters to the Kings of France and Spain, the text of which was promised in the last section. To understand them, however, it is necessary to recall the proposed plan of action he had announced to de Bernis on 22 July. He proposed to issue a Brief approving all that had been done by the two sovereigns to the Jesuits in their own States and to ask for the opinions of the clergy of their kingdoms; and he expressed the hope that by means of these two measures he might induce the other sovereigns to demand a suppression in their own States. His suggestion was that, when the latter heard the motives which had impelled the two Kings, and the confirmation of these by the opinions of the clergy, they would be convinced that the Kings were justified in what they had done, and had set an example which they ought themselves to follow. But for this he must have the motives of the two sovereigns communicated to him, together with the opinions of their Bishops; and in the light of the sequel one cannot help feeling that his proposal to take this preliminary step was nothing more than a *ruse* to get hold of the motives which so far had been concealed from him and from his predecessor. It was doubtless with the same object that he 'proposed to accord this Brief *motu proprio*'.[29] They must feel that it would be to their advantage to have a *motu proprio*, the force of which would be absolute, but if they wished for it it was indispensable they should submit their motives to his judgment.

The letter to the King of France in which he bound himself to suppress the Society, and asked for the information necessary to enable him to do so, was dated 30 September. It said that he had 'received with pleasure the latest project manifested to him in the King's name by the Cardinal de Bernis, in regard to the business of which they were aware. The project seemed well suited to attain its purpose, to their mutual satisfaction. He was, however, looking to receive through the same Cardinal the necessary documents, and when he had received them, he would give the King a mark of his constant affection.'[30]

[29] See de Bernis's despatch of 18 September, ap. Theiner, vol. 1. p. 384. A Brief granted *motu proprio* ('of mere motion'), in contrast with one granted in view of the representations of the petitioners, is one in which the Pope takes upon himself responsibility for the justice of the motives urged as requiring the grant. Such a Brief cannot afterwards be set aside on the ground that the representations made were false.

[30] To please the King Clement wrote this letter in French, and as he barely knew the language, and yet was afraid to divulge the fact of his negotiation to his Curia, the French was so bad as to be comical, and to amuse de Bernis highly. (See Masson, *Le Cardinal de Bernis depuis son Ministère*, p. 155, where the original is given.)

Clement could hardly have expressed himself less clearly, and we must see in the indefiniteness of his language another illustration of his desire to remain, as far as possible, unpledged. Still – as de Bernis points out to Choiseul in his accompanying despatch of 17 September[31] – at least this letter amounted to a written engagement the sense of which was interpreted by the circumstances, and the Pope so understood it, but wrote obscurely because he was afraid lest his letter should fall into the hands of the Jesuits. De Bernis also explained that the 'documents' for which his Holiness asked were the 'motives of the French expulsion and the opinions of certain Bishops and Doctors of Theology', and that he required them 'only for form's sake, that he might be able to observe the canonical rules', and (insinuates de Bernis) the sovereigns 'can draw up their *memorie* as they judge best'.

The letter to the King of Spain was more explicit; but it was not extracted till two months later and after further pressure had been applied. On 22 November, Azpuru sought an audience and assured the Holy Father that if the promised letter were not sent, the King of Spain might see himself forced to take extreme measures and to complete the rupture so injurious to the Church of Spain which had been commenced in 1767.[32] And after a conference with de Fuentes, the Nuncio had written from Paris to Cardinal Pallavicini, the Papal Secretary of State, to say that the King of Spain was so set on achieving his purpose that, if he were refused, it was feared he might go mad and take some extreme resolution.[33] Thus stimulated Clement wrote his letter to Carlos III, which was dated 30 November.

> We feel [he said] we cannot dispense ourselves from assuring your Majesty of our fixed intention to give you clear proofs of our desire to fulfil our obligations. We have caused to be collected all the documents we shall require for the promised *motu proprio,* by which we shall justify in the eyes of all the world the wise conduct of your Majesty in expelling the Jesuits as troublesome and turbulent subjects. As we have to bear alone and without assistance the entire weight of affairs ... some delay is still necessary ... but we are firmly resolved to act, and are preparing to give the public incontestable proofs of our sincerity. We will submit to your Majesty's wisdom and intelligence a plan for the unconditional suppression of this Society.

This letter was a trump card placed in the hands of the Spaniards,

---

[31] Theiner, *ibid.* p. 385.
[32] Theiner, *ibid.* p. 401. De Bernis to Choiseul, 23 Nov.
[33] Theiner, *ibid.* p. 374.

and de Bernis, who claimed for himself the entire merit of obtaining it, defined correctly its significance in his letter to Choiseul of 29 April 1770.[34] 'It is only in the matter of time,' he writes, 'that the Pope can now gain any point, for his Holiness is too enlightened not to perceive that, if the King of Spain were to cause his letter to be printed, he would be dishonoured if he refused to keep his word and suppress a society, his plan for whose destruction he had promised to communicate, and whose members he regards as dangerous, unquiet, and turbulent.'

Louis XV replied to Clement's letter to himself on 29 October.[35] His Majesty rejoiced to hear that the Pope had received his last proposals favourably, but courteously declined to send him the documents and expressions of clerical opinion for which he had asked. The Pope 'was too enlightened not to understand that the four sovereigns would never have banished a body of Religious whom they thought dangerous, without having first examined thoroughly the just motives which had determined their action.' He had already told his predecessor that they had been moved to solicit a Papal Suppression 'by their regard for the interests of religion, and of the Holy See itself, and for the tranquillity of their States'... 'nor could he believe that the Pope would refuse them a demand which they felt to be so necessary, when the matter affected no dogma, and lay well within the Pope's power'... that 'as for the clergy of his kingdom they would receive with submission and gratitude the suppression of an Order already banished from the kingdom; and the Pope might take his royal assurance of this as of more value than signatures which might have their inconvenience'... that as for the form of the promised Brief it was for the Pope to decide on that which pleased him best.

Possibly the Holy Father was 'enlightened' enough to perceive that if the King declined to supply him with any evidence to examine, it was because he had none to supply, and at least he will have been enlightened enough to perceive the impropriety of requiring the great Head of Christendom to play the part not of a judge, but of an executioner, in a matter affecting the lives and characters of many thousands of Religious. Still if right was on the side of his demand,

---

[34] Saint-Priest, *Histoire de la Chute des Jésuites,* p. 131. Apud de Ravignan, *Clément XIII et Clément XIV,* vol. 1. p. 296. The Spanish King's dissatisfaction with de Bernis, at times abated at times stimulated by the successive phases of his diplomacy, was never entirely laid aside, and one effect was that the Cardinal was kept in ignorance of the Pope's letter to the King of Spain till some time after its despatch and receipt. This explains the late date of the letter in which he comments on its significance.

[35] Theiner, *ibid.* p. 393.

might was on the side of the King's refusal, and there was nothing left save to submit As far as France was concerned no *data* were obtainable for judging whether the Jesuits were really guilty.

From Spain the Pope's application for documents met with a better reception. If he did not get all that he required to form a basis for his *motu proprio,* he got what after all was all that he had formally demanded of de Bernis, a more detailed statement of the charges and the opinions of certain Bishops. Even these were apparently given with reluctance.[36] The Conde de Fuentes, on 9 October, had told Choiseul[37] that his royal master would never dream of divulging them, and Azpuru, in conjunction with de Bernis and Orsini, had assured the Pope as much, as late as November[38] – an assurance which probably explains the Pope's silence on this subject in his letter to the King of Spain.

Still Don Carlos, to whom de Bernis's despatch of 18 September had been communicated, had been reflecting on the matter, and, perhaps because he despaired of otherwise bringing Clement to the point, resolved to comply with his demand at least to the extent just indicated. Moñino, one of the Procurators-Fiscal, was deputed accordingly to draw up a statement of the offences charged; and the resulting *memoria* – which was approved by the Extraordinary Council of Castile on 30 November as suitable to be laid before the Pope – was that of which use has already been made in a previous chapter.[39] It alleged, it will be remembered, that at his accession to the throne of Spain, Carlos III found that the Jesuits had everything in their hands, education, influence, patronage, the royal confessorship; and he determined to substitute a system more equitable to the other clergy. The Jesuits, however, had resented this invasion of their monopoly, and in revenge sought to stir up the people, first by pamphlets, sermons, and conversations in which the King and his Ministers were vilified, and eventually by exciting insurrections, chief among which was the Madrid rising of 1766. Such an indictment, it will be acknowledged, is just such as might have been concocted by adversaries of the Society out of a few isolated facts and much flimsy gossip. It might, on the other hand, have been attested by solid proofs. In short it was a document which could be of use to one who desired to form an independent judgment on the case only if accompanied by the *dossiers* of the various trials which it should have presupposed, that is to say, the depositions of the witnesses for

---

[36] That is, the *memoria* was given reluctantly. The opinions of the Bishops he may have given more willingly, as this was the precise thing which the Extraordinary Council of 30 November 1767, had recommended. See above p. 161.
[37] See Danvila, *Historia del Reinado de Carlos III*, p. 384. Masson, p. 159.
[38] Masson, p. 159. Bernis to Choiseul, 1 November.
[39] See above pp. 105ff.

both prosecution and defence, their examinations, confrontations, etc. Nothing, however, of this sort was either included in the *memoria,* or appended to it; and we have seen in a previous chapter just how little of the sort is to be found in the Spanish Archives, and that little how inconclusive.

To elicit the opinions of the Bishops an order was sent to them by the Ministry of Grace and Justice on 29 October. After reciting briefly what had been done by the King and the Bourbon Courts so far, it invited them to say 'with the utmost promptitude and reserve' whether the anticipations of the past (in regard to the tranquillity likely to result from the expulsion) had been so far realized, and whether the necessity of an entire suppression had not grown more imperative. Fifty-four episcopal opinions were collected in this way during the months of November and December, 1769, to which were added seven others that had been previously communicated to the Extraordinary Council in 1767, and one other which had been written by the Royal Confessor in 1768 when the expediency of demanding a Papal Suppression was first mooted. Of the sixty-two thus obtained eight were adverse to the suppression, eight declined to express any opinion, and forty-six considered a Papal Suppression necessary.[40] According to Danvila the originals of these opinions are at Simancas, and he summarizes the text of the seven given in 1767 and 1768. They are those of the Bishops of Palencia, Barcelona, Salamanca, Taragona, Albarracín, and Corduba Tucumán (in South America), and of the Royal Confessor, Don Joachim Eleta. They accuse the Society of being animated with the spirit of domination, of political intrigues, of avarice, of extensive trading, of teaching lax doctrine. There can be no doubt that these seven report against it *con amore,* though, strange to say, the alleged complicity of the Jesuits in the Madrid rising, which made so deep an impression on the King and was the immediate occasion of the expulsion, made on these seven prelates an impression so slight that they do not even include it in their indictment. Danvila tells us nothing of the tenour of the other opinions hostile to the Society, which is unfortunate, as one would have liked to compare many of them with the opinions of the same prelates previously expressed to Clement XIV, in the letters in which they solicited or applauded the *Apostolicum.*[41] One thing is at least clear, these earlier

---

[40] The list may be found in Danvila, *Historia del Reinado de Carlos III,* iii. p. 429.

[41] In the documents appended to Père de Ravignan's two volumes, lists are given of Spanish Bishops who wrote in this sense to Clement XIII. In some cases, too, the texts of letters thus sent and of Clement XIII's acknowledgments are given, and from these it will be seen that the episcopal commendations of the Society at this earlier date were rendered in effusive language and professed to rest on personal experience.

and later opinions were in conflict with one another. Are we then to assume that the authors had changed their views during the interval, or must we suppose that either the earlier or the later opinions did not express the real minds of the writers, and if so, which are most to be trusted? The reader must judge, but we cannot help reminding him of the reason given by the Extraordinary Council of 30 November 1767, for recommending the King 'to consult his Bishops separately and not assemble a Council', namely; that 'each Bishop would thus make his own reflections separately, and the danger would be obviated of allowing them to talk the matter over in common'.[42] When these opinions, together with Moñino's *memoria*, arrived in Rome at the beginning of February, 1770, further grounds were disclosed for suspecting that they were opinions which had not been obtained without resort to some sharp practice. Of course none of the opinions unfavourable to the idea of the suppression were sent on, nor any of the non-committal opinions, but, as only thirty-four out of the forty-six which were said to favour suppression were included in the budget, it looks as if another dozen had not replied to the King in language that was deemed altogether satisfactory. Moreover, Grimaldi's covering letter of 23 January 1770,[43] stipulates that both opinions and *memoria* are to be kept a dead secret, except from the Pope, de Bernis, and Orsini, and that even to the Pope Azpuru must communicate them only in his own name, not in that of his Court.

The King of Spain was well satisfied with the Pope's written assurance of 30 November 1769, and regarded the suppression as now certain, since it would be impossible to rely on anything in this world if the Pope were false to his word.[44] He was consequently willing to give his Holiness the time he required. So he told the Marquis d'Ossun, who wrote accordingly from Madrid. Choiseul was delighted at the opportunity to extricate his Court from some of the responsibility, and wrote to de Bernis on 16 January[45] renewing an order already given him in the previous December, to adopt henceforth an entirely passive attitude, responding to every demand of the Spaniards, but originating nothing himself. It was that attitude which the Cardinal preserved from this time onward till the end.

In this way the year 1770 appeared to be opening with fair hopes for the Courts of a satisfactory attainment of their wishes. And they took it as a further sign of the Pope's sincerity when he called to assist him in his heavy labours of preparation Mgr Marefoschi – 'the

---

[42] See above p. 161.
[43] Theiner, *ibid*. p. 546.
[44] D'Ossun to Choiseul, 1 Jan., 1770.
[45] Theiner, *ibid*. p. 544.

one prelate who understood the intrigues of the Jesuits and other Orders of Friars, and had few dealings with the cloistered Orders.'[46]

Still the Courts did not abate their solicitations, and the first occasion on which their demand for the suppression was renewed was on 23 January, and was at the instigation of Almada, the Portuguese representative – for the Courts of Rome and Lisbon had recently been reconciled, on the understanding that the Society was to be suppressed. News came from Lisbon that the King of Portugal, whilst out hunting, was on 4 January assailed by a peasant with a club, and somewhat wounded. Choiseul, who had just received the news, writes to de Bernis: 'You may be sure they are ascribing the deed to the Jesuits,'[47] and so it was. There was not a Jesuit in Portugal save the poor prisoners in their subterranean dungeons, but what matter? They must have done it, *Ergo* they did; and so Almada invited the other ambassadors at Rome to unite with him in a strong *memoria* which de Bernis undertook to compose. He felt himself in a difficulty, 'as there was no proof to hand yet that the Jesuits or their friends had had any hand in the outrage,'[48] but he was equal to the task and urged that 'an Order which was always being suspected of such deeds ought not to be allowed to exist.' The Pope, on receiving this fresh *memoria*, is said to have been deeply impressed, and was thought to feel at last that there must be no more delays.[49] There were the indications too of what Danvila calls a 'time of unusual activity' in the Papal Palace. The Pope charged Marefoschi to search the Archives and collect whatever materials were available for justifying the suppression. Somewhat later he was told to make out the draft of the *motu proprio,* and was even supposed to be making out the draft of a Bull of Suppression. And by 3 March his Holiness was enabled to assure Cardinal de Bernis that he had given Marefoschi 'his last orders concerning the *motu proprio,* and had told him to keep working at it without interruption; adding that he would not lose sight of the plan of the Suppression.'

No result, however, followed to fulfil these newly warranted

---

[46] Tanucci to Losada, 23 Jan., 1770. Apud Danvila, *ibid.* p. 413.

[47] Masson, *ibid.* p. 162. Fr Thorpe, whose diary was quoted in the previous section, mentions on 26 January an account lately received from Lisbon, according to which the asailant was the aggrieved father of a young girl whom the King had caused to be carried off for the service of his lusts. That is an account which at all events was in keeping with the character of Joseph I, and with the generally credited explanation of the plot for which the Tavora family suffered in 1759.

[48] Letter to Choiseul of 16 January. Apud Theiner, *ibid.* p. 543.

[49] Grimaldi to Tanucci, 6 February. Apud Danvila, p. 415.

expectations, and so it continued throughout the year 1770, which proved to be nothing but a 'year of suspicions and reassurances,' and of never-ending disappointments for the Courts. It is unnecessary and would be wearisome to tell in full the tale of this year's negotiations, the details of which may be found in the pages of Theiner, Danvila, and Masson. The following summary will suffice to give an idea of the way in which the Pope continued to put off the fatal day. 'By each courier,' says Masson,[50] 'de Bernis reported new promises made by the Pope, and new declarations in reference to the *motu proprio,* but there were no visible results.' In March, as we have seen, the *motu proprio* was nearly ready; in April its draft was found to need revision in the sense of fortifying it with stronger motives, so as to protect the Pope against the possibility of Jesuit revengefulness, and when Azpuru protested against the impropriety of these further delays, Clement told de Bernis[51] that if the Spaniards pressed him further he would resign the Papacy and retire into Sant' Angelo. In March (27th) Choiseul wrote to de Bernis[52] that 'he did not know if the Court of Madrid regarded the matter as finished, but that to himself it seemed not even commenced,' and on 29 May, to the Cardinal's plea that the Pope thought it prudent to proceed slowly towards his object, he replied that 'there should at all events be some difference between going slowly and not going at all.' By June the Court of Madrid became suspicious again, and sent word that the 'strongest reasons' must be used to persuade the Pope of the inexpediency of further delay.[53]

This elicited another autograph from Clement[54] to Carlos III, protesting that all was going well and the King would be delighted with the *motu proprio* when he saw it, but that he could not take his Ministers into his confidence over its composition. And to this Carlos III was constrained in sheer courtesy to write back[55] that he personally was sure of the Pope's *bona fide* intentions, but that the delays were most embarrassing, as they sowed undesirable ideas in the public mind.

At the beginning of July[56] de Bernis reports that the Pope talks of new Jesuit intrigues. 'He seems always decided against these Religious, yet always to fear them.' And the Cardinal adds a rumour

---

[50] Op. cit. p.163.
[51] Danvila, *ibid.* p. 418. Bernis to Azpuru, 1 May.
[52] Theiner, *ibid.* p. 548.
[53] Danvila, *ibid.* p. 419. Grimaldi to Azpuru, 6 June.
[54] Danvila, *ibid.* p. 421.
[55] Danvila, *ibid.* p. 422.
[56] Theiner, *ibid.* p. 551.

which has reached him that the General of the Order of the Passion[57] has warned his Holiness 'to look to his kitchen'. This incident is of interest for the testimony it elicited from Choiseul, who wrote back on 13 August[58] saying he found it difficult to believe the Pope was so credulous and pusillanimous; that 'the Jesuits had been dangerous to the countries from which they had been expelled because of their doctrines, their institute, and their intrigues, but they had not been accused of being poisoners, and it was only the base jealousy and fanatical hatred of a few monks which could suspect them of it.'

In this same month of July the *motu proprio* Briefs for the different Courts were reported by Marefoschi to be at last ready, but 'the Pope desired before publishing them to prepare the way by dealing the Jesuits some striking blow,'[59] or 'of letting the lightning precede the thunderbolt', as Clement himself expressed it to Orsini.[60] He meant to say that he would visit them with some afflictions which would set people talking, and suspecting that they must have been convicted of some misbehaviour in Rome itself and were not unlikely therefore to have offended elsewhere. And it was evidently in this mind that he not only took the Seminary of Frascati out of their charge, but forbade them to give Missions in the Monastery of St Clare, or to receive from the Congregation of Indulgences any special favours.

Indeed from this time began quite a progressive series of measures avowedly intended to afflict them, and ruin their credit with the Roman people. In this way the Bishops in the Papal States were recommended to deprive the Fathers in their dioceses of faculties to preach and hear confessions; first the Irish College, then the Roman Seminary, which for a long time had been administered by the Jesuits, were submitted to an Apostolic visitation over which Marefoschi and his two subalterns, Alfani and Carafa, presided. The ordinary methods of procedure were disregarded, the Jesuits were

---

[57] St Paul of the Cross, the General in question, is not in the least degree likely to have said anything of the kind, and Père de Ravignan *(Clément XIII et Clément XIV,* p. 303) quotes from a letter of the Saint, of which the original is in the Archives of the Roman College. 'Be sure,' he writes, 'that I feel much the extreme afflictions to which this illustrious Society of Jesus is subjected. The sole thought of so many calamities makes me groan and weep, seeing as I do so many innocent Religious persecuted in so many ways ... I continually pray that God who gives death and life will in His own good time raise this Society to life again with a still greater glory; this has ever been and still is my feeling.'

[58] *Ibid.* p. 553.

[59] Theiner, p. 552. Bernis to Choiseul, 27 July. Marefoschi added that he himself had suggested this to the Pope, as he wanted 'to accustom him to the sound of cannon'.

[60] Danvila, p. 422.

given no opportunity of putting in any defence, and judgment was pronounced against them, accusing them of negligence, domineering, defalcations, and other crimes; and the institutions were taken out of their hands. Nor were these the worst vexations to which they were submitted, as we shall have occasion to show in the next section.

But to return to the Pope's fencing with the Courts. There was still no sign of the Briefs appearing, and on 10 August Choiseul again expressed the opinion,[61] to which events certainly pointed, that all this talk of a coming *motu proprio* was merely a kind of artifice with which his Holiness was playing off the Courts – since he had now been on the throne more than a year and had done absolutely nothing save make the written promise of the Brief and of the Plan, which promise he seemed in no hurry to fulfil. And Carlos III himself at length began to feel that his dignity was more compromised than his desires promoted by the repeated remonstrances of ambassadors which were only met by rebuffs. Accordingly he ordered[62] them to remit these, or at least to confine themselves to purely formal repetitions of their demand, and so the year dragged out its course.

One point, however, we must not pass over of the results of this year's negotiations, as it has its bearing on the motives of the Pope's delay. He had a really strong point when he protested to the ambassadors that he could not grant an entire suppression of the Society as long as several of the sovereigns in whose dominions it was working had not solicited it. It was the Empress Maria Theresa he had particularly in mind, but a despatch from the Nuncio at Vienna of 20 May 1770,[63] had informed him that her Majesty would offer no opposition to such a measure. Her reply to the Bourbon Ambassadors had been, as she assured the Nuncio, that she did not wish to intervene in any way in the Jesuit question; that they had twisted this answer and reported her as saying that she too wished for the suppression; but that her point was this – she had never had reason to complain of the Jesuits in her States, and whether they were left untouched or reformed, or suppressed, she would not banish them from her States; but that she was prepared to leave it entirely to the wisdom of the Holy See what measures should be taken with regard to them. This excuse, therefore, for delaying to gratify the Bourbon Courts was taken from Clement XIV by the summer of 1770, nor had it ever existed to delay his approbation of the doings of the Bourbons in their own States. Clearly, therefore, the true cause of his procrastination must have been intrinsic to the subject matter; in other words, it must

[61] Apud Danvila, *ibid*. p. 423.
[62] Grimaldi to Azpuru, 4 Dec., 1770. Apud Danvila, *ibid*. p. 427.
[63] Theiner, *ibid*. p. 554.

have been his own personal feeling that the suppression was a measure in itself most undesirable.

With the close of the year 1770, came a political event which for the moment seemed to threaten the whole structure of the Bourbon attack on the Society. Choiseul's tenure of office had for some time been insecure. He represented a party in the French Court, and there was another party, that of the Duc d'Aiguillon, which was intriguing to supplant him. The underlying motive of hostility to him was unquestionably personal, but Choiseul was a protector of the *Parlements*, who had often said a good word for them to the King, whereas d'Aiguillon, together with his fellow-ministers Maupeou and the Abbé de Terray (although the two latter had been Parlementaires themselves[64]), were their sworn foes. There may also have been a real as there certainly was an alleged source of opposition in Choiseul's disposition to renew the war with England, to which the other party were adverse. Choiseul, however, would probably have held his ground had be not excited the wrath of Madame du Barry, the King's new mistress, who, finding that he refused to pay incense to her, determined to displace him. She succeeded – for Louis XV could refuse nothing to his mistresses. Choiseul got his *lettre de cachet* on 24 December, which gave him twenty-four hours notice to betake himself to his country seat at Chanteloup and remain there in detention. Temporarily, the seals of the Foreign Office were given to the Duc de la Vrillière, who held them till the following March, by which time the mistress was able to obtain her favourite's appointment. Of course their enemies accused the Jesuits of having worked this intrigue, but the accusation was absolutely without foundation and does not require discussion. Still as the great enemies of the Society in Paris had been the Parlementaires, and the advent of the new Government was followed at once by the banishment of all these Parlementaires and the substitution of an entirely new judicial body, the Jesuits hoped that the change of Ministry might prove to their advantage. In some respects it did, for, as it was the *arrêt* of *Parlement* in 1767, and not the Royal Edict of 1764, which had sent them into exile, they were now allowed to re-enter the country, though only as individuals. But did this mitigation of their troubles forbode a further mitigation to follow? They themselves were sanguine, and not unnaturally so, and they wrote jubilant letters to their friends in other countries. The effect was to cause much anxiety to Carlos III and his Ministers, who were also exercised at the same time by another source of solicitude.

[64] For their part in the campaign against the Society a decade previously, see pp. 37–39, 49 50 above.

In the previous October news had come to Europe that the Spanish Governor of Buenos Ayres, Don Francisco Bucarelli, had forcibly taken possession of Port Egmont, a recently founded English establishment in one of the Falkland Islands. The English people were indignant, and Lord North's Government ordered the British Envoy at Madrid to demand the instant restitution of Port Egmont and the repudiation of Bucarelli's action. Carlos III haughtily declined, and relying on the Family Compact, prepared to accept the alternative of war. It was just then, however, that Louis XV's letter to Carlos III announcing the change of Ministry, and the fall of the *Parlement*, arrived in Madrid. Louis XV[65] exhorted his royal cousin to make concessions to England, and so avoid a war, for which he himself in the present critical state of his affairs was not ready. Carlos III did as he was asked, but the tone in which he wrote[66] back to Louis XV marked clearly that the Family Compact was strained. Don Carlos doubtless realized that it was the French King's lust which really lay behind the change of Ministry, which coming at such a moment was most injurious to the interests of Spain; and did it not show that the French King's regard for these interests, to which the Family Compact should have attached him cordially, was after all but slight?

It was undoubtedly the consciousness that Carlos III's attachment to the Family Compact was thus weakened, which determined the resolution of Louis XV and his new Ministry to persevere in the policy of Choiseul against the Society, and it is of interest to English readers to note this. Had it not been for the fear lest England should attack France once more, and on the other hand the hope of forestalling her by a descent on her own shores,[67] the maintenance of the Family Compact would have been of less moment to France, and in that case, as Louis XV – who 'took no personal interest in the negotiations, and only out of regard for his Catholic Majesty had demanded the suppression'[68] – the suppression would in all probability never have come off – since, had France withdrawn, Spain alone would never have been able to bring Clement XIV to the point. As it was, an assurance was sent to Carlos III that the policy which Louis had been pursuing was his own, and did not change with his Ministers, whilst de la Vrillière wrote to de Bernis on 25 December 1770,[69] that he was to push the matter on with more

[65] Masson, op. cit. p. 174.
[66] *Ibid.* p. 175.
[67] See Lord Mahon's *History of England*, vol. v. Append. pp. xix–xxv (edition of 1857) for two *mémoires* for the invasion of England, drawn up under the direction of Choiseul in 1767 and 1768.
[68] D'Aiguillon to de Bernis, 18 June, 1771. Theiner, ii. 118.
[69] *Ibid.* ii, p. 106.

vigour than ever, whilst however still regulating himself by the direction of his Catholic Majesty.

None the less, the course of the negotiations with the Pontiff during the new year 1771 proved to be exactly what it had been in 1770. Clement continued to renew his promises, and at the same time to multiply his excuses, but absolutely no results followed. In February, de Bernis learnt[70] again that the *motu proprio* Brief was ready for despatch to Spain, Naples, and Parma (France and Portugal had declined to receive it), but that the Pope had had it put into his head that if he published the *motu proprio*, he could not avoid publishing a Bull of Suppression as soon as two months later; and this had alarmed him, as he had not yet come to an understanding with the non-soliciting Courts, nor made arrangements to continue the studies in the schools from which the Jesuits had been ejected. At this early stage of the new year Clement had also hit on a new and valuable pretext for delay. He had managed to gain over Carlos III to the scheme of making the publication of the Bull of Suppression[71] simultaneous with the Beatification of the Venerable Palafox, who in his days had been their resolute adversary and whom they were charged with having persecuted. Don Carlos was attracted by a scheme which would give so much more force and solemnity to the act of suppression; but de Bernis saw more clearly what the scheme meant. 'His Holiness,' he wrote[72] in the following autumn, 'has hitherto found a means of suspending the expedition of the Brief by flattering the King of Spain with the hope of seeing the Venerable Palafox beatified, and has told him that this is the necessary preliminary to the Suppression ... This Cause of Beatification is not yet at an end, and perhaps will take years to complete.' Of the remaining points of interest in the negotiations of 1771 we need only notice one: de Bernis began to feel that his influence with the Pope, of which he had previously boasted, must have either been less than he supposed or was slipping away from him. In his letter, already cited, of 9 November 1771, he gives an interesting description of the Pope's *entourage*. His Holiness keeps all at a distance save Marefoschi, Bischi, and a few others, but has besides them an inner circle about him, the principal figures of which are Fra Buontempi, his Secretary, and Fra Francesco, his major-domo, both friars of his own Order. It is Fra Buontempi who really rules the Pope, and this friar is jealous lest Marefoschi should dispossess him. From all which de Bernis deducts the necessity, if he is to hold his ground, of bribing

---

[70] *Ibid.* ii, p. 108.
[71] Azpuru to Grimaldi, 31 January, 1771. Apud Danvila, *ibid.* p. 439.
[72] Bernis to d'Aiguillon, 9 November, 1771. Apud Theiner, ii. 125.

Buontempi, or as he puts it delicately, 'of taking means in reference to P. Buontempi, who never quits the Pope's side.' D'Aiguillon's own character was not one to invite respect, but he answered on this occasion with dignity that 'the King of France does not think it consistent with his dignity to gain over these pretended depositaries of the secrets of the Vatican.'[73]

And so the year 1771 spun out its course, and left the Courts with the feeling that they were exactly where they were in the middle of 1769. The Pope had indeed given a written promise in the autumn of 1769, but he had several times reminded de Bernis that he had never tied himself to any fixed time of fulfilment. He had only tied himself to suppress the Society when a suitable opportunity arrived, and this apparently was never going to happen. And as for the ambassadors, all their counsels, all their remonstrances, all their implied threats had buried themselves vainly in the sandy ramparts of the Pope's reassurances. Or, as the pert Almada put it, as often as the ambassadors met together to concert measures, it was as if de Bernis sat in the middle and sang *Per omnia saecula saeculorum,* whilst Orsini and Azpuru responded *Amen.*[74]

III.[75] [The drawing-up of the Brief]

We have brought our narrative down to the opening of the year 1772. More than two and a half years have passed since the Conclave was coerced into electing Cardinal Ganganelli, and more than two years since the latter, as Clement XIV, engaged himself to the King of Spain by a written promise. Yet so far the Courts had not succeeded in getting him to take a single step towards fulfilling this engagement.

Nor to the shrewd eyes of Cardinal de Bernis did it appear likely that the wished-for object would ever be attained in its entirety.

> The total suppression [he wrote on 17 January, 1772[76]] cannot well be carried out as long as the other Courts, such as Vienna, Turin, Tuscany, Milan, and Genoa do not demand it or give their formal consent to the scheme ... and this one difficulty alone has always made me regard the total suppression of the Order of Jesuits as an operation almost impossible. The Pope cannot be expected to embroil himself with half the Catholic sovereigns in order to satisfy the others, on a delicate point on which he cannot decide with justice and honour except in accordance with

---

[73] Theiner, *ibid.* p. 119.
[74] Masson, op. cit. p. 205.
[75] *The Month*, **101 (1903)**, 383–403.
[76] Theiner, *Pontificat du Clément XIV*, ii, p. 202.

rules and forms prescribed by the canons, and in reliance on documents which give certain proof that the entire government of the Society is corrupt and incapable of reform ... [And hence he thinks that eventually] the Holy Father will make the Spaniards feel the impossibility of destroying the Jesuits in the States where they are protected, especially if the proofs of the total corruption of the government of this Order are not clearly established.

Here is a statement of great value for the vindication of the Society, for it is tantamount to an admission that no such proofs of total corruption were in hand, and this from one who was in the secrets both of his own Court and the Court of Spain, or at least, as regards the latter Court, sufficiently so to know of all they had laid before the Pope, and to infer correctly the quality of all they might have kept back.

In the absence of these proofs of total corruption the Cardinal de Bernis anticipated in the letter quoted, that Clement XIV would eventually subside into a decision to suppress the Society, or at least to reduce its power, by indirect means – 'by limiting the Jesuits' power, forbidding them all manner of commerce, placing their moral teaching under episcopal supervision,' and so on. Meanwhile, the Spanish Court had no thought of allowing itself to be played off either with half-measures or indefinite procrastinations, but had become only the more determined to bring the negotiations to a speedy issue. A more effectual agent at the Vatican was what Carlos III felt he needed, and opportunely at this moment Mgr Azpuru, whose health was failing, asked to be replaced by another ambassador. The Conde de Lavaña was first appointed to the post but died while on his journey Romewards, and the King's choice then fell on Don Joseph Moñino. This man was of humble origin, but had by his talents as an advocate attained to the position of a Procurator-Fiscal of Castile. Even thus his selection for a foreign embassy seems to have been contrary to established precedent, and excited much suspicion at Madrid, the more so as the intention to appoint him was kept secret from all save the Marqués de Grimaldi.[77] The chief motive for his selection was undoubtedly his personal character, and what this was the Auditor of the Spanish Nunciature reported to the Cardinal Secretary of State in the following terms:

---

[77] That is to say, even from Aranda, de Roda, and the Royal Confessor. A dissension had arisen among the ministers and counsellors of Carlos III, and according to d'Ossun (d'Ossun to d'Aiguillon, 30 March 1772, apud Masson, *Le Cardinal de Bernis depuis son Ministère,* p. 200), the appointment of Moñino represented the victory gained by Grimaldi over the party of Aranda.

> My disappointment is great ... because I know what kind of a man he is ... and how, notwithstanding his mild and conciliatory exterior and his affectation of moderation and piety, he is at heart hostile to Rome, to the Pontifical authority, and to the ecclesiastical jurisdiction ... He is, in short, full of artifice, sagacity, and dissimulation; and no one here is more set upon the suppression of the Jesuits – whether it be from motives of principle and personal dislike, or because he is pursuing his own interests.[78]

This formidable personage reached Rome on 4 July, and his fame had preceded him. All seemed anxious to postpone the day when they must begin to meet him, and he found himself almost deserted on his arrival. Azpuru was at the point of death, and in fact died three days later; Orsini and Almada contrived visits to the country; and the Pope, pleading hoarseness from the effects of a cold, put off his first audience till the 12th. Bernis also had intended to go into the country, and had he not prudently changed his mind, the newly arrived Ambassador would have been left without information as to the state of affairs. As it was these two met, and concerted their plans for future action; that is to say, Moñino, whose directions de Bernis had orders to follow, explained the method they must unite to pursue. The King of Spain insisted on a total suppression, and this being so their object must be to extort it speedily. As for the promise of a previous *motu proprio* approving what the sovereigns had done to the Jesuits in their own dominions, and the promise of a simultaneous Beatification of the Venerable Palafox, these were but obstacles interposed by the Pope as means for gaining time, and must now be discarded. They must go straight to their end, and require the Pope to direct his attention to the suppression itself and its prompt accomplishment. Viewed from their standpoint this was doubtless a sound policy, but after all it only removed out of the way two pretexts for delay, and there were other pretexts left of which the Pope would doubtless avail himself as dexterously in the future as in the past. It was understood, however, that the main difference between Moñino's and Azpuru's policy was to lie in a more resolute application of the method of intimidation.

> The King of Spain, he told de Bernis, in one of their early meetings,[79] has very little confidence left in the Pope's promises ... and will give him only a short time for making up his mind. In case he should meet us with a refusal (which would be regarded as a downright breach of faith) there would be danger of our breaking openly with the Holy See or, which would be much more dangerous for it, of our breaking with it tacitly. For in that case Spain and other States which till now have been called lands of obedience would become lands of liberty.

[78] Theiner, *ibid.* ii, p. 209.
[79] Bernis to d'Aiguillon, 5 August. apud Theiner, ii. p. 226.

On 12 July Moñino had his first audience, but it led to no definite results. The Pope expressed his dislike for the Jesuits, which he said was of many years' standing, but as for their Suppression, though he fully intended to decree it, he must await an opportune time, and must avoid giving a handle to those who suspected that he had purchased his election by promising such a measure. Besides, he was compelled to take a long time over the preparations, by the necessity in which he was placed of doing all the work himself, his Curia being unsympathetic – and in this connection he asked for more secrecy from the Courts and their agents. To this demand for secrecy Moñino induced the Courts to accede, but he took occasion to remind the Pope thus early that 'his master was a resolute prince, and if the result of these long delays should be to destroy his trust in the Pontiff, all would be lost for the latter.'[80]

So his first audience ended, nor could the Ambassador obtain another till several weeks had intervened. The Pope said he was suffering from a skin affection, as indeed he was, and must retire at once to Castel Gandolfo for a short season. This was annoying, but Moñino deemed it prematute to protest, and employed the interval in improving his relations with his colleagues and others who might be able to help him. Almada was in thorough sympathy with his policy, but was unfortunately 'a mad-cap', nor does he seem to have thought highly of Orsini's capacity. On the first instance he judged de Bernis to be playing a double game, and he desired his removal, but during the interval of waiting he changed his mind altogether about this diplomatist, and wrote to Grimaldi in high commendation both of his abilities and of the trust that could be reposed in his loyalty to the Courts;[81] and the effect of this and similar subsequent letters was that the Spanish Court laid aside for ever its suspicion of the Cardinal, the King of Spain even directing that a cordial acknowledgment of the value of his services should be sent to Paris.[82] Mgr Macedonio was another on whose assistance Moñino found he could count, as a source of information as to the Pope's real mind and the best way of dealing with him; and this prelate now assured him that it was the case that Clement had repented of his promises, and that it was merely in the hopes of evading their fulfilment that he kept repeating his excuses for delay. Another suggestion he got from Mgr Macedonio was that he should direct his attention especially to Fra

---

[80] Moñino to Grimaldi, 16 July. Danvila, *Reinado de Carlos III*, ii. p. 466; Theiner, *ibid*. p.219.
[81] Cf. letter of Moñino to Grimaldi, 3 September. Danvila, *ibid*. p. 474.
[82] Grimaldi to Magallon (Chargé d'Affaires d'Espagne at Paris), 21 September, *ibid*. p. 482.

Buontempi,[83] 'who was the only one able to work miracles on the Pope', and Moñino took the hint and had several interviews with this mysterious personage. He professed that he disliked the Jesuits, as no doubt he did, but Moñino distrusted him none the less, and suspected him of being in some part responsible for the excuses and delays by which the demands of the Courts had been so far frustrated. Accordingly, when the Pope's reply to Moñino's credentials was found to contain nothing more than vague allusions to the Jesuit question, he laid the blame on Buontempi, and about the beginning of August, when he was beginning to tire of the Pope's prolonged silence about future audiences, he saw the friar again and 'asked him plainly whether he wished to be a friend or a foe to the Court of Spain'; and as Buontempi, who was 'consummate in artifices and external demonstrations', replied that, if he were regarded as an obstacle, 'he would be only too glad to retire', he was told that ' the risks of a favourite were not confined to the possibility of having to retire, and that the protection of Princes like the King of Spain was worth much more than all other supports.'[84]

After six weeks' silence the Pope sent word that he was prepared to continue his audiences with Moñino, and would give him for the purpose every Sunday at ten in the forenoon. Now then the battle seemed about to begin in earnest, and it was arranged between the two Ambassadors that whilst Moñino was to drive the Pope onward by forcing him to adopt his own ideas and threatening him with the dire consequences of further prevarication,[85] de Bernis was to

[83] Ferrer del Río, *Reinado de Carlos III*, ii. p. 410.
[84] Moñino to Grimaldi, 6 August. Apud Theiner, ii. p. 232.
[85] Of the vehemence of this undue pressure and the effect it had on the Pope we may quote, as confirming what can be gathered from the Ambassadors' letters, the testimony of Padre Vasquez, the Augustinian General, whose correspondence with de Roda and whose intimacy with de Bernis has been mentioned above (pp.225–6). He was also intimate with Moñino and Azara, and was well acquainteed with the Holy Father. 'God,' he wrote in one of his later letters to Roda, 'destined this Pope (Clement XIV) for the Pontificate, but only allowed him to suppress the Jesuits and did not let him do anything else which was useful either to Church or State. To fit him for carrying out the suppression the Creator gave him a heart so timid that, as I have said to your Excellency before, the flight of a fly sufficed to trouble his footsteps. Knowing that he was thus pusillanimous our able Minister (Moñino) adopted a tone of severity and let him see that he was aware of his tergiversations, by which means he reduced him at length to such an extreme state of fear, that his fear of the Jesuits and their adherents was outbalanced and ceased to influence him ... (And as regards himself Padre Vasquez adds) our Minister has more than once told me that I am the bogey not only of Padre Buontempi, but most of all of the Pope.' The *Cartas* of Vasquez are we believe still unpublished; the above extract is taken, from the *Jansenismo en España* (p. 342) of Fraile Miguélez, himself an Augustinian Father.

approach his Holiness more as a personal friend, striving to elicit his confidences, and assuring him that the wisest course would be to assent to Moñino's proposals. It was this crafty method which they actually followed, as appears from many passages in their official despatches,

The second audience came off on Sunday 23 August, and was followed by four others on the four following Sundays. Save in one respect, however, little came of them. The Pope rang the changes on his usual pretexts for delay. He must first obtain the assent of the other sovereigns; he must get together the materials out of which the Bull was to be constructed; he must take precautions against the vengeance of the Jesuits and their partizans, with which they would be sure, if able, to visit him; he thought it wise to proceed to the final end by gradual stages, and was minded to begin by forbidding them to take any more novices. This last measure he reminded Moñino had precedent in its favour, as it had been tried by Innocent XIII, who shut up some of their colleges, suppressed some of their sodalities of laymen, and forbade the Fathers to preach and hear confessions, and who would by these gradual stages have worked up to an entire suppression, had he not unfortunately died and been succeeded by a Dominican monk who had undone all his work. Just so, was Moñino's reply to this account of the failure of Innocent XIII's plan, and such is bound to be the fate of half-measures, nor will the King of Spain be satisfied with anything less than the entire uprooting of the evil weed. But in his audience of 30 August, Moñino availed himself of these incessant pleas for delay to initiate an important move.[86] The Pope could not see his way to any present plan for a total suppression which would not involve serious risks; might he, the Ambassador, suggest one to his Holiness; and with this he pulled a roll of paper out of his pocket, and made as if he would read it. Clement XIV, however, refused to look at it, on which Moñino, with an expression of disgust, put it back in his pocket, and renewed his previous warnings of the danger of delay. 'It excited the suspicions of the sovereigns' and 'might have the unpleasant effect of inducing the King of Spain to take up the idea which had already commended itself to some other sovereigns – that of destroying *all* the Religious Orders by the indirect process of forbidding their members entrance into his kingdom, except on condition that they first renounced their exemption from episcopal jurisdiction.'

Apparently this threat was not lost on the Pope for at the next audience on 6 September,[87] he asked to see Moñino's plan, which the

---

[86] Despatch of 3 September. Apud Ferrer del Rio, *ibid*. p. 387.
[87] Despatch of 3 September. Apud Ferrer del Río, *ibid*. p. 393.

latter then gave him, though only after a pretence of reluctance, on the ground that it was an idea personal to himself, and had not been contemplated in his instructions – which latter limited him to two points only; first, to continue soliciting the suppression by pacific means as long as there was any hope of thus obtaining it; and secondly, should this hope fail, to convince his Holiness that the King was firmly resolved to use the power which belonged to him as Protector of the Church now disturbed by the Jesuits, and as Sovereign of the State now invaded by this rebellious and persistent body. It was also at this audience that Moñino, with the intention of further encouraging Clement XIV to grant what was required of him, assured him that as soon as the suppression was decreed Avignon and Benevento should be restored to the Holy See. So barefaced an avowal of what was none the less perfectly understood between them was too much for the Holy Father, who replied nobly that he 'would never do one thing in order to obtain another'.

Nothing of consequence came out of the audience of 13 September except that the Pope referred to the measures he was about to take against the Roman Jesuits by depriving them of the Roman Seminary and the Irish Seminary, both which measures were carried out within the next few days. He also spoke of an idea he was then turning over in his mind (and which he afterwards carried into effect) of confiding to Cardinal Malvezzi, the Archbishop of Bologna, and Mgr Aquaviva, the President of Urbino – two men whom he felt he could thoroughly trust in this affair – an operation against the Jesuits within their jurisdiction, which would be the first step towards opening the door to the total suppression. In the audience of 20 September[88] his Holiness announced that the time for his *villeggiatura* was come, and that he must, therefore, intermit the audiences for a time, but that he intended to advance the matter by some steps whilst at Castel Gandolfo. Moñino came away from this audience much depressed, and with the feeling that the real reason for the Pope's fresh retirement into the country was to gain a pretext for further delay – a feeling confirmed by the Pope's silence about the plan given to him on 6 September, and likewise by the marked disposition of his Holiness during this interview to go back on his engagements, on the plea of the strength of the Jesuit party with which he would have to place himself in conflict. This much Moñino told de Bernis when the audience was over, adding that if, when the *villeggiatura* was over, the Pope still remained unresolved, he should consider that there was nothing further left for him to do, and that he must now leave it to

[88] Despatch of 3 September. Apud Ferrer del Río, *ibid.* p. 405.

the Courts to take what measures they deemed expedient. De Bernis was meant to report this by way of a confidential communication to the Pope, which he accordingly did on the next day, and received in reply this much of reassurance, that there was no ground for their fears, and that he would not have accepted the plan had he not intended to reply to it, but that they must remember that if they had but one matter to engage their attention, he had very many.

The plan which Moñino submitted for the Pope's consideration on 6 September, is a document of considerable importance, as it was eventually adopted by the Pope and formed the type to which the Brief of Suppression is conformed in almost every respect. Not having access to the original text we may borrow from the pages of Theiner, who gives a summary of its contents.[89] It contains eighteen articles of which the first two are here quoted from Theiner *in extenso*.

1. 'The Pope will do well to expound all the motives he has already alleged for destroying the Society of Jesus; and those which he still guards in his breast, and these motives should be relative to the peace of the Church and the tranquillity of Catholic nations. It will, however, be desirable that he should not enter into too great detail, so as not to give occasion to discussions, which would be injurious to religion and not less so to the Jesuits themselves, and would only defame the latter unnecessarily. Before all things it will be good to make it clear that the Pope does not wish to ill-treat these Religious, but on the contrary to treat them with paternal benevolence. It is thus that he will disarm most easily the wrath of the Jesuits and their partizans.'
2. 'It will be necessary to develop the thoughts expressed in the preceding paragraph, and for this end it would be of use if the Pope were to forbid all members of the clergy, secular and regular, of whatsoever rank and condition, and even the members themselves of the said Society, to attack or defend the measure of its suppression, its causes and motives, or the Institute of the Society, its rule, its government, or anything else connected with the question; or to write or speak on it without express permission from the Roman Pontiff. And likewise his Holiness should enjoin that no person be injured for his attitude to this question, either in speech or writing, in public or private, under pain of excommunication reserved to the Pope. By this means every impartial man will see that the Pope wishes to treat the Jesuits with the greatest charity, to recommend them to the protection of sovereigns, and to protect their Institute against all unjust attack.'

Paragraphs 3 and 4 suggest that the Christian Princes be exhorted to

[89] *Ibid.* p. 251.

facilitate the execution of the Bull, and that the faithful everywhere be exhorted to remember that they are all disciples of Jesus Christ and children of the Church, our Holy Mother, and all brothers who ought to love one another, abhor schisms, discords, etc. - which the enemy of mankind under the guise of scholastic doctrine, or under the pretext of spiritual advancement, employs to trouble the peace and tranquillity of the Church. The object of this clause, says Moñino, is to convince the faithful of the rectitude of the Pope's intentions, and to dispose them to accept the suppression with resignation.

The remaining paragraphs are to decree what form the suppression shall take for each class of members of the Order. (5) The novices are to be sent home at once. (6) The professed who are not yet priests (i.e., the scholastics) are to have their vows dissolved and be left free to embrace the mode of life which their conscience and strength suggest to them. (7) Priests are either to join other Orders, or live under the Bishop as secular priests. (8) Those Professed who wish to remain in their present abode, through want of a maintenance, may remain there till this has been provided for them, but meanwhile must wear the dress of the secular clergy. (9 and 10) The Bishops are to appoint a committee of three of their clergy in each place where there is a residence of the Society, to take over its property, and to allot it partly to the maintenance of the members, partly to pious purposes. (11 and 12) The Bishops may employ the ex-Jesuits for ministerial works if they find them fit. (13) When any ex-Jesuit leaves the College where he has been permitted to reside for a time, his place is not to be filled up by another. (14) At Rome the houses of the Jesuits are to be disposed of by a Congregation of Cardinals, which Congregation is to have the right of interpreting the Bull and deciding any difficulties which may arise as to its execution. (16) The Propaganda to be left free to make provision for the former Jesuit missions, in doing which however it must be mindful of the spirit of the Bull. (17) The authority of the General and other Superiors to cease for ever. (18) Princes to support the execution of the Bull by supplying troops in case of resistance.

These are the eighteen points, but a supplementary note recommends that as soon as the Bull is published the General and his Assistants, together with the Procurator General and all Rectors, shall be sent away from Rome, each to a secure place of detention that they may have no communication with one another. This, it is said, is necessary, as when once they are liberated from dependence on their Superiors, all the other ex-Jesuits will submit at once, as experience proved at the time of the expulsion from Spain.

The clauses in this plan which determine how the suppression shall be carried out, are drawn up wisely enough, but what must seem strange to a thoughtful reader is the recommendation in the first paragraph, that the Bull should not enter into too much detail. The plea that this abstention is motived by consideration for the Jesuits themselves, may be set aside as a piece of transparent hypocrisy, and when it is said that harmful discussions will in this way be obviated, we can only suspect Moñino's real meaning to have been that there were no details producible which could stand the test of an honest public discussion – a meaning which accords with the insights we have been able to obtain into the real motives of the Spanish Court. But whatever may have to be thought on this point, it is interesting to find Grimaldi (for Moñino had sent his plan on to Madrid for the King's consideration) writing back on 29 September, to say that 'the King quite approved of it, and especially liked his method of suppressing the corporate body without inflicting any injury on the individuals – whose personal well-being his Majesty was as anxious to secure, as he was anxious to terminate the conditions under which they were harmful.'[90]

Moñino had taken advantage of the Pope's *villeggiatura* to pay a visit to Naples and have some colloquies with Tanucci. He returned thence to Rome on 18 October, and the Pope returned to Rome from Castel Gandolfo on 28 October. It was not however, till 8 November, and only then in response to an express solicitation for an audience, that he was admitted again into the Pope's presence. He felt very unhopeful in consequence, and wrote to his Court to say that unless the Pope came to the point before the end of November, it would be well for Tanucci to be instructed to reassert the right of Naples to the territory of Castro and Ronciglione.[91] Nor did his next audience remove his anxiety. The Pope spoke of soon giving him the minute of his own plan for the suppression that he might send it on to Madrid, but added that he trusted the King of Spain would then solicit for him the consent of the other sovereigns, including Vienna, Venice, Tuscany, Sardinia, Genoa, and Modena, so that he might be able to insert a clause *'ex communi consensu principum'*. Moñino writes that he never felt more indignant, and was on the point of asking if his Holiness also required the consent of the Grand Turk, the potentates of Asia and Africa, etc. etc. He refrained, however, and merely observed that whatever his Holiness did he should do within the month, as his Sovereign's faith in him was well-nigh extinguished. A further and curious passage in this same despatch must not be

[90] Danvila, *ibid*. p. 485.
[91] Despatch of 12 November. Apud Ferrer del Río, *ibid*. p. 427.

omitted. The Pope, after referring to his previously-expressed anticipation that Padre Ricci being old would soon die, in which case he would have suspended the election of his successor, and so suppress the Society indirectly – intimated that, as the General showed no signs of dying, he had ideas of making him a Cardinal, and arriving at his end in that way. Moñino was aghast at the thought of the influence Ricci might exercise as a Cardinal, and suggested as an alternative that he might perhaps be made a Bishop or Archbishop, to which the Pope replied that that would not do, as he would be sure to refuse the mitre. Surely they could not have thought the Father General very guilty if they could speak thus of him, and yet if the head Superior were worthy of promotion, and the members generally were as innocent as Moñino's plan supposed, where could the general corruption of the Order lie?

Moñino after this audience reported his dissatisfaction to de Bernis and to Buontempi, telling the former that he feared a rupture between his Court and that of Rome could not be avoided, and the latter that if it came about, 'he (Buontempi) should be the first victim of the King's displeasure.'[92] According to the standing arrangement Bernis reported this to the Pope, on whom also Buontempi was doubtless quickened to exercise his thaumaturgic powers. More, therefore, came of the next audience, which was on 15 November.[93] It began, however, unsatisfactorily for Moñino, the Pope pleading the necessity of satisfying his conscience; his fears lest his conduct at the Conclave should become suspected; and his anxieties lest the other Courts should be displeased at his interference with the Jesuits in their dominions. Moñino laughed down all these excuses for delay, but still nothing came of the audience save that public prayers were ordered to be made in all the churches till Easter-time, for the Pope's special intention.

At the same time the critical moment for the Pope's policy was close at hand. The skilful strategy according to which Moñino's calm though vague threats were rubbed in by de Bernis's private and professedly friendly counsels, had at last convinced the Holy Father that there was no escape from the trap in which he had become enclosed, save by granting to the King of Spain all that he demanded. If too we can believe de Bernis,[94] even Cardinal Colonna, a known friend of the Jesuits, now advised him to take this course – which, matters having gone so far, was, it must be confessed, hardly avoidable. Consequently, on 22 November, he read to Moñino the

---

[92] Bernis to d'Aiguillon, 17 November. Apud Theiner, ii. p. 260
[93] *Ibid.* See also Danvila, p. 419.
[94] Despatch of 2 December. See Theiner, *ibid.* p. 263.

substance of the proposed preamble to the Brief, and told him he might communicate it to his Court, which he did at once in a transport of joy, by an extraordinary courier.[95] On 29 November[96] the Pope expressed himself still more decisively, surprising Moñino by the unusual gaiety of manner with which he said he had now quite made up his mind, and Moñino might tell the King that it was on this the First Sunday of Advent, which was also the eve of St Andrew's, that he had finally extricated himself from the perplexity in which he had so long been involved. But what was more to the purpose, he announced that he had decided to entrust Cardinal Negroni with the Composition of the Bull, and he invited the Ambassador to talk with that Cardinal, show him his own plan, and collaborate with him on the work of composition. Moñino was perplexed by so sudden a change, and could not at once lay aside his suspicions; still what had occurred was so much to the good, and he rejoiced over it.

On the following Sunday the sky had clouded again. Negroni was not yet recovered from an illness which confined him to his house and, as the Pope did not care to take a subordinate into his confidence, he had so far done nothing save tell Negroni to come to him as soon as he was sufficiently convalescent.[97] Moñino thought it wise, therefore, to show his teeth again, and on 13 December the Pope, finding that Negroni was not even yet recovered, proposed to Moñino to substitute Mgr Zelada.[98] It was a name which did not recommend itself to the Ambassador, being 'that of one out of the two persons whom he had set down in his own mind as least to be trusted in such a matter.' Still the chief thing was to come to the point at once, and 'even if the Holy Father had offered him the General of the Jesuits for the work he would not have denied him', but would have trusted in his own power to bend him to his ideas. Events proved, however, that Zelada was already sufficiently bent in the direction required.

We come now to a most important passage in the history of the Suppression. We have seen how Moñino was the author of the plan eventually followed in the Brief *Dominus et Redemptor*. We have now to see that this same man sketched out the minute of the Brief itself, and even directed and supervised the composition of its text, so that it may be truly said of it that, if as regards its legal authority it was the Pope's Brief, as regards its authorship it was Moñino's – Zelada's part in it being little more than that of a secretary. In his despatch of 17 December the Ambassador informs his Court that, as

---

[95] *Ibid.*
[96] Moñino to Grimaldi, 3 December. Apud Danvila, *ibid.* p. 495.
[97] Despatch of 10 December. *Ibid.* p. 498.
[98] Despatch of 17 December. *Ibid.* p. 499.

soon as he learnt of Mgr Zelada's appointment, he 'set to work himself on the text of the Bull,[99] sketching out, in accordance with the plan previously submitted, the introduction, the causes and grounds for the suppression, following as far as he understood them the Pope's intentions, and the desires of his own Court.' His idea was that, if the draft brought him by Zelada did not satisfy him, he should at once propose his own as a substitute, to be modified by such additions as they might agree upon together.

On 24 December[100] Moñino wrote to say that things were going on better. He had seen Zelada, whom he had reminded of the great *rôle* he was called upon to play, and how much he had to gain or lose by it, enjoining on him three things, secrecy, harmony, and promptitude. He read to him his own recently-composed minute, impressed on him what was important in it, and then gave it into his hands.[101] Zelada seemed to like it, and, a week later, brought it back and praised it as well-arranged and in every way satisfactory. He merely proposed four small changes, which they agreed to make; and on the 28th it was taken to the Pope, who also made a few changes, some of which Moñino thought might have been spared, both for the sake of the Courts and of the Holy See itself. These corrections made, Zelada was now charged to incorporate the minute into a proper Brief, equipped with all the requisite forms of style. Moñino imagined that the whole of January would be required to complete this work, but Zelada had finished his part by 4 January, having given the minute a form which favourably surprised Monino and was admired by the Pope.[102] It was then left with the Pope, who said he wished to examine it privately, and observed that no time would be thus lost, as it could not be sent to Paris till Giraud had been recalled, because otherwise that prelate would be sure to get a sight of it, and communicate its contents prematurely to the Jesuits at Rome.

Having thus got the minute into his own hands the Pope *more suo* used the opportunity to cause a fresh delay. On 10 January[103] he reported that he liked the minute, but had not gone through it all; on 17 January he had gone through the greater part, but wished for certain changes which would not affect the substance; on 24 January[104] he was still unprepared to give the minute his final

---

[99] Moñino and the Courts anticipated that the suppression would be by a Bull, and so they spoke of it. When it was actually published it proved to be a Brief.
[100] Danvila, *ibid*. p. 499.
[101] Despatch of 31 December. *Ibid*. p. 502.
[102] Despatch of 17 January. *Ibid*. p. 503.
[103] *Ibid*. p. 504.
[104] *Ibid*. p. 507. Bernis to d'Aiguillon, 27 January. Apud Theiner, p. 323.

approval, but referring to his long delays justified himself on the ground that before the suppression could be published it was necessary 'to destroy the feeling in favour of the Jesuits,' he meant by involving them in suspicions of misconduct. He said it was with this intent that he had ordered the visitation of the Irish Seminary and of the Roman Seminary, which had resulted in the discovery that the funds of these institutions had been improperly administered by the Jesuits, out of whose hands they had therefore now been taken. 'Till now the Jesuits had never lost any of their suits, but at present they are losing more than they gain.'[105]

Here we must digress for a moment to note this strange avowal of an intention which, had it not been so formally avowed, one would not have ventured to impute to the Pontiff. If it were really the case that the reports reaching him seemed to demand an inquiry into the mode in which the Jesuits were administering their trust-funds, one

[105] The Roman Seminary had been founded by Pope Pius IV for the training of the young Levites destined to form the clergy of the Roman diocese. Its administration had been entrusted by that Pope to the Society of Jesus. In their hands it had remained ever since, enjoying the approbation and favour of the successive Popes, and could claim to have educated four future Popes, ninety-six future Cardinals, and innumenable future Bishops, not to speak of other pupils who subsequently attained to distinction in Church or State. Pius IV did not provide it with endowments, but for its support imposed an annual tax on the Roman clergy. In 1772, it was alleged that there was no further necessity for this contribution, and a Commission was accordingly appointed to visit the Seminary and inquire into the state of its administration and its finances. By the terms of Pius IV's foundation the right of visitation belonged to the Cardinal Vicar, but as in 1772 this office was held by Cardinal Colonna, a known friend of the Society, the two names of Cardinals Marefoschi and York were added to his, that they might be able on all points to outvote him, and the real work was done by Marefoschi, the prelate whom we have heard Tanucci describe as 'the one prelate who understands the intrigues of the Jesuits and other Orders of Friars.' He took possession of the account books of the Seminary, and gave them over to a certain Smurraglia, whose name became a byword in Rome. This man, after privately examining them for some months, returned with a report accusing the Jesuit administrators of having diverted into their own exchequer no less than 300,000 scudi. The verdict was hardly taken seriously, but none the less the Jesuits were ejected from the management, and indeed the Seminary remained closed till the reign of Pius VI, when, if Father Boero (*Osservazioni sopra l'istoria di Clemente XIV scritta dal P. Theiner,* p.72) is to be believed, the cost of maintaining it was found to be not less but more than previously. The Irish College was for educating clergy for the Irish Mission, and had been founded in the previous century by Cardinal Ludovisi. This also was visited by Marefoschi. Its finances had long been in an unsatisfactory state, and several previous Apostolic visitors, after careful inquiry, had attributed the deficiency to economic causes of a public character. Marefoschi, on the other hand, ascribed it without hesitation to the maladministration of the Jesuits, from whose care he recommended the Pope to withdraw it.

would surely have anticipated that, in view of the circumstances of the time, a just-minded Pope would in his arrangements show a special solicitude that the trial should be fair and impartial. And yet what we find is that, on the one hand, it was entrusted to persons apparently selected precisely because of their prepossessions against the Society, these prepossessed persons being further authorized to disregard the usual forms of justice and to shroud their inquiry in secrecy, whilst, on the other hand, the Pope avows to the ambassadors that his whole end and object in instituting the inquiries was to obtain some means of exciting popular feeling against the Order it was intended to destroy. Presently there followed a still more glaring instance of this endeavour to bring them into discredit with the public, which had hitherto thought well of them. One day in February, Zelada was with the Pope and exhorted him to delay no longer.[106] 'On Friday next you will see what I have already done,' was the reply. Clement referred to the Brief which on 10 February he addressed to cardinal Malvezzi, the Archbishop of Bologna,[107] a Brief which commissioned him to visit the Jesuit houses in his diocese, and secularize any members of the Society who might ask for the favour. What, however, he did when in March he opened this visitation, was to call the Superiors of the various houses together and order them to cease from all spiritual ministrations and shut up their churches; to cease from all educational work and send back their pupils to their homes; and likewise to dismiss all their novices and scholastics. No fault of any kind was imputed to them; nor was any cause of so unexpected an order indicated; but, this omission notwithstanding, they obeyed so far as to close their churches and schools, and to send away their novices. As regards their scholastics however, their Superior, Father Belgrado, the Rector of Sta Lucia, felt a conscientious difficulty in complying. These students were bound by vows of Religion which could only be dispensed by the Pope, or one to whom he had delegated his authority for this purpose. Father Belgrado, therefore, respectfully begged the Cardinal to show him the Brief which gave him authority to grant this dispensation. It was obviously his duty to solicit this, but the Cardinal refused to let him see the Brief, and, on his still persisting in his inability otherwise to dismiss the scholastics, put him into prison for contumacy; after which his Eminence undertook himself to send the scholastics back to their parents, having first caused them to be forcibly divested of their Jesuit habits.[108] Such is in outline the

---

[106] Danvila, *ibid.* p. 507.
[107] Theiner, *ibid.* p. 326. Bernis to d'Aiguillon.
[108] See Padre Boero's *Osservazioni,* already cited, p. 73.

history of a strange episode which apparently Clement XIV intended to have repeated in all the dioceses of the Papal States.[109] Malvezzi was in the confidence of the Pope, and although in enforcing secularization on those who did not ask for it he exceeded the power, which, according to de Bernis, was contained in his Brief, it is likely enough that he did hold that power from the Pope. Why then did he refuse to show his authorization, knowing as he must have done, that Belgrado could not conscientiously comply until he had seen it, and yet if he did see it would comply at once? It is difficult to resist the conclusion – especially after hearing as we have done from the Pope's own lips his motive for ordering these visitations – that Cardinal Malvezzi refused to show his Brief, because he had no other offence to impute to the Jesuits of Bologna, but foresaw how by this means he could create a situation which would enable him to represent them as contumacious.

To return to the Pope's negotiations with the Ambassador. When Moñino heard of the Brief to be issued to Malvezzi he was not pleased, but irritated at the news. It appeared to him to be merely one more subterfuge in the eternal series by which his Holiness sought to escape from his engagements, and accordingly he spoke to him very seriously at his audience of 6 February.[110] The effect of this remonstrance exceeded the Ambassador's expectations, for the Pope in reply handed him a *resumé* containing the substance of the minute, and told him that this was the form in which he might communicate to his Sovereign. Thus was the most important stage in the process of extorting the suppression accomplished to the satisfaction of the Courts.

The next step was comparatively easy, for it was to obtain for this minute which Moñino had dictated, the approval of the four Kings and of the Empress. It had been agreed that the Pope should only send it through Moñino to the King of Spain, and that this monarch should communicate copies to the other sovereigns under cover of his own autograph letters. This was to secure secrecy by obviating (though it hardly succeeded in doing this) the necessity of despatches passing through the officials of the different Foreign Offices;[111] it was also acceptable to the King of France and the Empress, as it

[109] See above p. 250.
[110] Danvila, *ibid*. p. 507.
[111] Masson (op. cit. p. 212) notes that from the commencement of 1773 all important news was communicated by Bernis to his Court by private despatches which are to be found not in the Archives of the *Affaires Etrangères,* but in the private Archives of de Bernis. Through not having access to these latter Theiner incorrectly supposed that Moñino and Bernis knew little or nothing of the Pope's work in preparing the Brief, until it was actually published.

emphasized their personal indifference to a measure to which they assented merely to please the King of Spain. This Sovereign's own approval of the minute was communicated by Grimaldi to Moñino on 2 March.[112] The King was well satisfied with it and judged it to be 'according to the principles of justice and equity'. His Majesty's letters to the other sovereigns were dated 5 March.[113] The letters to the four Kings were purely formal; the letter to the Empress was more persuasive in its tone, trusting that her answer would be favourable to the desires of the Holy Father and that she would see her way to tranquillize them all, as they had no other object in view save by the suppression of this Order to extinguish the divisions of opinions and the factions which so disturbed religion and the State. The approval of the King of Naples and of the Queen Regent of Portugal was a matter of course. The King of France gave his assent with an *insouciant* readiness which the Court of Spain found most irritating. On 25 January, d'Aiguillon, foreseeing that the minute would soon be reaching Paris, had written to de Bernis: 'If Spain is content we shall be ... we shall approve (the Bull of Suppression) without even reading it.'[114] And Louis XV's reply to Carlos III, dated 11 March, was quite in this spirit. He expressed no opinion on the contents of the minute, but 'was delighted to hear that (his Catholic Majesty) was satisfied and felt confident that the Brief sent would restore '*to the dominions of your Majesty* the tranquillity which I desire for them no less than does your Majesty.' The Empress wrote back on 7 April.[115] She still felt in regard to the Jesuits what she had said of them to the Kings of France and Spain in 1770 – that is, that she had no personal causes of complaint against those in her dominions, but that if the Holy Father thought it just, convenient, and expedient for the Catholic religion to suppress them, she would put no obstacle in his way – but that she 'would never consent that the Holy Father should deprive her of her power to dispose of the persons and property of the Jesuits who were her subjects.'

By the end of April the Empress's answer reached Madrid, and Grimaldi at once wrote the news to Moñino, with orders to obtain the few changes in the minute for which her Imperial Majesty had stipulated.[116] Moñino, therefore, could not have received this despatch which enabled him to go on with his negotiation till the middle of

---

[112] Danvila, *ibid*. p. 509.
[113] Danvila, *ibid*. p. 511.
[114] Masson, *ibid*. p. 217.
[115] Apud Danvila, *ibid*. p. 512.
[116] Gimaldi to Magallon, 26 April. Apud Masson, *ibid*. p. 218.

May. During the interval of waiting, however, he had not been without occupation. He had been distributing rewards on the part of Spain to Zelada and Buontempi, in acknowledgment of the services they had rendered to that Court in the Jesuit question. Buontempi received a large gift of money, and Zelada, who was likewise made a Cardinal on 19 April, received several rich benefices, the patronage of which belonged to Spain.[117] There was also another question which had been the subject of negotiations throughout the first half of 1773. It was an understood thing that the Kings of France and Naples would restore to the Holy See the territories of Avignon and Benevento, which had been annexed by these powers chiefly that they might hold them as a gage till the suppression was accorded. It was now, therefore, time for them to be restored, but the Pope was most anxious that the restitution should precede the suppression, the better to forestall the suspicions of those who might connect the two together. Moñino and Bernis had also recommended that this sequence should be observed, but the King of Spain had not altogether laid aside his distrust of the Pope's intentions, and on 22 June, much to the latter's disappointment, Grimaldi wrote to say that the Suppression must come first.[118]

Still, however, the Pope kept disappointing the ambassadors and perplexing the Courts by putting off the evil day. On 8 June he signed the Brief,[119] though only after another sharp remonstrance from Moñino, but he still kept it in his own hands, and continued to insist on the necessity of preliminaries. The archives and goods of the Jesuits must be preserved from destruction or removal, and with this object on 25 June he sent Mgr Alfani to affix his seal on those of the Novitiate at Rome, and urged his legates at Ferrara, Urbino, and the other legations of the Papal States, to do the same in the Jesuit houses under their jurisdiction. This brought Moñino down on him again,[120] and caused him to promise that he would at once issue a Brief

---

[117] Danvila, *ibid*. p. 516.
[118] Danvila, *ibid*. p. 520; Masson, *ibid*. p. 220.
[119] According to Theiner (*ibid*. p. 334) the Brief was signed on 21 July, but that it was really signed much earlier is clear from the diplomatic correspondence. Thus on 16 June Bernis, in a private letter to d'Aiguillon, says 'the Pope has signed the Brief;' and he had previously written (on 9 June), 'the Pope promised Moñino that he would sign yesterday.' (See Masson *ibid*. p.221.) Similarly, Moñino on 17 June wrote to Grimaldi that it had been actually signed, and on 1 July Grimaldi wrote back to congratulate Moñino on having obtained the signature. (Danvila, *ibid*. pp. 524–526.) Still it must be remembered that the minute is all that the Pope signs; he does not sign the Brief itself. Perhaps therefore the latter was expedited on 21 July.
[120] Bernis to d'Aiguillon, 30 June (private). Apud Masson, *ibid*. p. 218.

appointing the Congregation which was to preside over the execution of the Brief of Suppression. Another month, however, was to elapse before this other Brief was actually published to Marefoschi, Casali, Zelada, Corsini, and Carafa, the five Cardinals who were to form the said Congregation. All through the month of July he still held out, relying, as we learn from de Bernis's weekly letters, first on one plea, then on another: before 12 July, on the necessity of ascertaining exactly what property the Order possessed; before 21 July on the propriety of allowing the Religious to celebrate together for the last time the feast of their Founder, and of not interrupting the studies in their Colleges before the end of the school term; before 28 July, on the necessity of first getting the Brief printed, and of sending back an answer to the Empress to inform her that the alterations she had demanded had been made. By this time Moñino again thought it necessary to remonstrate – the more so as the Pope had at the beginning of July gone for a six weeks' retirement into the country to drink the waters.[121] He wrote, therefore, a very sharp letter to Buontempi, which had the usual result of constraining his Holiness to a further step. This time it was a really decisive step which he was compelled to take, for on 29 July, Buontempi came back to the Ambassador with printed copies of the Brief to be sent off to Madrid, Versailles, Naples, Lisbon, and Vienna. They were despatched at once and, as they bore the date of the contemplated publication, this date could no longer be deferred. The Congregation of five Cardinals, to which Mgr Macedonio was attached as secretary and Mgr Alfani as assessor, was constituted on 8 August, and at once held its first meeting for the publication and execution of the Brief. It is important to notice that it was not published, either then or subsequently, according to the established custom, by being proclaimed in the Campo dei Fiori and affixed to the gates of the Vatican; but by the terms of the Brief establishing the Congregation of five Cardinals, was to be published separately in each house of the Society throughout the world. This was done at the Gesù and other houses of the Society in Rome on the night of 16 August, the date which the Brief bears on its face. But the circumstances under which it was thus published and intimated to the members of the suppressed Order, form a history which must be deferred to the next chapter.

---

[121] Bernis, 28 July and 14 August. Apud Masson.

Chapter Seven

The Execution of the Brief of Suppression

I.[1] [Prior to the death of Clement XIV]

Clement XIV's negotiation with the Powers was, as has been seen, shrouded in the strictest secrecy, and the perusal of such a diary as Fr Thorpe's shows how imperfectly the doomed victims realized the fullness of their peril. At the beginning of the new Pontificate opinions were divided among the Roman Jesuits, some taking a despondent some a hopeful view of the prospects it held out to them. Fr Thorpe belonged to the latter class, and perhaps his estimate of the state of feeling among his brethren may have been coloured in this sense. Still we can safely gather from his pages that the hopeful view was the more prevalent, and grew in force as the months passed by without yielding any decisive act for their destruction. They understood clearly that the Spaniards were their relentless foes, though they suspected de Bernis to be on their side; but they were confident that Clement XIV was doing his best to protect them. It was true he repelled them from his presence and kept on afflicting them by one oppressive measure after another. Still their trust in him did not fail. They only concluded that he was seeking to appease the Courts by reducing their influence, and perhaps intended to remodel their Constitutions, but they persisted in believing that he would never consent to their entire destruction. Meanwhile they were trying to pursue the quiet tenour of their lives. Some few of them indeed wrote anonymous though singularly temperate replies to the many slanderous charges which were circulating to their discredit; and others spoke in bitter terms of their persecutors and the injustice of their methods. Was this unnatural considering their circumstances, or is it imaginable that any other equally numerous body of men if subjected to the same treatment would have exercised a fuller self-

[1] *The Month*, 101 (1903), 498–516.

restraint? Still these were the exceptions. As a whole, and as represented by their leading men, the Jesuits of the old Society in those anxious days of its last agony were not fomenting any counter-agitation, but were quietly pursuing, so far as it was possible the course of their ordinary religious duties, the domestic duties of their community life, and the external duties of teaching, preaching, and hearing confessions, – consoled to find that in the midst of all that was being said and done against them, their schools, their pulpits, and their confessionals continued to be well attended.

And what is thus said of the Religious generally was specially true of their chief Superior. Some of his subjects thought he might have been more strenuous in his endeavours to ward off the coming ruin; and it is possible, though far from certain, that a stronger ruler might have been better fitted for the times. Still what we now desiderate is a trustworthy estimate of his character, to set by the side of that given by the Bourbon Ministers, according to whom he was the very 'focus of intrigue and fanaticism'. Let us hear, then, the Augustinian Padre Miguélez, who, after the perusal of Ricci's correspondence with Père Nectoux in 1775, writes:[2]

> This man has been much slandered by those who have called him a Machiavellian. I, who have before me his authentic letters, signed with his own hand, and written on paper at times sufficiently coarse, small, and excessively written over – points which testify, I fear, to the straits of poverty in which he then was – discern in these letters the faithful portrait of a beautiful soul, of a man of spotless life, of vast culture, of consummate prudence, and of a most solid piety which makes him lament over the abuses which have crept into his Order, in the sincere desire to correct them in silence and with closed doors. He did not fail to perceive the dark clouds impending over the Society throughout Europe; and like a man of great understanding and devout spirit, looked with a penetrating eye through that formidable Conspiracy against it, and perceived clearly the finger of Providence pointing out the road of persecution as that by which their gold was to be purified and its dross removed.

And in illustration of Fr Ricci's peaceful spirit, Padre Miguélez notes how

---

[2] *Jansenismo en España*, p. 301. Père Nectoux had been Provincial of Aquitaine before the expulsion from France, when he took refuge in Spain and resided in San Sebastian. His correspondence with the Father General fell into the hands of the Spanish officials at the time of the Spanish expulsion, and is now at Simancas. The two Fathers were men of kindred spirit, and the subject-matter of their letters was the sad state to which the Society was reduced, and what course its exiled members should pursue.

The Execution of the Brief of Suppression 255

> He exhorted all the Spanish Jesuits to prudence and circumspection in their present circumstances, and bade them let nothing censurable be found in their conduct such as might hasten the approach of the calamities and persecutions they were fearing.

This is how the last General of the old Society appears to an impartial observer in the mirror of his private letters and the seven beautiful letters which between[3] 1758 and 1773, he addressed to the entire Society, reflect the same image. The theme of them all is the right use of tribulation, and the necessity of looking beyond human agencies, to the Providence which desires through their instrumentality to spur on His servants to a more diligent exercise of the Christian virtues and a more earnest spirit of prayer.

> Let us try to defend the honour of the Society [he wrote on 13 November, 1763, when the persecution was beginning to spread], by the purity of our lives, by the holiness of our speech, by our unwearied zeal for the salvation of souls, but not by the tainted sounding of our own praises, nor by evil-speaking or contempt of others. [And in the very last of these letters, which bore the date of 21 February, 1773, he wrote] ... infuse into your prayers by an exact and fervent discharge of your spiritual duties, by your mutual charity to one another, by respectful obedience to those who stand to you in the place of God, by your patience in bearing labour and trials, poverty and insult, by your spirit of retirement and solitude, by the prudence and Evangelical simplicity with which you act, by your exemplary conduct, by your pious conversations. It is a Society instinct with this spirit whose preservation we ask of God. If (our Society) should be deprived of this spirit, which may God avert, it would matter little if it ceased to exist.

Such were the Jesuits and such was their General at the time when the fatal blow struck them. It was desirable that readers should have the picture set before them, but we can now return to the history of the downfall.

The Brief, *Dominus et Redemptor*, has two main divisions, of which the former enumerates the Pontiff's motives for suppressing the Society, and the latter contains the actual decree of suppression, together with the prescriptions for disposing of the persons of its former members. For the student solicitous to form a judgment on the guilt or innocence of the Jesuits, the former is the valuable part and it will be necessary to examine it carefully and compare it with the historical incidents to which it refers. It would be inconvenient,

---

[3] *Epistolae Praesulum Generalium ad Patres et Fratres Societatis Jesu*, vol ii. pp. 284, 300. Edit. of Ghent, 1847.

however, to break into the course of the narrative in which we are engaged, and we may therefore postpone this examination till afterwards, contenting ourselves in the meanwhile with a passage from the Protestant historian Schoell, who writes:

> This Brief condemns neither the doctrines, nor the morals, nor the discipline of the Jesuits. The complaints made against the Order are the sole motives for its suppression which are alleged, and the Pope justifies the measure by citing previous examples of Orders suppressed in deference to the demands of public opinion.[4]

In other words, the Pope reasons that the Society, as long as it exists, will be a bone of contention between its friends and its foes, and the peace of the Church will suffer; for the sake of peace then it ought to be suppressed. That the Brief should take such a form would be significant enough if its wording had originated with the Pope, but we have seen how its real author was Moñino (now created in reward for his services the Conde de Florida Blanca). May we not take this singular fact as an implicit acknowledgment, not merely from Clement XIV, but also from the Spanish Ministers, that they had no evidence in their possession which sufficed for a condemnation of the Society?

In its second and operative part the Brief (1) 'extinguished and suppressed' the Society; (2) it took away from it all its offices and administrations, its houses; schools, etc., and abrogated all its statutes, its habits and customs, its decrees, constitutions, etc.; (3) it cancelled the authority and jurisdiction of all its Superiors, and forbade the admission of new members, or the advancement of present members to profession or other grades.

And as regards the future, 'just as the Pope's intention was to consult for the utility of the Church and the tranquillity of the people, so in the paternal love which he bore for every one of the (Society's) individual members his intention was to grant them solace and aid, whereby, being freed from the contentions, dissensions, and distresses by which they had been hitherto vexed, they might cultivate the Lord's vineyard more fruitfully, and work more profitably for the salvation of souls.' Wherefore (1) all the scholastics of the Society were to leave its houses within the space of a year, and being freed from the simple vows they had taken, might on leaving embrace any mode of life to which they felt called; (2) all in priest's orders must either enter another religious order or place themselves as secular priests under the jurisdiction of the Bishop

---

[4] *Cours d'histoire des Etats Européens,* xliv. p. 83.

The Execution of the Brief of Suppression 257

where they might reside, their maintenance being secured to them from the revenues of the house to which they were attached at the time of the suppression; (3) those of the Professed for whom maintenance of this kind was not attainable, or who had no place to which they could go, or were aged or sick, might be gathered together in some house or houses of the extinct Society, there to remain, if necessary, till their death, but under the government of some secular cleric, and no longer wearing the Society's dress; (4) the Bishops might if they thought them suitable, employ the ex-Jesuit priests in preaching and administering sacraments, those excepted who were remaining in the houses formerly belonging to the extinct Society; (5) any of the ex-Jesuits, priests or scholastics, might be employed to teach in schools and colleges, provided they had no part in their government, and that they gave no offence by the character of their opinions; (6) the future administration of the foreign missions in which the Jesuits had been employed, the Pontiff reserved to himself for future settlement; (7) the ex-Jesuit priests might henceforth hold benefices.

Another point in this Brief which needs to be noticed is that it is a Brief not a Bull. The binding force of each is the same, but a Brief is a less solemn Papal utterance than a Bull, and is wont to be used when the object in view is of a less important kind. It was against all precedent to use this form for an object so serious as the suppression of a great Religious Order, which involved the abrogation of more than twenty previous Bulls. Why then, we ask, was it the form chosen by Clement XIV? As no reason was given in any of the communications to the ambassadors – at least so far as we know – we are left to our own conjectures. One reason may have been that Clement XIV, who resolved on the suppression so reluctantly, may have wished to facilitate the restoration of the Society, if better days should come – for a Brief, just because it is a less solemn document, is wont to be more readily revoked. Probably, however, the chief motive which determined the selection, was that it required him to take fewer people into his confidence. A Brief requires only two signatures, those of the Cardinal Secretary of Briefs and of his Secretary Substitute; and Cardinal Negroni, the Secretary of Briefs, happened to be one of the very few Cardinals whom Clement was prepared to take into his confidence. A Bull would have had to be prepared in the Papal Chancery, there to pass through several hands, and before it was expedited to receive the signatures of the Cardinal Pro-Datary and of about twenty other officials. Moreover, it would have been hardly decent to withhold it from the inspection of the assembled Cardinals in Consistory, whereas Clement XIV wished to keep the Decree of Suppression an absolute secret from all his Cardinals until it had been intimated to the Order and it was too late to recall it.

Notice has already been taken[5] of a further deviation from the usual procedure in the issue of this document. It was not promulgated in the usual way by being proclaimed in the Campo dei Fiori and placarded at the gates of the Vatican, nor, we must now add, was any alternative method of promulgation prescribed in its text. Theiner, who notes this circumstance, accounts for it on the ground that 'it would have been ridiculous and cruel to observe this formality in the presence of so solemn an intimation.' A suggestion so grotesque we may safely set aside. Doubtless the real reason was again the desire to keep the meditated blow a secret till the moment when it was to fall. Had there been the usual promulgation it must have preceded the intimation to the assembled communities, and in that case the news of what was to come would have reached them prematurely. Still, the defect of a promulgation *urbi et orbi* led to after results which the Pope did not perhaps foresee.

As there was to be no public promulgation, what was done was to create a Special Congregation *pro rebus extinctae Societatis*. It consisted of five Cardinals – Corsini (the President), Marefoschi, Zelada, Casali, and Carafa. These were assembled and instructed by Clement on 6 August, but the Brief, *Gravissimis ex causis,* by which they were formerly constituted, did not issue till 13 August. To this Congregation was entrusted the duty both of intimating the Brief to the Jesuits, and of taking all such subsequent measures as might be found necessary for its full execution. On the night of 6 August this Congregation sent official Visitors, attended by detachments of soldiers and police, to each of the Jesuit residences in Rome. The soldiers were to suppress any disturbances on the part of the populace, who were credited with a strong attachment to the condemned Religious; and for the same reason the Cardinals of the Special Commission held a session at the Carafa Palace, close to the Gesù, to be ready for any such emergency. The visits were simultaneous, and took place about nine o'clock. The Jesuits had received no previous warning, and were taken completely unawares. Fr Thorpe, who lived at the Penitentiary of St Peter's, relates that the community had just sat down to supper when a loud and imperious ring at the door was heard; and, as probably all the houses had their meals at the same time, we may assume that the commu-

---

[5] Cf. p. 252 above.

nity of the Gesù were similarly engaged. Mgr Macedonio was the Visitor sent to this mother-house of the Society. The police were left outside to line the streets.[6] The soldiers entered with Macedonio, and were at once distributed through the house to guard all its entrances and the doors to all its chambers. The beds were then dragged out of the rooms into the corridors, and it was there that the community were compelled to spend the night – it cannot be said to sleep – each being guarded by one sentinel and the General by eight. The night was almost entirely taken up by the invading party in searching the sacristies, the libraries, the rooms, and even the cellars. We have heard how the Society was accused of having turned its foreign missions into commercial associations, and of having thereby accumulated enormous wealth. It had been confidently stated that the greater part of this wealth was stored up at the Professed House, and a principal reason for making this sudden raid upon the communities was to get possession of their treasures before they could be removed elsewhere. The story was entirely imaginary, and as might have been expected, a comparatively small sum of money was in the house, in fact, about 40,000 scudi, the great part of which was money collected and set apart for the expenses of certain canonizations. This of course they secured, and they also set seals on all the papers and on every article of value in the sacristy or elsewhere. When the search was completed and the morning had come, the General and his community were bidden to assemble in a large hall, where the entire text of the Brief of Suppression was read to them by the Visitor. They listened to it submissively, and when the reading was finished the Father General bowed his head and protested they were prepared to render an entire and respectful obedience to the commands of his Holiness. On the evening of the 17th Cardinal Corsini, the President of the Special Commission, sent his carriage for the General. The message brought was couched in the form of a friendly invitation to take refuge in the English College. Thither, accordingly, he went in the clothes

---

[6] Although, however, notwithstanding the lateness of the hour, a large crowd had gathered round the Gesù, they were perfectly quiet. De Bernis, and after him Theiner, interpreted this as meaning that, though led to the spot by curiosity, they were indifferent to what was happening. But Mgr, afterwards Cardinal, Pacca, is a more trustworthy witness. He was in Rome both in 1773 and in 1814, and he tells us in his *Memorie Storiche* (part iii. c. viii. p. 362) that 'surprise and grief were to be seen on the countenance of almost every inhabitant on the publication of the Brief *Dominus et Redemptor*, whilst on the other hand it was impossible to count the cries of joy, the exclamations and plaudits of the good people of Rome when on 7 August 1814, he accompanied Pius VII, to the Quirinal where the Bull of Restoration was to be read.'

in which he stood up – for he was allowed to take nothing else with him – but when he arrived he found that there also he was practically a prisoner, forbidden to hold communication with any save the single lay-brother who was confined with him. The Jesuits left at the Gesù and other houses were detained there for eight days during which time new habits were being prepared for them. It was considered to be a mark of his kindness that the Pope took upon himself the expense of these garments, and so perhaps it was in the intention of his Holiness, but what happened was, as Fr Thorpe puts it, that the Pope's treasurer 'made a job of the tailors and the tailors made a job of us', the result being that their habits were made out of the coarsest cloth, ill-fitting, and coming down hardly below the knees, whilst their shoes were so narrow and of such bad quality that they could not walk in them without stumbling, and their feet quickly burst through the leather. Thus were they sent forth to excite the laughter of the people who called them Priests of the Warehouse, with the as yet unfulfilled promise of twenty crowns to start them in facing the hard world. True they were to receive periodically a scanty pittance levied on the possessors of their former residences, but with the humiliating condition attached that on each application for these remittances they must bring with them an attestation of good conduct from the *Cura* of the parish in which they resided. Yet still their cup was not, in the estimation of their persecutors, sufficiently bitter, and on 1 September the Special Congregation, reversing a humane clause in the Brief of Suppression, forbade the Bishops to grant to any of them faculties to preach or hear confessions, thus condemning them to objectless lives.

Thus was an end made to the corporate existence of the Society in the Papal capital. To end it elsewhere, Cardinal Corsini, in the name of the Special Commission, despatched on 18 August an Encyclical Letter *ad omnes Episcopos*,[7] acquainting them with what had been done in Rome, and authorizing and enjoining them to 'proclaim, publish, and intimate the Briefs *Dominus et Redemptor* and *Gravissimis ex causis* (copies of which were enclosed) to the Jesuits assembled in every one of their houses, colleges, or residences, or wheresoever any of the individual members were to be found' within the jurisdiction of the respective Bishops. They were then to expel the ex-Jesuits from the said houses, and take possession of them, and of the letters and all the property in them or belonging to them,

---

[7] The text of this Encyclical is given in Ravignan's *Clément XIII et Clément XIV*, vol. i. p. 560.

holding these till they should receive orders from his Holiness assigning the purposes to which they were to be applied.

During the next few weeks intimation of the Brief of Suppression was made under this Encyclical to the Jesuits in the Papal States, and also in some other parts of Italy. But, in regard to the Bourbon States, and likewise in regard to the Empire, a serious difficulty arose. The Empress had declared that if she assented to the suppression, she still claimed for herself the right to dispose of the persons and possessions of the ex-Jesuits who were her subjects; in France the civil power had actually exercised this power of disposition since the date of the Edict of 1764; in Portugal also, and Spain and Naples, the Crown had taken possession of the goods of the Society after the expulsions of 1759, 1767, and 1768; and, moreover, it was one of the cherished principles of Regalism that the goods and possessions of ecclesiastical corporations, being temporal, fell under the jurisdiction of the Crown. And yet whilst the Brief *Dominus et Redemptor* ignored this past allocation of Jesuit property by the civil power, the Brief *Gravissimis* empowered the Special Commission to inflict ecclesiastical censures on all persons 'of whatever state, degree, quality, or dignity' who might be retaining, holding, or hiding any of the former Jesuit property. Had the Brief *Gravissimis,* like the Brief of Suppression, been submitted to Moñino before its issue, it is morally certain that he would have noted this provision, and have insisted on its transformation into one more acceptable to the Regalist mind. Probably it was to evade this danger – at least it is difficult to assign another reason for the step – that Clement had recourse to one of his petty expedients. He left the ambassadors uninformed both of the issue of the *Gravissimis* on the 13th (the Cardinals being placed by its terms under an oath of secrecy), of the intimation of the *Dominus et Redemptor* on 16 August (of which they only learnt through popular rumour on the day following), and of the despatch of the Encyclical and the two Briefs on 18 August. They were not allowed to have any part in the transmission of the Briefs to their own Governments,[8] for the Pope caused them to be sent by the Congregation to the Nuncios, with the directions that they should communicate them to the sovereigns to whom they were accredited and to the Bishops of their kingdoms. Only when these despatches to the Nuncios had been actually sent off, was a laconic note conveyed to the ambassadors informing them of what had been done. Nor had they the means of protesting against these proceedings, because the Pope had for some time previously gone into a retirement during which he was invisible

[8] Theiner, *ibid.* p. 341

to everybody, and from which he did not issue till it was too late. The ambassadors were very displeased at this manoeuvre,[9] but in a sense it succeeded, for it relieved the Pope from the necessity into which otherwise his weakness might have been coerced, of setting down in writing an arrangement at variance with the traditional views of the Holy See as to the character of Church property. Still the provision made in the Encyclical was resisted by the Powers, and the Pope, declaring it to be a blunder on the part of Cardinal Carafa, the author of the letter, readily allowed its application to be restricted to the Papal States.[10] Even then, however, the language of the two Briefs remaining, they were distasteful to the Courts, and the result was that in France they were never published at all, though they were unofficially communicated to the Bishops; and that in the Two Sicilies their publication was forbidden by Tanucci under pain of death.[11] On the other hand, in the Spanish and Portuguese dominions, European and colonial, the Brief of Suppression was published, but in the former country the publication of the *Gravissimis* was withheld on the ground that 'it might suggest sinister interpretations.'[12] And even as regards the Brief of Suppression it must be remembered that the Jesuits of both countries having been long since expelled there were few left to whom it could be intimated, whilst the lack of promulgation *urbi et orbi* at Rome deprived of the necessary basis any merely general promulgation in other countries. In the dominions of the House of Austria it was also published, and here, as the Jesuits were still in their colleges, it could be intimated according to the terms of the Encyclical. Still the Empress had her way about the property.

But even then a difficulty was felt in carrying out all the provisions of the Brief of Suppression, and Cardinal Migazzi,[13] the Archbishop of Vienna, wrote to lay it before the Pope. After describing the consternation which the Brief had caused among the people, and commending the submissive spirit in which the Jesuits of those parts accepted it, he explained that if he did not preserve them as teachers in their former colleges, particularly in the grand Teresian College at Vienna, the whole educational system in those parts would break down, for it was impossible to provide at short notice an equally competent staff of teachers to take their place. Moreover it would be injurious to this College if its former superiors, to whom

---

[9] *Ibid.* p. 345.
[10] *Ibid.* p. 385.
[11] Ravignan, *ibid.* vol. i. p. 408.
[12] Danvila, *ibid.* p. 538.
[13] Ravignan, *ibid.* vol. ii. p. 401.

its striking success had hitherto been due, did not continue to govern, and most injurious to the spiritual welfare of the pupils as well as of the surrounding inhabitants, if the Jesuits engaged in teaching are not also allowed to continue preaching and hearing confessions.

It was a difficulty the like of which was felt in other regions and particularly in Silesia and White Russia. These two Catholic provinces had lately been annexed to the Crowns of Prussia and Russia respectively, their new sovereigns having at the time of annexation promised to preserve to the inhabitants their Catholic institutions; and here too the Jesuits were the only available teachers. Accordingly, both Frederick the Great of Prussia and Catharine II of Russia forbade their Bishops to intimate the Brief to the Jesuits in their dominions. This led to an anomalous state of things to which we can only refer briefly. The Jesuits remained in their houses, justifying their action on the ground that until the Brief had been intimated to them they were not called upon to obey it – a ground which appears defensible, in view of the defect of any promulgation *urbi et orbi* at Rome. On the other hand, the Special Congregation declared these Prussian and Russian Jesuits to be 'refractory' for not abandoning their houses and their corporate organization in spite of their sovereigns' prohibition. With what face ambassadors of the Courts could take this line is hard to understand: they claimed for their sovereigns as temporal rulers a certain right to stay the enforcement of any Papal Bulls or Briefs sent into their dominions, and they were prepared to inflict the severest punishments on any of their subjects who ventured to prefer to obey the Pope's commands rather than their own. If the Kings of Spain and France had this power, Frederick of Prussia and Catharine of Russia must have it also. Whether, judged by a sounder standard, the conduct of these Prussian and Russian Jesuits, if technically defensible, was also becoming is a question which cannot be judged offhand. There are other aspects to be considered, and particularly the question whether Clement XIV, and after him Pius VI, did not privately give some encouragement to the continuance of an arrangement which officially they were forced by the Bourbon Courts to condemn. This, however, at least we may conclude, that this action of a small body of Jesuits – which in Prussia lasted till 1780, and in White Russia lasted till it obtained recognition from Pius VII – could not compromise the other members of the suppressed Society or its deposed rulers, who had absolutely no part in recommending or sustaining it.[14]

[14] Cf. on this subject Fr. Zalenski's *Les Jésuites de la Russie-Blanche*, t. ii, chaps. i-viii.

Now that we have taken note of the way in which the suppression was carried out in the different countries, we must go back to relate what befell the General and his Assistants at Rome. The General, as has been already stated, was taken to the English College on the night of 17 August. There he remained, in strict confinement, guarded by soldiers for more than a month, after which, on 23 September, he was transported to the Castle of Sant' Angelo, whither also were taken his five Assistants – Fr Gorgo, the Assistant of Italy, Fr de Montes, of Spain, Fr de Guzman, of Portugal, Fr Rhomberg, of Germany, Fr Koricki, of Poland, and Fr Comolli, the Secretary General of the Society. The General was placed in a sufficiently large room, but its windows which looked on the Vatican were boarded up with planks, save just at the top. The food given him was always cold, and not a scrap of fire was allowed him even in the depth of winter, though he was an old man of seventy; nor was he allowed, during the lifetime of Clement XIV, either materials for writing, or books for reading. A sentinel was always at his door, but neither with him or with any one else was he allowed to exchange a word. The Assistants, and certain other Fathers imprisoned in the same fortress either at the same time or subsequently, were even worse treated, being cast into dark and damp cells in which the rats had free range. It has been noticed that in the Brief Clement XIV is made to declare his intention of treating all the members of the suppressed Order, without distinction, with paternal care and affection, and it is conceivable that he was under the impression that his prisoners at Sant' Angelo were being kindly treated. But a Sovereign who allows himself to be surrounded by suspect persons and will listen to no others is bound to be deceived, and in appointing Mgr Alfani to be their custodian, he handed them over to the tender mercies of one who was little better than a tiger.

We can readily understand why the Bourbon Courts should have wished to have the General and his counsellors arrested and imprisoned. If it were really true that the Jesuits were guilty of all the crimes with which the Courts had charged them; if they had enriched themselves by a vast commerce; if they had incessantly plotted and intrigued against Kings and Bishops; if they had stirred up insurrections and even plotted against the lives of the sovereigns – all this guilt must attach to some individual members of their body; and if, as their accusers freely confessed, the great majority of Jesuits were innocent and well-intentioned, and only dangerous because they were by their rule and training blind instruments in the hands of their Superiors, then it must follow that the Superiors who were at the head of the whole body – the General and his Assistants – were the primary culprits. The question, then, of the guilt or innocence of these few men was a test question, on the issue of which depended the solution of the further question whether the campaign against the Society, which had now terminated in its suppression, had been based on motives of justice or injustice. If the Courts themselves did not wish to accept this issue, public opinion would enforce it on them, and hence it was of vital consequence to their reputation that they should succeed in convicting the General and his Assistants of complicity in, or rather of the prime authorship of, all the crimes in their indictment

Nor could this issue be any longer avoided on the plea that the requisite papers were kept back by the accused. Half a century previously Don Melchior de Macanáz, a Regalist lawyer, had declared that the Jesuits were the great enemies of temporal rulers, and that the way to obtain clear proofs of the fact was to visit all their houses simultaneously and take possession of all their papers. Señor Ferrer del Río[15] reasonably assumes that the report containing this recommendation strongly influenced Don Carlos and his Extraordinary Council in 1767. The recommendation was carried out in the Spanish houses, but, as we have seen, the Spanish State Papers bear no trace of any adequate results having been obtained. Now, however, a far better opportunity had arisen; the papers not only of one Province, but of the head-quarters of the whole Society, were in the possession of their judges. Surely if the Jesuits were intriguers and sedition-mongers after the manner supposed, abundant proofs to secure conviction must be now in hand.

We can understand then why the Superiors of the Society were arrested, and the rumour circulated that discoveries had been made which showed them to be guilty of enormous crimes. But can we pierce the veil of secrecy in which the transaction was involved, and ascertain whether the imprisonment was justified or not?

We naturally turn first to the diplomatic correspondence, and find Florida Blanca, in his despatch of 21 August, writing that, as the Pope has explained to him, 'the General is to remain in custody both because it is not desirable for him to reside in Tuscany, his native country, whither he would otherwise have to be sent; and because some papers have been found which raise the presumption that he has designs for maintaining the system of the Society by a secret union of its members.'[16] And de Bernis, on 25 August, writes that 'before the General is released they want to obtain from him information about

---

[15] *Reinado de Carlos III*, vol. ii. p. 515.
[16] Danvila, *ibid*. p. 534.

several matters, particularly about the money he is supposed to have deposited somewhere, or to have sent out of the ecclesiastical state. His Assistants will be likewise interrogated;'[17] and on 22 September he writes that 'a secret instruction by the General has been found, in which he orders all the Jesuits, in case the Society should be suppressed, to go on living according to their Constitutions and continue to receive novices. I have,' he says, 'this most extraordinary fact from the Pope himself. They have also found other documents which when they are known will reconcile all good men to the destruction of an Order which had become restless, ambitious, and proud, less than forty years from the time of its foundation.'[18]

Is this all? is surely the first question which arises in the mind when one reflects how much more was necessary to justify all that the Courts had been doing. In their credulity they had persuaded themselves that the Jesuits possessed vast wealth, but with all their searches they had found only a few paltry sums. If their credulity still endured it was natural that they should try to force the prisoners into disclosure. But their past action, if justified, presupposed that there was also deposited in the Jesuit houses a mass of papers of a seditious, treasonable, and even regicidal character – many of which, since they were connected with recent Jesuit intrigues, should have been of recent date. Yet we hear of no compromising papers referring to the recent past – only of a few, discovered not at the Gesù, but at the Spanish Embassy, appertaining to events that happened two centuries ago.[19] Whatever else these diplomatists announced as having been discovered in the Jesuit papers referred to the future, not the past, and could not therefore convict them of any past ill-conduct such as had been alleged to require their suppression.

Still, if they had found papers showing that the General and his brethren intended to resist the Papal Brief and carry on their Society just as before, under the cover of a secret union of its members, though the find was wholly insufficient for what the Courts had to prove, it must convict the Jesuits of an offence grave enough to deprive them of the sympathy of loyal Catholics. Was there, then, such a find? Florida Blanca, in the passage quoted, hints cautiously at

[17] Theiner, *ibid.* p. 345.
[18] Masson, *Le Cardinal de Bernis depuis son ministère*, p. 242.
[19] The negotiation to which these belonged is noticed in a clause of the Brief of Suppression, so that the discovery in question must have been prior to the suppression. When we come to examine the text of the Brief we shall have to consider this point. For the present it is enough to say that in the judgment of Gregory XIV, Sixtus V's successor, and in the revised judgment of Philip II, the blame on that occasion attached not to the Superiors and main body of the Society, but to a little knot of innovators among its Spanish members.

a presumption raised, but de Bernis speaks boldly of a hard fact, the certainty of which the Pope himself had guaranteed. The French Cardinal's later despatches show how much he had been overstating.

It is a curious fact that although Louis XV had joined so readily with Carlos III in demanding the suppression, as soon as it was granted, he began to think of re-establishing the Order, not indeed as a world-wide Society, but as a Congregation, having the same rules and government within the limits of his own States. It was because the loss of the Jesuits in education was acutely felt, and his Carmelite daughter, Madame Louise, had united with the French Bishops to induce him to grant this solace to the outraged feelings of so many devout Catholics. The King was not unwilling to grant the request, but d'Aiguillon was against the idea, and tried his best to stop it. The latter was accordingly delighted with de Bernis's despatch of 22 September. He represented to the King that the ex-Jesuits should, as a preliminary condition to their reorganization as a national Congregation, be required to accept the Brief of Suppression, and renounce their former state; and he then wrote back to de Bernis telling him it was of the highest importance that the latter should send him a copy of Fr Ricci's alleged Instruction. This pressure of events, requiring the Cardinal to make good his rash words, put him in a tight corner. 'He (de Bernis) thereupon,' says Masson, 'became less affirmative each time he wrote.' Thus on 3 November he writes, 'I have no other means of ascertaining the real truth about the Instruction they pretend to have found among the General's papers, save by asking the Pope to communicate it to the King, and I feel sure his Holiness will not refuse this if the paper exists, as I was assured it does.'[20] By 29 December, de Bernis was still unable to report the finding of any such paper as he had announced. 'It passed as certain,' he pleaded, 'that the Roman Jesuits had renewed their vows just before their suppression, and promised to be faithful to the Society ... If they had done this at Rome, who could say but what they had done the same in other countries.'[21] Who could say, indeed? Rather, who could adduce any solid proof that this had happened either at Rome or elsewhere – at least in the sense in which Bernis meant it? Still he went on labouring the same point, and on 12 January wrote that the Pope had told Alfani to give him the authentic documents which prove that before the suppression of the Jesuits their General, as he then was, had authorized them to continue following their Institute, to receive novices, and hear confessions,

[20] Masson, *ibid.* p. 244.
[21] Masson, *ibid.* p. 248.

even if the Brief of Suppression when published should prove to interdict them that power. 'It is precisely this,' he adds, 'which they are now doing in Silesia.'[22] It has been already told how in Silesia the King of Prussia would not allow the Brief to be intimated by the Bishops to the Jesuits in his States, and how, in consequence, the latter deemed themselves justified in remaining in their houses and continuing their former mode of life. No doubt their conduct lent itself to the construction de Bernis put upon it; but we have argued that even if these Silesian Jesuits, after the extinction of the General's power, chose to act disloyally, the General and his Assistants could not be held responsible. At least it must be otherwise proved that he had sanctioned what they were doing. Again, some allowance must be made for the Silesian Jesuits themselves, whose contention that till the Brief was canonically intimated to them their vows still held good, was a contention which, even if unsound, was not unintelligible. And in the last place is it not significant that we should find de Bernis writing again on 14 November to say that 'the Pope will ... do nothing against the Jesuits of Silesia'? Does it not look as if there were some truth in the impression felt by many that Clement, though for fear of the Courts he was openly condemning them, was secretly encouraging them to go on?

It is unnecessary to pursue further the history of the ex-Jesuits in Prussia and White Russia, and as regards their fate in France a very few words must suffice. Any hopes they may have founded on the favourable dispositions of Louis XV, and the influence exercised over him by his Carmelite daughter, were terminated by his sad end on 10 May, 1774. With the accession of Louis XVI came also the end of d'Aiguillon's Ministry, who was succeeded by the Comte de Vergennes. Louis XVI, though his reign was destined to be unfortunate, was an upright and religious-minded man. Had he come to the throne some twenty years sooner it is not likely that the anti-Jesuit faction would have succeeded in its designs. But this new King was young and inexperienced, and besides the suppression was now a *fait accompli,* and could not well be reversed at once. The French ex-Jesuits were left free to accept service under the Bishops for the discharge of clerical functions, but the idea of forming them into a purely French Congregation lapsed for the time, to be revived when the storms of the First Revolution were spent.

We must now return to Rome and to the efforts that were being made to convict Fr Ricci and his Assistant of the crime of rebellion. According to the method of judicature then in force, the prosecution had

---

[22] Masson, *ibid.* p. 252.

(1) to collect evidence against the accused from their confiscated papers or other sources; (2) on the basis of this evidence to administer interrogatories to the accused and take down their answers; (3) promptly to complete the *procès* from these materials, and either cause the accused to be pronounced innocent and released, or bring them before their judges. All the proceedings in the present instance were kept absolutely secret; but, this notwithstanding, the General wrote down an account of his interrogatories, the truth of which has not been contested, and certain facts became public about the interrogatories of the others. In the next section we shall examine these sources of information, but there is one external and significant fact which can be noticed at once. According to Fr Ricci, his interrogatories ended about the middle of January 1774; he was asked no further questions after that. Accordingly he expected that he would soon be released, as interrogatories so trivial could not surely point to a grave charge. But when the days ran on without his receiving any communication, he sent in a *supplica* asking that at least he might be told what he was accused of, and brought to trial. To this he got back from the Special Congregation the brief reply, that 'the matter should be attended to.' That was all, and even that slender promise was not fulfilled. The months ran on, and nothing was done either to release the captives or to complete their *procès*. It is too evident that the primary object of the Special Congregation, or of Florida Blanca who overawed it, was to keep these poor victims in perpetual imprisonment, and that all else was but means to this end. If they could have convicted them of grave crimes, that would have suited them best, as they could then have made the trial public and ruined the reputation of the Jesuits for ever. As, however, they could find no proofs to sustain such a charge, the next best thing was to keep the *procès* indefinitely pending. If in that case nothing were published, the people would still suppose that it had been completed, and had gone against the accused – for they would never suppose that innocent men could be detained in prison for so long. Thus in either case the imprisonment would be prolonged indefinitely, the credit of the Society destroyed, and the action of their persecutors proportionately deemed to be just.

What caused this scheme eventually to break down was the death of Clement XIV on 23 September 1774. The mental troubles of his Pontificate had undermined his originally good constitution, and the result had been particularly noticeable in the months subsequent to the suppression. About the end of February of the ensuing year, 1774, his health underwent a considerable deterioration, and from that time onwards it was continuously failing. On 10 September he broke down while driving out into the country and was brought back to his palace. A fever had set in and he sank quickly, dying on the 23rd of the same month.[23] When they knew that the end was approaching, the anti-Jesuit Cardinals were anxious that he should first proclaim the names of certain prelates of their party whom he was known to have reserved *in petto*. The accession to their strength in the Conclave would have been important for their interests. Clement, however, refused.

Enough has been said in criticism of his character and his conduct. There is much, no doubt, in both which, with the best of wills to judge him favourably, one cannot but condemn – his refusal to hear both sides, or to take the counsels of his Cardinals; his want of straightforwardness in declaring his motives and intentions; his policy of reconciling public opinion to the coming suppression by first undermining the credit of the doomed Religious. A stronger and more clear-sighted Pope, even if he had decided on the suppression, would have prepared for it and enacted it in a juster and more dignified way. Yet Clement was at heart a good and well-meaning man, and, if weak and incompetent, he still struggled bravely according to his lights to bring the Church safely through a dangerous crisis.

With St Alfonso then let our chief feeling for him be one of compassion: 'Poor Pope,' said the Saint, a few days after receiving the Brief, and on hearing the Pope severely blamed for it, 'Poor Pope! what could he do in the circumstances in which he was placed, with all the sovereigns conspiring to demand this suppression. As for us we must keep silence, respect the secret judgments of God, and hold ourselves in peace.'

II.[24] [Pius VI and the death of Fr Ricci]

So far the narrative has been brought down to the autumn of 1774, that is, to the death of Clement XIV on 23 September of that year. The General and his Assistants, and a few other ex-members of the suppressed Order, were still detained in the Castle of Sant' Angelo, although more than a year had elapsed since their arrest, more than eight months since the termination of their interrogatories, and more than six months since Fr Ricci – strong in the consciousness or his innocence, and finding that the questions addressed to him pointed to no charge which savoured in any way of criminality – had asked to be released, or at least told of what he was suspected. He had

---

[23] Of course their adversaries suggested that the Jesuits had poisoned him, but Dr Saliceto's report proved that his death was due to natural causes.

[24] *The Month*, 101 (1903), 604–23.

got back from the Special Congregation a reply to this *supplica* that 'it should receive attention', but so far nothing had been done to relieve his legitimate anxiety. It must not be forgotten that all this delay was in flagrant opposition to the principles of judicature then in vogue, according to which, when the needful *indicia* had been gathered by the prosecution from the papers of the accused or other sources, he was entitled to be at once interrogated on all the points contained in the *indicia,* his answers constituting his defence to the charges; and when the interrogatories had been obtained and compared with the *indicia,* he was entitled to be brought before his judges and have his case heard and decided. We have suggested the motives which probably actuated the Special Congregation, and the Spanish Ambassador behind them, and induced them thus to violate all judicial proprieties in their treatment of their prisoners. 'The *procès* of the General,' says Masson, 'was the necessary consequence of the Suppression; to release Ricci absolved, to release him unsentenced, would be to condemn the Pope who had imprisoned him;'[25] or as we should ourselves prefer to put it, 'would be to condemn those who forced the Pope to imprison him, and pledged their word that proofs of his guilt had been found in his papers'. And the tedious delay in the proceedings meant that, as nothing incriminating had been discovered, the only way by which these diplomatists could save their faces seemed to them to be by continuing the detention of the prisoners, on the plea that their *procès* was not yet finished, and meanwhile doing nothing to forward it, so that it might lie dormant indefinitely.

Such was the state of things when Clement XIV expired, and such it must needs continue for some months longer. The Sacred College, as represented by the majority of its members, would have been only too glad to insist on the trial of the accused being promptly despatched, but their power during the vacancy of the Apostolic See was limited, and Florida Blanca had menaced them with the displeasure of his master, 'who held them responsible for the custody of the prisoners.' Nothing, therefore, could be done on behalf of these unfortunates till the new Pontiff was elected.

Meanwhile the Courts repeated in the new Conclave the strategy which had served them so well in 1769. By intimating dark threats of schism, they contrived to delay the election for four months; and when their lists had been matured, and the Cardinals from their dominions had at last been permitted to arrive, they proceeded to exclude one candidate after another of those proposed by the Zelanti,

---

[25] Masson, *Le Cardinal de Bernis depuis son Ministère,* p. 322.

with the object of thus forcing at length the acceptance of some candidate of their own nomination. The conditions, however, were no longer so favourable to their designs as in 1769. The Zelanti Cardinals had learnt a lesson from the events of the late Pontificate, and were determined that they would not be duped again. On the other hand, the few Cardinals whom the Ambassadors deemed entirely satisfactory – Malvezzi, Marefoschi, Zelada, Casali, and Simoni – had revealed their dispositions quite unmistakably and had made themselves hopelessly impossible. Negroni too, was unacceptable. Accordingly it was necessary for the Court Cardinals to moderate their aims, and to rest content with the election of some member of the Zelanti party whose opinions were thought to be of a less pronounced type. It was thus that, after some ineffectual efforts on either side to carry Colonna, Visconti, or Pallavicini, the united votes of the Electors came to fall on Cardinal Angelo Braschi. Cardinal de Bernis in his despatches claimed to have originally proposed and finally carried this candidature, and although we cannot altogether trust his assertions when he is engaged in exalting his own achievements, it is likely enough that he did by his advocacy materially contribute to the result, especially by gaining over the somewhat hesitating Moñino. Still, according to Beccatini,[26] it was by Cardinal Giraud's influence, both with the French Court and with the Albani party in the Conclave, that the candidature of Braschi was chiefly forwarded.

Cardinal Braschi, who took the name of Pius VI, was only fifty-eight at the time of his election. A native of Cesena in the Romagna, he was sent to the Jesuit College in that city, and there made good progress in his studies. Although belonging to a noble family and the only son of his parents, he resolved to embrace the ecclesiastical state. Through an uncle he became known to Cardinal Tommaso Ruffo, who attached him to his own household and, when later he himself became Bishop of Ostia and Velletri, made him the Auditor of his Episcopal Court. On the death of this Cardinal in 1753, Benedict XIV made him a Canon of St Peter's, and used him as his private secretary. In 1755 Clement XIII advanced him to be the Auditor, and in 1764 to the still more responsible office of Treasurer, of the Apostolic Chamber, and in these two offices he was retained throughout the Pontificate of Clement XIV. On 29 April 1773, he was created Cardinal by the latter Pontiff, along with his fellow-auditor, Mgr Delci – eleven others being then reserved *in petto*. He was thus the youngest Cardinal but one in

[26] Beccatini, *Storia di Pio VI*, vol. i. pp. 35-38.

the Sacred College at the time of his election. During the Conclave he kept in the background, and even when in the first instance his name was brought forward but soon withdrawn, he showed no signs of disappointment. Nor could it be laid to his charge that he had entangled himself in any compromising engagements, or even statements; and when the Cardinals gathered round him to do him homage, it was with evident sincerity that 'he cast himself on his knees and uttered a prayer so moving that it drew tears from all,' and then rising, said: 'Venerable Fathers, your gathering is now ended, but its result is too appalling for me.'[27]

Throughout his life he had been known for his integrity of character, for his genuine piety, for his amiability, as well as for his business capacity and his industry. He was not the man to put himself forward, and he had never been accounted a strong partizan. Still he was not afraid to speak out his mind, and he had made no secret of his disapproval of the treatment accorded to the Jesuits. On the other hand, Carlos III of Spain was indebted to him for services rendered on two notable occasions during his Neapolitan sovereignty – once in 1744, when as Auditor to the Cardinal Bishop of Velletri he saved the King's papers from falling into the hands of the Austrians, by whom his troops had just been defeated; and again in 1747, when Benedict XIV sent him as a secret agent to Naples, where he arranged successfully a dispute about jurisdiction between the spiritual and secular courts.[28]

It may have been the recollection of these past services which induced the Spanish Court to look favourably on his candidature, though it is not likely that they would have accepted it had there been a possibility of carrying a candidate belonging to their own party. Still they persuaded themselves that he would suit their purpose, and Grimaldi told Tanucci that the 'election had been good, and had proved that Florida Blanca possessed a good pair of nostrils.'[29] Bernis, though he claimed credit for having created the new Pope, was more guarded in expressing his opinion. In his despatch of 8 February 1775, he described him as 'inclined by his temperament as well as by his principles to respect the sovereigns, and seek their support for the Holy See; and as one who, although promoted by Rezzonico, had also been a pupil of Benedict XIV, and was more attached to the ideas of his master than to those of his benefactor',[30] and on 15 February, the day of the election, he wrote still more hesi-

[27] Beccatini, *ibid.* p. 39.
[28] *Ibid.* pp. 8, 14.
[29] Danvila, *Reinado de Carlos III*, vol. iii. p. 602.
[30] Masson, *ibid.* p. 313.

tatingly: 'As far as I can judge Braschi will prove a worthy occupant of the high dignity to which he has been called, and the enlightened classes generally have conceived a favourable opinion of him, whilst no one can deny that he has intelligence, piety, and a strict integrity which has never been found wanting ... His entire conduct indicates that he is honest, courageous, firm, prudent, and moderate. Nevertheless, I do not venture to hold myself responsible for his future behaviour ... God alone knows the hearts of men, and we can only judge by appearances. I can assure your Majesty that he cherishes a great regard for your Majesty, for all the august House of Bourbon, and for the French nation. His future government will show whether before his election he showed his real countenance or only his mask.'

Nor was it long before similar misgivings began to disquiet the Spanish diplomatists. On 23 March, Florida Blanca reported the rumour current in Rome that 'the Pope was at heart addicted to the Jesuits, and was about to take some step on their behalf', and Grimaldi, in his reply of 11 April, though 'discrediting the notion that his Holiness intended to restore the Society', expressed his belief that 'he would try to preserve some of its seed in view of future possibilities.'[31] And Florida Blanca in a further despatch of 20 April, after reporting that 'the Pope was said to have seen the Advocate Andreetti, about the case of the Duchess de Lante and about the illness of Padre Ricci', disclaims knowledge of the inner thoughts of Pius VI, but thinks it likely that he fears the Jesuits and their advocates, and is hoping to purchase security for his life by dealing mildly with the prisoners in Sant' Angelo. Still the Ambassador did not believe that his Holiness would take any decisive measure in their regard without first communicating with the Catholic King.[32]

It was the case that Pius VI did not sympathize with the designs of the Courts, and that they were destined to find him a far less pliant instrument than they had found his unfortunate predecessor. His position, however, was most difficult. The Courts were as determined as ever to carry on their Regalistic campaign, and to pursue to the uttermost the shattered remnants of the Order which had stood in its path; and they still had both the power and the will, should their demands be refused, to extend their persecutions to other Religious Orders and ecclesiastical institutions; indeed they were already engaged in suppressing convents.

In dealing with a situation so anxious the new Pope could not but

---

[31] Danvila, *ibid*. p. 604.
[32] *Ibid*. p. 605.

feel the need of extreme caution, nor can we be surprised to find him conceding much and tolerating much, which in his heart he must have disliked extremely in the hopes of thereby preserving to the Church institutions of still more vital consequence to her welfare. To restore the Society, though it may have seemed feasible to some enthusiasts, was of course quite out of the question, and if, as is highly probable, he was desiring 'to preserve some of its seed in view of future possibilities', in other words, to encourage the corporate existence of the Prussian and Russian Jesuits, he must abstain from all overt acts in their favour, and be content with such private encouragement, administered through indirect channels, as could quiet the consciences of these Religious, but was incapable of being publicly cited in their defence. It is, however, with his action in regard to the prisoners at Sant' Angelo that we are at present concerned, and we have to see with what discretion and with what results, working under these difficult conditions, Pius VI managed this test case in which not only the Jesuits but also their accusers were virtually put on their trial.

Shortly after his election he sent for Andreetti, the criminalist who had administered the interrogatories to the prisoners. He questioned him as to the present state of the investigation, and gave him strict orders to complete it promptly. His next step, taken about the end of April, was to put all the papers into the hands of Florida Blanca, and invite him to examine them and send him back a confidential report on their contents.[33] Florida Blanca accepted the task with pleasure. He took the invitation to mean that his Holiness intended to be guided by the views of the Courts, but it is more likely, indeed is certain, that the Pope's intention was to force out of the diplomatists themselves the acknowledgment that there was no evidence to sustain a conviction.

Florida Blanca was always prompt in his actions, and by 31 May presented the Report in question. Copies of the same were also communicated to the King of Spain, who in turn sent one to Tanucci for the King of Naples. From the copy preserved at Simancas, Sr Danvila has summarized the contents which are to the following effect.

After a pious preamble on the importance of preserving the peace of the Church, and respecting the memory of Clement XIV, and after rebutting the contention that the Jesuits should not have been condemned unheard, he comes to the point.

The crimes 'more or less established' as having been committed by the Jesuits are (he considers) those of '*lèse-majesté in primo capite,*

---

[33] Danvila, *ibid.* p. 562.

treason, rebellion, sedition, schism, superstition, disobedience, lying, and perjury. The persons who appeared most culpable were the ex-Assistants Gorgo and Rhomberg [that is, the Assistants of Italy and Germany], who could with difficulty be cleared from the spirit of sedition under which they had acted. Not only were there *indicia* that the ex-General Ricci knew of and connived at the negotiations, risings, and compacts directed against the Pope and his authority, but there was also proof of disobedience in his Instruction for maintaining the body of the Society after the suppression; that Koricki, Montes, and Guzman [the Assistants of Poland, Spain, and Portugal] were suspected of the same offences; and Faure, Forestier, Benincasa, Zuzzeri, and Catrani had been their accomplices.'

'The *procès* of all the accused should be completed according to the laws of God and man, civil and canonical [Moñino is always grand in such phrases as these]; the accused should then be heard, and receive a just sentence, being either absolved or condemned, in proportion to the guilt attaching to each respectively.' And here, to forestall the animadversion that all this should have been done long since, he notes that 'the completion of the Valentano investigations had been delayed by the death of Clement XIV and the resignation of the Judge Commissary, and that the Roman investigations remained incomplete because they had not finished registering the innumerable letters which had been found, and from which the *indicia* had to be gathered.' Also 'nine months had passed without the Special Congregation being in a position to do anything, whereas there were things useful and useless in the *procès,* between which it was its business to discriminate, after which it should proceed to inquire into the truth without partiality.'

Florida Blanca's final conclusions are that (1) those of the accused whom the Congregation judged might be set at liberty, even though found guilty of some offence, might be released at once, the needful precautions being taken; (2) the Congregation should advise what should be done with the less important among the accused, in consideration of the length of time they had been in prison; (3) it should ponder carefully the precautions which would be necessary to prevent the ex-General and his Assistants from uniting together, and entering into an understanding with the rest of the ex-Jesuits – lest they should organize disobedience to the Brief of Suppression, in opposition to Papal authority, to the detriment of the peace and tranquillity of the Church and the States; (4) no step should be suspended or omitted which was necessary for the full establishment of the offences committed, or for the exemplary chastisement of those implicated in the Valentano case, the crimes in which were so horrible, or of those implicated as principal authors in the crimes of schism and sedition which might be established in the Roman case.

This was the report drawn up by the Spanish Ambassador for the guidance of Pius VI, and we may be thankful for the insight it affords us into his ideas of judicial propriety; for it must not be forgotten that he had been a procurator-Fiscal to the Extraordinary Council of Castile, and that it was on the basis of his and Campomanes's joint-reports that this Council delivered the famous *Consultas* which were the direct cause of the Spanish and subsequent Papal suppressions of the Society. Viewed under this aspect the report summarized by Danvila is worth scrutinizing sharply, and there are points in it the significance of which may be appreciated at once. Are we to suppose it an honest verdict on overwhelming evidence which lay before him? That is the supposition with which one ought to begin, but there are these difficulties in sustaining it. The offences the report declares to have been established are serious enough, but why is there no detailed discussion of the evidence? It was written for Pius VI, himself a trained lawyer and former judge, to assist him in forming his judgment; but how could he be assisted by these few generalities? And why are the terms used so vague and non-committing – 'crimes more or less established'; 'could with difficulty be cleared from the spirit of sedition'? And why again, coupled with the opinion that the crimes established are most grave, and the recommendation that the principal authors should be severely punished, is it assumed that the General and his Assistants will have to be forthwith released? Suppose, however, we take another view of the Report, and regard it as an attempt to extricate the writer and his principals from a position found to be no longer tenable – does not its curious character then become intelligible? The vague allegation that serious crimes have been brought home to the accused, coupled with the suggestion that, if the time for their release has come, it is because they have now been sufficiently punished, thus becomes an ingenious device for covering the past misconduct of their accusers; whilst the tacit admission that their further detention cannot be reasonably demanded, betrays the consciousness that nothing had been found to convict them of guilt – for had he really before him evidence sufficient to convict them of crimes so grave as *lèse majesté in primo capite,* treason, rebellion, &c., Moñino was the last man in the world to accept a two years imprisonment as adequate expiation.

The value of this analysis is that it enables us to convict this protagonist of the anti-Jesuit campaign out of his own lips, but the reader will naturally ask how far the inference thus drawn can be supported by the direct testimony of the papers.

These papers, collected by the Special Congregation, and referred to Florida Blanca by Pius VI, are, we believe, preserved at Rome, and copies of the same are certainly preserved at Simancas. Unfortunately we have not been able to consult them personally, nor will we cite the estimate of Crétineau-Joly, who had seen them, lest it be deemed too partial. But we may reasonably lay stress on a testimony invoked by the Spanish historian, Danvila. This writer tells us that Don Cayetano Manrique, the joint-author with the Marqués de Montesa of the *Historia imparcial de la legislación española,* made a diligent collection of all the documents relating to the Jesuits in the *Archivo General* at Simancas. Danvila tells us he has seen the collection and that 'at the foot of the opinion of Florida Blanca, dated 3 May 1775, – that is, the Report we are concerned with – the aforesaid historian (Manrique) has written with his own hand the following note: "These two folios contain extracts from the *procès* formed against Fr. Ricci and his five Assistants, Rhomberg of Germany, Montes of Spain, Guzman of Portugal, Gorgo of Italy, Koricki of Poland, all of whom were imprisoned in the Castle of Sant' Angelo. In this *procès*, Moñino may say what he likes, but we have not found the grave crimes of *lèse majesté,* etc., which he supposes, and that they are not to be found there is also proved by the fact that after the death of Ricci all the other prisoners were sooner or later released, without any evidence whatever being found on which to condemn them."'[34] Danvila remarks that 'after this impartial judgment coming from one who strongly approved of the expulsion of the Jesuits, all further commentary is unnecessary'.

With these presumptions in favour of the ex-Jesuit prisoners we may be the less indisposed to listen to their own testimony, and we have a valuable account from Fr Ricci of the interrogatories put to him in Sant' Angelo and his answers to the same. He wrote it in the spring of 1775, and says of it in the document itself: 'These are all the interrogatories put to me, unless my memory deceives me, for I am writing this account a year and some months after the termination of the *procès* [which was in the middle of January, 1774]. Still, I think that it does not deceive me, for in order to keep myself from forgetting I have many times gone through the *procès* mentally. I have written it down from time to time on scraps of paper, which I afterwards burnt; I have told it to several persons, and I have at least a moral certainty that no other interrogatory of any importance was

---

[34] Danvila, *ibid.* p. 568.

put to me.'[35] Nor, it may be added, has the accuracy of his account been disputed, whilst the few papers from the *procès* which have been published, and the references to the events in the diplomatic correspondence, especially that of Bernis with d'Aiguillon and Vergennes, exactly tally with it.

The matter of his interrogatories, according to this account, referred to three main subjects – the steps be was suspected of having taken to maintain the Society even after the suppression (Questions 1–13, 16–18, and 23, 24); the money and other valuables he was suspected of having concealed (Questions 19–22); and the state of the Society during his Generalate (Questions 14, 15). If the Courts sought for a justification of their past actions the last of these three topics should have principally interested them, but the General was merely asked what defects had existed in the Order during his rule, and he replied, 'None, by the mercy of God, which were in any way common; and that on the contrary, there had been exhibited much regularity, much piety, much zeal, and in particular, much union and charity'; that 'there had of course been those occasional defects in individuals which would never be wanting whilst human nature remained what it is, but that these had been met by the proper remedies.' Not a word beyond this is found in the *procès* relating to the past.

On the money question the Prosecution naturally laid great stress, and Andreetti told Ricci it was believed that some fifty millions of *scudi* had been hidden away, a sum which he afterwards reduced to about twenty-two or twenty-four millions. Ricci's answer was that absolutely nothing had been hidden away in secret vaults, or deposited in foreign banks, or anywhere else; that some money had recently been sent to Venice but that was for the use of certain foreign missions to which it belonged, and the amount of it would be found in the Procurator-General's books; that very little money was

---

[35] The full text of this account is in the Appendix XIV to Fr Boero's *Osservazioni* on Theiner's *Clément XIV*. The restrictions imposed on the prisoners, which were considerably relaxed under Pius VI, had been extremely rigorous during the reign of Clement XIV. It is this which explains why Ricci was reduced to such expedients during the earlier reign, to preserve an exact record of his interrogatories. These interrogatories, as they are given in the body of the account, are twenty-two in number – but in an addition written subsequently to June 1775, he tells us that a text of his *procès* had at that time been printed and circulated in Rome. He recognizes from the accounts supplied to him the accuracy of this published text, and says it reminds him of two more interrogatories which he had forgotten in his own report. These he now adds, bringing up the number to twenty-four. We have not been able to learn anything further of this unauthorized publication of his *procès*.

accustomed to be sent to Rome from other countries, and only such as was required to support the General and his Curia, and to meet the expenses common to the whole Order; that the maintenance of the Portuguese exiles, to whom no pensions had been paid by their Sovereign, had been a most serious charge on the Order, especially after the break-up of so many provinces, and that it had only been by stinting themselves, and selling their church plate, for which they had received faculties from Clement XIII, that they were enabled even imperfectly to supply the necessary funds. And Fr Ricci might have added that, as the Special Congregation had captured all the papers in the Gesù, it must have in its hands his correspondence with the different provinces, and thus have unmistakable proofs of the pecuniary straits to which they had been reduced.

But the majority of the interrogatories bore on the supposed intention of the Jesuits to maintain their Order by a secret union, in defiance of the Brief. Had not Fr Ricci recently appointed a Vicar-General to succeed him in the case of his death; and if so, why had the letter of appointment been withdrawn from searchers; and what was the name of the person chosen? Did he recognize the authorship of a letter shown him? and did it not prove that he had granted to the Sicilian Jesuits certain faculties in regard to the choice of confessors and the use of money, of which they were to avail themselves in case they should be suppressed? Did he recognize the authorship of another letter (written to a Spanish Provincial), and did it not prove that he had sent out an Instruction encouraging the Spaniards rather to forfeit their pensions and go begging than accept secularization from the authorities of the Church? Had he not written to the King of Prussia, beseeching him to maintain the Jesuits in his own States? And did not these various acts point to an intention to resist the operation of the Brief of Suppression, and maintain the Society under the rule of its own chosen Superiors?

We have not given these questions literally as they were put to Fr Ricci, but summarized and paraphrased so as to indicate the object as well as the nature of the inquiries made. Such a paraphrase seems convenient both for the sake of brevity and of clearness, but its fidelity will not be disputed; and it gives the substance, the entire substance, of the questions asked – among which the part about the Instruction to the Spaniards should be read in comparison with de Bernis's despatch of 22 September, 1773, speaking of 'a secret instruction by the General [which] has been found, in which he orders all the Jesuits, in case the Society should be suppressed, to go on living according to their Constitutions, and continue to receive novices.'[36]

[36] Masson, *ibid.* p. 342. See above p. 266.

When we turn from these Questions to Fr Ricci's Answers it is really ludicrous to find how simple and intelligible were the few facts out of which this preposterous charge of schism had been manufactured. When a General dies there must be some one appointed to carry on the government during the *interregnum*, and to preside over the Congregation called to elect the new General. The Society's custom is that each General, when elected, should appoint a Vicar-General for this purpose; but the appointment is made secretly, by enclosing the name in a sealed packet, not to be opened till after the existing General's death – even the person chosen being left in ignorance till then. This P. Ricci had done, and this is all he had done, save that when the suppression was announced to him he had forthwith burnt the sealed packet, for which there was no longer a purpose. When they asked him for the name of the Father chosen, he demurred, as it was a fact so entirely internal to his own mind, but on their insisting, he gave it under a promise of secrecy, declaring it to be that of P. Rhomberg, the Assistant of Germany. This was all that underlay the suspicion that he had provided for the handing down of his authority *after* the suppression.

Under normal circumstances Jesuits, like members of other Religious Orders, can go to confession only to priests of their own Order, who receive faculties for this purpose from their own Superiors; nor can they have money in their own keeping, or the free control of its expenditure; nor must they clothe themselves otherwise than in the dress of their Order. But when, in 1764, the French Jesuits were turned out of their houses, dispersed through the country, and forbidden to wear their habits, some dispensations from these practices were absolutely necessary, and they were accordingly granted by Fr Ricci in a paper entitled, *Faculties granted to the French*. Later, when the exiled Sicilians were expecting to be similarly forbidden to wear their habits or live in community, they applied for an extension of the same faculties to themselves. The letter from a Sicilian Jesuit to which the interrogatory referred was a letter of inquiry as to what amount of dispensation had been thus granted.

In short, what the persecutors of the Society did was to construe an act of legitimate spiritual authority exercised during the time of merely civil suppression, and exercised precisely in order to enable the Religious to conform, without violation of conscience, to the demands of the civil power, into an act of usurped spiritual authority, exercised with a view to the time of Papal suppression, when the General's power would be utterly extinguished. And the General's so-called Instruction to the Spanish Provincial was misconstrued in exactly the same way. Some time before the Papal suppression had extinguished his authority, the Spanish exiles were expecting an order from their Court requiring them all to apply to the Church authorities for secularization, under pain of losing the pensions which were their only means of subsistence. Their Provincial wrote to the General, asking whether, if such orders reached them, they should comply, or whether it would not be nobler to preserve their religious state, and trust to God's Providence for their support. The General responded by an Instruction recommending compliance.

At the beginning of 1773 a letter written by Frederick II of Prussia to d'Alembert was in all the Gazettes. The King said that the General had sent him an Ambassador asking him to declare himself openly the Protector of the Society. It was in view of this royal letter that Ricci was asked in Sant' Angelo if he had written to the King, the suggestion being that he had asked the King to prevent the Papal suppression, if it should come, being carried out in Silesia. The General's answer was that he had once written to the King of Prussia to ask his protection in the matter of a serious lawsuit in which the Silesian Fathers were engaged. Evidently he was referring to a letter written at some earlier date, and did not own to having sent an Ambassador to the King of Prussia in the sense of that monarch's letter to d'Alembert. A letter[37] dated 10 January 1774, and written by a Viennese ex-Jesuit, Fr Pintus, to Cardinal Zelada, explains the mystery of the King's statement. It seems that Fr Pintus, on his own behalf, and without the previous knowledge of the General, had visited the King of Prussia at Potsdam, and had asked him 'to save if he could our Society which was verging towards its ruin, and if possible to support the Holy Father in resisting those who were pressing for our destruction.' It is surely hard to blame him for thus seeking to save his Order by means which were not unlawful; but in any case his act was the act of an individual, which in no way compromised the General or the Jesuits as a body.

One more question, in connection with this suspicion of schismatic designs, was put to the General. Did he believe that he still retained any authority over the Society now that it was suppressed, and what authority did he imagine he would have had if, instead of entirely suppressing it, the Pope had preferred to alter its Constitutions? The answer was what might have been expected. As it was suppressed entirely he had now no Authority at all over it; if its Constitutions had been altered he would have had just that authority which his Holiness had left with him.

---

[37] Ravignan, *Clément XIII et Clément XIV,* vol. 1. p. 307.

One would like to supplement this account of the interrogatories administered to the General by an account of those administered to his fellow-prisoners; but, although these were eventually released from prison, they were first made to take an oath of secrecy which sealed their lips, nor was there ever an official publication of their *procès*, nor, we imagine, are the official records now in existence. Still, notwithstanding the vigilance of their gaolers, a few facts concerning them leaked out through confidential channels during the time of their imprisonment, and therefore before the oath was exacted; and these are recorded in a useful little volume entitled *Le Oui et le Non*.[38] From this source we learn that Fr Comolli, the Secretary-General, who did not long survive his examination, was merely asked about the vaults at the Gesù where the treasures were hidden, to which he replied that he knew neither of any such vaults or any such treasures.[39] Fr de Guzman, the Assistant of Portugal, a bed-ridden old man of seventy-eight when he was arrested, does not appear to have been asked any questions at all, and Fr de Montes, the Assistant of Spain, a nonogenarian, was told at his first and perhaps his only examination, that he was under arrest not on any charge, but merely that his person might be secured. It is not known what questions were put to Fr Koricki, the Assistant of Poland, but Fr Rhomberg, the Assistant of Germany, was pressed very much to say whether he had been aware of his appointment as Vicar-General. Of course he had not and said so, and he too was told by Andreetti, at his first hearing, that 'he was not accused of anything, and would probably soon be delivered.' The examination of Fr Gorgo, the Assistant of Italy, came by some unknown means to be published in

---

[38] *Le Oui et le Non, ou Lettres sur la Procédure faite contre les Jésuites au Château Saint-Ange*, Paris, 1777. According to Père Sommervogel (*Bibliothèque des Ecrivains de la Compagnie de Jésus*, sub nom. Sauvage), this little volume of letters bears no author's name, but is attributed, rightly or wrongly, to Père Sauvage, a French Jesuit who with Père Grou composed the *Réponse aux Extraits des Assertions*. Whoever he was, the author was at least one who had access to interesting and on the whole trustworthy sources of information. Père Sommervogel tells us (ibid.) that the copy in the Jesuit Library at Louvain has some MSS notes wrttten in 1800 by the ex-Jesuit Fr Cornelius Geerts. From these notes we learn that the letters were first circulated in Rome, where they 'were composed from memoranda collected at the palaces of Cardinals Colonna, Albani, and Torregiani.'... 'The houses of these Cardinals,' says the note, 'were open to the prisoners as soon as any of them were set at liberty, and it was there that all such information about their interrogatories as did not fall under their oaths of secrecy was disclosed; and for two years these Cardinals incurred expenses and made researches to ascertain the truth.'

[39] *Ibid*. Lettre Xe – which contains all that was known about the examinations of the Assistants.

various Gazettes, and although after his release Fr Gorgo's own tongue was tied, his fellow-prisoners declared, says the author of *Le Oui et le Non,* that the published account corresponded with what they had learnt from him during his imprisonment.[40] This same author gives the examination in full. The questions relate almost entirely to the system that had been followed during recent years for supporting and employing the Spanish and Portuguese exiles. There is not a point among them all which could conceivably be made into matter of accusation.

Besides the Assistants a few others were arrested and imprisoned either in Sant' Angelo or elsewhere. Stefanucci and Togni (a laybrother); Romano and Zuzzeri (another lay-brother); Forestier, Benincasa, Faure, Gaultier, and Catrani (the latter a secular priest). The volume referred to, tells all that was known about the causes of complaint against them. Stefanucci, Togni, and Romano had destroyed some papers, which apparently were letters of conscience. Forestier had written a paper comparing the doctrines of Palafox with those of the Church and of Jansenius respectively; Benincasa may perhaps have done the same, but nothing is known; Zuzzeri had in his possession a copy of the *Irreflessioni* of Fr Benvenuto,[41] who had escaped to Prussia; Faure and Catrani had perhaps secreted some papers relating to the Malvezzi affair at Bologna; Gaultier was suspected, probably falsely, of warning Corletti to leave the country – the latter being a scholastic who had written, as he afterwards acknowledged, a letter signed 'the Jesuits' to the Archbishop-Elector of Mayence, asking him to protect them in case of their suppression. None of these appear to have been grave offences, and that there was none besides of a more serious kind may be inferred from the circumstances of the subsequent release of the accused.

All these persons were in what was called the Roman *procès,* besides which there was the Valentano *procès,* so called because the persons primarily concerned were a nun, Sister Teresa Poli, and a peasant girl, Bernardina Renzi, both belonging to that district. As much stress was laid on this Valentano *procès* by the Society's accusers it is necessary to say a brief word about it,[42] though it had little or nothing to do with the question of the guilt or innocence of the General and the Society. These two women were in repute for

---

[40] *Ibid.* pp. 210–214.
[41] These *Irreflessioni* were a temperately expressed criticism on the *Reflexions des Cours des Bourbons sur l'affaire des Jésuites.* The latter which were spread about Rome in 1770, contended that the Pope having made a promise to suppress the Society could not in honour refuse to fulfil it.
[42] See *Le Oui et le Non, Lettres XIIIe, XVIIe.*

The Execution of the Brief of Suppression   285

holiness of life; and had taken much to heart for some years past the calamities which were afflicting the Jesuits. They also from time to time imagined themselves to be recipients of heavenly predictions, mostly of an encouraging kind. Sister Teresa's confessor was an Abbate Mayoli, and Bernardina's the Abbate Azzaloni, Arch-priest of Valentano. Both these priests used to seek counsel as to the direction of their penitents from the Jesuit Fathers Coltraro and Venizza, and Fr Coltraro is said to have shown some of these prophecies to Fr Ricci for his consolation. In the spring of 1773 Bernardina predicted that Clement XIV would not live to open the Jubilee (of 1775), but would die in September. This much happened as she predicted, but she seems to have predicted other things, as that the Society would never be actually suppressed, which were falsified by the event. According to Danvila[43] she also said that Clement would die of poison, but Danvila in this part of his book is palpably inaccurate in several particulars, and cannot be relied on. Still it may have been so, though there are no traces of it in the account in *Le Oui et le Non*. Sister Teresa had made some similar but less definite prophecies. The two women, together with the Prioress of the convent at Valentano, the Abbati Azzaloni and Mayoli, and the two ex-Jesuits, Coltraro and Venizza, were arrested in May 1774, and the four priests after an interval were all placed in Sant' Angelo. The intention was to connect these prophecies with the alleged poisoning of Clement XIV, but, as has been related, there were no signs of poisoning or other violence in the circumstances of the death of this Pope, so that the very *corpus delicti* was wanting; nor was there reason for supposing that these priests and prophetesses were other than quiet if over-credulous people, still less that they had engaged in any plot to ensure the fulfilment of the predictions. And still less was there any evidence to connect Fr Ricci with their actions, real or supposed – he who had been in strict custody for a year and more before the Pope's death, and was never asked a question about these predictions in his examinations. We are entitled then to say that the entire Valentano *procès,* however much or little it may have compromised the individuals immediately concerned, is wholly irrelevant to the wider question of the Society's good name.

We now know sufficiently what evidence lay before Florida Blanca when on 31 May 1775, he delivered his strange report to Pius VI. We can return then to the history. Pius VI on receiving the report reassembled the Special Congregation and caused it to continue and promptly finish the investigations. He made, however, certain

---
[43] Danvila, *ibid.* p. 571.

changes in its *personnel* by dismissing Macedonlo and Alfani, and adding Giraud to the number of the Cardinals: he also required them to keep him fully cognizant of all their procedure. They held a session under these new conditions on 19 June, and one result was the immediate liberation, without sentence of any kind, of Forestier, Gaultier, and Zuzzeri. On 7 August they held another session – and this time they declared that though Benincasa, Faure, and the Archpriest Catrani were implicated in the *procès* (it was not said how), they might be liberated, but must he sent out of Rome – a restriction which Pius VI at once remitted. On 20 September Florida Blanca, foreseeing that it would be impossible to retain the General and his Assistants in prison any longer, addressed a memorial to Pius VI demanding that they should be forbidden to meet together after their release, that they should be interned each in a particular district, that they should be forbidden even to communicate with each other or to talk about the suppression, that they should all take an oath to observe secrecy on these points, and finally that they should be watched by spies.[44] In this same month were released Frs Guzman and de Montes, that is to say, the Assistants of those very countries in which the Jesuits had been declared to be particularly guilty. The Commission strove to delay the release of the other three Assistants as long as possible and told Pius VI that there were sixty-three new questions on which they must still examine them. It was his policy to let them have their way and so compel them to pronounce with their own lips the sentences of acquittal, which they had eventually to do on 16 February 1776. These Fathers, like the rest, were made to take an oath of secrecy, but no judgment was pronounced against them, though Moñino had declared two of them to be clearly guilty of sedition. On 7 March Coltraro and Venizza were liberated without sentence or punishment, though tied by the oath of secrecy. These were all the Jesuits. Azzaloni and Mayoli were released soon after, the latter being inhibited from hearing confessions any more, and the former ordered to make a two months' retreat in a monastery. The women also were released about the same time, some slight penances being imposed upon them and a retractation of their prophecies exacted. These penances assigned to the prophetesses and their confessors were perhaps deserved, but surely they are not consistent with the notion that their crimes had been, as Florida Blanca calls them, 'horrible', and certainly not consistent with the supposition that they had been convicted of a plot to poison Clement XIV.

But what about the issue of this *procès* for the chief of all the

---

[44] Danvila, *ibid.* p. 566.

accused? Pius VI, as we have seen, kept pressing the Special Congregation to hasten on its inquiries, but probably Fr Ricci was kept in ignorance of these efforts on his behalf. At all events, at the end of August, 1775, he wrote another *supplica,* in which he represented to the new Pope the injustice with which he was being treated, and gave a moving description of the rigours of his imprisonment. The effect, according to Fr Boero, who gives the text of the *supplica,*[45] was to induce Pius VI to insist still more strongly on the speedy termination of the *procès,* and it is doubtless this which explains Florida Blanca's letter of 20 September, the letter in which the Ambassador assumes that the General's release will have to be permitted. Yet still the Congregation managed to procrastinate, and on 24 November 1775, death transferred the sufferer to the bar of a higher court. Five days previously he had asked for the Viaticum, which was brought to him in his cell at Sant' Angelo, and there, whilst the priest with trembling hands held up the Blessed Sacrament before him, in the presence of the Vice-Governor of the Castle and several others, he read a solemn protestation which he had prepared.

> Believing that the time has now come when I must stand before the tribunal of infallible truth and justice – for such is the tribunal of God – after having long and maturely reflected, and after having humbly begged my merciful Redeemer and terrible Judge not to let me be swayed by passion, or bitterness of spirit, or any unholy affection or object, – solely because I judge it my duty to render justice to truth and innocence, I make these two declarations and protestations.
> 1. I declare and protest that the suppressed Society of Jesuits gave no grounds whatever for its suppression. I declare and protest this with the moral certainty that a Superior can have who was well-informed as to the state of his Order.
> 2. I declare and protest that I have given no grounds whatever, not even the slightest, for my imprisonment. I declare and protest this with that absolute certainty and evidence which each man has concerning his own actions. And I make this second protestation solely because it is required to vindicate the good name of the suppressed Society of Jesus, of which I was the Superior-General.

The dying man then went on to protest that he did not wish by his words to impute blame to any of the authors of the suppression, the beliefs and motives of human hearts being known only to God; and that he pardoned all who had wrought the ruin of himself and his brethren, even as he hoped himself to obtain pardon from God.[46]

[45] *Osservazioni,* pp. 117–120.
[46] *Ibid.* p. 115.

'The Pope', wrote de Bernis, 'need not be distressed at the death of a person so embarrassing; Providence arranges all for the best.'[47] But the Pope was most distressed that he should have died just when the hour of his vindication was near. He sent him, however, his blessing to console his last moments, and when he was dead caused the body to be buried with honour at the Chiesa dei Fiorentini, and thence transferred to the Gesù, where it was laid near the bodies of his predecessors.

---

[47] Despatches of 21 and 22 November. Apud Masson, *ibid.* p. 326.

Chapter Eight

The Brief of Suppression[1]

With the dying declaration of Fr. Ricci, testifying to the innocence of the Religious whom he had governed for so many years, we can fitly end this account of the history of the Suppression. We have still, however, to examine the text of the Brief of Suppression, and then to conclude with a comprehensive survey of the various causes which led up to the final catastrophe.

In the present chapter we shall examine the text of the Brief,[2] and we shall examine it from the point of view under which at the very moment of its issue it presented itself to the mind of Fr Cordara, who tells us in his *Commentaries* that before reading the Brief

> he had feared lest the Pope should give as his reason for suppressing the Society, that its members had been guilty of the thousand and one crimes with which their adversaries charged them, commerce, laxity of moral doctrine, disobedience to the Apostolic commands, betrayals and assassinations of kings, idolatry, etc.... Ganganelli, however, ... had charged them with no crime, no guilt, and had so drawn up its text that the suppression might appear to be not a punishment, but a concession to the necessity and condition of the times.

This estimate of the character of the Brief has been also taken not merely by other Jesuit writers such as Cahour,[3] but also by independent writers like Schoell, whose judgment, already quoted, is that 'this Brief condemns neither the doctrines, nor the morals, nor the discipline of the Jesuits. The complaints made against the Order are the sole motives for its suppression which are alleged.'[4]

---

[1] *The Month*, **102** (1903), **46–63**.
[2] [Readers wishing to consult an English translation of the Brief, cf. Thomas M. McCoog, S.J., ed., *'Promising Hope'*, 2003, Appendix I, where the original Latin text is also given. *Ed. N.*]
[3] *Des Jésuites, par un Jésuite*, pp. 278–283.
[4] *Cours d'Histoire des Etats Européens*, xliv. p. 83 [see p. 256 above, *Ed. N.*].

That it is desirable to interrogate the Brief from this point of view will not be denied, for if the Brief declares the guilt of the Jesuits to have been established, the weight of such a solemn Papal condemnation must ever press as a heavy burden on their reputation. If, on the other hand, the Brief, whilst recounting the number and gravity of the charges brought against the Order, noticeably omits to declare whether they have been established or not, and bases the Suppression on the consequences arising out of the mere fact of their being brought, so significant an avoidance of responsibility cannot be overlooked, but must point to the same conclusion to which the collateral evidence has already led us, the conclusion that the accusers of the Order had been unable to support their charges by any proofs worthy of the name. And, be it added, this conclusion will appear all the more impressive when we recollect that Moñino, the prime framer of the indictment against the Society in Spain, was also the literary framer of the Brief, which Clement XIV accepted from his hands not willingly, but only under stress of the gravest and most persistent threats.

The Brief contains two main divisions – the *recitatory* part which comes first and recites the reasons which in the judgment of the Pontiff require the suppression of the Jesuits, and the *operative* part, which actually decrees its suppression, together with the various provisions for carrying it out, and regulating its consequences. Of the operative part, enough has been said in the previous chapter. It is the recitatory part which we have now to consider, and this again falls into two divisions, the former stating the principles by which a Pope should be guided in retaining, or reforming, or suppressing a Religious Order instituted by his predecessors, the latter applying these principles to the case of the Society. The statement of principles occupies the first fifteen paragraphs, the application takes up the next nine.

In its initial paragraph the Brief strikes what we may call its keynote. Our Lord and Redeemer, Jesus Christ, came down on earth as the Prince of Peace. His ministry was a ministry of peace and reconciliation, and He bequeathed this ministry to His Apostles. They were sent forth to announce peace to the entire world, and were to implant in the hearts of those born in Christ a solicitude to preserve the unity of the Spirit in the bond of peace among themselves. In the next paragraph the Pontiff goes on to declare that from the time of his exaltation he had felt how heavy was the responsibility laid upon himself to preserve this peace to the Church, and how he must be prepared not only to plant and build up institutions calculated to promote it, but likewise to root up and destroy, if found to be injurious to it, institutions the parting with which would cause him the greatest grief and distress of mind.

In the third paragraph he begins to gather precedents. Among institutions dear to the Apostolic See, Religious Orders had always counted in the front rank, and it had frequently assisted their labours for the welfare of Christendom by the sanction of its approbation, and by the bestowal of many favours and privileges. None the less, whensoever any of these Orders had ceased in the course of time to yield the same good fruits as formerly, and had perhaps even become a source of disturbance rather than of profit to the peace of nations, it had never hesitated to interpose by its authority, so as either to recall the members to the primitive austerity of their profession, or to alter their constitutions, or even to destroy their Order altogether.

In the ten following paragraphs he enumerates past instances in which the Holy See had thus reformed or altered or suppressed Orders previously approved and favoured. In 1312, Clement V suppressed by Bull the Order of Templars on the ground that it had fallen into universal disrepute (*in universam diffamationem*), although the Ecumenical Council of Vienne had distinctly refused to pass a definitive judgment on the charges brought against it. In 1571, St. Pius V suppressed by Brief the Order of Humiliati, on the ground that its members had quarrels among themselves and with externs, which destroyed all hopes of their future usefulness, that they were disobedient to the commands of the Apostolic See, and that some of them had even conspired against the life of St Charles Borromeo, their Protector, who had been sent to them as an Apostolic Visitor. In 1626, Urban VIII suppressed by Brief the Reformed Conventuals on the ground that their Institute had not yielded the fruit anticipated from it, and that they had quarrels with the unreformed Conventuals. In 1643, the same Urban suppressed by Brief the Order of SS. Ambrose and Barnabas *ad nemus,* and in 1645 Innocent X confirmed this suppression by Bull. In the same year, the latter Pontiff converted by Brief the Religious of the Pious Schools of the Mother of God from a Religious Order into a Secular Congregation, on the ground that grave disturbances had arisen among the members – a conversion which in this instance was subsequently revoked. In 1650, the same Pontiff, Innocent X, suppressed by Brief the Order of St Basil of the Armenians, on the ground that disagreements and dissensions had arisen; and in 1651, he likewise suppressed by Brief the Congregation of the Priests of the Good Jesus, on the ground that they offered no promise of future spiritual utility. Finally, in 1668, Clement IX suppressed three Orders by one and the same Brief –

namely, the Canons Regular of St George in Alga, the Hieronymites of Fiesole, and the Jesuats of St John Columbanus – all on the ground that no advantage or utility to the Christian people was to be anticipated from their survival.

In the next paragraph it is claimed that in all these ten suppressions of Religious Orders previously approved and cherished by the Holy See, the Popes

> did not cause any forensic investigations to be held, in which the doomed Orders could plead in their own defence, and attempt to refute the accusations or reasons in view of which their suppression had been determined on, – feeling that it would be better to rely upon the counsels of their own prudence, and act not as judges [in a criminal suit] but as supreme administrators of the Christian community, so as to prevent the strifes, contentions, and manifestations of party spirit which the other method would be calculated to excite.

Here ends the statement of the principles which if verified in the case of the Society will, in the judgment of Clement XIV, require its total suppression. Before however we pass on to the paragraphs in which the application is made, it may be well to bring into greater prominence the precise points of precedent which the Pontiff intends to gather from the ten instances enumerated.

These points appear to be three in number, of which the first and most important is that the case in which a body of Religious have been found guilty of serious offences is not the only case in which the suppression of their Order may be justifiably decreed, but that the Holy See may propose to itself a broader scope, and resort to this means whensoever the general welfare of the Church demands the extinction of an institution disturbing to its tranquillity or, it may be, only the transference of vocations and endowments to more useful purposes. That this is so may be gathered not only from the initial paragraph which declares the peace of the Church and not the vindication of justice to be the ruling motive of the suppressions, but also from the diversity of the causes recited as having influenced the Holy See in the ten previous cases. In only one of them – that is, in the case of the Humiliati, who had been disobedient to the commands of the Holy See, and had conspired against the life of St Charles Borromeo – is guilt imputed by Clement XIV to the suppressed Religious. In one other case, it is true, namely, in that of the Templars, the cause alleged is 'a universal persuasion of guilt', but even there the Pontiff is careful to point out that the General Council appointed to judge their case had formally refused to pass a definitive sentence on the evidence laid before it. And in all the remaining cases[5] the causes indicated are either dissensions that have arisen among the members or between them and other bodies, the mere existence of which, on whichever side the rights or wrongs may have been, were sources of disturbance and rendered the members incapable any longer of rendering useful service to the Church; or else the mere fact that the Order has for some unnamed reason become useless, and should give place to something more profitable.

The second point of precedent on which Clement XIV obviously desires to insist is that his predecessors in suppressing Religious Orders have proceeded by way of administrative measure, and not of judicial sentence. And we can understand his reason, for we have seen that the Courts, which insisted on the suppression, insisted likewise on its being carried into effect without any previous investigation, by Commission or otherwise, into the conduct of the accused, and the defence they might be able to offer for themselves.[6]

The third point of precedent which he wished to gather from the acts of his predecessors was that, if at times they suppressed by Bull, there had also been occasions when they suppressed by Brief, which was what he himself had felt constrained to do for reasons which have already been sufficiently discussed.[7]

---

[5] That is to say, in the Brief of Clement XIV misconduct on the part of the members is not assigned as a cause of suppression save in two at most out of these ten cases. But if we turn to the Briefs by which the other eight Orders were suppressed, we find that in two of these – that is, the Ambrosians *ad nemus,* and the Basilians – irremediable misconduct is the cause assigned: whilst of the six remaining Orders, the Order of the Priests of the Good Jesus and the three Orders simultaneously suppressed by Clement IX, had so few members and did so little work, that their large endowments were being practically wasted; the Order of Pious Schools was not so much 'suppressed' as changed in character on the plea of its own advantage; and the Reformed Conventuals were not so much suppressed as fused into other branches of the Order to which they belonged. It was in fact quite unprecedented to suppress a large and active Religious Order on grounds other than the discovery in their ranks of deep-rooted and wide-spread guilt. To say this, however, is not to say that a suppression for other causes lay beyond the Pope's power, or could not be a just and expedient measure.

[6] At the same time here also the precedents invoked rather prove the opposite. The suppression indeed of an Order could hardly be carried out otherwise than by an administrative measure, but in each of the previous instances, as the Briefs and Bulls show, the administrative measure of suppression was preceded by an inquiry in which the members were examined and put on their defence before a Commission which followed the substance if not always the technical formalities of a judicial process.

[7] At the same time here also the precedents point the other way. The eight orders suppressed by Brief were comparatively small bodies. On the other hand, the

Having fixed the principles to be followed, Clement XIV passes in Paragraph XVI to apply them to the case of the Society, and begins by declaring that having a 'vehement desire to proceed (in the business before him) with a convinced mind and firm footsteps, he had spared no labour and omitted no inquiry that seemed necessary in order to ascertain all that related to the origin, history, and present state of the Religious Order commonly called the Society of Jesus; and that he had found that it was instituted by its Holy Founder for the salvation of souls, the conversion of heretics, and especially of pagans, in short, for the furtherance of piety and religion,' etc. This passage is sometimes cited as testifying that the Jesuits were not condemned unheard. But we have seen that they were in no single case heard in their defence until after the Brief was published, and it is not likely that the Pontiff meant to contradict so patent a fact. Besides the character of the Pope's diligent researches are indicated to us by the results to which he declares they have led him, and which he embodies in the summary account of 'the origin, growth, and present state of the Society', incorporated in the Brief. It is to this account therefore, and the terms in which it is given, that we must look for the means of answering the question stated at the beginning of this chapter, and determine whether this Brief is a Brief of condemnation, declaring the Jesuits guilty of grave crimes and misconduct, and inflicting their suppression upon them as a punishment, or whether it is not rather a simple Brief of Suppression, which refrains from imputing guilt to either side, and cites as the sufficient justification for its enactment the character of their Institute, of their teaching, and their mode of action, which, whether meritorious or defective in themselves, have at all events had the effect of exciting much opposition and causing dissensions, injurious to the peace of the Church. Let us then scrutinize the paragraphs next following from this point of view.

Paragraph XVII is a simple account of the foundation of the Society by St Ignatius, of the special features in its Institute, and of their approval in their successive stages by Paul III.

Paragraph XVIII begins by noting how the original approbation of

---

Bull which suppressed the Humiliati was of a specially solemn kind, being signed by the Pope and all the Cardinals; whilst the Bull which suppressed the Templars – the only Order out of the ten which, in view of its size and importance, was at all comparable with the Society – was of the most solemn kind known, being Promulgated in a General Council, and declared by its text to emanate *sacro approbante Concilio*. Still it is beyond dispute that it lay within the absolute Apostolic Power to suppress a Religious Order of whatever size and importance by the simple form of Brief.

The Brief of Suppression 295

Paul III was confirmed and enlarged by the further grants of Julius III, Paul IV, Pius IV, St Pius V, Gregory XIII, Sixtus V, Gregory XIV, Clement VIII, Paul V, Leo XI, Gregory XV, and Urban VIII, not to speak of other Pontiffs.

In Paragraph XIX begins the statement of the case for suppression.

> From the tenour itself and the language of the Apostolic Constitutions [i.e., the Bulls of Approbation just enumerated] it is clearly seen that very soon after the foundation of the said Society various seeds of discord and jealousy sprang up, and embroiled its members not only among themselves but also with other Religious Orders, with the secular clergy, with Academies and Universities, public schools of letters, and even with Princes into whose dominions the Society had been admitted.
>
> And [it is further seen] that those strifes and disagreements had been stirred up
>
> (1) at times *in reference* to the nature and character of the vows, to the time when the members should be admitted to their vows, to the right of expelling them, to the custom of promoting them to Holy Orders, contrary to the decrees of the Council of Trent and of Pius V of holy memory, without either provision for their congruous maintenance or the bond of solemn vows;
>
> (2) at other times *in reference* to the absolute power which the General of the same Society claimed to exercise, and to other matters affecting the Society's system of government;[8]

[8] The Institute of the Society of Jesus innovated in many respects on the provisions hitherto usual with Religious Orders. Whereas in other Orders the noviceship lasts but a single year, after which solemn vows are at once taken, both by the choir-religions and the lay-brothers, in the Society the noviceship lasts two years, after which the vows taken are 'simple', and, in case further experience proves the candidate unfit, can be dispensed by the General, whilst solemn vows are not taken till ten or more years later, and then only by a fraction of the Fathers. Again, whereas in other Orders promotion to the subdiaconate is not permitted till after the taking of the solemn vows, in the Society the last vows cannot be taken till after promotion to the priesthood. This difference of method doubtless means more than at first sight appears. Promotion to the subdiaconate and succeeding Orders is by the law of the Church not permitted until a *congrua*, i.e., some title or security for the maintenance of the candidate, is guaranteed. In a Religious Order this guarantee is supplied by the 'title of Poverty', or the obligation of the Order in which such a vow is taken, to provide a livelihood for its members. But if, urged the early adversaries of the Order, ordination is permitted to candidates tied to their Order only by the less durable bond of simple vows, the effect will be to let loose on the Church a number of priests exposed to temptation because unprovided with the means of living, or else of forcing the Bishops to maintain priests for whom they never made themselves responsible. And the danger, they urged, was the more serious because in the Society, unlike other Orders, it was not necessary before expelling a member to hold a formal trial with the hearing of witnesses, but the Superior was left unfettered, except for the obligation to see that he observed the substance of justice. It

(3) at other times *in reference* to various points of doctrine, to schools, exemptions, and privileges, which the local Ordinaries and other persons of high position in Church and State, declared to be injurious to their jurisdiction and rights;

(4) nor [in addition to these complaints about their Institute, etc.] have there been wanting grave accusations brought against the members themselves, which [accusations] have disturbed not a little the peace and tranquillity of Christendom.[9]

In this section at all events it will be conceded that the Brief confines itself to recording the bare fact that serious charges were brought against the Society and its members, and refrains from deciding how far they were justified. 'Grave seeds of discord, etc.', it says, have sprung up, and it enumerates under four headings the questions 'in reference to which' the discord has raged; and there it ends. Moreover, of these four headings, the two first, which are placed on the same footing as the rest, were about points of the Institute every one of which had been approved and decreed by the Holy See itself in its various Bulls of Foundation and Confirmation up to that time; and it is inconceivable that the members should be condemned for their obedience to such Constitutions. In the third heading the

---

was thus they objected to the novelties in the Society's Institute, and it is not disputed that there was weight in the objections. Still the Institute would not have been approved in regard to these particulars so often by the Holy See had there not been a deal to say on the other side, and in our own times the distinction between first and last vows, respectively simple and solemn, has even been extended by the Holy See to the other Orders. On the other hand, in our own days, when by the impoverishment of the episcopal funds the difficulty about maintenance of expelled Religious has been intensified, the Holy See has sought to meet it by some prudent legislation. Also in other Orders the local Superiors were elected by the chapters of the monasteries, whilst in the Society they were appointed by the General whose power, though far from absolute and unlimited, was much more extensive than in the older Orders. These and other innovations on past usage were all motived by the requirements of the special work which the Society set before it, and as such were most distinctly sanctioned by the Apostolic See; at the same time they excited the animosity of other Orders, who also took offence at the many privileges bestowed by the Popes on the Society, and not unnaturally laid stress on the decrees of Trent which sanctioned their own usage.

[9] Moñino, it will be remembered, advised that in stating the historical reasons for the suppression, the Brief should abstain from entering into details. The text of the Brief offers convincing proof that he followed his own recommendation. It will be difficult, for instance, to gather what precisely is referred to here under the phrase 'grave accusations against the members themselves'. Still there were no doubt grave accusations against individual Jesuits, just as there were against individual members of other bodies.

contentions indicated had been over the meaning and application of the Church's teaching and the privileges granted to the Society for the furtherance of its work, and it is otherwise known from history of the events that when the authority of the Holy See was invoked to settle this class of controversies, at times the decision was adverse to the Jesuits, but as often in their favour. In the fourth heading the conduct of the members is no doubt in question, but the abstention from deciding how far the accusations brought against them were well-founded or not is here particularly marked. This, however, is a point on which we are anxious not to be misunderstood. We are far from affirming that members of the Society were never to blame in the cases where charges were brought against them by others, either in this early stage of their history to which the present section belongs, or in its sequel. Of course they were, on many occasions, as likewise were their opponents. How could it be otherwise in a long course of years when oppositions of interest embroil large bodies of men who on neither side are altogether free from the infirmities of human nature? Still, what we claim now is that Clement XIV nowhere in this section decides between the contending parties, or declares that the blame was preponderantly on the Jesuit side, but merely argues that as there were certain features in the Society's Institute which were special to itself and excited the opposition of others, with results disastrous to the peace of the Church, it had better be suppressed.

The two next following paragraphs supply more details as to these 'early seeds of discord' of which the Society was the cause or occasion, and they are details the character of which tends to confirm what we have been saying. These complaints, the Brief says, were laid before Paul IV, Pius V, and Sixtus V, being supported by the instances of certain princes, notable among whom was Philip II of Spain. This King, it explains, having 'received from the Spanish Inquisitors protests against the immoderate privileges of the Society', and certain articles of complaint even from certain 'members of the Society conspicuous for their learning and piety', had transmitted them to Sixtus V asking him for an Apostolic Visitor to inquire into the matter.[10]

[10] The Provincial of Castile had judged and expelled one of his subjects for a crime which the Spanish Inquisitors claimed as belonging exclusively to their competence. They also contended that he was usurping their jurisdiction by granting permission to his subjects to read heretical books. The members of the Society who addressed complaints to Philip II were a small knot of Spanish Fathers who were anxious on their own account to change the Institute in some particulars, and their opposition to Father General Aquaviva on these grounds formed a

'Sixtus V acceded to this request, which he held to be just, and chose for the office of Apostolic Visitor a Bishop remarkable for his prudence, virtue, and learning; and he also nominated a Congregation of Cardinals who were to see to the execution of the design.' This Pontiff, however, 'dying prematurely, his salutary plan remained frustrate, and (the new Pontiff) Gregory XIV by his Bull of 28 June, 1591, re-confirmed the Institute of the Society, and ratified all the privileges granted to it by his predecessors, especially the privilege by which it was enabled to expel a member by a summary process, instead of by the usual formal trial.' Gregory XIV also forbade under pain of excommunication any further attack upon the Institute, Constitutions, or Decrees of the said Society – 'allowing only a recourse to the Roman Pontiff for the time being, on the part of any person who should desire to see them changed in any way.'

By applying the term 'salutary plan' to the contemplated measure of Sixtus V, Clement XIV no doubt insinuated his regret that the Jesuit Institute had not been then changed; still in narrating what was done by Gregory XIV, under whose Pontificate the dispute was decided,

---

painful episode in the early history of the Society which could, not inaptly, be called 'seeds of dissension springing up'. The prime motive of their dissatisfaction was that, whereas the Society was of Spanish origin and its first three Generals had been Spanish, and even the fourth a subject of the Spanish Crown, Aquaviva was an Italian, and was deemed by these few discontented Spaniards to be governing without due regard for the condition of their country. Hence they were working to get a practically independent Superior, or Commissary, for the Spanish Jesuits, and for their Provincial Congregation a certain right of legislating and electing Superiors – two points for which precedents could be found in other Orders. The chief among these Fathers were Fr Hernandez, Fr Diego Vazquez (to be distinguished from Fr Gabriel Vasquez, the theologian), and, when the controversy revived a few years later, the four brothers Acosta, Fr Henriquez de Henrique, and probably Fr Mariana, who took no open part in the movement, but whose book (if it is his), abstracted from his papers and published by a member of some other Order, gives in detail and with much skill a catalogue of their complaints. These men had considerable influence with Philip II and other powerful persons, and in this way were able to obtain results out of proportion to their numbers and personal importance. Philip II had a great esteem for the Society which he protected and encouraged throughout his reign, but like all despots he magnified his own authority, and was pleased with the idea of changes which would place the Society more effectually in his hands. Hence it was that he consented to ask Sixtus V to allow a Visitor (the Bishop of Cartagena) to inquire into the state of the Spanish Provinces, so as to prepare the ground for the desired changes. Sixtus V assented very willingly to the proposal, being himself anxious to remove from the Institute its exceptional features. Two things however combined to prevent these changes from being made – for Fr Persons, sent by Aquaviva to Philip II, persuaded him for the time to forego his design, and Sixtus V was succeeded, after the thirteen days' reign of Urban VII, by Gregory XIV, who instead of carrying out the designs of Sixtus, confirmed afresh the peculiar features of the Institute and condemned the innovators.

he was constrained to make his own Brief testify that at least as far as concerned these 'early seeds of discord', the judgment of his See had acquitted the main body of the Society and condemned the assailants of their Institute.

Another section now follows in the Brief of Suppression in which it laments that all these endeavours on the part of the Holy See had no success in silencing the clamours and complaints against the Society, but that on the contrary –

1. The entire world was filled more and more by contentions *concerning the Society's doctrine,* which many people denounced as contrary to the orthodox faith and to sound morality.[11]
2. *Dissensions* among the members grew bitter, and *accusations* multiplied, and they were *denounced as* animated by an excessive cupidity for worldly goods. From all which sources originated those well-known disturbances which caused the Holy See so much grief and trouble, and caused some princes to take measures against the Society.

Here again, the structure of the sentence shows that only the existence of dissensions arising out of accusations made and leading to disturbances, is declared, without there being a single word, at all events of direct statement, to affix the guilt in any quarter. An account is, indeed, added of a Bull of Paul V, dated 1606, which the Jesuits had been 'compelled to ask of him', and in which he confirmed certain decrees enacted by the Jesuits in their Fifth General Congregation, held in 1593, one of which decrees Clement XIV quotes *verbatim* from the Bull of Paul V, introducing the quotation by these words:

> In these decrees it is acknowledged in discreet language that it was domestic quarrels and disturbances within its own body, and complaints

---

[11] By the doctrine 'which many denounced as contrary to the orthodox faith' must be meant Molina's doctrine of *scientia media,* by which it was attempted to harmonize the apparently incompatible doctrines of divine predestination and human free-will. It was denounced by the Dominican theologians, and gave rise to the famous discussions between the two Schools and to the Congregations *de Auxiliis.* Clement VIII was inclined to decide against the Molinist doctrine, but Paul V finally determined that both it and the opposing Thomistic doctrine might be taught, each side being bidden to refrain from denunciations of the other. It is not so easy to say what were the Jesuit doctrines denounced at that time as 'contrary to sound morality', for the campaign against the Moral theologians of the Society originated with the misrepresentations of Pascal, and belonged to the next chronological stage – in the paragraph describing which there is curiously no reference to them.

and charges brought against it by externs, which had impelled the Jesuits assembled in General Congregation to pass the decree quoted.[12]

But here also nothing is affirmed save the existence of certain complaints and charges, quarrels and consequent disturbances, and the measures taken by the Society to remove all possible occasion for them; nor is there any blame.

The third section surveys the next chronological stage, a stage extending from the beginning of the seventeenth century to the accession of Clement XIV. It is of the same character as the preceding, and begins by lamenting that 'neither the aforesaid measures or the many others afterwards taken' had proved to 'be of sufficient force and authority to eradicate and disperse the disturbances, the accusations, and the complaints brought against the said Society.' And it enumerates as having laboured in vain for this end, 'Urban VIII, Clements IX, X, XI, XII, Alexanders VII, VIII, Innocents X, XI, XII, XIII, and Benedict XIV'.

These Pontiffs, it says,

> strove to restore to the Church the desired tranquillity by publishing many salutary Constitutions:
> (1) *about* secular transactions such as ought not to be undertaken either apart from Sacred Missions or in connection with them;[13]
> (2) *about* grave disputes and quarrels with local Ordinaries, Religious

---

[12] In this paragraph Moñino's hand is particularly discernible. It is so worded as to convey the idea that Paul V was displeased with the Society, and had only consented to confirm their Institute on condition that they cut off the source of their internal dissensions by passing a decree in their General Congregation which should put an end to their interference in politics. There is, however, no ground for this under the Bull of Paul V, which grants the Society a most cordial approval, condemns strongly the actions of 'the members of the Society conspicuous for their prudence, piety, and virtue', whom it calls 'disturbers of their Order and instigators to rebellion', and orders the General to punish them severely. In approving, too, the decree against meddling with politics this Bull has not a single word to suggest that the decree had been exacted. It was, in fact, passed in a Congregation held during the previous Pontificate, and gave expression to a very earnest feeling on the part of Aquaviva and the Fathers of the Congregation. Several Jesuit Fathers had been drawn into the troubles in France caused by the civil wars of the League and the disputed succession. Aquaviva had tried his best to stop them, but Kings and even Popes had stood in his way; and just on that account, lest the same thing should happen again, the Congregation was anxious now that its decree should be corroborated by Papal authority.

[13] No such Constitution directed specially against the Jesuits was ever published; but the Bull of Clement IX (1669) is probably meant. This, however, is addressed to the missionaries of all classes and Orders, and the Jesuits are only named among several others. Moreover, the Bull is directive not condemnatory.

Orders, [Guardians of] Pious Places, and Communities of one sort or another, in Europe, Asia, and America – which had been acrimoniously stirred up by the Society to the immense loss of souls, and the astonishment of populations;[14]

(3) *about* the interpretation which had been widely given to certain of the rites of the native races (*ethnicorum*),[15] and to the practice of these,

[14] Here is another paragraph so vague and general that it is difficult to identify the occurrences meant. Still, as they excited much attention, it may be presumed that by 'quarrels with the local Ordinaries' are meant the disputes with Bishop Palafox of Los Angelos, Bishop Cardenas of Asunción, and Archbishop Pardo of Manila. Of these, however, the only one which can be taken seriously is the first-named, and of it the chief wonder is that, considering the efforts then being made by the Spanish Court to obtain the beatification of Palafox, nothing more definite is said in the Brief about his controversy with the Society. As for the facts, the controversy turned on the question whether the Society really possessed certain exemptions, namely, from the obligation of paying tithes to the parish priests for their lands, and from the necessity of obtaining the Bishop's permission to preach and perform other spiritual ministrations. The controversy caused much friction and led to further steps taken on either side, the lawfulness of which became again matter of controversy, and all was eventually referred to Rome in 1646. The decision of the Holy See is contained in the Bull of Innocent X (16 April 1648), from which also the details of the dispute may be learnt. The decision was on the whole in favour of the Bishop, though in some points in favour of the Society. A subsequent letter, bearing the date of 1648, and purporting to be from Bishop Palafox, brings serious and general charges against the Society, charges so exaggerated that the Bishop's character rather than the Society's has been compromised by its language. This letter, in fact, was treated by the Congregation of Rites as a powerful argument against his beatification; its authenticity was, however, questioned.

[15] This clause refers to the famous controversies about the Chinese and Malabar rites. The missionary to heathen races usually finds himself confronted by a serious difficulty in their attachment to their native practices. When these are free from all religious meaning (and of course free also from a moral taint), there is no reason why they should not be tolerated, just as on the other hand there can be no question of tolerating them when they are clearly idolatrous. But between these extremes there can be cases such that it is uncertain to which of these two categories they should be referred, and in particular there may be cases where some practice which had a religious and therefore superstitious meaning has lost it, and become purely civil through some general change in the ideas of the people – as has happened in regard to the names of the days of the week, which now-a-days suggest to no man the heathen gods to which they were once dedicated. Such was the controversy about Chinese and Malabar rites. The Chinese had a custom of honouring Confucius and their own ancestors, by certain prostrations, incensings, and oblations, and the Hindus emphasized their caste distinctions by certain purifications, etc., and particularly by wearing round the neck cords twisted out of differently coloured threads, the colours of which indicated their descent from the gods. Persecutions loomed in the distance if these were forbidden to the converts; but the Jesuit missionaries thought they could be tolerated on the ground that the more educated natives had ceased to regard them as other than merely civil ceremonies, and the converts could be taught to do the

with the omission of rites duly approved by the Universal Curch;[16]

(4) *about* the use and meaning of propositions which the Apostolic See has deservedly condemned as scandalous, and clearly opposed to sound moral conduct;[17]

(5) or *about* other matters of great importance and most necessary for preserving the purity of Christian dogmas, and from which in our age, not less than in past times, many evils and inconveniences have resulted – to wit, tumults and disturbances in some Catholic regions, and persecutions in certain provinces of Asia and Europe.

This is the portion of the Brief in which the nearest approach is made to the language of condemnation, for it cannot be denied that there is an implication running through it that the Jesuits had been in the wrong in regard to the various matters which had called forth these 'many salutary Constitutions'. Still it is not by mere implication that

---

same. The missionaries of other Orders took a stricter view and thought that the converts must be absolutely forbidden to take part in them. The question was referred to the Holy See as early as 1645; but owing to the difficulty of ascertaining the truth about the facts, which the opposite parties reported differently, the investigation was prolonged till the time of Clement XI, who decided it against the Jesuit missionaries for India in 1704, and for China in 1710. This closed one stage in the distressing history; but unfortunately some of the missionaries withheld compliance with Clement XI's decision on various pleas, such as that the facts had not been correctly represented to the Holy See. In this way the controversy was prolonged till the days of Benedict XIV, who in 1742 for China, and in 1744 for India, issued dogmatic Bulls in which he confirmed the decisions of his predecessors in the most solemn manner, and terminated the controversy for ever. There is nothing in either Clement's or Benedict's Bulls to show that they blamed the Society as a whole for its part in the controversy; but it is clear that they both regarded some of the Jesuit missionaries as guilty of disobedience to the orders of the Holy See, and not, as it would appear, without solid reason. One might accordingly have expected the Brief of Suppression to profit by this occasion, and recite not merely the fact that this controversy had caused solicitude to the Holy See and drawn forth from it salutary constitutions to remedy the evil, but also that it had condemned the missionaries. It abstained, however, from availing itself of this opportunity, and kept here as elsewhere to its purely negative attitude.

[16] The natives of India were scandalized at the use of saliva, of salt, and of insufflations in the administration of Baptism, and the missionaries thought therefore that these ceremonies, not being essential, might be omitted for a time till the Indians were better instructed; and Clement XII, in 1734, gave a dispensation to this effect to last for ten years, a dispensation which Benedict XIV, in 1744, renewed for another ten years, after which the omission was to cease altogether.

[17] Here again the vagueness of the allusions makes it difficult to identify their object. Probably what are meant are certain benignant interpretations put by some of the missionaries on certain propositions to be found in the works of Confucius and other Chinese authorities, as well as affirmations of the suitability of a certain Chinese term to denote the God of the Christians.

Briefs of Condemnation are wont to pronounce their judgments on the guilty, as may be seen in the Briefs suppressing the Humiliati, the Religious of SS. Ambrose and Barnabas, and the Basilians, which express their sense of the misconduct of these Religious in the directest form and in no measured terms. And it is precisely this direct language of condemnation which is conspicuous by its absence in the Brief *Dominus et Redemptor*, in the present section as well as in the foregoing – for here as there, all that is directly stated is that previous Popes made certain 'salutary Constitutions' *about* certain disputes over secular transactions etc., the terms and purport of the Constitutions being in no wise specified.

But the section does not terminate here. It goes on to say that the persistence of the tumults, disturbances, and persecutions in so many places

> caused much grief to the successive Popes, among whom Innocent XI felt himself in consequence compelled to forbid the Jesuits to continue to receive novices; Innocent XIII felt obliged to threaten them with the same penalty;[18] and Benedict XIV deemed it necessary to order a visitation of their houses and colleges in Portugal,...whilst on the other hand no consolation to the Apostolic See, or support to the Society, or advantage to Christendom, resulted from the recent letter, extorted rather than petitioned,[19]...of our immediate predecessor Clement XIII of recent memory...in which the Society of Jesus was highly commended and again approved.

---

[18] The only reference we can find to this is a declaration of Propaganda, cited by Crétineau-Joly (Tome 4e, p. 376), in which Innocent XI is recommended 'to forbid the Father General and the whole Society to receive novices, or admit to vows, simple or solemn, under pain of nullity and other penalties according to the pleasure of his Holiness, until they obey effectually and prove that they have obeyed the decrees and ordinations which have been made in reference to the said missions.' This refers to the case of the Chinese and Indian rites, in regard to which, as has been said, it was thought that the missionaries were resisting the Apostolic orders, and that the General was not taking sufficiently drastic measures to compel their submission. This prohibition was, on a petition from the General, shortly after withdrawn, but Père Norbert, in the Preface to the fifth volume of his *Mémoires Historiques,* says that Innocent XIII contemplated a similar prohibition in 1720. This however was never actually issued, and Benedict XIII in 1725 withdrew the proposal to inflict it, after hearing from Father General Tamburini what efforts he had made.

[19] From the fact that such words occur in a Papal Brief, we can infer that such a document can be 'extorted rather than solicited'. The external history, on the other hand, would seem to show that to the *Dominus et Redemptor* of Clement XIV, rather than to the *Apostolicum* of Clement XIII, this characterization applies.

At least this portion, it will be said, lays the blame at the door of the Jesuits. But it is not so.

The insinuation no doubt continues; but there is as little as ever of direct condemnation. It is the tumults and discussions themselves, not the conduct of the Jesuits in exciting them which is said to have caused grief to the Popes and moved two of them to provide, by forbidding the further admission of novices, for the gradual extinction of the Order.

The next section is concerned with the reign of Clement XIII.

> After all these fierce storms and tempests it was the hope of every right-minded person that a time of peace and tranquillity would at length dawn. (On the contrary, during the Pontificate of Clement XIII) the times became more difficult and disturbed than ever. The clamours and complaints against the Society grew daily more loud; and things got so bad that dangerous seditions sprang up in some places, together with tumults, dissensions, and scandals which burst the bond of Christian charity, and kindled in the minds of the faithful party aims, hatreds and enmities; whence it came to pass that the Kings of France, Spain, and Portugal, and the Two Sicilies, who till then had regarded it as their hereditary right to show liberality to the Society, were compelled to banish all its members from their dominion; deeming this to be the only remedy for all these evils, and absolutely necessary if Christian populations were to be prevented from tearing one another to pieces in the very bosom of our holy mother the Church. Moreover, as these sovereigns felt that this their remedy could not be securely established unless the Society itself was utterly extinguished and suppressed, they represented their wishes to the said Clement XIII and uniting their instances urged him with all the authority they possessed, to provide in this effectual way for the security of their subjects, and the good of the Universal Church. The unexpected death of that Pontiff stayed the course and conclusion of these negotiations in his days, but as soon as by Divine clemency we were ourselves placed in the same See of Peter the self-same prayers, petitions, and desires were laid before us, along with the desires and opinions of several Bishops and other persons conspicuous for their station, learning, and piety.

This is the last paragraph in the historical part of the Brief. The previous chapters of this book have supplied the materials from which it can be judged in what relation this representation stands to the facts, but we are still chiefly solicitous to note how, whatever may be the force of the implied suggestion, there is the same curious avoidance of any words which could directly lay the blame for the dissensions excited at the door of the Society.

To this extent then it is the case that the Brief of Suppression, although it suppresses the Society, does so without condemning it, and - we will venture to repeat it once more - the significance of such a fact is very great, not only whilst we regard the Brief as emanating from the Holy See which clothed it with its authority, but still more when we regard it as emanating from the Spanish Court which first composed its text and forced its acceptance by the direst threats on the unwilling Pontiff - significant from the former point of view, because it leaves the Society's reputation untouched, more significant from the latter, because the Spanish Court had used the most direct and unqualified language of condemnation in its own *Consultas* and *Memorials,* and we may be sure that Moñino would not have watered it all down into the evasive non-committal phrases we find in the Brief, except for the consciousness that he had absolutely no proofs of guilt to produce.

Still this undercurrent of insinuation does run through the Brief, and it would be unsatisfactory to leave its significance unestimated. We may put the case thus in the words of Gutiérrez de la Huerta:

> From this portrait [of the Society, drawn by direct statement in the Spanish *Consultas,* and after them by implied suggestion in the Brief of Suppression] one might gather that the history of the Society of Jesus from its foundation to the moment of its abolition, had been the history of crimes, malefactions, impieties, sacrileges, and parricides: that in this corporation not a single one of the religious and social virtues had ever been exercised, and that since its foundation, far from rendering any useful services or yielding any salutary fruits, in the States which had admitted and protected it, it had been the abiding domestic cause of all the commotions, upheavals, and scandals that had afflicted those States in the course of time.

And if this portraiture of the Society is there in the Brief, is not that condemnation?

But granted that this is so, there are two considerations which blunt the edge of the latter question. (1) The fact remains that the condemnation is not pronounced in the straightforward language of direct statement, but is merely insinuated with the aid of dexterous phrasing. Now so tortuous a method is quite unusual in a Papal decree, and occurs here in a document the whole history of which shows it to have been *extortum potius quam impetratum.* Are we not justified then in perceiving here the hands indeed of Esau but the voice of Jacob? - especially as the authority of a Papal Brief is seen most in its operative part? (2) And if so, are we not entitled to take note of what is unquestionably the most remarkable feature in the Brief?

'The fiscal [says Gutierrez of himself] has not failed to observe how dexterous pencils have contrived to trace this picture by bringing together all the strongest hues without feeling obliged to tone them down by including the shades.' In other words, Moñino's method was to leave out everything that might tell to the credit of the Society, and had gained for it words of commendation from a whole series of Popes, and to pick out and mass together all the episodes in its history which rightly or wrongly lent themselves to the composition of an unpleasant picture. Is there a Religious Order in the world, one asks, at least one that has endured for a lengthened period, had a varied life, and engaged in work calculated to arouse oppositions of interest, or any institution or body of men, but must needs have its character hopelessly blackened if the admissibility of such a test is acknowledged?

Conclusion[1]

We have followed the history of the Suppression through all its stages, but it may be convenient to conclude by summarizing the results to which we have been led.

The first thing to note is that the destroying legions were not homogeneous. They belonged to different classes who, whilst uniting in the same means, were employing it for different ends. The oldest enemies of the Society were the legal families in France, who by a kind of prescription had come to form almost exclusively the *personnel* of the French *Parlements*, especially of the powerful *Parlement* of Paris. These families were by a three-fold title the traditional enemies of the Jesuits. As the representatives of the civil law and exercising many of the functions of State government, they had been ever since the time of the Pragmatic Sanction the great stronghold of Gallicanism in the country, and were proportionately adverse to an Order dedicated in a special manner to the defence of the rights of the Holy See. As intimately connected with the University of Paris, whose *personnel* had likewise through many centuries been largely recruited from their ranks, they had shared its jealousy of a religious Order which first entered Paris at a time when the University was temporarily decadent, and resented the rivalry of Colleges which taught gratuitously and were staffed by teachers of the highest qualifications. As closely connected with the original Jansenists – the Arnaulds, the Pascals, and others, who sprang from the same family stock – they identified themselves with Jansenism throughout, and were once more brought into conflict with the Order which from first to last was the uncompromising opponent of that heresy. We are far from meaning to imply that there were no exceptions to the anti-Jesuit spirit thus engendered among the Parlementaire families, for there were some conspicuous exceptions. But the general trend of

[1] *The Month*, 102 (1903), 171–84.

feeling among these families, and the bodies they constituted, was one of bitter hostility to the Society; and this hostility, as often happens, had hardened in intensity with the course of time and the repetition of conflicts, and by the middle of the eighteenth century had been rendered specially acute by the controversies over the Bull *Unigenitus*.

The Jansenists were hostile to the Society because of its rigid orthodoxy, but had this in common with it that they believed in Christianity. The Encyclopaedists, though allied with the Jansenists in intriguing for its destruction, were actuated by a downright hatred for the Christian religion. For prudential reasons they disavowed this hatred in their public speech, and professed to be loyal sons of the Church. But it formed a common topic in their private correspondence with one another, and was the mainspring of their secret intrigues. They saw no great distinction between Jesuits and Jansenists, except that the Jesuits appeared to them the more dangerous foes; and they desired the extinction of both, but of the Jesuits first, because, if this were first achieved, they believed that the other would quickly follow. The writings of Voltaire and d'Alembert at this time are full of such sentiments. Thus

> the nation [writes the latter, in his essay, *Sur la destruction des Jésuites*[2]] is beginning to grow enlightened, and will become so increasingly ... Disputes on religion will be despised, and fanaticism [by which name these people were wont to designate Catholic faith and piety] will be held in horror. The magistrates who have proscribed the fanaticism of the Jesuits are too enlightened, too good citizens, too conformed to the spirit of their age, to suffer another fanaticism to succeed to theirs ... The Jesuits were the regular troops, recruited and disciplined under the standard of superstition; they were the Macedonian Phalanx which it behoved Reason to see broken up and destroyed. The Jansenists are merely the Cossacks and Pandours whom Reason will make cheap work of, as soon as they have to fight alone and dispersed.

The third class distinguishable among the allied foes of the Society were the Regalists. These were few in number, but being Ministers of State, actual or potential, had the Royal power in their hands, and so could execute the measures which the Sectarians and Encyclopaedists could only demand and intrigue for. Regalism is but an aspect of Despotism, being its attitude towards the ecclesiastical jurisdiction. For despotism chafes under every limitation set to its power, and when it is brought in conflict with the ecclesiastical juris-

[2] Published in 1764, just after the promulgation of the Royal Edict banishing the Jesuits from the kingdom.

diction inevitably seeks to enslave it. Regalism is thus a malady of the civil power to which it has been liable in all ages, but was never more pronounced or more virulent than in the eighteenth century – two things then conducing to this result, one that the absolute monarchs on the thrones of Continental Europe held the most despotic ideas; the other that by that time able lawyers and theologians in the service of the State had wrought the principles of Regalism into a coherent scientific system. Thus the end in view which, working on these lines, the eighteenth century Regalists set before themselves was well described by Clement XIII in his protest against the action of the Government of Parma in 1768. It was

> to detach the faithful and keep them apart from the Head of the Church, the sheep from their Shepherd, and the result is to oppress the ecclesiastical jurisdiction, to overthrow the sacred hierarchy, to diminish the Rights of the Holy See, to subordinate his authority to the civil power, and to enslave the Church of God, which is free.

There have been Jesuits attached to Courts who have yielded to the atmosphere there prevalent, and advocated the claims of Regalism. Of such a character, as Fraile Miguélez proves,[3] was P. Rábago, confessor to Ferdinand VI, and the last of the Jesuit royal confessors at the Spanish Court. But the Society as a whole was identified with the opposite principles, and the influence of its writers, its professors, its preachers, above all of its central government, was exercised in that direction. It lay, therefore, across the path which the Regalists were pursuing.

Still another set must be taken into account which, though less virulent in its animosities, contributed to swell the torrent of hostility by which the Society was eventually swept away. This was a party composed not indeed of the secular clergy or the other religious orders as entire wholes – for to many of these the Society was indebted for sympathy and aid in the time of its troubles – but of numerous sections of their members who resented the preponderant influence which the Society had acquired for itself, principally through the means of its schools. There is no reason to suppose that these ecclesiastics believed in the monstrous crimes imputed to the Society, or that they would have wished in the first instance a measure so drastic as the entire suppression of the Order. But when they saw the turn events were taking, and that this was the goal towards which they were tending, they welcomed it as a means of

[3] *Jansenismo y Regalismo en España*. By Fraile Miguelez, O.S.A. See the letter of P. Rábago to Cardinal Portacassero in the Appendix.

deliverance from distasteful competitors, and perhaps did not advert to the enormous injustice to individuals inseparable from the actual execution of such a measure.

These four classes were broadly distinguishable among the foes of the Society, but of course they overlapped and interfused one another to some extent, besides which they were reinforced by others who were either the dupes of their misrepresentations, or else were State servants, like de Bernis, prepared to execute the commands of their masters, whatever these might be.

We have seen, however, from the foregoing narrative that, if the Society had powerful enemies leagued together for its destruction, it had also friends to take its side, who, if less powerful, were probably more numerous, and were not inconspicuous for their virtue and piety. These certainly must not be excluded from the reckoning, if we are to form a correct estimate of the circumstances under which the suppression was carried out. Such was the French episcopate with hardly an exception which testified so strongly in their favour in 1762; such were the Bishops of Spain and other countries who solicited and applauded the *Apostolicum* in 1764. Such was the mass of the Cardinals and prelates at Rome, who created such a difficulty for the skilful negotiators of the suppression, – compelling them to involve their proceedings in a dense secrecy, and to set aside the usual and becoming methods by which a measure like the suppression should have been prepared. Such was the multitude of their adherents and defenders in every country, priests, religious, and laity, whom it pleased their enemies to call Tertiaries, and of whose resistance to their policy they were so continually complaining. It is impossible to estimate the proportion in which they stood to the opposite party, but we can gather something from the acknowledgment of a contemporary writer like the traveller Duclos, himself an Encyclopaedist in his sympathies, for, 'I do not hesitate to declare', he says, 'and I have been a closely-placed spectator of the transactions, that the Jesuits had and still have more partizans than adversaries ... Speaking generally the provinces [of France] regret the loss of the Jesuits, and they would, if they were to reappear among them, be received with acclamation;'[4] we may gather something too from 'the multitude of representations from the provinces, cities, towns, and villages of Spain', of which Ferdinand VII speaks in his Ordinance[5] of 29 May, 1815 – at the time when the storms of the Revolution were temporarily appeased – as 'daily addressed to him by Archbishops, Bishops, ecclesiastics, and some laymen', and 'supplicating him to re-establish

[4] *Voyage en Italie*, p. 52.
[5] Apud de Ravignan, *Clément XIII et Clément XIV*, i. p. 547.

the Society throughout his dominions', for are we not entitled to see in these multitudinous representations the distant echoes of the regrets passed down to their descendants by those who had been witnesses of the expulsion and its consequences? And may we not draw a like inference from the language of Pius VII's Bull of Restoration,[6] which speaks of petitions addressed to him in the same sense from many regions of the earth?

Our study has also shown what part in the campaign against the Society was taken by the different classes of its enemies. Although their hostility was of long standing they do not seem in the first instance to have formed any definite plans for concerted action, or to have contemplated an end so drastic as entire suppression. One thing led on to another. It was Pombal who set the ball rolling, and although the antagonism between his ideals of life and those of the Catholic Church must sooner or later have involved him in a conflict with the Society, it would appear that the accident of the troubles over the Treaty of Exchange was what first kindled his wrath against the Order. When it was seen how easily he was able to expel it from the Portuguese dominions, the hopes of its enemies elsewhere were raised, and they began to ask themselves whether a similar policy might not be successful in other countries. The diffusion of virulent anti-Jesuit pamphlets now began. It had indeed already been initiated by Pombal, who circulated everywhere his *Brevis Relatio* with its imaginary account of a Jesuit empire founded across the ocean. But it was now taken up energetically by Jansenists and others who started special presses for the purpose at Paris and Lugano, as also at Rome itself where Don Manuel de Roda and a few others formed a kind of head-centre for the administration of this campaign of defamation.

These pamphlets were quite uncritical, and scattered unauthenticated charges, scandalous inventions, rehashes of ancient calumnies, in the most virulent language, and with reckless disregard for responsibility – much in the same way that ultra-Protestant agencies or newspaper correspondents do now. They were mostly anonymous and were often circulated from hand to hand by private means. Spain, Italy, and France were particularly flooded with them, and the Bishops in their letters to Clement XIII make frequent mention of the harm they did. Thus Cardinal de Solís, the same who afterwards at the bidding of his Sovereign forced on the election of Clement XIV, says in his letter to Clement XIII of 19 June 1789: 'It is impossible to count the defamatory libels, the satires, the impious and calumnious

---

[6] The *Sollicitudo Ecclesiarum*, of 7 August 1814 [also now available in English, cf. Thomas M. McCoog, S.J., ed., '*Promising Hope*', 2003, pp. 323–330. *Ed. N.*].

writings (grieved over and condemned by the Bishops, the Supreme Councils of the Inquisition and Castille, and every prudent and God-fearing man) which envy and malice has stirred up for the ruin of the good name and high credit of the venerable Order and Institute.'[7] We know how easily simple-minded people can be taken in by literature of this kind, and can readily believe that the effect must have been to convert many former friends of the Society into its adversaries, and prepare the ground for the action of the statesmen.

The Lavalette affair gave the Paris *Parlement* its opportunity, and it may be that its original idea was merely to weaken the Society by draining off its financial resources. In any case, the subsequent idea of inquiring into the Constitutions was cleverly devised and led on to all that followed; but according to d'Alembert it was only the extraordinary energy of the Abbé Chauvelin and one or two others which was able to carry the business through and bring it to an issue so antecedently improbable. 'I know not,' he wrote to Voltaire on 31 March 1762, 'what will become of the religion of Jesus, but His Society has come to rags and tatters. What Pascal, Nicolas, and Arnauld could not do, it appears that three or four absurd fanatics will prove able to carry through.' Still even these three or four fanatics would not have been able to carry through what was, after all, a gross invasion of the royal power, as embodied in the various edicts by which the Society and its many houses were authorized, had not the royal power at this particular time been in the hands of so weak and *insouciant* a monarch; and it was here that Madame de Pompadour's quarrel with the Society was of so much service to them. Had it not been for the accident of her applying for absolution to a Jesuit confessor, who had no course save to refuse it, Louis XV would never have been gained over as he was, to tolerate and even to confirm by Royal Edict the decrees of the *Parlement*. And it is in this sense, though the woman did not live to see the final results, that her influence over her royal paramour must be accounted one of the determining causes of the Suppression.

The Encyclopaedists took no open part in the transactions of the campaign, but they claimed it none the less as their own campaign, conducted under their orders and for their interest. 'The sections of the *Parlement*', wrote d'Alembert on 4 May 1762, 'are not going sluggishly to work. They think they are serving Religion, but it is Reason they are serving, though without suspecting it. They are the executioners of high justice, on behalf of Philosophy, whose orders they are taking without knowing it.' What he means, and what was

---

[7] Ravignan, *ibid.* ii. p. 132.

the case, is that this party was exercising its influence against the Jesuits through the press and the *salons,* and particularly through its intimacy with the leading statesmen, such as Choiseul, de Terray, d'Aiguillon, Bernis, Aranda, Tanucci, and others.

In Spain, as we have seen, the Jesuits were fully aware that a strong party wished to see them destroyed there as well as in Portugal and France; but they imagined the King and his Ministers to be their protectors. They had grounds for so thinking, for they had not been reprehended in any way by the authorities, but, on the contrary, were receiving constant marks of the royal confidence. Hence when the blow fell on 1 April 1767, it came upon them as a bolt from the blue. Now, however, we know from the private correspondence between the King and his confidential advisers, that they were concealing their real sentiments until the dramatic moment should come, but had determined on a Regalist policy, and a *coup* against the Jesuits, as far back as 1759, when Carlos III passed from the Neapolitan to the Spanish throne. To this extent, therefore, the King must have acted with a full knowledge of what he was doing; but something more is required to explain the intense aversion and the ruthless cruelty with which he pursued his Jesuit subjects, and afterwards the entire Society, as though they were men unfit to live in a civilized land. In this respect we have seen reason for believing that he was the dupe of others. Though a man of principle he was not a man of much intelligence, and never realized the necessity of giving both sides a hearing; and his unscrupulous Ministers, by a dexterous manipulation of Jesuit writings, and a dexterous manipulation of the facts of the Madrid riot, had succeeded in persuading him that the Jesuits did not scruple to assassinate sovereigns who refused to be subservient to their interests. It was through the false persuasion thus introduced into a stubborn and vindictive mind that the movement acquired the force and solidity which henceforth characterized it, and made the total destructipn of the Order inevitable.

The expulsions from Naples, Parma and Malta were the necessary consequence of the expulsion from Spain; and so too, for the reason just given, was the demand for an ecclesiastical suppression by the Holy See. But the history of this final stage of the campaign brought into prominence another very striking feature, namely, that of those who were the principal actors at this stage none save the Spanish King and his Ministers were acting from personal conviction. We have heard from the lips of Choiseul himself that the French Court was moved to co-operate in demanding and compelling the suppression, not because it desired it for its own sake, but because having once committed itself it could not withdraw without incurring the humiliation of a seeming defeat, and still more because its co-operation with the Spaniards was the price to be paid for maintaining the anti-English alliance. In other words, as far as the French Government was concerned, the suppression was a mere political job. Again, we have heard from the lips of Cardinal de Bernis, that he himself felt no more personal interest in the business he was negotiating than did Choiseul, which was as much as to say, that he was as ready to negotiate the suppression of any other religious order or institution if only his Court put him to the task; nor is it easy to believe that Cardinal de Solís, the Spanish agent at the Conclave of 1769, had changed his mind concerning the Jesuits since 1759, when he wrote of them in such glowing terms to Clement XIII; or Cardinal Orsini, the representative of Naples at the same Conclave, since the time, so shortly before, when he used Fr Ricci as his confessor. The view taken by these Cardinals and probably many others, was that their business was to sink personal convictions, and do the bidding of their Courts. Of the unwillingness of Clement XIV to consent to a measure which he only accorded after long resistance and to avoid still greater misfortunes, it is not necessary to add more than has been already said. It comes then to this, that of the many persons who played leading parts in the miserable drama, only a few were independently anxious for the destruction of the Society. Pombal and his few adherents in Portugal, the Abbé Chauvelin and his adherents in the *Parlement* of Paris, Carlos III (himself only duped) and his Regalist Ministers in Spain and Naples, and the Voltairian leaders and their sympathizers in the four countries concerned. And this is exactly what Clement XIII thought, as we learn from Cardinal Calmi, 'to whom', testifies the Cardinal in his conversation with Pius VI,[8] 'he said repeatedly that the war against the Society had been caused by four or five Ministers who had circumvented their sovereigns, and, having first succeeded in making themselves despotic in their cabinets, proceeded to form cabals – the existence of which they kept secret from their sovereigns – and maintained them active and united as a means of combating the Society and the Apostolic See.'

To indicate the chief agents in the suppression of the Society is to indicate the motives by which they were led. In the Jansenists it was the desire to see their chief theological opponents destroyed, and to ensure the triumph or at least the revenge of their own sect. In the Philosophers it was the desire, as they expressed it themselves, to see the Jesuits destroyed first, that the Catholic Church might be more easily destroyed afterwards. In Pombal and the Spanish Ministers it was the desire to remove an obstacle from the path of their Regalist policy. These were the true reasons for the suppression. As for the reasons which were

---

[8] Conversation with Pius VI on 1 April 1780. Apud Boero, *Osservazioni*, p. 185.

paraded in the *comptes-rendus* of the *Parlements*, the memorials of the four Courts, and the publications of the anti-Jesuit printing-press, the course of time has itself exposed the hollowness of many of them. No one now-a-days could without making himself ridiculous maintain that the Jesuits had set up an empire in South America under the rule of a Jesuit monarch, Nicholas I. Nor could any responsible writer in these days fail to acknowledge that the conditions of the Treaty of Exchange were sufficient of themselves to account for the rebellion of the natives, without attributing it to their Jesuit missionaries. The houses and papers of the Jesuits fell everywhere into the hands of their adversaries, but no traces were found of the extensive commerce through which the wealth of the Indies was supposed to have been converted into gold stored away in their vaults. And if, as they themselves acknowledged, they did on a large scale exchange the exports of the Reductions for European imports, the documentary proofs are now accessible which show that this was not trade in the sense prohibited by the Canon Law; that it was done in their capacity as procurators for the native converts, they themselves receiving from it not a penny of profit even under the form of commission or salary; that it was fully justified by the necessities of the case, the Indians being unable otherwise to protect themselves against the rapacity of the European colonists; and finally, that it had been again and again formally sanctioned by the Holy See and the Spanish and Portuguese Courts. Nor, again, would it be possible for a responsible modern historian to maintain that the Spanish and Portuguese Ministers had any evidence before them to convict the Jesuits of complicity in the Madrid riots, or the Lisbon attempt at regicide. None such is to be found in the State Archives of the two countries, or was ever submitted to a legal investigation; on the contrary, the whole character of their diplomacy in requiring the Holy See to punish the Order, whilst refusing to supply it with the proofs of its guilt which they professed to hold in their hands, is evidence which can be no longer disputed that they were perfectly well aware that no such proofs existed.

On the other hand, a collection like the *Extraits des Assertions*, which was perhaps the most effective of their libels, can still deceive honest minds incapable of detecting the fraud underlying its composition. The secret of the success of such a book is simply in its size, for only in a series of lengthy volumes which few readers would ever care to peruse would it be possible to expose all the acts of misquotation, excision, interpolation, and distortion of contexts, by which so many propositions are made to bear a sense which never entered into their authors' heads. We can, however, appeal to the authority of a witness unimpeachable in this respect, who describes the collection as we have ourselves done – 'as so barefaced a fraud that one does not know which to wonder at the most, the dishonesty or the audacity of the men (who composed it).'[9] We can appeal also, as in an earlier chapter,[10] to the exposure of the true character of the *Extraits des Assertions* contained in Archbishop de Beaumont's famous Pastoral of 28 October 1763, to which many French Bishops shortly afterwards gave in their adhesion, others preferring to write Pastorals of their own to the same effect. Nor did these prelates confine themselves to Pastorals, but wrote also to Clement XIII, who in his replies, for instance in his letter of 17 November 1762, to the Bishop of Sarlat, associated himself with their protests.

So much on the true motives by which the adversaries of the Society were led, and the false motives under which they endeavoured to conceal the true. But there is another aspect under which the sad story of the Suppression may present itself, and we have no wish to overlook it in this study. Granted, it may be said, that the chief authors of the Suppression were led by unworthy motives, were there not also some real defects in the conduct of the eighteenth century Jesuits sufficient to explain why truly good men – we refer particularly to the members of other religious orders – could take part with their enemies, and be glad rather than sorry to see their candlestick removed? This is practically the question raised by a modern writer whom we have more than once quoted, Fraile Miguélez, the author of *Jansenismo y Regalismo en España*.[11] Fraile Miguélez is an Augustinian, that is to say, a member of the Order whose General, Padre Vasquez, was, in association with Don Manuel de Roda, a leading spirit in the anti-Jesuit campaign. Fraile Miguélez, however is no mere partizan, but distributes praise and blame with impartial hand, on the basis of authentic documents, and on the whole justly. What he complains of and assigns as the true reason why so many religious communities belonging to other Orders took part with the enemies of the Society and worked for its suppression, or at all events sympathized with it, has already been noticed, namely, the enormous predominance over other Orders which the Society had gradually acquired. It had almost exclusive possession of the schools in which the youth of the higher classes were educated, and occupied the principal chairs in the Universities. This of course meant influence all round, for the link established between the Fathers and their

---

[9] Döllinger's Continuation of Hortig's *Manual of Church History*, ii. § 2, p. 792. We take this extract from Fr Duhr's *Jesuiten-Fabeln* (p. 437), to whose instructive chapters on the charges against Jesuit moral doctrine and their alleged defence of tyrannicide we are glad to be able to refer our readers.

[10] See above, ch. 2, pp. 68–69.

[11] pp. 308–312.

pupils tended to cement them together in afterlife, when the latter had themselves entered into positions of power. Thus the pulpits and confessionals of the Jesuits were frequented to the neglect of others, and their churches gleamed with the offerings of their many admirers. They had penetrated, too, into the Courts of Kings, where in like manner they seemed to absorb everything, being the confessors of kings and statesmen, and the instructors of their children. It does not appear that there was any serious fault in the Superiors of the Society, who had sanctioned the various offices and employments out of which this far-reaching predominance had sprung. That had happened to the Society which in turn has happened to each of the great religious orders; for each has had its 'booming-time' when by the very success of its methods and their adaptation to the particular age it was best able to offer to kings and people what these wanted. But it is not good that any one religious Order should have such a monopoly, for it is sure to irritate the others who find themselves excluded, and in the less noble characters to stir up resentments and jealousies; and this is precisely what it did. Nor is it good for the Order itself. We are not prepared to admit that the Old Society, on the whole, used her monopoly badly. On the contrary, when the true facts are liberated from the multitude of calumnies by which they have been overwhelmed, it seems to us that she honestly and on the whole successfully strove to use it for the promotion of God's glory and the diffusion of a just and Christian spirit through the ranks of her adherents. Still, human nature remains even under the habit of the Religious, nor is it good for human nature, particularly when under that habit, to be surrounded by so many subtle incitements to pride and self-complacency. And that these incitements had their effect is acknowledged by Fr Cordara, who in the concluding part of his *Commentarii,* sets it down as the providential reason why God allowed the terrible calamity to overtake his Order. We cannot indeed accept as true all that P. Cordara writes on the subject, for he can be very childish at times in his reflections, and is especially liable to be carried into exaggerations of the particular point he happens at the time to be labouring. Still, he was an eye-witness excellently placed, and, if we bear in mind that an Order is liable to get characterized by the conduct of its least, not its most perfect members, we can accept his testimony as substantially the truth, as we may also accept his judgment that the providential purpose of the suppression was to cut off excesses and teach lessons of moderation.

Nor must we finish with Fraile Miguélez without taking note of his other complaint against the Jesuits of the eighteenth century, namely, that they were too given to heresy-hunting. Of course vigilance is necessary to call attention to unsound and dangerous doctrines, which often lurk in the dark till they have acquired strength to do mischief. But there can be excess which finds unsound doctrine where it does not exist, and is over-ready to impute heterodox sentiments to theologians of adverse schools; and there can be a controversial acrimony introduced into treatises which should be conciliatory as well as firm in their tone. It was a charge against the Jesuits of those days that they were prone to scent Jansenism everywhere, just as some of their enemies were prone to scent Jesuitism everywhere; and certainly they do not appear to have been free from blame in the episode which specially stirred up the bile of the Augustinians against them, that is, in the agitation to get Cardinal Noris's *History of Pelagianism* put on the Index. It had been published at Rome as far back as 1673, and in spite of the efforts of Fr Macedo (once a Jesuit, then a Capuchin), who soon afterwards brought it before the Holy See, had not been put upon the Roman Index. It was unwarrantable therefore of Fr Cansani, SJ, to use his influence with the Grand Inquisitor to get it put upon the Spanish Index in 1747, and still more unwarrantable was it for Fr Osorio to contend that the book ought to remain on the Spanish Index, after Benedict XIV in 1749, had insisted on its removal.

These shortcomings in certain of the members of the condemned Order, and the part they had in swelling the forces of its adversaries, needed to be acknowledged, but they do not counterbalance the verdict which must be passed on the real authors of the Suppression, and the real motives which actuated them. It is for the reader now to consider, with the aid of the materials we have laid before him, what this verdict should be. But we may at least claim to have established one point, the point from which this publication commenced, and may contend that the question of Jesuit guilt or innocence of the many vices and crimes imputed to them is not to be decided against them straight off – according to the easy method which some have recommended – from the bare fact that Catholic rulers have at times expelled them from their dominions, and a Pope once suppressed them altogether.

Afterword

The Suppression of the Society of Jesus viewed from the twenty-first century

R. W. Truman

Early in June 1773 Clement XIV signed the papal brief *Dominus ac Redemptor* suppressing the Society of Jesus. Professor Owen Chadwick has commented that it was the most popular such document ever to come from a Pope. It was also 'the most tremendous use of power in the Church ever achieved by a Pope. To abolish the strongest of religious orders without an enquiry, and with no reason alleged, was a unique act of international supremacy. It could not have been done if St Ignatius Loyola had not made obedience the supreme virtue of a religious life'.[1]

Clement XIV had finally been brought to issue the Brief by the combined pressure of the Bourbon Powers of Portugal, France, Spain, and Naples. These had already brought the existence of the Order as such in their territories to an end in 1759, 1764, and (in the case of Spain and Naples) 1767 by appropriating its property and expelling its members.

The Bourbon States

In each case such action was justified by those taking it as a response to a scandalous situation arising from recent events. In the case of Portugal, it was the resistance of the Jesuits in Paraguay to the home government's orders that the native Indians living in a number of the reservations or 'reductions' established for their protection from incoming traders and settlers must be moved to the further side of the River Uruguay in order to conform with a new agreement with Spain

---

[1] Owen Chadwick, *The Popes and European Revolution* (Oxford: Clarendon Press, 1981), p. 383.

over territorial boundaries. This resistance prompted claims that these largely autonomous areas – also largely closed to outsiders – brought the Jesuits great wealth to which they were not entitled – this being to the detriment, moreover, of a legal monopoly in trade enjoyed by others. Further difficulties with the Jesuits in the New World were reported back to Lisbon and became greatly exaggerated in the process. In Portugal 'the great strength of the Jesuits lay in their intimacy with the crown through the royal confessors, their direct influence over the people, whether through their preaching, their unrivalled collection of relics, or their energy in raising funds'.[2] José de Carvalho e Melo (later, Marquis of Pombal and, from early 1756 Chief Minister) set himself to undermine their position, seeing them as a challenge to his policies and a threat to his own power. In May 1757 the Jesuits belonging to the Royal Household were discharged. In 1758 the Order found itself under rapidly mounting pressure. In February, Carvalho renewed his attacks on its alleged misconduct on both sides of the Atlantic and closed its university at Évora; in April, Benedict XIV, in response to demands from the government, issued a Brief ordering the Cardinal Patriarch of Lisbon to enquire into charges against Jesuit activities in the New World and to reform the Society in Portugal; in May, its members were forbidden to engage in 'illicit trading', and in June were forbidden to preach or hear confessions. In July their Superior was banished from Lisbon. After an attempt had been made on the King's life in September, the verdict of the court (which met *in camera*) on those charged with the crime alleged complicity on the part of the Jesuits. In January 1759, they were confined to their colleges by royal edict. On the first anniversary of the attempted regicide, a further royal edict outlawed and expelled the Jesuits from Portugal 'for ever'.[3] After the expulsion had been accomplished, Carvalho announced his achievement to the wider world in a series of pamphlets. These were soon fully reported in Paris in the brilliantly successful underground newspaper, the *Nouvelles ecclésiastiques*, which was strongly inclined towards the Jansenists.[4]

This came shortly after the inventive commercial activities undertaken by Fr Antoine Lavalette, head of the Jesuits in the French West Indies, for the benefit of their missionary purposes, had ended in financial collapse and a major scandal in France. As the Jesuit General in Rome, Fr Lorenzo Ricci, acknowledged, this did more

[2] H. V. Livermore, *A New History of Portugal* (Cambridge: C.U.P, 1966), p. 220.
[3] Ibid., pp. 226, 230.
[4] See John McManners, *Church and Society in Eighteenth-Century France*, 2 vols (Oxford: Clarendon Press, 1998), ii, 423–24, 545–46.

harm to the position of the Order in France than its worst enemies could have achieved. Lavalette's indebtedness was subsequently found to amount to over six million *livres*. The Courts first made the Jesuits in the French dominions at large, and then the Order as a whole, legally responsible for Lavalette's debts, and in May 1761 ordered that they pay his Marseilles agents 1.5 million *livres*. Being incapable of doing this, they found all their properties in France sequestrated a year later for non-payment. In the eyes of many – frequently eager on other scores to believe it – the episode confirmed even the worst that the Portuguese had claimed about the Jesuit pursuit of wealth, and so of power, in Paraguay, and reinforced hostility towards the Jesuits in France itself. In March 1762 a royal edict placed the latter under the authority of the bishops and required the General of the Order to transfer his authority to the provincial superiors of France within six months. The admission of further novices was forbidden until this was done. Jesuit houses were to continue, but would have to be reformed and regulated. However, already – the month before this – the *parlement* of Normandy had ordered that all Jesuit houses within that province of France be closed by 1 July. This, in the words of McManners, was 'the decisive blow which brought down the whole Order in France'.[5] Others followed suit, with varying degrees of eagerness. Finally, in November 1764, a further royal edict proscribed the Order throughout France.

In Spain a curiously trivial element contributed, it seems, to the crisis that led to the Jesuit expulsion there: the decision of one of the King's ministers, the Marchese di Squillace, to order men to wear their hats with the broad brims turned up so that criminals could less easily escape arrest. Attempts to enforce this led to a riot in Madrid on Palm Sunday 1766. The next day, with a violent crowd outside his palace, the King, Charles III, accepted demands that his Neapolitan minister, Squillache, be sent into exile, that his edict concerning dress be rescinded – and that the price of foodstuffs be lowered. The demand for cheaper bread was pressed during disturbances that took place in other cities and towns of central Spain a month later. Increasingly alarmed, the government set up a commission of enquiry. This included four bishops and an archbishop; however, its conclusions were decisively influenced by the reports supplied to it by the strongly reformist *fiscal* of the Council of Castile, Pedro Rodríguez de Campomanes. He was eager to draw parallels between what had just happened in Spain and what had happened so recently

---

[5] *Church and Society in Eighteenth-Century France*, ii, 554.

in Portugal and France, and in doing so drew on the arguments of Pombal and the French *parlements*. He had praise for both. Moreover, the same charges as before were again brought against the Jesuits: that they had used their position in Central and South America to accumulate vast riches for their Order and had done so by illegitimate and corrupt commercial operations; in this and in other respects they had acted against the royal authority to which they were properly subject; more generally, they were committed to the secret undermining of the system of Enlightenment monarchical rule and, beyond that, held 'horrible doctrines' concerning regicide. Applying the doctrine of corporate responsibility on the part of the Order for any anti-government act of which its individual members might be held to be guilty, Campomanes presented the Spanish Jesuits at large as heavily implicated in initiating the Spring riots of 1766. Charles III signed the edict for their expulsion from Spain and its dominions on 20 February 1767. By this time detailed arrangements for putting the edict into effect had been secretly and efficiently prepared. Ten days later, all Jesuits were taken in requisitioned coaches to assembly points; from these they went, on foot and under armed guard, to designated ports, and so to Italy. There Naples and Sicily enacted and executed similar edicts of expulsion towards the end of that same year.

The Process of Expulsion

In October 1759, 133 Portuguese Jesuits were deposited without warning at Città Vecchia in the Papal States. Eventually over 1,000 of the 1,678 Jesuits in the Portuguese branch of the Society (including the Portuguese Empire) found themselves there. Of the 453 Jesuits in Brazil and Paraguay, 170 left the Order and remained there. In Portugal itself, Pombal imprisoned about 124 Jesuits in a fort near the mouth of the Tagus and kept them without trial, in part because Rome refused his demand that Portugal be granted a perpetual right to bring the higher clergy and religious Orders into a secular court when charges of high treason were preferred. The Patriarch of Lisbon and most of the bishops did not protest. Forty-five were still prisoners when the death of the King in 1777 at last brought them liberation.

French Jesuits received more humane treatment, finding protection from the Crown against further measures proposed by the *parlements* and receiving modest life-pensions for their subsistence (the former Royal Confessors were treated vastly more generously). Some older men went at once into retirement; some younger men became secular priests; others contrived to live by their pens in one way and another as laymen; others joined missions in the Far East; perhaps most joined Jesuit houses in Spain.

In the first hours of April 1767 all the latter, with their colleges and churches, were placed under guard and sealed. Papers, books title-deeds, and funds belonging to the Order were seized; inventories were made of precious objects. It was laid down, however, that individual Jesuits should be allowed to take their personal effects with them. And as in France, they were given pensions for life: 100 *pesos* a year for priests and ninety for lay brothers, to be paid in monthly instalments by the Spanish minister in Rome. The worst of their troubles awaited them when they arrived in Italy. The ships carrying them into Cività Vecchia found the guns of the Papal States denying them entry. The King of Spain had not told the Pope that he was sending him the Jesuits of his home and overseas territories; it was a time of severe food shortages; and already there were many Jesuits there to be supported. So the Spaniards found themselves deposited for the time – in deplorable conditions – in Corsica; and when Corsica came under French sovereignty in 1768, Genoa was persuaded to allow them entry there on their way to the still reluctant Papal States, unwilling to yield openly to Spanish pressure. In the year before the expulsion there were 5,376 Spanish Jesuits (2,746 in Spain and 2,630 in Latin America and the Philippines). Of the 2,746, 2,503 found entry to the Papal States, the loss of nearly nine per cent being accounted for by death. In the following five years, another nearly nine per cent (243) of those who had arrived from Spain died, while nearly fifteen per cent of them (371) became secularized. There was a substantial loss of novices in Spain at the outset.

The Case of Spain

The complex of factors that led up to these events can be illustrated in more detail by the case of Spain. First, there was the attitude towards the Jesuits of Charles III, who ordered their expulsion. As John Lynch has written:

> Charles III had an ingrained prejudice against Jesuits. As far as he was concerned they were an insidious and wealthy organisation who had once defended regicide [that is, in Juan de Mariana's famous treatise on kingship]. They still retained their special vow of obedience to the pope and their reputation of papal agents, while their loyalty to the Spanish crown in the American colonies was also suspect. An order with an international organisation whose headquarters were outside Spain was regarded as inherently incompatible with absolutism, and in seeking to

implement the concordat of 1753 Charles III believed that he had to reckon with its resistance in Spain and in Rome.[6]

He resented their opposition to the canonizing, which he strongly supported, of Juan de Palafox, the strongly anti-Jesuit seventeenth-century bishop of Puebla, in Mexico; more generally, their ubiquitous presence in Church and State left him convinced that they were troublemakers and a challenge to royal power. As for the Count of Campomanes, *fiscal* of the Council of Castile from 1762 and foremost among the royal policy-makers, he saw unchallengeable royal authority as the essential prerequisite for the programme of institutional reform in Spain to which he was committed. On both scores he was the enemy of the Jesuits.

He was also the enemy of the *colegios mayores*. Established in the sixteenth century, their stipulated purpose had been to enable poor students who had obtained their baccalaureate to progress to higher degrees ... and thus join an intellectual élite. In time, these people came to achieve great preponderance over other graduates – the *manteístas* – in the obtaining of university chairs. Beyond that, the *colegios mayores* became institutions open only to a small and wealthy social élite, whose admission to such places brought with it subsequent privileged access to high positions in the royal administration and the Church. Campomanes – in this typical of Charles III's ministers – was a university-trained lawyer, from the lower ranks of the nobility and a *manteísta*, not a *colegial*, who was convinced that the reform of Spain's government and institutions required radical reform of the *colegios mayores*. In all this were further grounds for hostility towards the Jesuits, with their connections with these *colegios*, with their own schools for the sons of the nobility, their own connectedness with the world of social and political privilege, significance, and weight. After the riots of 1766, it was Campomanes (as we have already noted) who undertook the secret inquiry into the event and drew up the official report. This set out by every means to place the blame on the Jesuits and concluded by recommending their expulsion. Without this he did not see how the reform of the *colegios mayores*, on which so much else depended, could be achieved.

The Spanish Jesuits found little support and much hostility from other significant quarters: the bishops and the religious Orders. One important reason for this was the part played in government by the Jesuit Francisco Rávago, Royal Confessor over the years 1747 to 1755 to Charles III's predecessor, Ferdinand VI, and much more than Royal

---

[6] John Lynch, *Bourbon Spain 1700–1808* (Oxford: Basil Blackwell, 1989), p. 281.

Confessor: in effect, the minister for ecclesiastical affairs and adviser to the Crown on ecclesiastical appointments – all the more important a role since the 1753 Concordat which had extended the Crown's long-held right of nomination to bishoprics to nearly all canonries, prebends and benefices. This brought Rávago – and through him the Spanish Jesuits – many enemies among disappointed candidates. As for the bishops themselves, when both Pope and government sought their opinions on the possible suppression of the Society, four out of five gave their support on the grounds that it was a measure necessary for the Church's recovery and well-being. Subsequently, some bishops reiterated their support publicly in pastoral letters.

As for the other religious Orders, the Jesuits' chief enemies among them were the Augustinians and Dominicans, who had been the principal losers in rivalries over the obtaining of university chairs and, more broadly, the safeguarding and promotion of their respective theological positions. Their heads, in Rome, along with the Spanish Ambassador, played a significant part in bringing the Pope to the point of signing the Brief abolishing the Society. In Spain, the Jesuits and their supporters, in the months leading up to their expulsion, launched a fierce counter-attack in the form of pamphlets directed principally against Augustinians and Dominicans. This in turn provoked more hostility from them and from the government.

None of these antagonists was without thoughts of the material advantages to be derived from the suppression of the Society. Among these, the reformers in government had in mind buildings for schools; and bishops, buildings for seminaries and for parish use; other Orders would have their own uses for Jesuit property; while Jesuit finances offered the prospect of recompense to all those involved in bringing about the expulsion and suppression.

The Brief of Suppression

The five Catholic states (France, Spain, Portugal, and the Two Sicilies, with Spain taking the leading role) sought the suppression of the Society in order to complete what they had achieved with the expulsions and to give permanence to the situation to which they had for the most part publicly committed themselves. Clement XIII had already reacted strongly against the Jesuit expulsion from Portugal and France, declaring in a powerfully stated Bull of January 1765 that the vows of the Jesuits were pleasing to God and that the Society was a nursery of saints. It was clear that he would not willingly move from this position. However, just three years later, he provided the same Catholic Powers with grounds for renewing and increasing their pressure. In January 1768 Ferdinand, Duke of Parma, nephew of Charles III of Spain, issued an edict establishing, in various regards, his practical control of the Church in his duchy and interposing his own authority between it and Rome. Within a fortnight Clement XIII replied with a Brief (known as the 'Monitorium') declaring the Duke's edict to be null and void: it was, he said, a document full of wicked doctrine which diminished the rights of the Holy See, placed them under lay control, and reduced the Church of God to a state of slavery. He invoked the Bull *In Coena Domini*, issued each Thursday of Holy Week, with its series of excommunications directed against appellants from Rome to the secular power, against secular judges who brought members of the clergy before their courts, and against those who published or used decrees to limit the liberties of the Church. Clement's response to the Duke of Parma was therefore seen as a dramatic exercise of papal power that challenged the prerogatives of sovereigns as regards ecclesiastical matters within their own territories and especially as regards the action they themselves had taken in expelling the Jesuits – an Order that they in any case viewed as a semi-autonomous body within their territories.

In January 1769 France, Spain and Naples made a formal request to Clement XIII that the Jesuits be suppressed. The Pope died, however, at the start of February, and so the issue fell to be dealt with by his successor, the Franciscan Lorenzo Ganganelli – Clement XIV – in whose election the following May the influence of the Catholic Powers played a decisive part. Two months later, the French ambassador, acting for Naples and Spain as well as France, renewed the request that the Jesuit Order be suppressed. This confronted the new Pope with complex problems. He knew that most of the cardinals would be against such a step, and he had to calculate, in the interests of his own authority, how the Catholic Powers that had not expelled the Jesuits would react. And how should the colleges that provided a Catholic education across Europe be preserved? So, though he had soon written to Louis XV and Charles III promising to resolve the Jesuit question speedily, he in fact temporised, limiting himself to withdrawing customary marks of favour towards the Jesuits, restricting their activities in Rome and the Papal States, giving his support to the process of beatification of Juan de Palafox, and stopping the pension paid to the Portuguese Jesuits deposited in Italy by Pombal. Diplomatic relations with Lisbon having been restored (Pombal had suspended them in 1760), he confirmed the latter's nominees as bishops and made Pombal's brother a cardinal. On Maundy Thursday 1770 he suspended – as the Bourbon Powers greatly desired – the reading of the now notorious *In*

Coena Domini and it was not revived. But the suppression of the Society still did not come.

Early in 1772 the Spanish government sent a new ambassador to Rome – José Moñino, the future and famous Count of Floridablanca – to force the issue. The Pope countered by proposing a process by which the matter could be resolved over a period of time. The Order would be turned into a set of religious societies operating in the different countries; these would continue the work of education and the missions hitherto pursued by the Jesuits; but they would no longer be allowed to preach and hear confessions and there would be no more novices. This plan was unacceptable to the Powers because it failed to bring about the immediate dissolution of the Order to which they were committed. In September 1772 Clement XIV finally accepted that he had no other option, and by the end of the year a draft edict (at first, a Bull, subsequently a Brief) had been prepared – by Cardinal Zelada and Ambassador Moñino, with the collaboration of the Spanish heads of the Dominican, Augustinian, and Franciscan Orders. A copy was submitted to Charles III; he wrote to Maria Theresa of Austria; and when she indicated a willingness to accept what the Pope thought best for the Church, the way was open for the issuing of the decree, *Dominus ac Redemptor*, dated 21 July 1773 and published on 16 August. Its text spoke of the difficult relations between the Jesuit Order and temporal rulers, its alleged inability now to fulfil the purposes for which it had been founded, its difficult relations also with other religious Orders, and the damage that all this did to the peace of the Church. A commission of cardinals was at once established to put the provisions of the decree into effect. Among the European countries where Jesuits were still present, only Prussia and Russia (after the First Polish Partition of 1772) forbade promulgation of the brief. Clement XIV died the following year, in September 1774.

Sydney Smith and the Nineteenth-Century Debate

The suppression of the Society of Jesus found an immediate and widespread welcome within the Roman Catholic Church as well as outside it. The Order had become the object of criticism and hostility from a variety of quarters for a variety of reasons. That hostility was intensified by a sense of the success, influence, and power of the Jesuits. They unquestionably controlled the higher education of the Catholic world through their colleges and carefully systematized curriculum and pattern of religious formation. This brought its own reaction from adherents of the eighteenth-century Enlightenment, who viewed the Jesuit curriculum as now unacceptably narrow and fixed in the past, believed that education should include the teaching of history and the natural sciences, and in any case deplored what they saw as the underlying authoritarianism of the Jesuit educational enterprise which was rooted in the Counter-Reformation, its aims and its values. Nevertheless, this educational role had long given the Jesuits ready access to the world of the upper and middle classes, where the influence with which they were credited was made all the greater by their role as confessors. Their prominence in this role, and the system of moral theology ('Probabilism') with which they especially came to be identified, had exposed them, from the mid-seventeenth century onwards, to prolonged and even virulent attack from the Jansenists and their sympathisers on the one side (as most famously in Pascal's *Lettres provinciales*) and from the Dominicans on the other. At the start of the eighteenth century, Clement XI's condemnation of much Jesuit practice in the matter of the Chinese Rites drew vast publicity to itself. A decade later, that same pope's Bull *Unigenitus*, which renewed papal condemnation of Jansenist positions, far from strengthening the Jesuit position, led to the most heated controversy of the eighteenth century Church – a controversy which brought dissension and division over many issues beyond the purely theological – with the result that the two papal determinations, different as they were from each other, together seriously damaged the reputation and weakened the position of the Jesuits. In France, *Unigenitus* strengthened Gallican sentiment as regards the relations of the French Church with Rome and this again worked to the disadvantage of the Jesuits, their Order being both widely international and strongly unified, with its central authority embodied in its General in Rome and its members bound by an oath of obedience to the Pope. This brought them widespread hostility both from rulers and from the episcopates of the states whose governments were to play the greatest part in bringing about their suppression.

The latter at once prompted discussion in print of the event itself and in particular of the roles and characters of the two popes most closely involved. Nineteenth-century discussion of the Suppression is better called debate since its underlying purpose and nature were to a large degree polemical. This, in turn, was due not only to the continuing significance that was read into the Suppression itself but also to the continuing contentiousness of the Order after its restoration by Pius VII in 1814. Witness to that contentiousness is found in the varying fortunes of the Order throughout the century, when it was several times expelled – entirely or partially – from France and Spain or otherwise inhibited in its teaching functions. Against that background we can usefully look briefly at the nineteenth-century works on the Suppression on which Sydney Smith chiefly draws, for, clearly, he saw himself as contributing, for the benefit of English readers, to the tradition of debate which those earlier works represented. He not only refers to them or otherwise engages with them but, in several cases, draws heavily on them, especially for the documentary evidence that they offered.

The first of these authors was Jacques Crétineau-Joly (1803–1875), historian of the Guerre de la Vendée (his native region) and spokesman for the Legitimist cause. His six-volume *Histoire religieuse, politique et littéraire de la Compagnie de Jésus* (Paris, 1844–46) was followed in 1847 by his *Clément XIV et les Jésuites* (published in Spanish the next year at Madrid). His work on this combined task was greatly assisted by the Jesuit General of the time, Fr G. Roothaan, who made available to him not only the documentary resources of the Jesuit headquarters in Rome but also those of the Society elsewhere on the Continent. He was thus writing in the years when Jules Michelet published his *Des Jésuites*, of 1843, a work where he argued that 'the Society of Jesus reduced human beings to the status of obedient machines the better to control, manipulate and enslave them; Jesuitism was the enemy of progress in science and in law'.[7] If Crétineau's project was partly conceived as a response to anti-Jesuit feeling in France such as one finds here, it in turn provoked lively polemic and prompted the writing of the next of these studies – the one, in fact, to which Smith refers more often than any other – the Oratorian Augustin Theiner's *Geschichte des Pontificats Clemens' XIV*, of which the two-volume French edition (translated 'sous les yeux de l'auteur') was published in Paris in 1852. It was (it seems) Pius IX, no less, who gave Theiner the task of writing a history of Clement XIV's pontificate that would serve as a reply to Crétineau's negative portrayal. Having been appointed (by the Pope) Coadjutor to the Prefect of the Vatican Archives in March 1851, Theiner was all the better placed to draw on that rich source of documentary material for his own study, which runs to over 1,000 pages. His concluding reflections, at the end of the whole work, make his position as regards his subject entirely clear:

> Before leaving our readers, we cannot permit ourselves not to make at this point a solemn declaration and say that all the works written by Jesuits and their friends, named or unnamed, since the death of Clement

[7] Ceri Crossley, *French Historians and Romanticism* (London and New York: Routledge, 1993), pp. 228–29.

XIV, and even in his life-time, down to our own day, on the subject of this Pontiff and the suppression of the Society of Jesus, are the fruit of the most deplorable illusions, filled with errors without number, among these works there being even some that are not free of mendacity. We therefore beg those who are lovers of truth to read [such works] only with the greatest circumspection.[8]

It is not surprising that such sentiments from so authoritative a figure produced a further reaction. Crétineau-Joly quickly published two *Letters* addressed to Theiner on the subject. That same year Giuseppe Boero (another of Smith's sources and himself a Jesuit and archivist at the headquarters of the Society in Rome) published his *Osservazioni sopra l'istoria del pontificato di Clemente XIV scritta dal p. A. Theiner* (two vols, Modena, 1853 and again in 1854). The fullest response, however, came from a French Jesuit, Gustave-Xavier Delacroix de Ravignan (1795–1858), in his massive study: *Clément XIII et Clément XIV* (2 vols, Paris, 1854). Ravignan, still more than Boero, was an important source for Sydney Smith. The same Jesuit General, Roothaan, who had helped forward Crétineau's work, encouraged Ravignan to undertake this further study. Ravignan explains in his Preface that Roothaan had been much distressed by Theiner's book, where he not only found the Society of Jesus attacked but saw the Holy See and Clement XIV poorly defended from attack and even compromised. He thought (with notable magnanimity, surely) that a better apologia could be presented on behalf of the pope who had suppressed the Society, and he had conveyed such reflections to Ravignan.[9]

At Notre-Dame in the decade after 1835 Ravignan had acquired a great reputation as a preacher. However, the tone that he adopts in his *Clément XIII et Clément XIV*, while fundamentally a reply to Theiner, is, for the most part, notably eirenic and restrained. He has written, he says, without bitterness and in no spirit of contention; his sole concern is with truth, and with the truth that emerges from the relevant documents when these are allowed to speak for themselves. It is for that reason that he has felt obliged, he says, to quote from them so often and at such length.

It is not to imply bad faith on Ravignan's part to note again, however, that the overall direction of his argument was one in which he had been encouraged by Roothaan shortly before his final illness; and it is not irrelevant to note that, in stressing his concern solely with the truth, at the start and the conclusion of his Preface, he each

[8] Augustin Theiner, *Histoire de Clément XIV*, 2 vols (Paris, 1852), ii, 532.
[9] Xavier de Ravignan, *Clément XIII et Clément XIV* (Paris, 1854), vol.i, pp. iii–iv.

time borrows words from so strongly traditionalist and authoritarian a thinker as Joseph de Maistre, quoting from his *Du Pape*, of 1819, and taking the epigraph for his own study from that same source: 'Les Papes n'ont besoin que de la vérité'.[10]

What these writers have in common is a desire to give an account of the successive stages of the expulsions and suppression of the Jesuits in the context of the parts played by monarchs, their ministers and diplomatic representatives on the one hand, and by popes and papal secretaries of state on the other – the whole detailed narrative being based on an abundant use of primary documentary material. Sydney Smith follows them in this. While he nevertheless disowns any claim to have engaged in primary research himself, he has clearly devoted much attention to the works of those before him who had done so, and the way in which he incorporates his reading of the documentary evidence they offer into a strong, well-paced, elegantly expressed, and cogent narrative of his own is deeply impressive. It is striking too that he makes telling use of (for him) so recently published a work as the Spaniard Manuel Danvila y Collado's *Reinado de Carlos III [Reign of Charles III]*, of the earlier 1890s, one of the volumes of which, with its six-hundred pages and more of text and supporting documents, is entirely devoted to the matter of the Jesuits.[11] Smith's linguistic range should not be left unnoticed.

The air of calm, sustained, earnest reasoning that so largely prevails in his analysis of events and how they came to pass and what they signified, together with his repeated stress on the issues that

---

[10] The strength of feeling underlying his work finds eloquent expression in its 'Conclusion', which begins: 'L'Église, dans tous les temps, fut plus ou moins en butte aux attaques de différentes classes d'adversaires: l'histoire des deux pontificats de Clément XIII et Clément XIV nous les a montrées toutes réunies et conjurées sous un même drapeau qui portait pour devise: *haine aux jésuites*. Mais, dans la réalité, la ligue ne fut formée, la guerre entreprise, la victoire obtenue que pour enchaîner et asservir l'épouse de Jésus-Christ aux volontés de ceux que le fanatisme de l'opinion avait établis maîtres souverains du monde. C'était bien du reste le moyen le plus sûr d'arriver à détruire l'Église, si elle pouvait être détruite: car la liberté est sa vie' (ii, 459).

[11] Welcoming the final, full restoration of the Order by Leo XIII, Danvila saw it as the role of the Jesuits now to 'preach obedience to the principle of authority, respect for law, and love of princes'. He closes with the words: 'It is pleasant to reflect that, after three centuries of struggle, the principle of authority has triumphed'. See *Historia general de España* ... bajo la dirección de Antonio Cánovas del Castillo, 6 vols (Madrid, 1894), iii, 624–25. His position was thus very much at odds with that of his fellow Academician Antonio Ferrer del Río (to whom Sydney Smith also refers), vol. 2 of whose *Historia del reinado de Carlos III en España*, 4 vols (Madrid, 1856), is wholly given over to the subject of the Spanish Jesuits. Ferrer del Río adopts a strongly pro-Charles III and pro-Suppression viewpoint.

require to be considered by his readers – and considered with due and impartial respect for the facts of the matter – as steps towards a final judgement regarding the justice or injustice of the suppression of the Society of Jesus, when taken together, give his series of articles something of the character of a written legal submission. We find ourselves reading what is, in its totality, an extensive and powerful piece of reasoned advocacy.

Its power derives not only from the course of argument but also from its author's commitment to a particular point of view. That commitment has within it – as is to be expected – a psychological and emotional component as well as an intellectual one; and this affects the underlying attitudes that find expression – mostly very discreetly – in Smith's treatment of his subject. Consciously or unconsciously, he puts things at times in terms tending to draw the reader into an emotional response matching his own – as, for example, when he puts the emphasis he does on the physical unsightliness of the Abbés Chauvelin and De Terray (p. 35); or when he points out (while conceding the irrelevance of the detail) that the son of M. Lepelletier de Saint-Fargeau ('a rigid Jansenist') 'became a fanatical revolutionist, and was very prominent among those who voted for the execution of Louis XVI', even though 'a man is not necessarily responsible for the sins of his sons, but it is of interest to know that ...' (p. 40, n. 24). Jansenists and adherents of the Enlightenment (of which his thumb-nail sketch will be recognized as something of a caricature) are routinely pigeon-holed ('the notorious Voltairian Abbé Galliani' [p. 138] and the like). And then there is Döllinger: 'Even a writer like Döllinger ...' (p. 53). As Smith sets about his account of a further stage in the process by which Clement XIII was brought under pressure by the Sovereigns of the Bourbon Powers to suppress the Society: 'We have now to continue this scandalous history' (p. 148). In the course of it we read that 'Carlos III with his bull-dog tenacity thought not of withdrawing [from his campaign to achieve his purposes] but of driving his fangs deeper into the heart of the afflicted Pontiff' (p. 153). To point these things out is not to deny to Sydney Smith a genuine desire to present a truthful account of the process leading up to the Suppression; but in view of his repeated pleas that the rights or wrongs of that Suppression shall be judged by his readers in a reasoned and unbiased fashion, it is relevant to note that Smith could not escape the general human predicament of looking at what he took to be 'the truth' through the lenses of his own mind and dispositions.

He is wholly unambiguous in his overall assessments of the two popes at the centre of his story. His chapter on Clement XIII concludes: 'He had fought a good fight; he had offered a noble spectacle of moral force contending against physical violence, and, although his reign was one long chronicle of calamities, he must always count among the great Popes' (p. 157). This is – more briefly put – the same judgement as Ravignan's, who had found in this pope 'the truest marks of grandeur and glory that have ever belonged to the most illustrious pontiffs', so that he could be compared with Innocent III, Gregory VII, and others of like kind (*Clément XIII et Clément XIV*, ii, 235). Of Clement XIV, however, Smith declares: 'He was essentially a weak man and an opportunist, and had what so often accompanies a weak man's opportunism, a deficient sense of the justice due to individuals' (p. 202). The contrast thus drawn between the two was (as L. Cajani and A. Foa point out), one found both in Ravignan and Crétineau-Joly and, more broadly, among those who, in the middle decades of the nineteenth century, contributed to what these two modern scholars describe as 'la storiografia cattolica intransigente'.[12]

It would be of interest (though a substantial task) to investigate in detail how far Sydney Smith's view of his subject as a whole corresponds to that of his Jesuit predecessors just mentioned, along with Danvila and the others on whom he chiefly draws (the cases of Theiner and Ferrer del Río are manifestly different). Here, however, in conclusion, it must suffice to note a few points of difference and similarity between Smith and scholars of our own time.

First, the question of the treatment received by the Spanish Jesuits when Charles III's edict for their expulsion was so dramatically put into effect. Their collective arrest must indeed have been a traumatizing experience, and Sydney Smith gives a vivid account of this (pp. 91–92):

> [The Fathers, he writes], were told that they were to depart at once on their painful journey, leaving everything behind, even the MSS on which some had spent the labour of a lifetime, everything save the clothes in which they stood up, their breviaries, and a single prayer-book, and, which was spoken of as a signal act of royal considerateness, any snuff and chocolate or small change which it was supposed they might have at the time in their possession.

A Spanish scholar of our own times, Professor Teófano Egido, has quoted the terms of the government instructions on these matters.[13] The Jesuits were to be allowed to take with them 'all their clothes

---

[12] *Dizionario biografico degli Italiani* (Rome, 1960–), xxvi (1982), 341.
[13] 'La expulsión de los jesuitas de España', in *Historia de la Iglesia en España, IV: La Iglesia en la España de los siglos XVII y XVIII*, Biblioteca de autores cristianos: Serie maior 19 (Madrid: Editorial Católica, 1979), ch. 8 (see pp. 752–53).

and usual changes of the same, without diminution; their personal boxes, handkerchiefs, tobacco, chocolate [no mention of this being a special act of favour] and useful articles of such kind: breviaries, diurnals and portable prayer-books for their acts of devotion'; also 'the money that belongs to them personally' – an addition for the benefit of the Madrid Jesuits, it seems. Beyond these specific provisions, the government instructions are emphatic that the Jesuits shall be treated with 'the greatest propriety, attention, humanity and assistance during the implementation [of the Edict]. Special arrangements are mentioned for the old and the sick. Now, in all this, a crucial question is that of how far these gestures of humanity prescribed by the Instructions were put into effect, or were expected to be, or even intended to be. Nevertheless, the fact that such instructions were issued by the highest authorities needs now to be taken into account.

Larger issues where modern studies of the Suppression differ in their emphasis or conclusions from Smith's account of them include episcopal attitudes towards the Jesuits (in Spain above all), and, along with that, the attitudes and behaviour of the other religious Orders at this dramatic juncture – this being an issue about which Smith says very little before his Conclusion.

Modern scholarship has probed more deeply than he did into the complex sociological as well as political and specifically religious reasons for the hostility of which the Society found itself the object in the years leading up to the Suppression. However, it strongly endorses his central contention: that the Suppression, along with the expulsions that preceded it, was an act of remarkable injustice on the part of all those who brought these things about, varied (one must add) though their motives were. We noted, at the start of this Afterword, Professor Owen Chadwick's comment that 'to abolish the strongest of religious orders without an enquiry, and with no reason alleged, was a unique act of international supremacy'. To say that the abolition took place 'with no reason alleged', is perhaps surprising in view of the justification of the event attempted in *Dominus ac Redemptor*; but there is no disputing the fact that this Brief established no intellectually adequate case for the doing of a deed with such vast destructive consequences; nor was the Society ever given the opportunity to confront and contest the charges directed at it in any appropriate forum.

One senses a touch of discomfort over this failure in the Pastoral Letter issued by Archbishop Lorenzana of Toledo, Primate of Spain, in October 1773. Here the Papal Brief of Suppression is reproduced within the setting of the Primate's own reflections upon it.[14] He

---

[14] Bodleian Library, MS Arch. Sigma 115 (22) [=fos.291r–328v].

refers back, implicitly, to Charles III's edict of expulsion issued in 1767, where the King speaks – beyond his duty to maintain peace and justice among his subjects – of the 'other pressing, just, and necessary reasons which I reserve in my Royal breast',[15] and Lorenzana expatiates on the subject's duty to take such things on trust when spoken by God's vicegerents on earth and to respond with interior as well as exterior obedience. The Brief, he claims, has served 'to free the Faithful from the least scruple, quieting their consciences and dissipating their old fears'. 'From its very first lines', he says, 'this document, coming as it does from the Church's Universal Shepherd, makes manifest to even the feeblest vision a particular unction of the Holy Spirit'.[16] Any of the hard-headed compilers of the document reading this would surely have felt a touch of sardonic satisfaction.

Lorenzana's presentation of the process leading up to the Brief of Suppression, when set against the facts of the matter, is of some interest as a notable eighteenth-century example of the art of 'spin' as practised by a very senior prelate who was both a convinced opponent of the Jesuits and one who owed his episcopal elevation to the Spanish government. He writes:

> We doubt whether any other matter in the history of Christendom has been examined in the Court of Rome with more mature deliberation or a greater abundance of information. Our Most Holy Father, Clement XIV, whom God preserve, heard first the Catholic Sovereigns of Europe; he [then] sought information from many prelates of the Church; he brought together all the documents showing the steps that had been taken, and he has pondered this difficult and gravest of matters ever since he ascended the Papal Throne. Now finally, he has issued his Bull [sic] which is word for word as follows ...[17]

If the Suppression did great injustice to the Order as a whole, it also brought – at the least – displacement, dislocation, disorientation,

---

[15] See Smith, p. 90.
[16] Ff. 292v, 321r.
[17] Fol. 293r. It should, however, be added that Lorenzana was a man of scholarly interests and that these were of some benefit to the Spanish ex-Jesuits and their books. L. Sierra records that Lorenzana 'bore the cost of countless publications of the ex-Jesuits exiled in Italy, and principally, among them, the works of Diosdado Caballero y Arévalo'. He also created for the Infante Luis A. J. de Borbón a collection of 9000 books that had belonged to Jesuits. This at least helped to preserve them. Lorenzana gave his financial patronage to a number of scholarly projects, especially in the field of Spanish ecclesiastical history. See *Diccionario de historia eclesiástica de España*, dirigida por Q. Aldea Vaquero et al., 4 vols (Madrid, 1972) and Supplement I (1987), ii, 1346–47, s.v. 'Lorenzana'.

deprivation, and often worse, into the lives of its individual members. Perhaps the French Jesuits, many of whom remained in France, came off least badly on the whole as they found new lives for themselves. Those who suffered worst were the Portuguese, whether those deposited in Italy or those kept in long imprisonment by Pombal and the King. Symbolic of the sufferings of so many was the experience of their former General, Fr Ricci, who, a year after the Brief of Suppression, found himself a prisoner in the Castel Sant' Angelo, along with his five assistants and seven other ex-Jesuits, guarded by sixty German mercenaries.[18] He died there two years later, before the various interested Powers had managed to agree on terms for his release.

In this survey of the nineteenth-century debate about the Suppression, the works that we have seen Sydney Smith reading and responding to in one way or another have all been works produced on the Continent. His own sources include no works in English primarily devoted to the subject – for the sufficient reason, one concludes, that they did not exist. Nor does he make any reference to attitudes in his own country – and in the Roman Catholic Church in England – towards the Jesuits and their suppression. One cannot, therefore, learn anything here of how far a concern with this aspect of his subject may have contributed to his decision to undertake this series of articles. That there were grounds for such concern is evident from the reflections on the Society of Jesus carefully and deliberately set down by Cardinal Manning in a private diary in 1889, near the end of his life.[19] He writes that 'I wish to put down carefully my judgement as to the Society of Jesus, because I have often been thought and said to be opposed to it'. He sets out the grounds for his personal spiritual indebtedness to Jesuits, and says with perfect clarity: 'I have had none of the traditional anti-Jesuit prejudices'. Furthermore, he sees the establishment of the Society in 1540 as 'a creation of God by St Ignatius, raised up for a special work'. But he still sees the suppression of the Society as 'a work of our Divine Master in behalf of the Church'. His grounds for saying so are that 'there can be no doubt that [the Society's] corporate action has been excessive', whereas 'no Society can take the place of the Divine Order of the Universal Church'. Manning further argues that, 'if the Society had not been suppressed in 1773, the English Hierarchy would not have

[18] Owen Chadwick, *The Popes and European Revolution*, pp. 375–76.
[19] See Francis Edwards, S.J., *The Jesuits in England from 1580 to the Present Day* (London: Burns & Oates, 1985), pp. 298–302 [= 'Appendix I: Cardinal Manning and the Society of Jesus']. I am grateful to the Editor for bringing this to my attention.

been restored in 1850' ... this on the grounds that, until the Suppression, the colleges and seminaries of Rome were in the hands of the Jesuits, who drew the brightest and best of their students into the Society, whereas, in the decades after it, those same colleges and seminaries bred up for the diocesan clergy a new race of men 'of a higher and more vigorous kind' than they had provided before, men 'restored to their independence and self-formation': 'the English College produced Cardinal Wiseman'.

The suppression of the Society of Jesus by Clement XIV was a remarkable event which continues to offer every kind of interest for historical and sociological investigation as well as material for Christian reflection. It can safely be said that Fr Sydney Smith's account of this chapter in the life of the Society remains by far the fullest, most wide-ranging, and most detailed treatment of the subject available in English. It represents much devoted labour and a very considerable intellectual achievement. The Editor of this volume comments that what Sydney Smith has produced here is 'a piece of high-class propaganda journalism', and it has been pointed out now in some detail that Smith's account does have in certain respects to be read with a wary eye. Nevertheless, it presents a great deal that is, beyond question, both true and historically important; and even at points where it may fail to convince, it will serve as a lively stimulus to further enquiry. Smith's series of essays was published in *The Month* a century after the first steps were being taken for the reestablishment of the Order at large and within a few years of the abrogation of Clement XIV's Brief by that of Leo XIII. They remain of interest after a further century and deserve a recognized place in the English historiography of the subject. One welcomes their republication now.

Modern Studies Consulted

Aldea Vaquero, Quintín *et al.*, *Diccionario de historia eclesiástica de España*, CSIC, 4 vols (Madrid, 1972–75) and 'Suplemento I' (Madrid, 1987).

Chadwick, Owen, *The Popes and European Revolution* (Oxford: Clarendon Press, 1981), ch. 5.

Crossley, Ceri, *French Historians and Romanticism* (London and New York: Routledge, 1993).

Dizionario biografico degli Italiani (Rome: Istituto della Enciclopedia Italiana fondata de Giovanni Treccani, 1960–), xxvi (1982), 328–62, s.vv. 'Clemente XIII' (by L. Cajani and A. Foa) and 'Clemente XIV' (by M. Rosa), each with extensive bibliographies, cf. pp. 342–43 and pp. 360–62.

Dominus ac Redemptor. Text in A. Barbèri and A. Spetia (eds.), *Bullarii Romani Continuatio*, vol. 4 (Rome, 1841), pp. 607–18; main clauses given by C. Mirbt, *Quellen zur Geschichte des Papsttums und des römischen Katholizismus* (4th edn., 1924), pp. 404–11 (no. 546). [Both the Latin text and the first complete English translation are now available in Thomas M. McCoog, S.J., ed., *'Promising Hope': Essays on the Suppression and Restoration of the English Province of the Society of Jesus*, Appendix 1 (Rome [Institutum Historicum Societatis Iesu], 2003).]

Edwards, Francis, S.J., *The Jesuits in England from 1580 to the Present Day* (London: Burns & Oates, 1985), pp. 298–302 [='Appendix I: Cardinal Manning and the Society of Jesus'].

Egido, Teófanes, 'La expulsión de los jesuitas de España', in *Historia de la Iglesia en España, IV: La Iglesia en la España de los siglos XVII y XVIII*, Biblioteca de autores cristianos: Serie maior 19 (Madrid: Editorial Católica, 1979), ch. 8.

Herr, Richard, *The Eighteenth-Century Revolution in Spain* (Princeton, NJ.: Princeton U.P., 1958), ch. 2.

Livermore, H.V., *A New History of Portugal* (Cambridge: C.U.P., 1966), ch. 8 (2).

Lynch, John, *Bourbon Spain 1700–1808* (Oxford: Basil Blackwell, 1989), ch.7.

McManners, John, *Church and Society in Eighteenth-Century France*, 2 vols (Oxford: Clarendon Press, 1998), chs. 42, 43.

Shirley, William, *Observations on a Pamphlet lately Published, entitled The Genuine and Legal Sentence pronounced by the High Court of Judicature of Portugal upon the Conspirators against the Life of his Most Faithful Majesty, with the just Motives for the same*, by William Shirley, late of Lisbon, Merchant (London: Printed for M. Cooper, MDCCLIX), pp. 5–6, 21–22, 30ff. [Probably a rare kind of testimony from an English observer of the Lisbon scene, who makes it clear that he was no friend of the Jesuits, but was a fair-minded and intelligent man: his general theme is that the charges brought against the alleged conspirators were not supported by the evidence shown.]

Spencer, Philip, *Politics of Belief in Nineteenth-Century France: Lacordaire – Michon – Veuillot* (London: Faber and Faber, 1954).

Index

Ablitas, Xavier (S.J., Spaniard, exiled) 93
Aiguillon, Armand Louis de Vignerot, Duc d' (adversary of Choiseul, Foreign Minister) 231, 234, 250, 268, 279, 313
Aimerich, Mateo (S.J., Spaniard, exiled) 82
Albani, Cardinal Alexander (in conclave 1769) 174, 187
Albani, Cardinal J.F. (in conclave 1769) 168, 169, 171–3, 174, 187, 190, 192–7, 283n.
Alembert, Jean le Rond d' (encyclopaedist) 25, 27, 28–30, 34, 282, 308, 312
Alexander VI 191
Alexander VII 13, 150, 300
Alexander VIII 300
Alfani, Cardinal 229, 251–2, 264, 267, 286
Alfonso Liguori, St (comment on Clement XIV) 270
Almada (Portuguese ambassador at Vatican) 11, 143, 206, 227, 234, 236, 237
Alphonso VI (Portugal) 12
Alva (Alba), Duque de (member of *junta* for expulsion) 80, 90
Ambrose and Barnabas *ad nemus*, Order of SS. (suppressed order) 291–2, 303
Andreetti (advocate; interrogates Fr Ricci and Assitants) 274–5, 279, 283
Andreucci, Padre (S.J., Italian, recommends Lorenzo Ganganelli) 203

Annat, Père (S.J., confessor to Louis XIV) 33
Antilles 37
Apologie Générale 56
Apostolicum (Bull in defence of Society) 72, 78, 212n., 219, 225, 303n., 310
Appel à la Raison 55–6
Aquaviva, Claudio (General of Society) 57–8, 297n., 300n.
Aquaviva, Mgr (President of Urbino) 240
Aranda, Conde de (head of Council of Castille) 79, 89–91, 94, 100, 103–4, 110–11, 114–15, 117–19, 121, 131, 235n., 313
Aranjuéz 86, 99, 116
Arnauld, Antoine (Jansenist) 31, 307, 312
Assertions see *Extraits*
Aubeterre, Joseph Bouchard, Marquis d' (French Ambassador to Vatican) 72, 139–41, 150–1, 153, 155, 204–5
 role in election of Clement XIV 161–76
Augustinians see Pinelli; Vazquez
Aveiro, Duke de (implicated in plot against Joseph I) 15–16
Averdy, Clément de l' (member of the *parlement* opposed to Society) 34, 36–7, 44
Avignon (dispute over possession) 135, 140, 149–50, 166, 180, 197, 204, 240, 251
Ávila (assistant to Alcalde of Madrid) 113

342 The Suppression of the Society of Jesus

Azara, Nicolo d' (first Secretary at Spanish Embassy to Vatican) 131, 140, 166, 171, 173, 175, 178, 182n., 187
Azcoitia 85, 87
Azpeitia 85
Azpuru, Mgr Tomás Jiménez (Spanish chargé d'affaires at Vatican) 96, 102, 135, 140, 151, 156, 205-6, 213, 222, 224, 226, 228, 234, 236
  role in election of Clement XIV 162-99
Azzaloni, Abbaste (involved in Valentano case) 285-6
Balanchán, Juan (accused of Madrid insurrection, 1766) 118-19, 121
Basil of the Armenians, Order of St (suppressed order) 291, 303
Beaumont, Christopher de, Archbishop of Paris 22, 31, 49, 59, 68-9, 316
Beauteville, Mgr de, Bishop of Alais 69
Belgrado, Father (S.J., Rector in Bologna) 248
Bellarmine, St Robert 47
Benedetti, Abbate (chamberlain of Card. Torregiani) 140
Benedict XIII 150, 303n.
Benedict XIV 11, 13, 14-15, 30, 50, 150, 162n., 200, 203, 272-3, 300, 301n., 302n., 303, 318, 320
Benevente, Miguel de (S.J., implicated in Madrid insurrection) 119
Benevento (Papal citadel on frontier with Naples, Duchy) 135, 149-50, 153, 240, 251
Benincasa, Fr (S.J., imprisoned with Fr Ricci) 276, 284, 286
Benvenuto, Fr (S.J., writing in defence of Society) 284
Bernis, Cardinal de (French ambassador at Vatican) early career 25, 182-3
  attitude to Jesuits 220, 253, 259n., 265-6, 268, 279, 280, 288, 310, 313-14
  pressure on Clement XIV to suppress Society 202-52
  role in election of Clement XIV 163-99
  role in election of Pius VI 273-4
Berryer, Nicolas (*Intendant de Police*) 34, 52

Bischi, Mgr (counsellor to Clement XIV) 233
bishops
  attitude to the Society 14, 18, 52, 59-65, 69, 72-3, 77, 90, 142, 182n., 212n., 219, 225, 267, 310, 316, 324-5, 328, 334
Boero, Giuseppe (S.J., historian) 247n., 279n., 287, 314, 330
Bologna (Jesuits in) 248-9
Borromeo, Cardinal (in conclave 1769) 174, 187, 195
Borromeo, St Charles 291-2
Boschi, Cardinal (in conclave 1769) 161, 174, 187
Bossuet 31
Bourbon Courts (France, Parma, Portugal, Spain, Two Sicilies, i.e. Naples and Sicily) 3, 133, 135, 182n., 204, 230, 261, 304, 319
  plan for suppression 5, 128, 137, 142, 148, 153-5, 167, 210, 214, 218, 220, 225, 263, 264, 325-6, 332
  role in election of Clement XIV 162-3, 171, 176, 178, 197
  supposed demand for written promise to suppress Society 180-6, 191, 195, 198n.
Bousemart, Gabriel (S.J., Spaniard, exiled) 93
Branciforte, Cardinal, Archbishop of Palermo (in conclave 1769) 161, 174, 187
Braschi, Cardinal Giovanni Angelo *see* Pius VI
Brevis Relatio see *Short Relation*
Brief of Suppression 111, 137-8, 221, 227, 233, 234-52, 261, 276, 325-7, 335, 337
  analysis 289-306 (suppression or reform of other orders 291-3; reasons for suppressing the Society 294-305); see *Dominus et Redemptor*
British (Museum) Library 83
Broglie, Comte de 24
Bucarelli, Francisco (occupies Falklands) 232
Buffalini, Cardinal (in conclave 1769) 161, 171, 174, 187, 195
Bull (as distinct from Brief) 293, 327

Index 343

Buonacorsi, Cardinal (in conclave 1769) 174, 187, 195
Buontempi, Fra (O.F.M., counsellor to Clement XIV) 233-4, 238, 244, 251-2
Caballero, Bernado (involved in Secret Inquiry) 104
Caballero, Ramón Diosdado (S.J., writer) 80, 83, 93
Cahour, Arsène (S.J., historian) 289
Cajani, L. see *Dizionario biografico*
Calatayud, Pedro (S.J., Spaniard, exiled) 81-2, 93, 123
Calini, Cardinal (in conclave 1769) 174, 187
Calmi, Cardinal (friend of Pius VI) 314
Campo dei Fiori 252, 258
Campomanes, Pedro Rodríguez de (fiscal of Council of Castile) 80, 84, 104-5, 114, 117, 119, 144, 277, 321-2, 324
Canali, Cardinal (in conclave 1769) 174, 187
Cano, Melch(i)or (theologian) 143, 148
Canons Regular of St George in Alga (suppressed order) 292-3
Cansani, Fr (S.J., heresy-hunter) 318
Capefigue, Jean-Baptiste (historian) 24, 25, 34
Capuchins 11
Caradeuc de la Chalotais (*Avocat-Général* at Rennes) 51, 65
Carafa, Cardinal 229, 252, 258, 262
cardinals 161, 173-4, 189; Old College 192
  see Crown Cardinals, Indifferents, Zelanti
Carolos III (Spain) 74-5, 78-80, 82, 85-91, 94-5, 96-109, 110-11, 117, 121, 126, 128-9, 132, 133, 138, 179, 193, 231-2, 273, 275, 313-14, 321-4, 333, 335
  campaign for suppression 140-3, 151, 153, 213-15, 221-2, 224, 226, 228, 230, 233-4, 235, 239, 243, 249-52, 265, 267, 326
  secret motives against Society; 101-2, 108, 124, 224
  death forecast 125
Carlos IV (Spain) 78
Carne, M. de (historian) 34

Car(r)accioli, Marchese (editor of letters of Clement XIV) 201, 203
Carraccioli (misspelt Caraciolo and Carraciolo), Cardinal (in conclave 1769) 168, 174, 187
Cartagena 92, 93
Casali, Cardinal (member of Congregation of Cardinals) 252, 258
Castan, Friar (O.F.M., resident in Avignon) 204
Castel Gandolfo (Pope's summer residence) 237, 240, 243
Castelli, Cardinal (in conclave 1769) 161, 174, 187, 196
Castel Sant' Angelo 264, 270, 275, 278, 283n., 285, 287, 336
Castro (Papal citadel/State belonging to Duchy of Parma) 141, 149, 151, 243
Catharine II (Russia) 263
Catrani, Fr (secular priest, imprisoned with Fr Ricci) 276, 284, 286
Cavalchini, Cardinal (in conclave 1769) 168, 174, 187, 188, 193-4, 203
Caveirac, Abbé (author of *Appel à la Raison*) 56
Centomani (lawyer, *chargé d'affaires* for Naples at Rome) 173, 175
Cerda, Cardinal de la, Patriarch of the Indies (in conclave 1769) 179, 185
Cerutti (former Jesuit scholastic, author of *Apologie Générale*) 56n.
Cevallo(s), General 13, 75, 79, 125
Cevallos, Don (Alcalde in Madrid) 113-14
Cevallos, Fernando (San Jerónimo monk) 120
Cevallos, Padre (S.J., witness of Madrid insurrection) 121
Chadwick, Owen 319, 334
Chaise, Père del la (S.J., confessor to Louis XIV) 32, 59
Champion de Cicé, Mgr, Archbishop of Auxerre 64
Charles III (Spain) see Carlos III
Charles IX (France) 42
Chauvelin, Abbé 34-5, 41-8, 52, 54, 136, 312, 314, 332
Chigi, Cardinal (in conclave 1769) 161, 162, 174, 187, 193
Choiseul-Beaupré, Cardinal de, Bishop

344 *The Suppression of the Society of Jesus*

of Besançon (brother of the Duc de Choiseul) 64
Choiseul, Etienne François, Duc de 27, 29, 34, 52, 59, 65, 72, 79, 102, 141, 147, 153, 156, 313–14
  early life 25
  attitude to Society 214
  first to suggest suppression of Society 138–9
  role in election of Clement XIV 161–99
  role in supression of Society 151, 204–8, 211, 215–16, 220, 222, 224, 226–31
  fall 231
Choiseul-Beaupré, Mgr. Archbishop of Chalons 64
Chomé, Padre (S.J., work and death in South America) 83, 95
Città Vecchia 17, 94, 151, 323
Clémencet (Clémency?), Dom C. (O.S.B., author of *Extraits?*) 49, 54
Clement V 291
Clement VIII 150, 203, 295, 299n.
Clement IX 291, 300
Clement X 300
Clement XI 150, 300, 301n., 328
Clement XII 13, 158, 300, 302n.
Clement XIII (Carlo della Torre Rezzonico) 15, 52, 57–8, 66, 69–70, 72–3, 74, 77, 94, 97–100, 108, 127, 158, 160, 162, 165, 170, 175n., 179, 182n., 201–3, 205–6, 210, 272, 273, 280, 303, 304, 311, 314, 316, 323, 325–6, 332–3
  character 151–2, 270
  harrassing of 133–47
  on ecclesiastical rights 4
  final days 147–57
  see *Apostolicum*; Rezzonico, Carlo della Torre
Clement XIV 105, 128, 272, 311, 329–30, 333
  attitude to the Society 203–5, 211–12, 216–18, 228, 237, 238n., 253, 256–8, 262–4, 279n.
  first six months as Pope 200–34
  delaying tactics over suppression 216, 221–2, 228, 230, 233, 236, 238–41, 243–52, 314, 326
  letters 201, 203
  death 269–70, 285–6

  see Brief of Supression; Ganganelli
Clément, Abbé (Jansenist) 151
Clément, Jacques (assassin of Henri III), 44
Codallos, Felipe (judge in Madrid) 119
Coelestium munerum (Papal brief renewing concessions to Society) 208–10, 213, 214
colegios mayores 324
Colmenarez, Eugenio de (S.J., Spaniard, exiled) 82
Colonna, Cardinal M.A. (in conclave 1769) 174, 187–90, 193, 244, 247n., 283n.
Coltraro, Fr (S.J., involved in Valentano case) 285, 286
Comolli, Gabriel (S.J., Secretary General of Society) 264, 283
conclaves, regulations 158–60
conclave (of 1769) preparations and delays 158–67
  commencement 167
  late arrivals 170
  negotiations within the conclave 176–86
  election of Ganganelli 186–99
conclave (of 1774) 271–2
confessor to Carlos III see Elata, Joachim
confessors, Jesuits as royal 27
confiscation of Society property 250–2, 259–62, 321
Gongregation of Cardinals for suppression of Society 252, 258, 260, 263, 269, 271, 276, 278, 285, 287, 327
Conseil de Roi 19–20
  see *Gens du Roi*
Constitutions (of Society) 41–5, 51–2, 54, 57, 62, 67, 137, 253, 280, 282, 296
Consulta (29 Jan. 1767) 90, 96, 108, 109, 115, 132, 277
Consulta (30 April 1767) 100–1, 277
Consulta (30 November 1767) 144–7, 155, 224, 226, 277
Consulta (21/23 March 1768) 149–50, 155, 278
Conti, Cardinal (in conclave 1769) 168, 174, 187, 188
Cordara, Giulio Cesare (S.J.) 80, 162n., 172, 192, 195–6, 201–3, 289, 317

Index   345

Corletti (S.J. scholastic, letter requesting protection) 284
Corsini, Cardinal Andrea (in conclave 1769, president of Congregation for suppression) 168, 174, 187, 252, 258-9
Corsini, Cardinal Neri (in conclave 1769) 168, 174, 187, 188
Corsica 94, 95, 323
Corvo, Ponte (Papal citadel on frontier with Naples) 149-50
Cosío, Juan (S.J., Spaniard, exiled) 94
Coxe, Archdeacon William (historian) 79
Crétineau-Joly, Jacques (S.J., historian) 198n., 278, 329-30, 333
Croix, Père de la (S.J., French Provincial in Paris) 58-9
Crown Cardinals 161, 167-70, 176-8, 185, 188, 190-3, 197
Croze, Adriano (S.J., writer in defence of Society) 125
Cunninghame-Graham, R.B. (historian) 6
Damiens, Robert François (supposed assassination attempt on Louis XV) 114
Danvila y Collado, Manuel (historian) 104, 109, 114, 118-19, 121-2, 125-8, 130-1, 138, 166, 173, 225, 227-8, 277, 278, 285, 331, 333
Davila, Pedro (judge in Salazar case) 121
Deshaises, Abbé (conclavist to Card. de Bernis) 196, 198n., 215
Desmaretz, Père (S.J., confessor to Louis XV) 30
Dictamen (1811 or 1815) 86n., 96, 103-5, 111
Dictonnaire de Biographie Nationale Universelle 35-6
Didérot, Denis (Encyclopaedist) 26, 122
Dizionario biografico degli Italiani 333
Döllinger, Johannn Joseph Ignaz von (historian) 53, 70, 316, 332
Dominicans 325
Dominus et (or ac) Redemptor 2, 245-6, 255-62, 319, 327, 334
see Brief of Suppression
Du Barry, Countess (mistress of Louis XV) 231
Duclos, Charles Pinot (writer) 18, 310

Dumoulin, Charles (anti-Jesuit writer) 76
Durini, Cardinal (in conclave 1769) 174, 187
Dutillot, Marchese de Felino (chief minister in Parma) 133
Egido, Teófano (historian) 333-4
Eleta, Joachim de (Joaquín de Osma, O.F.M., confessor to Carlos III) 90, 99, 106, 215, 225, 235n.
Encyclopaedists/Philosophers 25, 26, 31, 33-5, 49, 51, 76, 127, 136, 219, 308, 312, 314,
England 38, 74, 111, 204, 206, 214, 231-2
English College 264
Enlightenment 327, 332
see Encyclopaedists
Ensenada, Marqués de la (deposed minister of Carlos III) 106, 111, 119, 122, 131
Erceville, Rolland d' (anti-Jesuit French lawyer) 34-5
Escandón, Padre (S.J., Spaniard, procurator for Paraguay, exiled) 75, 79, 82
exclusiva 168-9, 177
expulsions of Jesuits from France, 71, 136, 321-3, 336
from Malta 136, 313
from Naples 134, 136, 313, 322
from Parma 133, 135, 313
from Portugal 17, 320, 336
from South America 11, 95, 322-3
from Spain 84, 90-5, 313, 322-3
from Two Sicilies 133, 322
Extraits des Assertions 48-54, 67-71, 76, 315-16
see *Réponse*
Extraordinary Council/Tribunal (set up by Carlos III for expulsion of Society) 86, 89-90, 96, 100, 104-8, 110, 113, 115, 117, 125, 126-7, 132, 149, 224, 226, 265, 277, 321
see *Consulta*
Falklands 232
Family Compact 133, 232
Fantini, Abate (secretary to Card. Torregiani) 140
Fantuzzi, Cardinal (in conclave 1769) 162, 174, 187-90, 193, 195

Farnese, Elizabeth (mother of Carlos III), 78, 135n.
Farnese family 141
see Farnese, Elizabeth, Paul III
Faure, Fr (S.J., imprisoned with Fr Ricci) 276, 284, 286
Felino, see Dutillot
Fénelon, François de Salignac de la Mothe, Bishop of Cambrai 31
Ferdinand, Duke (Parma) 3, 4, 133-5, 141, 151, 167, 179, 196-7
Ferdinand IV (King of Naples) and I (King of Two Sicilies) 78, 102, 129, 133-4, 136, 167, 250-1, 275
Ferdinand VI (Spain) 9, 75, 78, 79, 81, 82, 111-12, 309
Ferdinand VII (Spain) 103, 310
Ferrer, Padre (Augustinian, wrongly identified with Isidro López) 117
Ferrer del Río, Antonio (historian) 104-5, 109, 114-16, 118, 122, 125, 154, 265, 331n., 333
Figueira, Fr (S.J., missioner in Paraguay) 10
Fitz-James, Bishop of Soissons 64
Flesselles, Jacques de (secretary to Royal Commission to examine Society) 57-8, 63
Florentin, Comte (minister of Royal Household) 60
Florida Blanca, Conde de see Moñino
Foa, A. see Dizionario biografico
Forestier, Germain Le (S.J., imprisoned with Fr Ricci) 276, 284, 286
Francesco, Fra (O.F.M., major-domo to Clement XIV) 233
Frascati (Jesuits banned) 216, 229
Frederick II, the Great (Prussia) 263, 268, 280, 282
Freire de Andrada, Gómez (Portuguese Governor of Rio de Janeiro) 10, 11
Franciscans 327
Fuentes, Conde de (brother of Pignatelli) 94, 103, 166, 178, 214, 222, 224
Gal(l)iani, Abbé 138, 332
Gallicanism 59, 307, 328
Gándara, Miguel de la, Archdeacon of Murcia (supposed role in Madrid insurrection) 114-18, 120
Ganganelli, Cardinal Lorenzo (baptised Giovanni Vincenzo Antonio),
 Clement XIV, early life 200-1
 election as Pope 162, 166, 174-6, 184, 186-9, 234, 326
 shortcomings 202
 see Bourbon Courts (supposed written promise); Clement XIV
García Ros, Balthasar (defends Society in Paraguay) 12
Gaultier, Fr (S.J., imprisoned 1773) 284, 286
Geerts, Cornelius (S.J., notes on Le Oui et le Non) 283n.
General Council, threat of 142-3, 145
Genoa 211, 216, 234, 243, 323
Gens du Roi 43-6
Giraud, Mgr (Papal nuncio at Paris) 214, 246, 286
Gobel, Jean-Baptiste, Archbishop of Paris 49
Gonzáles (González), Antonio (S.J., author of Life of Idiáquez) 82, 86, 113
González, Ignatio (S.J., implicated in Madrid insurrection) 119
Gorgo, Giuseppe Antonio (S.J., Italian Assistant to Fr Ricci) 264, 276, 278, 283-4
Goujet, Abbé (author of Extraits?) 48, 54
Granada de Ega, Duque de 82, 87, 123
Gravissimis ex causis (Papal brief setting up Congregation of Cardinals to oversee supression of Society) 258, 260-2
Gregory VII 333
Gregory XIII 42n., 295
Gregory XIV 266n., 295, 298
Gregory XV 158-9, 295
Griffet, Père (S.J., connected with Apologie Générale) 56n., 58-9
Grimaldi, Marqués de (Minister of Foreign Affairs, Madrid) 79, 88, 90, 99, 103, 140, 142, 148-9, 155, 205, 226, 235, 237, 243, 250-1, 273-4
 role in election of Clement XIV 166-99
Grou, Jean Nicolas (S.J., linked to Le Oui et le Non and to Réponse) 283n.
Grou & Son (of Nancy) 38-40
Guérin (doctor for Saint-Cyran and the Jesuits) 32

Guglielmi, Cardinal (in conclave 1769) 174, 187
Gutiérrez de la Huerta, Francisco (historian) 108–9, 114, 115–18, 305
  see Dictamen
Guzman (Gusmão), Joan (S.J., Portuguese Assistant to Fr Ricci) 264, 276, 278, 283, 286
Harlay, Achille de, Comte de Beaumont (criticism of Society) 22
Henry III, Emperor 135
Henri III (France) 42
Henri IV (France) 29, 21, 22, 42, 45, 50
Henry VIII (England) 6
Hermosilla (implicated in Madrid insurrection) 118
Hermoso, Lorenzo (implicated in Madrid insurrection) 114–16, 118, 120
Hieronymites of Fiesole (suppressed order) 292–3
Holbach, Paul Henri Dietrich, Baron d' (encyclopaedist) 26
Humiliati (Order suppressed) 291–2, 303
Ibañez, Bernardo (ex-S.J., anti-Jesuit writing) 75
Ibarra, Joaquín (Madrid publisher) 118
Idiáquez, Francisco (S.J., Spanish Provincial, exiled) 76, 82, 84–5, 87–9, 94, 123, 126–7
Ignatius Loyola, St 21, 66, 294, 319, 336
In Coena Domini 326–7
Indifferents (cardinals) 161
Innocent III 333
Innocent X 32, 291, 300, 301n.
Innocent XI 148, 150, 300, 303
Innocent XII 300
Innocent XIII 239, 300, 303
Irish College/Seminary, Rome (removed from Society) 229, 240, 247
James I (England) 144
Jansenism 21–3, 26, 28, 31–5, 48–9, 65, 69, 76, 151, 204, 219, 284, 307–8, 314, 318, 320, 328, 332
  see Unigenitus
Jarente, Mgr, Bishop of Orleans (courtier of Louis XV) 36, 204
Jeréz de la Frontera 93
Jesuats of St John Columbanus (suppressed order) 292–3

John V (Portugal) 13
Joly de Fleury, Omer (anti-Jesuit French lawyer) 34, 37, 43, 45, 52, 64
Joseph I (Portugal) 3, 5, 11, 14, 65, 78, 152, 176, 227, 320
  see Bourbon Courts
Joseph II (Austrian Emperor) 167, 211
Julius II 158–9, 181
Julius III 295
junta for expulsion of Society from Spain 90
Keene, Sir Benjamin (English Ambassador at Madrid) 111
Koricki, Karel (S.J., Polish Assistant to Fr Ricci) 264, 276, 278, 283
Lacretelle (French historian) 34
Laffrey, Arnoux (historian) 19
Lamoignon, Guillaume de (Chancellor) 63
Lances (Lanze), Cardinal des (delle) (in conclave 1769) 174, 187
Lante, Cardinal, Archbishop of Turin (in conclave 1769) 161, 169, 174, 187
Lante, Duchess de (case of) 274
Larreátegui, Pedro Colón de (member of Extraordinary Council) 104
Latila, Bishop (confessor to King Ferdinand of Naples) 134
Lavallette, Antoine (S.J., financial problems) 37–47, 312, 320–1
Lavaña, Conde de (briefly Spanish Ambassador at Vatican) 235
La Vrillière, Louis Phélypeaux, comte de Saint-Floretin, duc de (succeeds Choiseul) 36, 231
Leiza (assistant to Alcalde of Madrid) 113
Leo XI 295
Leo XIII 331n., 337
Leopold Duke of Tuscany 167, 234, 243
Le Oui et le Non see Sauvage, Henry Michel
Lepelletier de Saint-Fargeau (father and son) 40, 41, 332
Lessius, Leonardus (S.J., theologian) 47
Le Tellier, Père (S.J., confessor to Louis XIV) 32
Lioncy & Gouffre (of Marseilles) 38–40
López, Isidro (S.J., implicated in

348 The Suppression of the Society of Jesus

Madrid insurrection) 89, 114–117, 119, 121
Lorenzana, Mgr., Archbishop of Toledo (pastoral letter publishing Brief of Suppression) 334–5
Loreto (Jesuits banned) 216
Losada, Duque de (chamberlain to Carlos III) 130–2
Louis XIV 3, 20, 22, 33, 45, 61–2, 148
Louis XV 20, 36, 43–6, 48–9, 55, 57–60, 62, 65–7, 72, 78, 136, 140, 151, 153, 164, 165, 166, 197, 212n., 221, 223, 231–2, 249–51, 267–8, 321, 326
see Bourbon Courts; Pompadour
Louis XVI 167, 268, 332
Louise, Madame (daughter of Louis XV, Carmelite nun), 267–8
Loyola 85, 89, 132
Luciani, Cardinal (Nuncio at Madrid) 148–9
Ludovisi, Cardinal (founder of Irish College, Rome) 247n.
Luynes, Henri Charles, Cardinal de (Archbishop of Sens; in conclave 1769) 60, 165, 170, 171, 180, 182, 185
Lynch, John (historian) 323
Macanáz, Melchior de (lawyer) 265
Macedo, Fr (S.J., then Capuchin, critique of Cardinal Norris) 318
Macedonio, Mgr (confidant of Clement XIV) 237, 252, 259, 286
Madrid insurrection (1766) 85–6, 89, 102–6, 110–11, 113–21, 127, 129–31
Maistre, Joseph de 331
Mala, John de (defends Soceity in Paraguay) 12
Malagrida, Fr (S.J., executed by Pombal) 16
Maldonado, José (Relator) 118
Malvezzi, Cardinal, Archbishop of Bologna (in conclave 1769) 168, 174, 187, 188, 240, 248–9, 284
Manning, Cardinal 336–7
Manrique, Cayetano (historian) 278
Maranhão (mission, Paraguay) 12
Maraver y Vera, Andrés (member of Extraordinary Council) 104
Marefoschi, Cardinal (assists in drawing up Brief of Suppression and its implementation) 226–7, 229, 233, 247n., 252, 258
Maria Theresa, Empress (Austria) 25, 166–7, 211, 230, 249–52, 261, 327
see Vienna
Mariana, Juan de (S.J., book on regicide) 297n., 323
Martin, Henri (historian) 34, 36
Martinique (West Indies) 37, 38, 320
Masones, Jaime (member of *junta* for expulsion) 90
Masson, Frédéric (historian) 196, 228, 235n., 267, 271
Maupeou, René Charles (*premier président au parlement*) 36, 231
Mayoli, Abbate (involved in Valentano case) 285–6
Mello, Aires de la (Portuguese Minister at Madrid) 142
Memoria (18 January 1769, to Clement XIII demanding suppression) 153–5
Memoria Ministerial (of Moñino in 1768) 105–8, 109, 110–15, 120, 121, 224
Menduru, Padre (S.J., Basque, exiled) 82
Menoux, Père de (S.J., connected with *Apologie Générale*) 56
Michelet, Jules (historian) 329
Migazzi, Cardinal, Archbishop of Vienna 161, 262–3
Miguélez, M.F. (O.S.A., historian) 238n., 254, 309, 316–17
Milan 234
Minard, Abbé (author of *Extraits*?) 49, 54
Mirabeau, Honoré Gabriel Riqueti, Comte de 56n.
Modena 243
Molina, Luis de (S.J., theologian of *scientia media*) 299n.
Molino, Cardinal (in conclave 1769) 174, 187
Monita Secreta (anti-Jesuit propoganda) 124–5
Monitorium (decree of Clement XIII against Duke of Parma) 134–6, 141, 149, 150–1, 326
Montes, Francisco de (S.J., Spanish Assistant to Fr Ricci) 264, 276, 278, 283, 286,
Montigny, Père de (S.J., delivers Jesuit *Constitutions* to *parlement*) 42

Monzón, Augustín (S.J., biographer of St Joseph Pignatelli) 80
Moñino, Joseph/José, later Conde de Floridablanca (Procurator-Fiscal; Spanish Ambassador at Vatican) 105, 117, 144, 224, 226, 235-52, 256, 261, 265-6, 269, 271, 273-5, 285-7, 290, 296n., 300n., 305, 327
  report on imprisoned Jesuits 275-8
  see Memoria Ministerial
Mourin, Antonio (S.J., Spaniard, exiled) 81
Muniacín, Juan Gregorio, member of *junta* for expulsion 90
Múzquiz, Miguel de 87, member of *junta* for expulsion 90
Nava, Miguel María de (member of Extraordinary Council) 104
Navarrette, Juan Andrés (S.J., Spaniard, writer, exiled) 76, 80, 82, 83
Navarro, Benito (advocate, witness re. Madrid insurrection) 118-22
Navarro, Domingo (S.J., supposed treasonable letter) 125-6
Navarro, Pedro (S.J., Spaniard, exiled) 81, 93, 101n.
Nectoux, Charles Auguste Lazare (S.J., French Provincial) 254
Negroni, Cardinal (Secretary of State; in conclave 1769) 151, 157, 174, 187, 245
Neuville, Père de (S.J., French superior) 59, 71
Nicholas I (fictitious King of Paraguay) 75, 315
Nickel, Goswin (General of Society) 32
Nicolas, i.e. Nicole, Pierre (Jansenist) 312
Noailles, Cardinal de, Archbishop of Paris 22
Noris, Cardinal (*History of Pelagianism*) 318
North, Lord (demands return of Falklands) 232
Nouvelles Observations 42
Noyelle, Charles de (General of Society) 63
Oddi, Cardinal (in conclave 1769) 171, 174, 187
Oeyras, Count d' *see* Pombal
Olier, Jean-Jacques (known as 'Monsieur', founder of Saint-Sulpice) 31
Oliva, Paul (General of Society) 33
Orsini, Cardinal (Neapolitan Ambassador at Vatican; in conclave 1769) 156, 203, 205-6, 224, 226, 229, 234, 236, 237, 314
  role in election of Clement XIV 161-99
Osorio, Ignacio de (S.J., Spaniard, exiled) 82, 89, 318
Ossun, Marquis d' (French ambassador at Madrid) 102-3, 121, 226
Oviedo 82, 94
Pacca, Cardinal (Nuncio at Lisbon), verdict on Pombal 5, 259n.
Palafox, Venerable Juan de, Bishop of Puebla, Mexico 192, 204, 233, 236, 284, 301n., 324, 326
Palamares, Silvestro (implicated in Madrid insurrection) 119, 121
Pallavicini, Cardinal (Nuncio at Madrid; in conclave 1769; Secretary of State) 96, 99, 148, 174, 187, 214, 222
Pamphili, Cardinal (in conclave 1769) 174, 187
Papal States 95
Paracciani, Cardinal (in conclave 1769) 171, 174
Paraguay 6-11, 75, 79-80, 82-83, 111, 319-20, 322
Parlement of Paris 232
  nature 19-20
  hostility to Society 21-72, 84, 138, 307, 312, 314
Parlements of provinces 51, 84
Parma *see* expulsion of Society; Ferdinand, Duke of Parma; Ranuccio
Pascal, Blaise 299n., 307, 312, 328
Pasquier, Étienne (anti-Jesuit writer) 76
Paul III 135, 141, 294
Paul IV 295, 296
Paul V 144, 150, 299, 300n.
Paul of the Cross, St (General of Passionists) 229
Peralta, Gabriel (Dean of Cathedral of Paraguay, defends society) 12
Peramás, José Emmanuel (S.J., Paraguayan, writer, exiled) 80, 83
Perelli, Cardinal (in conclave 1769) 168n., 169, 174, 187

350 The Suppression of the Society of Jesus

Pérusseau, Père (S.J., confessor to Louis XV) 29
Philip II (Spain) 266n., 297
Philip V (Spain) 12, 13
Philosophers, see Encyclopaedists
Piacenza 135n.
Pignatelli, Saint José María (S.J.) 77, 80, 81, 84, 94, 182n.
Pinelli, Padre (Augustinian friar, member of *junta* for expulsion) 90
Pinto, Fr (S.J., missioner in Paraguay) 10
Pintus, Fr (S.J., letter to Cardinal Zelada) 282
Pious Schools of the Mother of God, Religious of (reformed order) 291, 293n.
Pirelli, Cardinal (in conclave 1769) 168n., 174, 187
Pitt, William (the elder) 214
Pius IV 150, 158–9, 247n., 295
Pius V 291, 295, 297
Pius VI (Giovanni Angelo Braschi) 247n., 263, 277
  election 272–3
  policies 274–5, 279n., 285–7, 314
Pius VII (publishes Bull for restoration of Society) 134n., 259n., 263, 311, 328
Pius IX 329
Platel, Norbert (ex-Capuchin, criticism of Society) 75
Poland 211, 216
Poli, Sr Teresa (involved in Valentano case) 284
Pombal, Sebastian Joseph Carvalho (=Sebastião Jose de Carvalho e Melo), Count d'Oeyras, Marquis of 3, 23, 52, 75, 77, 320, 322, 326, 336
  career 5–6
  brothers (i) Francis Xavier Mendoza 10–11, (ii) Carvalho, Cardinal Paul 16, 326
  campaign against Society in Portugal and South America 6–17
  campaign for the suppression 141–5, 311, 314
Pompadour, Jeanne Antoinette Poisson, Marquise de 23–4, 27–30, 33–4, 52, 71, 183, 312

Portugal 250
  see Bourbon Courts; Joseph I
Poyanos, Crispin (S.J., supposed defender of regicide) 125
Pozzobonelli, Cardinal (in conclave 1769) 162, 174, 187–90, 197
Pragmatic Sanction (Royal Edict) 92, 108, 114, 130, 307
Praslin, Duc de (cousin and colleague of Choiseul) 34, 72, 168n.
Priests of the Good Jesus, Congregation (suppressed congregation) 291–2
Priuli, Cardinal (in conclave 1769) 174, 187
'Probabilism' 328
prophecies 207, 285
Prussia 211, 263, 327
  see Frederick II
Rábago (=Rávago), Francisco (S.J., confessor to Ferdinand VI) 111, 309, 324–5
Ranuccio II (Duke of Parma) 141
Ravenna 135n.
Ravignan, Gustave-Xavier Delacroix de (S.J., historian) 14, 18, 57, 63, 64, 70, 198, 229n., 330–1, 333
Reductions 9, 10, 107
  see Paraguay
Reformed Conventuals (suppressed order) 291
Regalism 4–5, 6, 128–9, 133, 136, 149, 182n., 219, 265, 274, 308–9, 313–14
regicide 57–8, 125, 142, 323
Renzi, Bernardina (involved in Valentano case) 284
Retz, Fr (General of Society) 9
Réponse aux Extraits 69–70, 125, 283n.
Rezzonico, Cardinal Carlo della Torre
  see Clement XIII
Rezzonico, Cardinal (nephew of Clement XIII; in conclave 1769) 139, 157, 161, 169, 174, 175, 187, 190, 192–4, 196–7
Rezzonico, M. (in favour of suppression of Society) 139
Rhomberg, Ignaz (S.J.) (German Assistant to Fr Ricci) 264, 276, 278, 281, 283
Ric y Egea, Pedro (member of Extraordinary Council) 104
Ricci, Lorenzo (General of Society) 55,

Index   351

58, 65–6, 79, 100, 126, 151, 152n.,
  164–5, 182n., 205, 208–9, 220,
  244, 254–5, 264–6, 268–9, 270–1,
  274–7, 285, 289, 314, 320, 336
account of interrogatories 278–82
death 287–8
Richelieu, Cardinal 20
Richelieu, Louis François, Duc de
  Plessis (minister of Louis XV) 36
rites (Chinese and Malabar) controversy
  301n., 303n., 328
Rivera, Diego (S.J., superior of Jesuit
  house in Madrid) 125
Rochechouart, François Charles,
  Cardinal de (French Ambassador to
  Vatican) 65, 66
Rochefoucauld, Mgr. de, Archbishop of
  Rouen 64
Rochford, Lord (English Ambassador at
  Madrid) 103
Roda, Manuel de (Spanish Ambassador
  at Vatican; later Minister of
  Finance) 78, 80, 90, 99–100,
  121–2, 124, 140–1, 153, 155, 170,
  175, 188, 192, 201, 206, 215,
  235n., 311, 316
Rodríguez de Campomanes *see*
  Campomanes
Rojas y Contreras, Mgr, Bishop of
  Cartagena (president of Council of
  Castile) 77
Rolland (*parlementaire*) 34
Roman Seminary (removed from
  Society) 229, 240, 247
Romano, Fr (S.J., imprisoned in 1773)
  284
Ronciglione (Papal citadel/State in
  Duchy of Parma) 141, 149, 151,
  243
Roothaan, Jan (General of the Society)
  198n., 329–30
Rossi, Cardinal de (in conclave 1769)
  174, 187
Roussel de la Tour (author of *Extraits?*)
  48
Ruffo, Cardinal Tommaso (uncle of Pius
  VI) 272
Russia 263, 327
Sacy, Jean-Pierre de Tiremois de (S.J.,
  treasurer for French Jesuit
  Missions) 30, 38
Saint-Cyran, Jean Duvergier de
  Hauranne, Abbé de (Jansenist) 31
Saint-Priest, Alexis Guignand 29, 72,
  102–3
Saint-Victor, Jacques B.M. Comte de 41
Sainte-Beauve, Charles-Augustin de 32
Salamanca 94
Salas, Diego de (defends Jesuits in
  Paraguay) 13–14
Salazar Calvete, Juan de (executed for
  insults to Carlos III) 106, 121–2,
  125
Saldanha, Cardinal (Apostolic Visitor
  for Portuguese dominions) 14–15
Salgado, Padre (S.J., Spaniard, exiled)
  82, 94
Salmerón, Alfonso (S.J., theologian)
  47
Santander 93, 94
Santos, Eduardo dos (defends Society in
  Paraguay) 12
Saragossa *see* Zaragoza
Sardinia 211, 243
Sauvage, Henry Michel (S.J., author of
  Le Oui et le Non) 283–5
Schoell, Maximilien S.F. (historian) 34,
  256, 289
Semonis, M. de (French Minister at
  Lisbon) 141, 143
Serbelloni, Cardinal (in conclave 1769)
  162, 174, 187, 195
Sersale, Cardinal, Archbishop of Naples
  (in conclave 1769) 161, 162, 166,
  168, 170–1, 174, 175, 177, 185,
  187, 188, 193–4
Shelburne, William Petty, Earl of
  (English policitian) 103
Short Relation (anti-Jesuit work) 11–14,
  75, 77, 311
Silesia 263, 282
Simancas (archives) 121, 173, 225,
  254n., 278
Sismondi, Jean Charles de (historian) 34
Sixtus V 266n., 295, 297–8
Smith, Sydney Fenn, life vii–viii, work
  329–37
Smurraglia (entrusted with account
  books of Roman Seminary) 247n.
Society of Jesus, accusations against
  1–4, 11, 13, 18, 33, 48, 51–3, 74,
  76, 96–109, 123, 125, 142–3,
  153–5, 256, 264–6, 295–305,
  317–18, 327–8

attitude to suppression 253-4, 258-60
enemies 307-10
innovative features 295n., 297n.
restoration 259n., 263, 311, 328, 331n.
Spanish Jesuits, twelve exceptional 80-3
supposed wealth 278-80, 325
survival 263, 268, 275
writings in defence, *see Apologie Générale, Apostolicum, Appel, Réponse aux Extraits;*
see confiscation; *Constitutions*; expulsions; Ricci
Solís, Cardinal de, Archbishop of Seville (in conclave 1769) 123, 179, 182n., 185, 311, 314
Sollicitudo Ecclesiarum (Papal Bull restoring Society) 311
Sommervogel, Carlos (S.J., bibliography of Society) 283n.
Soubise, Charles de Rohan, Prince de 36
Spinola, Cardinal (in conclave 1769) 174, 187
Squillace, Marchese di (minister of Carlos III) 84-6, 88, 106, 116, 119, 321
Stefanucci, Fr (S.J., imprisoned in 1773) 284
Stonyhurst Archives 207
Stoppani, Cardinal (in conclave 1769) 162, 174, 187, 189-90, 191n., 193-5
Suárez, Francisco (Jesuit theologian) 47
Suárez, Abate (identified by Hermoso) 116
Tamburini, Michael Angelo (General of the Society) 303n.
Tanucci, Marchese (chief Minister, Naples) 102, 122, 124, 129-32, 133-4, 138, 140, 151, 155, 168n., 170, 173-4, 178, 243, 247n., 262, 273, 275, 313
correspondents 131
Tarragona 93
Tavora, Marquis of (implicated in attempt on Joseph I) 15
Templars (suppression of) 146, 291-2
Terray, Abbé Joseph-Marie de 34-7, 44, 46-7, 50, 54, 231, 313, 332
Theiner, Augustin (Oratorian, historian) 19, 33, 53, 70, 88, 126, 149, 152n., 156, 164-75, 187, 188-9, 191, 196, 198n., 206, 209, 228, 249n., 251n., 258, 259n., 279n., 329-30, 333
Thorpe, John (S.J., resident in Rome at time of suppression) 207, 209, 227n., 253, 258-60
Tinseau, Mgr, Archbishop of Nevers 64
Togni, Br (S.J., imprisoned 1773) 284
Toletus (Toledo), Francisco Cardinal (Jesuit theologian) 47
Tonegiani, Cardinal (in conclave 1769) 161, 171, 174
Torregiani, Cardinal (Papal Secretary of State, later Papal Secretary) 100, 126, 139-40, 142, 147, 148, 151, 152n., 153, 156, 157, 187, 283n.
trade 8
Treaty of Exchange/of Limits 10, 79, 111, 311, 315
Turin 234
Tuscany *see* Leopold
tyrannicide *see* regicide
Unigenitus (Bull against Jansenism) 23, 35, 197, 308, 328
Urban VIII 291, 295, 300
Uruguay 9, 12-13
Valdelirios (Spanish Governor of Paraguay) 10, 11, 13
Valentano case 276, 284-5
Valerani, Cardinal (perhaps misprint for Cardinal Veterani) 195
Valle Salazar, Luís del (member of Extraordinary Council) 104
Vazquez, Gabriel (S.J., theologian) 47
Vazquez, Padre (General of Augustinians) 170, 206-7, 238n., 316, 325
Venaussin, Comtat de 149-50
Venice 211, 216, 243
Venizza, Fr (S.J., involved in Valentano case) 285, 286
Vergara, Emanuel de (S.J., Provincial in Paraguay) 125-6
Vergennes, Charles Gravier, Comte de (minister under Louis XVI) 268, 279
Veterani, Cardinal (in conclave 1769) 174, 187
see Valerani

Veto (right of certain Courts to exclude a papal candidate) 175, 193n.
Vicar-General, appointment of 280-1
Vienna 234, 243, 263-4
Villaflores, Marqués de (implicated in Madrid insurrection) 114-18, 120
Villagarcía (Spanish novitiate) 94
Vincent de Paul, St 31-2
Vincente, Conte Ippolito (auditor at Papal Nunciature in Madrid) 99
Voltaire, François Marie Arouet *called* 22, 26, 53, 122, 129, 138, 308, 312, 314
von Reumont, Alfred (historian) 201n., 204
Waldeck-Rousseau, Pierre M.R. (19th-century French politician) 6

Wall, Richard (Spanish Minister) 13, 111, 130, 138
Wiseman, Cardinal 337
Ximenez (intermediary for Cardinal Albani) 172
York, Cardinal (in conclave 1769) 161, 168-9, 174, 187, 216n., 247n.
Zaragoza 81, 84
Zelada, Cardinal (helps to compose Brief of Suppression) 245-6, 248, 251, 252, 258, 282, 327
Zelanti cardinals 161, 163, 164, 168-73, 188-92, 195-6, 202, 271
Zubiria, Br (S.J., Spaniard, exiled) 94
Zuzzeri, Br (S.J., imprisoned with Fr Ricci) 276, 284, 286

www.ingramcontent.com/pod-product-compliance
Lightning Source LLC
Chambersburg PA
CBHW070823250426
43671CB00036B/1840